T0093019

Data Science and Its Applications

Data Science and Its Applications

Edited by
Aakanksha Sharaff
G. R. Sinha

CRC Press
Taylor & Francis Group
Boca Raton London New York

CRC Press is an imprint of the
Taylor & Francis Group, an **informa** business

A CHAPMAN & HALL BOOK

First edition published 2021
by CRC Press
6000 Broken Sound Parkway NW, Suite 300, Boca Raton, FL 33487-2742

and by CRC Press
2 Park Square, Milton Park, Abingdon, Oxon, OX14 4RN

© 2021 selection and editorial matter, Aakanksha Sharaff and G R Sinha; individual chapters, the contributors

CRC Press is an imprint of Taylor & Francis Group, LLC

ISBN: 978-0-367-60886-6 (hbk)
ISBN: 978-0-367-60887-3 (pbk)
ISBN: 978-1-003-10238-0 (ebk)

Typeset in Palatino
by SPi Technologies India Pvt Ltd (Straive)

Dedicated to my late grandparents, my teachers, and family members.

Aakanksha Sharaff

Dedicated to my late grandparents, my teachers, and Revered Swami Vivekananda.

G. R. Sinha

Contents

Preface

Data science is interpreted as either "data with a new platform" or "data used to make market strategy." Data mining, machine learning, artificial intelligence, data analytics, deep learning, and several other related disciplines are covered under the umbrella of data science. Several multinational organizations realize that data science plays an important role in decision-making and market strategy. The revolutionary growth of digital marketing not only changes the market game, but also results in new opportunities for skilled and expert professionals. Today, technologies are rapidly changing and artificial intelligence (AI) and machine learning are contributing as game-changer technologies that are not only trending but also very popular among data scientists and data analysts. Due to widespread usage of data science concepts in almost all emerging applications, there are several challenges and issues in implementation of data analytics and big data problems. Therefore, it is essential to bring out a book that can provide a framework for data handling and management methods so that the issues related to data science applications can be mitigated. This book discusses data science–related scientific methodology, processes, and systems to extract meaningful knowledge or insight for developing concepts from different domains, including mathematics and statistical methods, operations research, computer programming, machine learning, data visualization, and pattern recognition, among others. The book also highlights data science implementation and evaluation of performance in several emerging applications such as cognitive, computer vision, social media analytics, sentiment analysis, and so on. A chapter-by-chapter description of the book follows:

Chapter 1 presents a review of how data science is applied to address various critical problems in the area of big data analytics. It also explains the opportunities and challenges that come with the increase in new computational technologies. In Chapter 2, an overview of different types of real-world recommender systems and AI, along with challenges and opportunities in the age of big data, are provided. This chapter discusses recent growth in cognitive technology, together with advancement in areas such as AI (plus ML, DL, and NLP), as well as knowledge representation, interaction, and personalization, which have resulted in substantial enhancement in the research of recommender systems. Chapter 3 presents some discussion on practical issues and how to resolve them using ensemble learning and meta-learning techniques like bagging, boosting, and stacking. In this chapter, the theory and utility of various machine learning algorithms for data science applications are discussed. The data can be distinguished based on whether it is labeled or not. The major supervised and unsupervised algorithms considered in this chapter are linear regression, decision trees, naïve Bayes, support vector machines (SVMs), and clustering techniques like K-Means. For the sake of completeness, this chapter also presents techniques for making better predictions on the new (unseen) data with performance metrics used for evaluating machine learning algorithms.

Chapter 4 proposes an advanced convolutional neural network (CNN) technique for farming by classifying and recognizing citrus disease that helps grow healthy plants. The model proposed was trained using different training epochs, batch sizes, and dropouts. The dataset includes images of unhealthy and healthy citrus leaves and fruits that can be used to prevent plant disease by using deep learning techniques. The main diseases in the datasets are canker, black spot, greening, scab, and melanose. Chapter 5 presents a detailed discussion and analysis on credibility assessment of social media data. In addition, it discusses a deep learning–based approach for determining the credibility of user-generated healthcare–related tweets (posts on microblogging website Twitter) and the credibility of their authors by utilizing linguistic features. In particular, we focus on the superstition or misinformation that is spread by the people using such sites, which can lead to hazardous consequences in future. The presented model is based on a semi-supervised approach, where a subset of training tweets, derived from Twitter using web scraping, are labeled as true or false. The remaining tweets are labeled by the model itself. Next, BERT (bidirectional encoder representation using transformers) and CNN (Convolutional Neural Network)–based hybrid model are used for the credibility assessment of tweets. Experimental results show the efficacy of the presented work. Chapter 6 begins with linear filtering concepts of DSP, which are then correlated to time series analysis concepts in both time and spectral domain. The basic knowledge of DSP and random signal processing is assumed, and rigorous mathematical proofs for such concepts are avoided. The chapter then describes limitation of conventional linear filters; the remedy using adaptive filtering algorithms is also described. In addition, an application to forecast stock market index movement is also illustrated using a simulation exercise where the national stock exchange (NSE) index: NIFTY 50 closing values are used to train and test the time-series model. Chapter 7 describes a new framework and model, industry linked additive green curriculum using feed-backward instructional design approach, and a shift from Internet of Things to Internet of Learning Things to inform data science and learning analytics. The chapter traces the forces that shape educational systems, describes the current view of Data Science from educational system perspective including educational data mining and learning analytics, examines framework and features of smart educational systems proposed in literature, describes relevant socioeconomic and technical challenges in adopting learning analytics in educational systems. and concludes with the proposed new framework. In Chapter 8, the hypothesized computational algorithm solution has been illustrated in the method built for more practical learning.

In Chapter 9, a combination of network architectures is used, including question-answering (BERT) and image-captioning (BUTD, show-and-tell model, Captionbot, and show-attend-and-tell model) models for VQA tasks. The chapter also highlights the comparison between these four VQA models. Chapter 10 discusses the benefits of deep learning over machine learning for recommender systems by tuning and optimizing the hyperparameters of the deep neural network, and also throws light on the open issues in recommender systems for researchers. Chapter 11 represents the culmination of a major development project that can be used for the optimization of a single process or guidance during the development of similar supply chain management systems. Chapter 12 introduces various application areas where data science can be useful to analyze healthcare data. This chapter also discusses various issues and challenges faced by data scientists during the knowledge discovery process.

In Chapter 13, the authors have discussed how to solve optimization problems using Python and other tools. The intention of the authors is not to help the user become a skillful theoretician, but a skillful modeler. Therefore, little of mathematical principles related to the subject of optimization is discussed. Various aspects of optimization problems are covered in the case studies mentioned in the chapter. The chapter can be effectively used to create easy yet powerful and efficient models. In Chapter 14, the proposed model shows the numerous advantages of integrating the BioNER model. The proposed model successfully overcomes the problem of improper classification of the biomedical entity, and also improves the performance by leveraging multiple annotated datasets for various types of entities. The state-of-the-art performance of the suggested model increases the accuracy of text-mining applications related to biomedical downstream, or to find out the relation between the biomedical-entity relationships. In Chapter 15, the performance of various machine learning (ML) classification algorithms is estimated, such as logistic regression, K-nearest neighbor, support vector classifiers, and Gaussian naïve Bayes algorithms implemented on a Crime against Women dataset. Finally, the chapter concludes with the result based on the most reliable outcome from converting the imbalanced data to balanced data by using Python. In Chapter 16, a mathematical model is used to calculte iteration and find the best score of pages. Chapter 17 explains the several deep network architectures that are utilized in the current scenario for scene text analysis. It also compares the detection, recognition, and spotting results for popular approaches on the publicly available scene text datasets.

This book provides a unique contribution to the interdisciplinary field of data science that allows readers to deal with any type of data (image, text, sound, signals, and so on) for a wide range of real-time applications

Acknowledgements

Dr. Sharaff expresses her heartfelt appreciation to her parents, husband Sanju Soni, her loving daughter Aadriti, brother Rahul, sister Shweta, and her entire family members for their wonderful support and encouragement throughout the completion of this important book. This book is an outcome of sincere efforts that could be given to the book only due to the great support of family. This book is dedicated to her parents Mr. Laxman Sharaff and Mrs. Gayatri Sharaff for their entire support and enthusiasm.

Dr. Sinha, too, expresses his gratitude and sincere thanks to his family members, wife Shubhra, daughter Samprati, parents, and teachers.

The editors would like to thank all their friends, well-wishers, and all those who keep them motivated in doing more and more, better and better. They sincerely thank all contributors for writing relevant theoretical background and real-time applications of *Data Science and Its Applications*.

They express their humble thanks to Dr. Aastha Sharma, Acquisitions Editor, and all of the editorial staff at CRC Press for great support, necessary help, appreciation, and quick responses. They also wish to thank CRC Press for giving this opportunity to contribute on a relevant topic with a reputed publisher. Finally, they want to thank everyone, in one way or another, who helped edit this book.

Dr. Sharaff especially thanks her family who encouraged her throughout the time of editing book.

Editor Biographies

 **Dr. Aakanksha Sharaff** is a faculty member in the Department of Computer Science & Engineering at National Institute of Technology Raipur, Chhattisgarh, India, since July 2012. She has been actively involved in research activities leading to data science research and related areas. She holds Doctor of Philosophy in Computer Science & Engineering from National Institute of Technology Raipur (an Institute of National Importance) in 2017; Master of Technology from National Institute of Technology Rourkela (an Institute of National Importance) with Honours in 2012; and Bachelor of Engineering from Government Engineering College Bilaspur Chhattisgarh with Honours in 2010. She received gold medals during her graduation and post-graduation. To date, she pursues excellence and various academic success, including the Top Student in Post-Graduation Master of Technology (2012), Bachelor of Engineering (2010), and throughout her schooling. She has received the gold medal for being the Top Student in Higher Secondary School Certificate Examination (2006) and High School Certificate Examination (2004). She has completed all her degrees and schooling with Honours (Distinction) and studied from reputed national institutions. She has achieved various merit certifications, including All India Talent Search Examination, during her schooling.

She is the Vice Chair of Raipur Chapter of Computer Society of India and Secretary of IEEE Newsletter of Bombay Section. She is actively involved in various academic and research activities. She has received Young Women in Engineering Award for her contribution in the field of Computer Science and Engineering at the 3rd Annual Women's Meet AWM 2018 by Centre for Advanced Research and Design of Venus International Foundation. She has achieved the Best Paper Award for several research papers. She contributes to various conferences as session chairs, invited/keynote speakers, and has published a good number of research papers in reputed international journals and conferences. She is contributing as active technical reviewer of leading international journals for IEEE, Springer, IGI, and Elsevier. Dr. Sharaff has supervised many undergraduate and postgraduate projects. Currently she is guiding five research scholars studying for their PhDs. She has visited Singapore and Bangkok, Thailand, for professional as well as personal reasons. Her research areas focus mainly on data science, text analytics, sentiment analysis, information retrieval, soft computing, artificial intelligence, and machine and deep learning. She is editing one more book on *New Opportunities for Sentiment Analysis and Information Processing* with IGI Publisher.

G. R. Sinha is Adjunct Professor at International Institute of Information Technology Bangalore (IIITB) and is currently deputed as Professor at Myanmar Institute of Information Technology (MIIT) Mandalay Myanmar. He obtained his BE (Electronics Engineering) and MTech (Computer Technology) with Gold Medal from National Institute of Technology Raipur, India. He received his PhD in Electronics & Telecommunication Engineering from Chhattisgarh Swami Vivekanand Technical University (CSVTU) Bhilai, India. He was Visiting Professor (Honorary) in Sri Lanka Technological Campus Colombo for one year (2019–2020). He has published 254 research papers, book chapters, and books at international and national level, including _Biometrics_, published by Wiley India, a subsidiary of John Wiley; _Medical Image Processing_, published by Prentice Hall of India; and has edited five books with IOP, Elsevier, and Springer. He is an active reviewer and editorial member of more than 12 reputed international journals with IEEE, IOP, Springer, Elsevier, and others. He has teaching and research experience of 21 years. He has been Dean of Faculty and Executive Council Member of CSVTU and is currently a member of Senate of MIIT. Dr. Sinha has been delivering ACM lectures as ACM Distinguished Speaker in the field of DSP since 2017 across the world. His few more important assignments include Expert Member for Vocational Training Programme by Tata Institute of Social Sciences (TISS) for Two Years (2017–2019); Chhattisgarh Representative of IEEE MP Sub-Section Executive Council (2016–2019); Distinguished Speaker in the field of Digital Image Processing by Computer Society of India (2015). He is the recipient of many awards and recognitions, like TCS Award 2014 for Outstanding Contributions in Campus Commune of TCS, Rajaram Bapu Patil ISTE National Award 2013 for Promising Teacher in Technical Education by ISTE New Delhi, Emerging Chhattisgarh Award 2013, Engineer of the Year Award 2011, Young Engineer Award 2008, Young Scientist Award 2005, IEI Expert Engineer Award 2007, ISCA Young Scientist Award 2006 Nomination, and Deshbandhu Merit Scholarship for five years. He served as Distinguished IEEE Lecturer in IEEE India council for the Bombay section. He is a Senior Member of IEEE, Fellow of Institute of Engineers India, and Fellow of IETE India.

He has delivered more than 50 keynote and invited talks, and has chaired many technical sessions for international conferences across the world. His special session on "Deep Learning in Biometrics" was included in the IEEE International Conference on Image Processing 2017. He is also member of many national professional bodies like ISTE, CSI, ISCA, and IEI. He is a member of various committees of the university and has been Vice President of Computer Society of India for Bhilai Chapter for two consecutive years. He is a consultant for various skill development initiatives of NSDC, Government of India. He is regular referee of project grants under the DST-EMR scheme and several other schemes for Government of India. He received few important consultancy supports as grants and travel support. Dr. Sinha has supervised eight PhD scholars, 15 MTech scholars, and has been supervising one more PhD scholar. His research interest includes biometrics, cognitive science, medical image processing, computer vision, outcome-based education (OBE), and ICT tools for developing employability skills.

List of Contributors

Aakanksha Sharaff
Department of Computer Science and
Engineering
National Institute of Technology
Raipur, Chhattisgarh, India

Aaryan Kapoor
Department of Computer Science and
Information Systems
BITS Pilani
Pilani, Rajasthan, India

Abhilasha Chaudhuri
Department of IT
NIT Raipur, India

Ajay Dhruv
Research Scholar, Department of
Information Technology
Thadomal Shahani Engineering College
Mumbai, India

Alok Negi
Department of Computer Science and
Engineering
National Institute of Technology
Uttarakhand, India

Amin Beheshti
Macquarie University
Sydney, Australia

Ashutosh Kumar
National Institute of Technology Raipur
Raipur, India

Dr. Naresh Kumar Nagwani
National Institute of Technology Raipur
Raipur, India

Dr. V. Kakulapati
Sreenidhi Institue of Science and
Technology
Hyderabad, India

Emir Žunić
Info Studio d.o.o. Sarajevo and Faculty of
Electrical Engineering
University of Sarajevo
Bosnia and Herzegovina

Emmanuel S. Pilli
Department of CSE
MNIT Jaipur
Jaipur, India

G. R. Sinha
Myanmar Institute of Information
Technology
Mandalay, Myanmar

Hari Prabhat Gupta
IIT (BHU)
Varanasi, India

Haris Hasić
Tokyo Institute of Technology, Japan and
Info Studio d.o.o. Sarajevo
Bosnia and Herzegovina

J. W. Bakal
Department of Information Technology,
SSJCOE
Mumbai, India

Jahangir Alam
University Women's Polytechnic, F/o.
Engineering & Technology, AMU Aligarh
Alligarh, Uttar Pradesh, India

Jigarkumar H. Shah
Pandit Deendayal Petroleum University
Gandhinagar, Gujarat, India

Kerim Hodžić
Faculty of Electrical Engineering,
University of Sarajevo and Info Studio
d.o.o. Sarajevo
Bosnia and Herzegovina

Krishan Kumar
Department of Computer Science and
  Engineering
National Institute of Technology
Uttarakhand, India

Lavika Goel
Department of Computer Science and
  Engineering
Malaviya National Institute of
  Technology
Jaipur, Rajasthan, India

Mansi A. Radke
Visvesvaraya National Institute of
  Technology
Nagpur, Maharashtra, India

Meenakshi S Arya
Department of CSE, Faculty of E&T
SRM Institute of Science and
  Technology, Vadapalani Campus,
  Chennai, India

Meera S Datta
NIIT University
India

Mehdi Elahi
University of Bergen
Bergen, Norway

Mohit Dhawan
Department of Electrical and Electronic
  BITS Pilani
Pilani, Rajasthan, India

Monika Choudhary
Department of CSE, MNIT Jaipur
Jaipur, India
Department of CSE, IGDTUW
Delhi, India

P. Tamilarasi
Sri Sarada College for Women
  (Autonomous)
Salem, Tamil Nadu, India

Dr. R. Uma Rani
Sri Sarada College for Women
  (Autonomous)
Salem, Tamil Nadu, India

Rachit Rathore
Department of Computer Science and
  Information Systems
BITS Pilani
Pilani, Rajasthan, India

Randheer Bagi
IIT (BHU)
Varanasi, India

Ravindra B. Keskar
Visvesvaraya National Institute of
  Technology
Nagpur, Maharashtra, India

Robert B. Handfield
North Carolina State University and
  Supply Chain Resource Cooperative
NC, United States

Rutvij H. Jhaveri
Pandit Deendayal Petroleum University
Gandhinagar, Gujarat, India

Satyansh Rai
Department of Computer Science and
  Information Systems
BITS Pilani
Pilani, Rajasthan, India

Satyendra Singh Chouhan
Department of CSE
MNIT Jaipur
Jaipur, India

Sead Delalić
Faculty of Science
University of Sarajevo and Info Studio
  d.o.o. Sarajevo
Bosnia and Herzegovina

Sheri Mahender Reddy
Otto-Friedrich university of Bamberg,
  IsoSySc
Bamberg, Germany

Srinivasa Reddy Goluguri
Macquarie University
Sydney, Australia

Supriya Gupta
National Institute of Technology Raipur
Raipur, India

Tanima Dutta
IIT (BHU)
Varanasi, India

Tirath Prasad Sahu
Department of IT
NIT Raipur, C.G. India
Raipur, India

Ulligaddala Srinivasarao
Department of Computer Science and
    Engineering
National Institute of Technology
Raipur, Chhattisgarh, India

Vijay V Mandke
NIIT University
India

Yashvardhan Sharma
Department of Computer Science and
    Information Systems
BITS Pilani
Pilani, Rajasthan, India

1

Introduction to Data Science: Review, Challenges, and Opportunities

Ulligaddala Srinivasarao and Aakanksha Sharaff
National Institute of Technology, Raipur, Chhattisgarh, India

G. R. Sinha
Myanmar Institute of Information Technology (MIIT), Mandalay, Myanmar

CONTENTS

1.1 Introduction

Data science is a new area of research that is related to huge data and involves concepts like collecting, preparing, visualizing, managing, and preserving. Even though the term *data science* looks related to subject areas like computer science and databases, it also requires other skills, including non-mathematical ones. Data science not only combines data analysis, statistics, and other methods, but it also includes the corresponding results. Data science is intended to analyze and understand the original phenomenon related to the data by revealing the hidden features of complex social, human, and natural phenomena related to data from another point of view other than traditional methods.

Data science includes three stages: designing the data, collecting the data, and finally analyzing the data. There is an exponential increase in the applicability of data science in various areas because data science has been making enormous strides in data processing and use. Business analytics, social media, data mining, and other disciplines have benefited due to the advance in data science and have shown good results in the literature.

Data science has made remarkable advancements in the fields of ensemble machine learning, hybrid machine learning, and deep learning. Machine learning methods (ML) can learn from the data with minimum human interference. Deep learning (DL) is a subset of ML that is applicable in different areas, like self-driving cars, earthquake predictions, and so on. There are many pieces of evidence in the literature that show the superiority of DL over ML methods; DL methods include artificial neural networks, k-nearest neighbors, and support vector machine (SVM) in different disciplines, such as medical, social media, and so on.

Torabi et al. developed a hybrid model where two predictive machine learning algorithms are combined together [1]. Here, an additional optimization-based method has also been used for maximizing the prediction function. Mosavi and Edalatifar illustrated that hybrid machine learning models perform very accurately compared to single machine learning models [2].

This chapter presents a review of various data science methods and details how they are used to deal with critical challenges that arise when working with big data analytics. According to the literature, different classification, regression, clustering, and deep learning–based methods have often been used. However, there is an opportunity to improve in new areas, like temporal and frequent pattern discovery for load prediction. This chapter also discusses the future trends of data science, to explore new tools and algorithms that are capable of intelligently handling large datasets that are collected from various sources.

1.2 Data Science

Technological tools developed recently over the years have helped in many domains, including management and big data. Advancements in different areas of communications

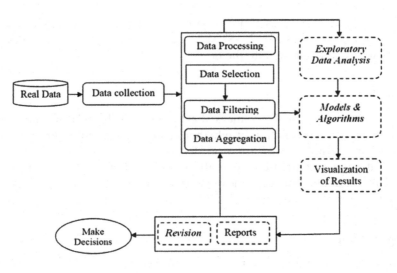

FIGURE 1.1
Data science process

and information technology—like email information privacy, market, stock data, data science, and real-time monitoring—have also been a good influence.

It is well known that data science builds algorithms and systems for discovering knowledge, detecting the patterns, and generating useful information from massive data. To do so, it encompasses an entire data analysis process that starts with the extraction of data and cleaning, and extends to data analysis, description, and summarization. Figure 1.1 depicts the complete process. It starts with data collection. Next, the data is cleaned to select the segment that has the most valuable information. To do so, the user will filter over the data or formulate queries that can erase unnecessary information. After the data is prepared, an exploratory analysis that includes visualizing tools will help decide the algorithms that are suitable to gain the required knowledge. This complete process will guide the user toward the results that will help them make suitable decisions.

Depending on the primary outcomes, the complete process should be fine-tuned to obtain improved results. This will involve changing the parameter values or making changes to the datasets. These kinds of decisions are not made automatically, so the involvement of an expert in result analysis is a crucial factor.

From a technical point of view, data science consists of a set of tools and techniques that deals with various goals corresponding to multiple situations. Some of the recent methods used are clustering, classification, deep learning, regression, association rule mining, and time-series analysis. Even though these methods are often used in text mining and other areas, anomaly detection and sequence analysis are also helpful to provide excellent results for text mining problems.

1.2.1 Classification

Wu et al. have classified a set of objects that predict the classes based on the attributes. Decision trees (DT) are used to perform and visualize that classification [3]. DTs may be generated using various algorithms, such as ID3, CLS, CART, C4.5, and C5.0. Random forest (RF) is one more classifier that will construct a set of DTs, and then predicts through the aggregation of the values generated from each DT. A classification model was developed by using a technique known as Least Squares Support Vector Machine (LS-SVM). The classification task is performed by LS-SVM by using a hyper-plane in a multidimensional space for separating the dataset into the target classes [4].

1.2.2 Regression

Regression analysis aims for the numerical estimation of the relationship between variables. This involves the estimation of whether or not the variables are independent. If a variable is not independent, then the first step is to determine the type of dependence. Chatterjee et al. proposed a regression analysis that is often used for predicting and forecasting, and also to understand how the dependent variables will change corresponding to the fixed values of independent variables [5].

1.2.3 Deep Learning

In deep learning, many hidden layers of neural networks are used to deeply understand the information that images are attempting to predict accurately. Here, each layer will learn and detect low-level features, such as edges. Further, new layers will be merged with the features of the previous layer to represent it better. Fischer and Krauss [6] have expanded the long short-term memory (LSTM) networks for forecasting out-of-sample directional movements in the stock market. Here, a comparative study has been performed with DNN, RF, and LOG, and it demonstrates that the LSTM model outperforms the others. Tamura et al. [7] have proposed a model for predicting stock values, which is a two-dimensional approach. In this model, technical, financial indexes related to the Japanese stock market are used as input data for LSTM to predict. Using this data, the financial statements of other companies have been retrieved and are also added to the database.

1.2.4 Clustering

Jain et al. proposed a clustering-based method using the degree of similarity [8]. In clustering, the objects are separated into groups called clusters. This type of learning is called unsupervised learning, as there is no prior idea over the classes as to which group the objects belong. Based on the similarity measure criterion, cluster analysis has various models: (i) based on the connectivity distance, connectivity models are generated, i.e., hierarchical clustering; (ii) by using the nearest cluster center, the objects are assigned, centroid models are generated, i.e., k-means; (iii) by means of statistical distributions, the distributed models are generated, i.e., expectation-maximization algorithm; (iv) based on high-density areas that exist in the data, the clusters are defined in density models; (v) graphs are used for expressing the dataset in graph-based models.

1.2.5 Association Rules

Association rules are suitable tools to represent the new information that has been extracted from the raw dataset. These rules are expressed to make the decisions in terms of implication rules, per Verma et al. [9]. The respective rules indicate the frequency of occurrence of the attributes with high reliability in databases. This example represents an association rules related to the database of the supermarket. Even though the algorithms like ECLAT and FP-Growth algorithms are available for large datasets, in the Apriori algorithm, for

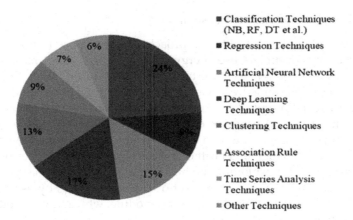

FIGURE 1.2
Data Science Techniques

example, the generalized rule induction algorithm and its adaptations are often used, per Tan et al. [10].

1.2.6 Times Series Analysis

Das provided a time-series analysis. Here the time-series data, which is collected over time, is used for modeling the data. Further, the model is used for predicting future values of the time series [11]. The often used methods are the following: (i) techniques for exploratory analysis, for example wavelets, trend analysis, autocorrelation, and so on; (ii) forecasting and prediction methods, for example signal estimation, regression methods, and so on; (iii) classification techniques that will be assigned a category to patterns related to the series; and (iv) segmentation that aims to identify a sequence of points that share particular properties. Hullermeier developed a fuzzy extension that allows for processing uncertain and imprecise data related to different domains [12]. Bezdek et al. have proposed a fuzzy k-means method. This method is similar to a type of clustering technique that has given efficient results in different scenarios, as it will permit the assignment of data elements related to single or more clusters [13]. Figure 1.2. shows different types of techniques used in data science and application.

1.3 Applications of Data Science in Various Domains

Data science is one subject that has gained popularity out of necessity, corresponding to real-world applications as a substitute to research domain. Its application began from a narrow field of analytics and statistics and has improved to be applied to different areas of industry and science. Consequently, this section explains the data science applications that can do the following: (i) economic analysis of electric consumption, (ii) stock market prediction, (iii) bioinformatics, (iv) social media analytics, (v) email mining, (vi) big data analysis, and (vii) SMS Mining, among other things!

1.3.1 Economic Analysis of Electric Consumption

Different electric companies or utilities approached data science to find out and understand when and how consumers use energy. There has been an increase in competition among companies that use data science to develop such information. Traditionally, this information has been determined via classification, clustering, and pattern analysis methods by using the association rule. Chicco et al. have grouped consumers as various classes based on their behavior and usage of electricity [14]. The comparative evaluation was made with self-organizing maps and an improved version of follow-the-leader methods. This was the first step initiated for a tariff of the electrical utilities. Figueiro et al. [15] have developed a framework for exploiting the historical data, which consists of two modules: (i) a load-profile module, which creates a set of customer classes by using unsupervised and supervised learning, and (ii) a classification module, which builds models for assigning customers to their respective classes.

1.3.2 Stock Market Prediction

An application of ML and DL techniques in the stock market is increasing compared to other areas of economics. Even though investing in the stock market gives profits, high risk is often involved along with high benefits. So, investors try to estimate and determine the value of a stock before they make an investment. The cost of the stock varies depending upon factors like local politics and economy, which causes difficulties in identifying future trends of the stock market. Fischer and Krauss [6] used LSTM to forecast future trends in the stock market. The results have been compared with LOG, DNN, and RF, and have shown improved results over the others. Tamura et al. [7] have proposed a new method for predicting the values of the stock. Here, financial data related to the stock market of Japan has been used as a prediction input in LSTMs (Long short-term memories). Further, the financial statements of the companies are recovered and then added to the database. Sharaff and Srinivasarao [16] proposed Linear Support Vector Machine (LSVM) identify the correlation among the words in content and subject of the emails.

1.3.3 Bioinformatics

Bioinformatics is a new area that uses computers to understand biological data like genomics and genetics. This helps scientists understand the cause of disease, physiological properties, and genetic properties. Baldi et al. [17] utilized various techniques to estimate the applicability and efficiency of different predictive methods in the classification task. The previous error estimation techniques are primarily focused on supervised learning using the microarray data. Michiels et al. [18] have used various random datasets to predict cancer using microarray data. Ambroise et al. [19] solved a gene selection problem based on microarrays data. Here, 10-fold validation has been used. Here, 0.632 bootstrap error estimates are used to deal with prediction rules that are overfitted. The accuracy of 0.632 bootstrap estimators for microarray classification using small datasets is proposed in Braga et al. [20]

1.3.4 Social Media Analytics

Joshi and Deshpande [21] have used Twitter data to classify the sentiments included in tweets. They have applied various machine learning methods to do so. A comparative study has been carried out by using maximum entropy, naïve Bayes, and positive-negative word counting. Wolny [22] proposed a model to recognize the emotion in Twitter data and performed an emotion analysis study. Here, the feelings and sentiments were discussed in detail by explaining the existing methods.

The emotion and sentiment are classified based on symbols via an unsupervised classifier, and the lexicon was explained by suggesting future research. Coviello et al. [23] have analyzed the emotion contagion related to Facebook data. The instrumental variable regression technique has been used to analyze the Facebook data. Here, the emotions of the people, such as negative and positive emotions during rainy days, were detected. Roelens et al. [24] explained that the detection of the people who influence social networks is a difficult task or area of research, but one of great interest so that referral marketing and spreading information regarding products can reac the maximum possible network.

1.3.5 Email Mining

There is a threat to internet security with spam emails. Spam emails are nothing but unwanted or unsolicited emails. Mailboxes will overload with these unwanted emails, and there may be losses in storage and bandwidth, which favors quick, wrong information and malicious data. Gudkova et al. [25] conducted a study and explained that 56% of all emails are spam emails. Caruana and Li [26] illustrated that the machine learning method is successful for detecting spam data. These include learning classifier models, which map data by using features like n-gram and others into spam or ham classes. Dada et al. [27] have demonstrated that email features may be either manual or automatic. Bhowmick and Hazarika [28] demonstrated that the manually extracted rules are known as knowledge engineering, which requires expert and regular updates to maintain good accuracy. Text mining methods are used for automated feature extraction of useful information like words, enabling spam discrimination, HTML mark up, and so on. Using these features, an email is represented as Bag-of-Words (BoW) as proposed by Aggarwal [29]. Here the unstructured word tokens are used to discriminate the spam messages with the others. The BoW assumes word tokens that are not dependent that will prevent from delivering the good semantic content to represent the email. Sharaff and Nagwani [30] have identified the email threads using LDA- and NMF-based methodology.

1.3.6 Big Data Analysis Mining Methods

Big data is one of the very fast-growing technologies that is critical to handle in the present era. The information is used for analytical studies to help drive decisions for giving quick and improved services. Laney [31] proposed that big data consists of three characteristics: velocity, volume, and variety. These are also called the 3Vs.

Chen et al. [32] explained that data mining is a procedure where potentially useful, unknown, and hidden meaningful information is extracted from noisy, random, incomplete, and fuzzy data. The knowledge and information that has been extracted is used to derive new comprehensions, scientific events, and influences business scientific discovery, per Liu [33].

Two articles have aimed at improving the accuracy of data mining. Han et al. [34] have proposed a new model using the skyline algorithm. Here, a sorted positional index list (SSPL), which has low space overhead, has been used to reduce the input or output cost. Table 1.1 shows an overview of data science methods used in different applications.

TABLE 1.1

An overview of data science methods used in different applications

S.no	Applications	Methods	Source
1	Economic analysis	Follow-the-Leader Clustering (FLC) K-Means	Chicco et al. [14] Figueiredo et al. [15]
2	Stock Market	Long Short-Term Memory (LSTM)	Fischer and Krauss [6] Tamura et al. [7]
3	Bioinformatics	Gradient Descent Learning (GDL) k-nearest-neighbors (K-NN) support vector machine (SVM)	Baldi et al. [17] Michiels et al. [18] Ambroise et al. [19]
4	Social Media analytics	Naive Bayes (NB) and Maximum Entropy Algorithms (MEA) Lexicon Based Approach (LBA) Regression Methods (RM)	Joshi and Deshpande [21] Wolny [22] Coviello et al. [23]
5	Email Mining	Machine and Non-Machine Learning Methods (NMLM) Deep Leaning Methods (DLM) Machine Learning Techniques (MLT) Latent Dirichlet Allocation and Non-Negative Matrix Factorization (NNMF)	Caruana and Li [26] Dada et al. [27] Bhowmick and Hazarika [28] Sharaff and Nagwani [30]
6	Big Data Analysis	Fuzzy Clustering (FC) Data Mining Methods (DMM) Skyline Algorithm (SA)	Chen et al. [32] Liu [33] Han et al. [34]

1.4 Challenges and Opportunities

This section summarizes the key issues, challenges, and opportunities that are related to data science in different fields.

1.4.1 Challenges in Mathematical and Statistical Foundations

The main challenge in mathematical fields is to find out why theoretical foundations are not enough to solve complex problems, and then identify and obtain a helpful action plan.

1.4.2 Challenges in Social Issues

In social contexts, the challenges are to specify, respect, and identify social issues. Any domain-specific data is to be selected, and then its related concepts—like business, security, protection privacy—should be accurately handled.

1.4.3 Data-to-Decision and Actions

It is important to develop accurate decision-making systems that are data-driven. These systems should also be able to manage and govern the decision-making systems.

1.4.4 Data Storage and Management Systems

One of the challenges include designing a good storage and management system that has the capability to handle large amounts data, stream-speed in real time, and can manage such data in an Internet-based environment, including cloud.

1.4.5 Data Quality Enhancement

Another important challenge is issues of data quality like uncertainty, noise, unbalance, and so on. The level of presence of these issues will vary depending upon the data complexity.

1.4.6 Deep Analytics and Discovery

Cao [35] proposed new algorithms to deal with the deep and implicit analytics that are not able to be tackled using the existing descriptive, latent, and predictive learning. Also, how to aggregate the model based with data-driven problem-solving solutions to balance the domain-specific data complexity, intelligence-driven evidence learning, and common learning frameworks.

1.4.7 High-Performance Processing and Analytics

Systems must handle the online, real-time, Internet-based, large-scale, high-frequency, data analytics and processing with balanced resource involvement that may be local and global. This requires new array disk storage, batch, and high performance parallel processing. It is also necessary to use complex matrix calculations, data-to-knowledge management, mixed data structures, and management systems.

1.4.8 Networking, Communication, and Interoperation

The challenge involved is how to support the interoperation, communication, and networking between various data science roles like distributed and complete cycle of problem-solving in data science. Here, it is necessary to coordinate management of tasks, data, workflows, control, task scheduling, and governance.

1.5 Tools for Data Scientists

This section presents the tools required for data scientists to address the aspects discussed above. These tools are classified as data and application integration, cloud infrastructure, programming, visualization, high-performance processing, analytics, master data management, business intelligence reporting, data preparation and processing, and project management. The researcher can use any number of tools depending upon the complexity of the problem being solved.

1.5.1 Cloud Infrastructure

Like Map R, Google Cloud Platform, Amazon Web Services, Cloudera, Spark, Apache Hadoop, and other systems may be used. Most of the traditional IT vendors at present are using cloud platform.

1.5.2 Data/Application Integration

This includes Clover ETL, Information Builders, DM Express Sync sort, Oracle Data Integrator, Informatics, Including Ab Initio, and so on.

1.5.3 Master Data Management

Master data management includes SAP Net Weaver Master Data Management tool, Black Watch Data, Microsoft Master Data Services, Informatica MDM, TIBCO MDM, Teradata Warehousing, and so on.

1.5.4 Data Preparation and Processing

Stodder and Matters [36] have used some platforms and data preparation tools like Wrangler Enterprise and Wrangler, Alpine Chorus, IBM SPSS, Teradata Loom, Platfora, and so on.

1.5.5 Analytics

Analytics includes commercial tools like Rapid Miner [37], Mat Lab, IBM SPSS Modeler and SPSS Statistics, SAS Enterprise Miner, and so on, in addition to some new tools, like Google Cloud Prediction API, ML Base, Big ML [38], Data Robot, and others.

1.5.6 Visualization

Some commercial and free software listed in KDnuggets [39] to visualize include Miner3D, IRIS Explorer, Interactive Data Language, Quadrigram, Science GL, and so on.

1.5.7 Programming

Additionally, Java, Python, SQL, SAS, and R languages have been used for data analytics. Some data scientists have also included Go, Ruby, .net, and Java Script [40].

1.5.8 High-Performance Processing

Around 40 computer cluster software programs, like Platform Cluster Manager, Moab Cluster Suite, Stacki, and others, have been listed in Wikipedia [41].

1.5.9 Business Intelligence Reporting

Some of the reporting tools [42] commonly used are SAP Crystal Reports, SAS Business Intelligence, Micro Strategy, and IBM Cognos, among others.

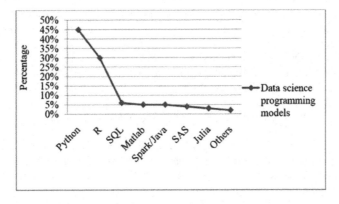

FIGURE 1.3
Data Science Programming Models

1.5.10 Social Network Analysis

Around 30 tools have been listed for social network analysis and to help visualize data. For example, Ego Net, Cuttlefish, Commetrix, Keynetiq, Node XL, and so on. [43]. Figure 1.3 shows the different types of programming languages that are used in data science.

1.6 Conclusion

This chapter has surveyed the modern advances in information technology, and the influence these advances have had on big data analytics and its applications. The effectiveness of different data science algorithms that can be applied to solve the challenges in big data has been examined. Data science algorithms will be extensively used in the future to address the problems and challenges in big data applications.

In various areas, the exploitation and discovery of meaningful insights from the dataset will be very much required. Big data applications are necessary in different fields like industry, government, and so on. This new perspective will challenge research groups to develop better solutions to manage large heterogeneous amounts of real-time data. It also deals with the uncertainty associated with it. Data science techniques reveal important tools that can extract and exploit the information and knowledge that exists in the user dataset. In the coming days, big data techniques will increase possibilities, and may also democratize them.

References

1. Torabi, M., Hashemi, S., Saybani, M. R., Shamshirband, S., & Mosavi, A. (2019). A Hybrid clustering and classification technique for forecasting short-term energy consumption. *Environmental Progress & Sustainable Energy*, 38(1), 66–76.

2. Mosavi, A., & Edalatifar, M. (2018). A hybrid neuro-fuzzy algorithm for prediction of reference evapotranspiration. In *International conference on global research and education* (pp. 235–243). Cham: Springer.

3. Wu, X., Kumar, V., Quinlan, J. R., Ghosh, J., Yang, Q., Motoda, H., … & Zhou, Z. H. (2008). Top 10 algorithms in data mining. *Knowledge and information systems*, 14(1), 1–37.

4. Suykens, J. A., Van Gestel, T., & De Brabanter, J (2002). *Least squares support vector machines*. World Scientific.

5. Chatterjee, S., Hadi, A. S., & Price, B. (2000). *Regression analysis by example*. New York: John Wiley & Sons Inc..

6. Fischer, T., & Krauss, C. (2018). Deep learning with long short-term memory networks for financial market predictions. *European Journal of Operational Research*, 270(2), 654–669.

7. Tamura, K., Uenoyama, K., Iitsuka, S., & Matsuo, Y. (2018). Model for evaluation of stock values by ensemble model using deep learning.

8. Jain, A. K., Murty, M. N., & Flynn, P. J. (1999). Data clustering: a review. *ACM computing surveys (CSUR)*, 31(3), 264–323.

9. Verma, M., Srivastava, M., Chack, N., Diswar, A. K., & Gupta, N. (2012). A comparative study of various clustering algorithms in data mining. *International Journal of Engineering Research and Applications (IJERA)*, 2(3), 1379–1384.

10. Tan, P. N., Steinbach, M., & Kumar, V. (2016). *Introduction to data mining*. Delhi: Pearson Education India.

11. Das, S. (1994). *Time series analysis*. (Vol 10). Princeton, NJ: Princeton University Press.

12. Hüllermeier, E. (2005). Fuzzy methods in machine learning and data mining: status and prospects. *Fuzzy Sets and Systems*, 156(3), 387–406.

13. Bezdek, J. C., Ehrlich, R., & Full, W. (1984). FCM: the fuzzy c-means clustering algorithm. *Computers & Geosciences*, 10(2–3), 191–203.

14. Chicco, G., Napoli, R., Piglione, F., Postolache, P., Scutariu, M., & Toader, C. (2004). Load pattern-based classification of electricity customers. *IEEE Transactions on Power Systems*, 19(2), 1232–1239.

15. Figueiredo, V., Rodrigues, F., Vale, Z., & Gouveia, J. B. (2005). An electric energy consumer characterization framework based on data mining techniques. *IEEE Transactions on power systems*, 20(2), 596–602.

16. Sharaff, A., & Srinivasarao, U. (2020). Towards classification of email through selection of informative features. In *2020 First International Conference on Power, Control and Computing Technologies (ICPC2T)* (pp. 316–320). IEEE.

17. Baldi, P., Brunak, S., Chauvin, Y., Andersen, C. A., & Nielsen, H. (2000). Assessing the accuracy of prediction algorithms for classification: an overview. *Bioinformatics*, 16(5), 412–424.

18. Michiels, S., Koscielny, S., & Hill, C. (2005). Prediction of cancer outcome with microarrays: a multiple random validation strategy. *The Lancet*, 365(9458), 488–492.

19. Ambroise, C., & McLachlan, G. J. (2002). Selection bias in gene extraction on the basis of microarray gene-expression data. *Proceedings of the national academy of sciences*, 99(10), 6562–6566.

20. Braga-Neto, U. M., & Dougherty, E. R. (2004). Is cross-validation valid for small-sample microarray classification? *Bioinformatics*, 20(3), 374–380.

21. Joshi, S., & Deshpande, D. (2018). Twitter sentiment analysis system. *International Journal of Computer Applications*, 180(47), 0975–8887.

22. Wolny, W. (2016). Emotion analysis of twitter data that use emoticons and emoji ideograms.

23. Coviello, L., Sohn, Y., Kramer, A. D., Marlow, C., Franceschetti, M., Christakis, N. A., & Fowler, J. H. (2014). Detecting emotional contagion in massive social networks. *PloS one*, 9(3), e90315.

24. Roelens, I., Baecke, P., & Benoit, D. F. (2016). Identifying influencers in a social network: the value of real referral data. *Decision Support Systems*, 91, 25–36.

25. Gudkova, D., Vergelis, M., Demidova, N., and Shcherbakova, T. (2017). Spam and phishing in Q2 2017, Securelsit, Spam and phishing reports, https://securelist.com/spamand-phishing-in-q2-2017/81537/, 2017.

26. Caruana, G., & Li, M. (2008). A survey of emerging approaches to spam filtering. *ACM Computing Surveys (CSUR)*, 44(2), 1–27.
27. Dada, E. G., Bassi, J. S., Chiroma, H., Adetunmbi, A. O., & Ajibuwa, O. E. (2019). Machine learning for email spam filtering: review, approaches and open research problems. *Heliyon*, 5(6), e01802.
28. Bhowmick, A., & Hazarika, S. M. (2016). Machine learning for e-mail spam filtering: review, techniques and trends. *arXiv preprint arXiv:1606.01042*.
29. Aggarwal, C. C., & Zhai, C. (Eds.). (2012). *Mining text data*. Springer Science & Business Media.
30. Sharaff, A., & Nagwani, N. K. (2016). Email thread identification using latent Dirichlet allocation and non-negative matrix factorization based clustering techniques. *Journal of Information Science*, 42(2), 200–212.
31. Laney, D. (2001). 3D data management: controlling data volume, velocity and variety. *META group research note*, 6(70), 1.
32. Chen, M. M. S., & Liu, Y. (2014). Big Data: A Survey. *Mobile Networks and Applications*, 19, 171–209.
33. Liu, L. (2013). Computing infrastructure for big data processing. *Frontiers of Computer Science*, 7(2), 165–170.
34. Han, X., Li, J., Yang, D., & Wang, J. (2012). Efficient skyline computation on big data. *IEEE Transactions on Knowledge and Data Engineering*, 25(11), 2521–2535.
35. Cao, L. (2017). Data science: challenges and directions. *Communications of the ACM*, 60(8), 59–68.
36. Stodder, D., & Matters, W. D. P. (2016). Improving data preparation for business analytics. Applying technologies and methods for establishing trusted data assets for more productive users. *Best Practices Report Q*, 3(2016), 19–21.
37. RapidMiner. 2016. RapidMiner. (2016). https://rapidminer.com/.
38. BigML. 2016. BigML. Retrieved from https://bigml.com/.
39. KDnuggets. 2015. Visualization Software. Retrieved from: http://www.kdnuggets.com/software/visualization.html.
40. Davis, J. (2016). 10 Programming Languages And Tools Data Scientists Used. (2016).
41. Wikipedia. 2016. Comparison of Cluster Software. Retrieved from https://en.wikipedia.org/wiki/Comparison_of_cluster_software.
42. Capterra. 2016. Top Reporting Software Products. Retrieved from http://www.capterra.com/reporting-software/.
43. Desale, D. (2015). Top 30 Social Network Analysis and Visualization Tools. KDnuggets. https://www.kdnuggets.com/2015/06/top-30-social-network-analysis-visualization-tools.html.

2

Recommender Systems: Challenges and Opportunities in the Age of Big Data and Artificial Intelligence

Mehdi Elahi

University of Bergen, Bergen, Norway

Amin Beheshti and Srinivasa Reddy Goluguri

Macquarie University, Sydney, Australia

CONTENTS

2.1 Introduction

In the times of Big Data, choosing the right products is a challenge for consumers due to the massive *volume*, *velocity*, and *variety* of related data produced online. Because of this, users are getting more and more desperate when making choices among an unlimited set of choices. Recommender systems are support apps that can deal with this challenge by assisting shoppers to make choices on what to purchase (Jannach, Zanker, Felfernig, and Friedrich, 2010; Resnick and Varian, 1997; Ricci, Rokach, and Shapira, 2015). Recommender systems can learn from *particular* preferences and tastes of users and build personalized suggestions that tailor to users' preferences and necessities rather than offering suggestions based on mainstream taste (Elahi, 2011; Elahi, Repsys, and Ricci, 2011).

Many recommender software options and algorithms have been proposed, up to now, by the academic and industrial community. Most of these algorithms are capable of getting input data from various data types and then exploiting them to generate recommendations on top of the data. These data types can describe either the item content (e.g., category, brand, and tags) or the user preferences (e.g., ratings, likes, and clicks). The data is collected and pre-processed, cleaned, and then exploited to build a model in which the items are projected as arrays of features. Recommendation lists for a specific user is then made by filtering the items that represent alike features to the rest of the item sets that user liked/rated high.

Enhanced capabilities of recommender techniques in understanding the varied categories of user tastes and precisely tackling information burden has enabled them to become an important part of any online shop that tackles the expansion of item cataloging (Burke, 2002; Elahi, 2014). Diverse categories of recommender engines have been built in order to generate personalized selection and relevant recommendations of products and services ranging from clothing and outfits to movies and music. Such a personalized selection and suggestion is usually made based on the big data of a huge community of connected users, and by calculating the patterns and relationships among their preferences (Chao, Huiskes, Gritti, and Ciuhu, 2009; Elahi, 2011; Elahi and Qi, 2020; He and McAuley, 2016; Nguyen, Almenningen, Havig, Schistad, Kofod-Petersen, Langseth, and Ramampiaro, 2014; Quanping 2015; Tu and Dong 2010). The excellency in performance of recommender systems has been validated in the diverse range of e-commerce applications where a choice support mechanism is necessary to handle customers' needs and help them when interacting with online e-commerce. Such an assistance improves the user experiences when shopping or browsing the system catalogue (He and McAuley, 2016; Tu and Dong, 2010).

In this chapter, we will provide an outline of different types of real-world recommender systems, along with challenges and opportunities in the age of big data and AI. We will discuss the progress in cognitive technology, in addition to evolutionary development in areas such as AI (with all relevant disciplines such as ML, DL, and NLP), KR, and HCI, and how they can empower recommender systems to effectively support their users.

We discuss that modern recommendation systems require access to and the ability to understand big data, in all different forms, and that big data generated on data islands can be used to build relevant and personalized recommendations tailored to each customer's needs and preferences. We present different application scenarios (including multimedia, fashion, tourism, banking, and education) and review potential solutions for the recommendation. The remaining parts of the chapter is organized as follows: Section 2.2 briefly describes popular methods and algorithms. Section 2.3 discusses different application scenarios, and Section 2.4 reviews real-world challenges and potential solutions. Section 2.5 extends the previous chapters by providing some advanced topics. Finally, in Section 2.6, we conclude the chapter.

2.2 Methods

2.2.1 Classical

Diverse recommendation approaches have already been developed and tested, which can be classified within a number of categories. A well-adopted category of methods is called **content-based** (Pazzani and Billsus, 2007). Methods within this category suggest items based on their descriptors (Balabanovíc and Shoham, 1997). For example, book recommender systems take terms within the text of a book as descriptors and suggest to the user other books that have descriptors similar to the book the user liked in the past. Another popular category is **collaborative filtering** (Desrosiers and Karypis, 2011; Koren and Bell, 2011). Collaborative filtering methods predict the preferences (i.e., ratings) of users by learning the preferences that a set of users provided to items and suggests to users those items with the highest predicted preferences. Methods within the **demographic** (Wang, Chan, and Ngai, 2012) category generate recommendations by identifying similar users based on the demographics of the users (Pazzani, 1999). These methods attempt to group existing users by their personal descriptors and make relevant suggestions based on their demographic descriptions. **Knowledge-based** (Felfernig and Burke, 2008) methods are another category that tries to suggest items that are inferred from the needs and constrains entered by users (Burke, 2000). Knowledge-based methods are distinguished by their knowledge about how a specific item fulfills a particular user's needs (Claypool, Gokhale, Miranda, Murnikov, Netes, and Sartin, 1999). Hence, these methods can mine inferences based on the connections within the user's need and the possible recommendation. **Hybrid** (Li and Kim, 2003) methods combine diverse individual methods among those noted earlier in order to handle the particular restrictions of an individual method.

2.2.2 Collaborative Filtering

Collaborative filtering (CF) is a recommender method used in almost all application domains. This method focuses on effective adoption of the user feedback (e.g., ratings) elicited from the users to make a profile of affinities. Such profiles are used to generate personalized recommendations. Hence, collaborative filtering relies on big data comprised of ratings acquired from typically big network of users (Desrosiers and Karypis, 2011). Using such data, collaborative filtering recommends items that a target user has not yet checked, but could probably like (Koren and Bell, 2011). Perhaps a cornerstone for these systems is to ability to estimate the feedback (or ratings) entered by users for items that they have not produced any rating for yet. Having the predicted ratings, collaborative filtering can sort the items based on the predicted ratings and recommend those with the highest ratings.

Classical methods in collaborative filtering systems are neighbor-based, which compute user-to-user or item-to-item similarities based on the co-rating patterns of the users and items. In item-based collaborative filtering, items can be computed as alike if the community of interconnected users have rated those items in a similar way. Analogously, in user-based collaborative filtering, users with similar rating patterns form neighborhoods that are used for rating prediction. Hence, ratings predictions are performed based on how the item has been co-rated by other users who were considered as like-minded compared to the target users.

Another category of collaborative filtering systems adopt Latent factor models in order to generate rating prediction. A well-adopted category of these methods is *matrix factorization* (Koren, 2008b; Koren and Bell, 2011). Matrix factorization builds mathematical models on top of ratings data and forms a set of factors for the users and items. These sets, with equal length, are learned from every rating elicited from users. Every factor of these sets is assigned to an item and represents the level in which an item projects a particular latent aspect of user preference. In the movie domain, as an example, item factors could be interpreted as the genre of the movie, while user factors could describe the taste of the users toward such genres.

In order to identify such factors, matrix factorization decomposes the rating matrix into different matrices:

$$R \approx SM^T \tag{2.1}$$

Where S is a matrix of $|U| \times F$, and M is a matrix of $|I| \times F$.

A well-known implementation of matrix factorization, *Timely Development* (2008), was proposed as Funk-SVD Funk (2006) and is capable of making predictions using this formula:

$$\hat{r}_{ui} = \sum_{f=1..F} s_{uf} m_{if} \tag{2.2}$$

where the s_{uf} describes the level of the user u preferences towards the factor f, and the m_{if} describes the strength of the factor f is in the item i (Koren, 2008b).

2.2.3 Content-Based Recommendation

Content-based methods are also widely adopted in recommender systems. Content-based methods adopt content-based filtering (CBF) algorithms in order to build user profiles by associating user preferences to the item content (Deldjoo and Atani, 2016; Deldjoo, Elahi, Cremonesi, Garzotto, Piazzolla, and Quadrana, 2016). As noted earlier, the user preferences are typically given as ratings to items and item content can be described with diverse forms of features. Content-based recommender systems exploit such content features and make a *vector space model* on top of the content data (Pazzani and Billsus, 2007). This model projects every item into a multi-dimensional space according to the content features (Lops, De Gemmis, and Semeraro, 2011). The content-based methods measure a relevancy score associated to user preferences proportional to the content features.

So far, a diverse spectrum of CBF approaches have been formulated and tested in the context of recommender systems. A well-adopted method is *K-nearest neighbors* (*KNN*) which exploits the similarities using items content and builds suggestions on top of it. The similarities scores among the item *j* and all the rest of the items allows us to build a set of nearest neighbor items (i.e., NN_j) containing the items with the maximum similarity scores to the item *j*. Accordingly, the preferences (e.g., likes/dislikes or the star ratings) that have provided for the items within the nearest neighbors set are then used to predict the preference $\hat{r}_{ij}$ for user *i* and item *j*:

$$\hat{r}_{ij} = \frac{\sum_{j' \in NN_j, r_{ij'} > 0} r_{ij'} s_{sjj'}}{\sum_{j' \in NN_j, r_{ij'} > 0} s_{sjj'}} \tag{2.3}$$

where $r_{uj} > 0$ reflects the elements of the preferences matrix, $\mathcal{R}$, i.e., user ratings included in the matrix of all ratings.

2.2.4 Hybrid FM

While the collaborative filtering method and content-based method have both been largely adopted by the recommender system community, they have a number of restrictions. These restrictions will be explained later on in this chapter. In order to address such restrictions, *hybrid* methods have been developed by hybridizing these methods (Low, Bickson, Gonzalez, Guestrin, Kyrola, and Hellerstein, 2012). While hybrid methods can also have diverse forms, we briefly introduce one of the most recent methods, called *factorization machines* (Burke, 2002; Rendle, 2012).

Factorization machines is a recommender method that is formed by extending the classical matrix factorization method TURI (2018). Factorization machines hybridizes matrix factorization by mixing it with a well-known machine learning method named *support vector machines* (*SVM*). This hybrid method enables the factorization machines to be capable of taking advantage of not only the user preferences (e.g., ratings), but also item descriptions, as well as any additional data attributed by users. This enables factorization machines to adopt a wide range of data, typically referred to as *side information*, or item descriptors (e.g., category, title, or tag) as well as user attributes (e.g., demographics, emotion, mood, and personality). Hence, factorization machines build mathematical models on top of user ratings, as well as item descriptors or user attributes in order it make preference predictions (Rendle, 2012).

Predicting the user preferences (e.g., likes and dislikes, or ratings) is conducted through the next formula:

$$\hat{r}_{ij} = \mu + w_i + w_j + \mathbf{a}^T \mathbf{x}_i + \mathbf{b}^T \mathbf{y}_j + \mathbf{u}_i^T \mathbf{v}_j \tag{2.4}$$

where μ denotes the bias factor, w_i is the user weight, w_j is the item weight, and $\mathbf{x}_i$ and $\mathbf{y}_j$ are feature set for user and item, respectively.

There other advanced models (such as Mooney and Roy, 2000; Ahn, Brusilovsky, Grady, He, and Syn, 2007) that go beyond traditional methods by building probabilistic models based on the user or item input data. For instance, in Fernandez-Tobías and Cantador (2014) and Manzato (2013), a model called *gSVD++* has been developed that can take advantage of content data attributed into MF Koren (2008a).

2.2.5 Modern Recommender Systems

Despite the effectiveness of the presented methods, in the age of big data and artificial intelligence (AI), the need for more advanced methods has been a strong force to build a modern generation of recommender engines. Several improvements in such recommendation engines have enabled them to make quick and accurate recommendations tailored to each customer's needs and preferences. To achieve this goal, modern recommendation systems have focused on three main aspects: data, knowledge, and cognition.

2.2.6 Data-Driven Recommendations

Modern recommendation systems require access to and understanding of the raw data generated on various data islands, including open/private/social data sources (Beheshti, Benatallah, Sheng, and Schiliro, 2019). This is important as the improvement in data communication and processing enable access to big data, and will enable intelligent and accurate recommendations. In this context, the main challenge in harnessing big data is the ability to ingest and organize the big data (from various data islands) onto a centralized repository. The concept of a *data lake* presents a centralized repository in which to organize the raw data generated on various data islands. Modern approaches, such as CoreDB (Beheshti et al., 2017a) propose the notion of data lakes as a service to facilitate managing and querying large amount sof information (from open, social, IoT, and private data islands) and to enable analysts to deal with the variety of data and non-standard data models. Figure 2.1. illustrates the CoreDB (data lake as a service) architecture.

To understand the raw data, it is necessary to leverage AI (artificial intelligence) and ML (machine learning) technologies to contextualize the raw data, and ultimately improve the accuracy of recommendations. This enables the adoption of popular recommender systems, and facilitate sthe journey from analytical models to deep learning models. The goal here is to generate better predictions by improving correlations between features and attributes. Hence, the concept of a *knowledge lake* has been introduced. Accordingly, data curation services can be adopted, which will enable automatic transformation of the raw data into curated data. Figure 2.2 illustrates the architecture of the knowledge lake.

As a motivating scenario, we may consider recommendations on social media, such as Twitter. Modern recommender systems would need to understand the content and context of tweets posted by social users. Considering a tweet as a raw data, the curation services (Beheshti, Tabebordbar, Benatallah, and Nouri, 2017b) in the knowledge lake would be able to extract information (e.g., keyword, phrase, named entity, topic, sentiment, etc.) from the text of the tweet or a URL in the tweet, and enrich them using external knowledge sources and services. A contextualized tweet (as illustrated in Figure 2.3.) will tell more stories compared to a raw tweet. For example, if we are able to extract "Barack Obama" from the text of the tweet, understand that it is a named entity or person, and link it to the entity Barack Obama (i.e., the 44th president of the United States) in Wikidata, the recommendation system will understand that this tweet may be related to the topic of politics. Similarly, if the tweet contains a keyword related to health or mentions the World Health Organization (WHO), the tweet would be classified as related to the topic of health..

2.2.7 Knowledge-Driven Recommendations

Intelligence RSs learn from domain experts' experience and knowledge in order to understand the domain that the items will be recommended (Beheshti, Yakhchi, Mousaeirad,

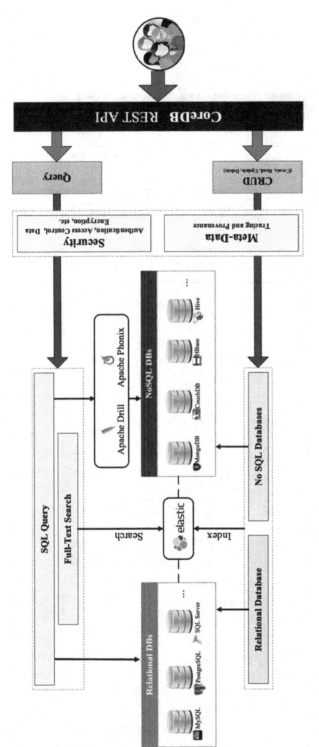

FIGURE 2.1

The data-lake-as-a-service architecture (CoreDB Beheshti et al., 2017a).

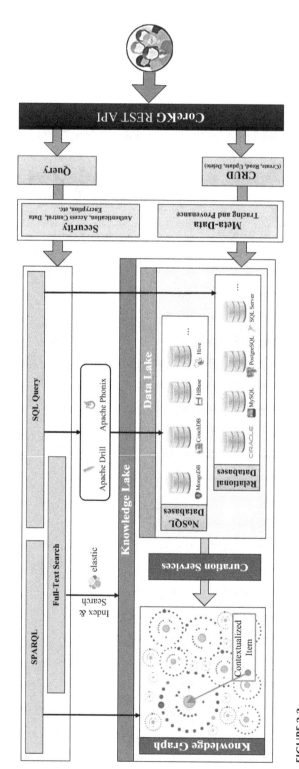

FIGURE 2.2

CoreKG: knowledge-lake-as-a-service architecture (Beheshti et al., 2018).

Ghafari, Goluguri, and Edrisi, 2020b). For example, a new line of research started (Beheshti et al., 2020b) to use crowdsourcing techniques to capture domain experts' knowledge and use them to provide accurate and personalized recommendations. Another line of work has been leveraged by intelligent knowledge lakes (KLs) to address the following two challenges: (i) The cold-start problem: leveraging intelligent knowledge lakes will bring informative data from a crowd of people and use it to generate recommendations.; (ii) Bias and variance: leveraging intelligent knowledge lakes will be able to guide recommender systems to choose the best next steps by following the best practices learned from domain experts. This is important, as features used for training recommenders may be gathered by humans, which enables biases to get into data preparation and training phases. To build an intelligent KL, it is important to mimic domain expert's knowledge. This can be done using techniques such as collecting feedback, organizing interviews, and requesting surveys. To achieve this goal, it is important to capture important events and entities (and relationships among them) that are happening in real time in various disciplines and fields, such as education and fintech.

2.2.8 Cognition-Driven Recommendations

To support accurate and intelligent recommendations, it is vital for a recommender system to identify similar users based on their behavior, activities, and cognitive thinking. Accordingly, a cognition-driven recommender system should: (i) facilitate understanding users' personalities, emotions, moods, and affinities over time. This task aims to empower the recommender models in exploitation of the cognitive signals and neural data, as noted in our previous work, Personality2Vec (Beheshti, Hashemi, Yakhchi, Motahari-Nezhad, Ghafari, and Yang, 2020a), to design mechanisms for personalized task recommendations and to facilitate discovering meaningful patterns from users' social behaviors. A cognitive RS may focus on dimensions such as explicit behavioral pattern and implicit behavioral patterns (Beheshti et al., 2020b). Explicit patterns may include text-based methods, location-based approaches, action-based methods, and feature-based methods. Implicit patterns may focus on social-based features, trust-based features, and action-based features.

Sequential recommender systems (Wang, Hu, Wang, Cao, Sheng, and Orgun, 2019) aim to understand and model user behaviors, however, they do not consider the analysis of users' attitude, behavior, and personality over time. Recent work introduces a new type of recommender system, cognitive recommender systems (Beheshti et al., 2020b), which focuses on understanding the users' cognitive aspects.

2.3 Application

2.3.1 Classic

2.3.1.1 Multimedia

Multimedia is probably the most popular application domain in recommender systems. Multimedia recommender systems can exploit different forms of preference data and can use different types of multimedia descriptors when creating recommendations (Elahi, Ricci, and Rubens, 2012; Hazrati and Elahi, 2020). While such features can have different forms, we can classify them into a two main categories: *high-level* and *low-level* forms of

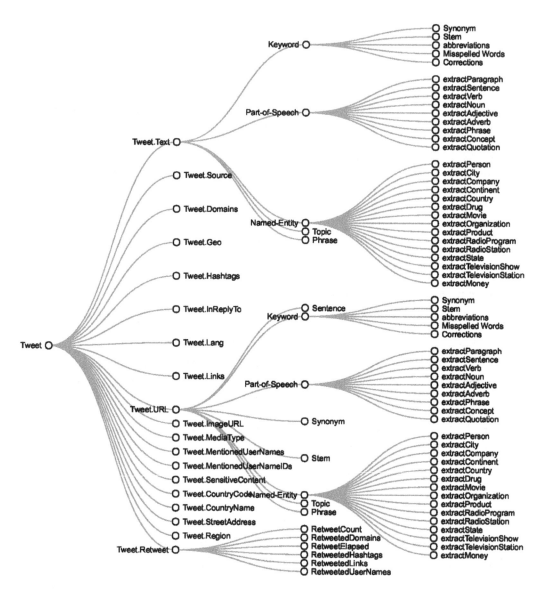

FIGURE 2.3
A contextualized tweet (Beheshti et al., 2019).

descriptors (Cantador, Szomszor, Alani, Fernandez, and Castells, 2008; Hazrati and Elahi, 2020).

High-level descriptors illustrate more of the semantic and syntactic characteristics of multimedia items and can be aggregated from either structured forms of metadata, e.g., a relational databases or an ontology (Cantador et al., 2008; Mooney and Roy, 2000), or from less structured form of data, e.g., user reviews, film plots, and social tags (Ahn et al., 2007; Hazrati and Elahi, 2020).

Low-level descriptors, on the other side of the story, are aggregated directly from multimedia files (e.g., audio or visual files). In the music domain, for instance, low-level descriptors can represent the acoustic configurations of the songs (e.g., rhythm, energy, and melody), which can be adopted by recommender systems to find similar songs and to generate personalized recommendation for a user (Bogdanov and Herrera, 2011; Bogdanov, Serra, Wack, Herrera, and Serra, 2011; Knees, Pohle, Schedl, and Widmer, 2007; Seyerlehner, Schedl, Pohle, and Knees, 2010).

In video domain, low-level descriptors can represent the visual aspects of the videos and thus reflect an artistic *style* (Canini, Benini, and Leonardi, 2013; Lehinevych, Kokkinis-Ntrenis, Siantikos, Dogruoz, Giannakopoulos, and Konstantopoulos. 2014; Yang, Mei, Hua, Yang, Yang, and Li, 2007; Zhao, Li, Wang, Yuan, Zha, Li, and Chua, 2011).

It is a fact that recommendation based on low-level features do not draw much attention to multimedia recommender systems. On the other hand, such features received massive attention in some related research fields, namely, in computer vision (Rasheed, Sheikh, and Shah, 2005), and content-based video retrieval. Despite the differences in objectives, these communities share objectives such as formulating the informative descriptors of video and movie items. Hence, they report outcomes and insights that can be beneficial to the context of the multimedia recommender systems (Brezeale and Cook, 2008; Hu, Xie, Li, Zeng, and Maybank, 2011; Rasheed et al., 2005).

2.3.1.2 Tourism

Another well-studied domain in the research on the recommender systems is tourism. This is a domain where *contextualization* plays an important role. We can define contextualization as the process of incorporating contextual factors (such as weather condition, travel goals, and means of transportation) in the recommendation generation. The idea is to make personal suggestions by incorporating diverse sources of user data, as well as the *condition* represented by contextual factors (Adomavicius and Tuzhilin, 2011). For example, a group of tourists may be interested in visting suggested indoor attractions (e.g., museums) during bad weather, but in nice weather they may prefer outdoor activities (e.g., hiking). Recommender systems that are capable of using such contextual factors are known as *CARS*.

CARS are empowered to exploit mathematical modeling in order to better learn user preferences in different contextual situations based on diverse sources of data, e.g., the temperature, season, the geographical position, and even the vehicle type. Due to the popularity of this research domain, a big amount of research has already been conducted in in this domain (Baltrunas, Ludwig, Peer, and Ricci, 2012; Chen and Chen, 2014; Gallego, Woerndl, and Huecas, 2013; Hariri, Mobasher, and Burke, 2012; Kaminskas, Ricci, and Schedl, 2013; Natarajan, Shin, and Dhillon, 2013). The majority of these works can exploit the context experienced by the user in the recommending process.

2.3.1.3 Food

There are a diverse categories of food recommendation systems that have recently been proposed by the community (Trevisiol, Chiarandini, and Baeza-Yates, 2014; West, White, and Horvitz, 2013). For example, Freyne and Berkovsky (2010) built a food recommendation system that, through an effective user interaction model, collects user preferences and generates personalized suggestions. Their system converts the preferences of the users for recipes into preferences for ingredients, and then merges these converted preferences to form user suggestions.

Elahi, Ge, Ricci, Massimo, and Berkovsky (2014) devised a different approach for food recommendation that can combine the predictions for food along diverse aspects (such as user food preferences, nutrition, ingredients, and expenditure) to measure a score for a potential food (or meal). The objective is to take into account measures that shall impact the user's food choices in order to make a more beneficial set of recommendations (Teng, Lin, and Adamic, 2012). In their next paper, the same authors performed an assessment of the rating prediction method, which used a variant of MF. This method exploits more data than utilizing only ratings, such as subjective tags paired to different recipes by users. It has been discovered that extra data input on the user preferences allows the technique to outperform other baseline methods, including those developed in Freyne and Berkovsky (2013).

Generally speaking, the preferences that are aggregated by a recommender system can have two forms, i.e., long-term affinities or short-term affinities. While obtaining and aggregating both forms of preferences is essential, the research on recommender systems does not identify the differences between these two forms. Only limited research works have considered such differences (e.g., Ricci and Nguyen, 2007). The noted example is one of the few works that developed a recommender system, which elicits both generic long-term affinities and specific short-term affinities.

We would like to point out that the traditional line of research on recommender systems typically undermines the importance of human-system interaction model, as an essential component for creating an industrial-grade system. Hence, they mainly concentrate on enhancing the core analytical models by supposing that the preference acquisition procedure is conducted only in the beginning, and then ended.

2.3.1.4 Fashion

Fashion is traditionally referred to as the prevailing form of clothing, and it can be formulated by the concept of *changing*. Fashion includes diverse characters of self-fashioning, such as styles in the street to the other calls of *high* fashion made by designers (Bollen, Knijnenburg, Willemsen, and Graus, 2010); Person, 2019). One of the biggest issues for this type of application is the growing diversity and expanding number of fashion products. This is an effect that can certainly lead to choice overload for the fashion consumers. This is not necessarily negative, since the more available options then there is a higher likelihood that consumers will find a desired product. However, such an effect may lead to the impossibility of actually choosing a product, i.e., the problem of receiving too many options, particularly when they are very diverse (Anderson, 2006).

Recommender techniques are powerful tools that can effectively tackle this issue by making relevant suggestions of products tailored to the needs of the users. They can build a filtering mechanism that eliminates uninteresting and irrelevant products from a shortlist of recommendations. They can thoroughly mine the user data in order to learn particularities among user preferences for each single user. For instance, Amazon can look into the purchase history of users and build predictive models that can ultimately be used to make personalized recommendation for the purchaser. Hence, the smart engine behind the recommender can actively understand the users' behaviors, and obtain diverse and informative forms of data describing the user tastes in order to obtain knowledge on the individual requirements of every user (Rashid, Albert, Cosley, Lam, McNee, Konstan, and Riedl, 2002; Rubens, Elahi, Sugiyama, and Kaplan, 2015; Su and Khoshgoftaar, 2009).

2.3.2 Modern

2.3.2.1 Financial Technology (Fintech)

Financial technology (fintech) aims to use technology to provide financial services to businesses or consumers. Any form of recommendation method in this field will need to understand three main dimensions to provide intelligent recommendations: (i) banking entities, such as customers and products; (ii) banking domain knowledge, such as how different banking segments operate across customers, sales and distribution, products and services, people, processes, and technology; and (iii) banking processes, to help understand the best practices learned by knowledge experts in processes such as fraud detection, customer segmentation, managing customer data, risk modeling for investment banks, and more.

The main shortcoming of existing RSs is that they do not consider domain experts' knowledge, and hence may not exploit user-side information such as cognitive characteristics of the user. These aspects are quite vital to support intelligent and time-aware recommendations.

To support data analytics focusing on customers' cognitive activities, it is important to understand customers' dimensions both from banking and non-banking perspectives, as depicted in Figure 2.4. Modern approaches, such as cognitive recommender systems (Beheshti et al.. 2020b), model the customer behavior and activities as a graph-based data model (Beheshti, Benatallah, and Motahari-Nezhad, 2016; Hammoud, Rabbou, Nouri, Beheshti, and Sakr, 2015) over customers' cognitive graphs to personalize the recommendations.

2.3.2.2 Education

One of the most popular application domains in recommender systems is the field of education. Education allows individuals to reach their full potential and aids in the development of societies by reducing poverty and decreases social inequalities. Recently, the world has experienced an increasing growth in this domain, both on quantity and quality measures.

This, in turn, has already generated several challenges in the education system, such as instructors' workload in dealing with assessments and providing recommendations based on students' performance and skills assessment.

In this context, recommender systems can be significantly important tools for personalizing teaching and learning by understanding and analyzing important indicators such as knowledge, performance (e.g., cognitive, affective, and psychomotor indicators), and skills (e.g., decision-making and problem-solving). An attractive planned work for the future could implement a time-aware deep learning model to construct and analyze learners' profiles in order to better understand students' performance and skills. The learning models would enable recommender systems to identify similarly performing students, which may facilitate personalizing learning process, subject selections, and recruitment.

2.3.2.3 Recruitment

Talent acquisition and recruitment processes are examples of ad hoc processes that are controlled by knowledge workers aiming to achieve a business objective/goal. Attracting and recruiting the right talent is a key differentiator in modern organizations, and recommender systems can play an important role in assisting recruiters in the recruitment process. For example, consider a recommendation engine that has access to LinkedIn profiles,

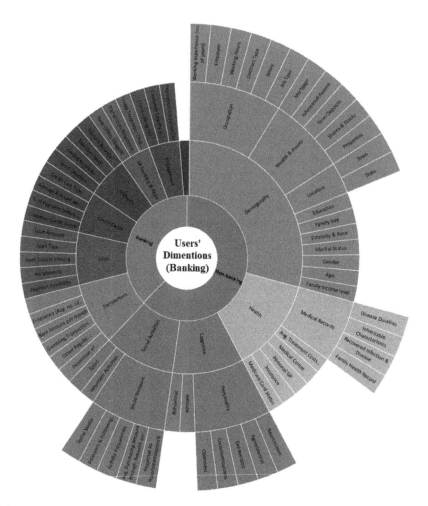

FIGURE 2.4
Users' dimensions in a banking scenario (Beheshti et al.,2020b).

is able to extract data and knowledge from business artifacts (e.g., candidates' CV and position descriptions), has access to curation algorithms to contextualize the data and knowledge, and is able to link them to the facts in the recruitment domain knowledge base.

Artificial intelligence (AI) has enabled organizations to create business leverage by applying cutting edge automation techniques (Shahbaz, Beheshti, Nobari, Qu, Paik, and Mahdavi, 2018): (i) improving the overall quality and effectiveness of the recruitment process; (ii) extracting relevant information from a candidate's CV automatically; (iii) aggregation of different candidate evaluations and relevant information; (iv) understanding the best practices used by recruiters; (v) extracting personality traits and applicant attitudes from social media sites, something that was traditionally only possible through interviews. All these techniques can be leveraged by recommender systems building effective ranking algorithms that optimize the recommendations and help maintain a priority pool of talent. AI-enabled recommender systems would be able to help match the behaviors of the most talented people in their organizations, and help businesses recruit the right candidates for open jobs by aggregating information from different sources and then ranking them based on their overall score. Another future line of work would be to use computer vision algorithms to assess interviews of potential candidates and compare them to the organization's best talent in order to make recommendations (Hirevue, 2019).

2.4 Challenges

Recommender systems typically exploit datasets that contain user feedback (e.g., likes and dislikes, or ratings) that represent preferences produced by a big crowd of interconnected users to a large list of items (Desrosiers and Karypis, 2011). Exploiting such data empowers the recommender systems to learn the patterns and connections among users, and use them to estimate the missing assessments (likes and dislikes, or ratings) of users for the unexplored items and then suggest items that may be attractive to a target user (Koren and Bell. 2011).

The above-mentioned procedure is oversimplified, and there are many grand concerns that have not been fully addressed so far. Hereafter, we briefly explain some of these concerns.

2.4.1 Cold Start

Recommender systems may still encounter a wide range of challenges due to different reasons, such as the lack of rating data for some of the users or items (Adomavicius and Tuzhilin, 2005); Schein, Popescul, Ungar, and Pennock, 2002). One of the problematic issues in building personalized recommendation is *cold start*, which is strongly related to low quality or the quantity of the input data. A sub-problem of cold start is called the *new user* situation, which refers to when a new user begins to use the system and demands suggestions prior to giving any preferences to any existing item. Similarly, in a *new item* situation, a new item is introduced to the item catalog waiting to obtain assessments from existing users (in terms of ratings, reviews, or tags). In addition to that, in spite of the fact that these are typical situations in a cold-starting recommender systems, there exists another problem called *sparsity*. Sparsity is a measure of the data density and is proportional to the number of available feedbacks (e.g., ratings) over the overall possible feedbacks:

$$1 - \frac{\# \, of \, existing \, feedbacks}{\# \, of \, all \, possible \, feedbacks} \tag{2.5}$$

In some of the acute situations of sparsity, the effectiveness of the recommender systems can be strongly deteriorated, consequently resulting in a significant decrease in the performance of the system. In such a condition, the quantity of available user feedback is largely smaller than the number of missing feedback, and the operating system has to build predictions with satisfactory level of quality (Adomavicius and Tuzhilin 2005; Braunhofer, Elahi, and Ricci, 2014).

Different cold start conditions can take place in the actual applications, namely *extreme* cold start and *moderate* cold start conditions.

- *Extreme cold start* condiction take place when a user starts using the system and asks for a recommendation before producing any feedback. The problem can also happen when a brand-new product is inserted into the catalog and has no associated data that can represent that item. This, in turn, can lead to a failure in suggesting that new product to an existing users. Both of these situations are critical issues that have to be handled activrely by the system.

- *Mild cold start* conditions happen once a small number of feedbacks are produced by a user to existing products, and the system can use this limited data to generate a recommendation. This problem may also take place for a new product when a small amount of content data are not fully produced. Mild cold start may take place as a combined condition of extreme and warm start. This can still lead to a failure if not be promptly addressed by the operating system.

2.4.2 Context Awareness

Although context may have different meanings in various domains, it typically emphasizes an event that will be helpful in order to be understood (Beheshti et al., 2020b). In general, context is represented by factors that influence computation but are still different from the input and output data (Lieberman and Selker, 2000). Time, location, and social relations are examples of a context for which motivated researchers may focus on contestaware techniques, such as location-aware and time-aware recommender systems.

For instance, time-aware recommender systems can be beneficial for the system to understand the development of users' affinities over a certain period of time, and can thus provide contextual recommendations for different times (e.g., seasonal, monthly, weakly, or daily with different weather conditions). As another example, social-aware recommender systems can benefit from big data generated on social media in different aspects, from the social characterization of users (including social relationships, followers, and shared content) to identify the personality, behavior, and attitude of social users (Ghafari, Yakhchi, Beheshti, and Orgun, 2018). For example, features such as intimacy, emotional intensity, along with location and time-aware context, can be calculated and used to provide accurate and context-aware recommendations.

2.4.3 Style Awareness

Modern recommender systems in various application domains are becoming more and more aware of the *style* of the items and products they recommend. Integration of product style within the recommendation process is in turn becoming increasingly important. In the multimedia domain, examples of style elements are lighting, colorfulness, and movement and sound.

There are diverse reasons for having lighting in films and movies. The most important one is to enable the perceived understanding of the space and to build observable objects that the audience is seeing. But lighting can also perhaps alter the way an occurrence seen, acting in a way that goes beyond the logical perception of a human.

Colors express a similar capability by setting up emotions derived by an encounter condition. The specific quality of colors disallows them to be perceived separately from space lighting. Likewise, colors tend to contribute to making a unique "perception" of a space in comparison to the other aesthetic characteristics functioning in the similar manner. Experts in media have a common belief that the impact of colors becomes larger as they are predisposed in making a particular emotional goal.

A number of research works on recommender systems have reported that users' preferences can be impacted greater by low-level descriptors in comparison to high-level descriptors (expressing the semantic or syntactic forms in films) (Elahi, Deldjoo, Bakhshandegan Moghaddam, Cella, Cereda, and Cremonesi, 2017; He, Fang, Wang, and McAuley, 2016; Messina, Dominquez, Parra, Trattner, and Soto, 2018; Rimaz, Elahi, Bakhshandegan Moghadam, Trattner, Hosseini, and Tkalcic, 2019; Roy and Guntuku, 2016). Examples of such low-level descriptors can be color energy, shot duration, and lighting key. (Wang and Cheong, 2006) have a proved to influence on user mood and emotion (Roberts, Hager, and Heron, 1994). In addition to that, various forms of motion (such as camera movement) can play a significant role and are commonly adopted by filmmakers when aiming to affect the perception of movie watchers (Heiderich, 2018). A range of methods and techniques have been adopted to address the task of learning visual descriptors from films (Ewerth, Schwalb, Tessmann, and Freisleben, 2004; Savian, Elahi, and Tillo, 2020; Tan, Saur, Kulkami, and Ramadge, 2000).

Despite of the importance of low-level descriptors, the usage of them has not drawn much consideration in recommendation systems (e.g., an example is Messina et al. [2018]). However, these audiovisual descriptors are thoroughly investigated in the related areas, namely within the computer vision community (Naphide and Huang, 2001; Snoek and Worring, 2005).

2.5 Advanced Topics

In the times of AI, an intelligent recommender system should be highly data driven, knowledge driven, and cognitive driven. Cognitive recommender systems (Beheshti et al., 2020b) have been proposed as a new type of intelligent recommender system that aims to analyze and understand users' preferences and explore mechanisms to intelligently understand the complex and changing environments. In this context, we categorize the advanced topics in recommender systems into the following categories: AI-enabled recommendations, cognition aware, intelligent personalization, intelligent ranking, and intelligent customer engagement.

2.5.1 AI-Enabled Recommendations

As discussed in Section 2.3, AI-enabled recommendations should benefit from data-driven and knowledge-driven approaches, such as data lakes (Beheshti et al., 2017a) and knowledge lakes (Beheshti et al., 2018, 2019).

Data-driven recommendations will enable leveraging machine learning technologies to contextualize the big data aiming to enhance the precision of automatic suggestions, facilitating the use of content/context, and moving from statistical modeling to advanced models based on multi-layer neural networks. These will improve mining patterns between item and user descriptors to build better suggestions for users.

Knowledge-driven recommendations empower simulating the expertise of the domain experts (e.g., using crowdsourcing methods [Beheshti et al., 2019]) and to adopt methods such as reinforcement learning to enhance making relevant and accurate recommendations.

2.5.2 Cognition Aware

Cognition refers to the mental procedure of eliciting knowledge and learning by thinking, experience, and the diverse sources of senses (Beheshti et al., 2020a). In this context, a cognition-aware recommendation will enable recognizing the users' personality and emotion, as well as study their particular characteristics and affinities over time. *Social cognition-aware recommendations* can refer to the processes that enable a recommender system to interpret social information and provide context-aware recommendations. This task can be quite challenging, as social cognition means different things to different people and can be quite subjective. Moreover, it can be involved in social interactions at a group level or on a one-to-one basis. This, in turn, makes group-aware recommendations a challenging task, as group-aware recommender systems support scenarios in which a *group*of users might be a target for items to be consumed.

Attention mechanism would be also an interesting line of future work in recommender systems as it can be used to simulate the neural activities of a person. This task could quite be challenging as the recommendation methods and algorithms would need to take into consideration the variation in the user's preferences. Applications could include in case-based and session-based recommendations, which may require taking the user's previous cases/sessions into account. A future line of work may focus on a hybrid model, leveraging the attention mechanism and context-aware approaches to learn the user's stable preferences and linking that with dynamic intents to make the best use the variation in the user's contextual preference in order to cope with the cold-start problem within sessions.

2.5.3 Intelligent Personalization

Personalization, i.e., the action of designing or producing something to meet someone's individual requirements, can support analytics around users' cognitive activities. This, in turn, can support intelligent and time-aware recommendations. In particular, product and content recommendations tailored to a user's profile and habits can facilitate understanding and analyzing users' behavior, preferences, and history. This, in turn, will boost users' engagement and satisfaction in real-time, in contrast to a uniform experience. This process requires automatic processing and curation of the data, identifying meaningful features, selecting the right algorithms, and using them to train a proper personalization model.

In this context, feature engineering (Anderson, Antenucci, Bittorf, Burgess, Cafarella, Kumar, Niu, Park, Ŕe, and Zhang, 2013), i.e., the procedure of using domain knowledge to obtain diverse forms of describing features from the raw data via data mining methods, is a key future work for intelligent personalization, and is necessary to improve and optimize a personalization model. To achieve this goal, features (i.e., the observations or characteristics on which a model is built) can be engineered by decomposing or splitting features (e.g., from external data sources from open, private, social, and IoT data islands), or aggregating or combining features to create new features (e.g., to understand users' behavior). However, the countless number of options of transformations that can be performed for training and optimizing a personalization model makes the task of effective feature engineering to meet someone's individual requirements very difficult.

2.5.4 Intelligent Ranking

The business's priorities, i.e., its value proposition and profit formula, are quite important and they require the organizations' recommendation engine to promote specific content or products, such as trending news or a promotional offer, over time. Learning the personalized recommendation list can be cast as a ranking problem. Ranking can be quite subjective as it requires determining the causal connections among various features and, more importantly, calculating and assigning weights and importance scores to the connections between features.

An intelligent ranking algorithm should be capable of being trained on top of the domain experts' knowledge and experience to understand the context, extract related features, and to determine the causal connections among various features over time. The goal here is to concentrate on the *change* from statistical modeling to novel forms of modeling, such as those based on deep learning, to improve potential similarities among descriptors and ultimately build a more accurate ranking. A future work direction may focus on empowering the exploitation of personality, behavior, and attitudes when generating recommendations that can be used to improve correlations discovery among features (Yakhchi, Beheshti, Ghafari, and Orgun, 2020).

2.5.5 Intelligent Customer Engagement

Customer engagement, i.e., the emotional connection between a customer and a brand, is a vital process for organizations as highly engaged customers buy more, promote more, and demonstrate more loyalty. Powering real-time personalized product and content recommendations can improve customer engagement. Most of the existing recommender systems have been designed to recommend the right products to users; however, very few recommender systems are focused on the emotional connection between a customer and a brand, to better understand their needs, feelings, and environment. Provenance (Beheshti, Motahari-Nezhad, and Benatallah, 2012), i.e., the logged records of an object (e.g., service, or product) or the documentation of procedure in an object's life stage that logs the sequences that the object was derived and evolved, can help in tracing customer activities and their interactions with specific products over time. A provenance-aware recommender system would be an interesting future direction as it will facilitate understanding and analyzing customer behavior and activities. Another future plan could be to adopt Gamification methods, i.e., the application of game-design units and game principles in non-game contexts, to learn from the users' activities (Beheshti et al., 2020b).

2.6 Conclusion

Choosing the right product in the age of big data and AI is becoming a growing challenge due to the enormous volume and variety of products and services. Recommender systems can deal with this problem by providing personalized suggestions of items that will likely match the user's requirements. In particular, recommender systems can improve the user experience in online applications by assisting users and allowing them to explore different types of items. In this chapter, we provided a summary of different types of real-world RSs, their methods, and applications, along with challenges and future opportunities in the age of big data and AI. We discussed how machine learning algorithms are adopted by recommender systems to obtain knowledge from diverse sources of input information, e.g., user data (ratings, reviews, and comments) and item data (categories, descriptions, and images) when generating personalized recommendations for users. We presented applications and motivating scenarios, and discussed how increasing growth of the cognitive technology mixed with development in areas such as AI, data science, and user personalization and engagement shows a clear opportunity to take the recommender systems the next level.

References

Gediminas Adomavicius and Alexander Tuzhilin. Toward the next generation of recommender systems: a survey of the state-of-the-art and possible extensions. *Knowledge and Data Engineering, IEEE Transactions on*, 17(6):734–749, June 2005. ISSN 1041-4347.

Gediminas Adomavicius and Alexander Tuzhilin. Context-aware recommender systems. In *Recommender Systems Handbook*, pages 217–253. Springer, 2011.

Jae-wook Ahn, Peter Brusilovsky, Jonathan Grady, Daqing He, and Sue Yeon Syn. Open user profiles for adaptive news systems: help or harm? In *Proceedings of the 16th international conference on World Wide Web*, pages 11–20. ACM, 2007.

Chris Anderson. *The Long Tail*. Long Tail : Why the Future of Business Is Selling Less of More (motamem.org). 2006.

Michael R Anderson, Dolan Antenucci, Victor Bittorf, Matthew Burgess, Michael J Cafarella, Arun Kumar, Feng Niu, Yongjoo Park, Christopher Ŕe, and Ce Zhang. Brainwash: A data system for feature engineering. *Cidr*, 40(3): 2013.

Marko Balabanovíc and Yoav Shoham. Fab: Content-based, collaborative recommendation. *Commun. ACM*, 40(3):66–72, March 1997. ISSN 0001-0782. URL: http://doi.acm.org/10.1145/245108.245124.

Linas Baltrunas, Bernd Ludwig, Stefan Peer, and Francesco Ricci. Context relevance assessment and exploitation in mobile recommender systems. *Personal Ubiquitous Comput.*, 16(5):507–526, June 2012. ISSN 1617-4909. URL: http://dx.doi.org/10.1007/s00779-011-0417-x.

Seyed-Mehdi-Reza Beheshti, Hamid Reza Motahari-Nezhad, and Boualem Benatallah. Temporal provenance model (tpm): model and query language. *arXiv preprint arXiv:1211.5009*, 2012.

Seyed-Mehdi-Reza Beheshti, Boualem Benatallah, and Hamid Reza Motahari-Nezhad. Scalable graph-based OLAP analytics over process execution data. *Distributed Parallel Databases*, 34(3):379–423, 2016.

Amin Beheshti, Boualem Benatallah, Reza Nouri, Van Munin Chhieng, HuangTao Xiong, and Xu Zhao. Coredb: a data lake service. In *Proceedings of the 2017 ACM on Conference on Information and Knowledge Management, CIKM 2017*, Singapore, November 06–10, 2017, pages 2451–2454, 2017a.

Seyed-Mehdi-Reza Beheshti, Alireza Tabebordbar, Boualem Benatallah, and Reza Nouri. On automating basic data curation tasks. In Rick Barrett, Rick Cummings, Eugene Agichtein, and Evgeniy Gabrilovich, editors, *Proceedings of the 26th International Conference on World Wide Web Companion, Perth, Australia, April 3-7, 2017*, pages 165–169. ACM, 2017b.

Amin Beheshti, Boualem Benatallah, Reza Nouri, and Alireza Tabebordbar. Corekg: a knowledge lake service. *Proc. VLDB Endow.*, 11(12):1942–1945, 2018.

Amin Beheshti, Boualem Benatallah, Quan Z. Sheng, and Francesco Schiliro. Intelligent knowledge lakes: The age of artificial intelligence and big data. In Leong Hou U, Jian Yang, Yi Cai, Kamalakar Karlapalem, An Liu, and Xin Huang, editors, *Web Information Systems Engineering – WISE 2019 Workshop, Demo, and Tutorial, Hong Kong and Macau, China, January 19-22, 2020, Revised Selected Papers*, volume 1155 of *Communications in Computer and Information Science*, pages 24–34. Springer, 2019.

Amin Beheshti, Vahid Moraveji Hashemi, Shahpar Yakhchi, Hamid Reza Motahari-Nezhad, Seyed Mohssen Ghafari, and Jian Yang. personality2vec: Enabling the analysis of behavioral disorders in social networks. In James Caverlee, Xia (Ben) Hu, Mounia Lalmas, and Wei Wang, editors, *WSDM '20: The Thirteenth ACM International Conference on Web Search and Data Mining*, Houston, TX, USA, *February 3-7, 2020*, pages 825–828. ACM, 2020a.

Amin Beheshti, Shahpar Yakhchi, Salman Mousaeirad, Seyed Mohssen Ghafari, Srinivasa Reddy Goluguri, and Mohammad Amin Edrisi. Towards cognitive recommender systems. *Algorithms*, 13(8):176, 2020b.

Dmitry Bogdanov and Perfecto Herrera. How much metadata do we need in music recommendation? a subjective evaluation using preference sets. In *ISMIR*, pages 97–102, 2011.

Dmitry Bogdanov, Joan Serra, Nicolas Wack, Perfecto Herrera, and Xavier Serra. Unifying low-level and high-level music similarity measures. *Multimedia, IEEE Transactions on*, 13 (4):687–701, 2011.

Dirk Bollen, Bart P Knijnenburg, Martijn C Willemsen, and Mark Graus. Understanding choice overload in recommender systems. In *Proceedings of the fourth ACM conference on Recommender systems*, pages 63–70. ACM, 2010.

Matthias Braunhofer, Mehdi Elahi, and Francesco Ricci. Techniques for cold-starting context-aware mobile recommender systems for tourism. *Intelligenza Artificiale*, 8(2):129–143, 2014.

Darin Brezeale and Diane J Cook. Automatic video classification: A survey of the literature. *Systems, Man, and Cybernetics, Part C: Applications and Reviews, IEEE Transactions on*, 38(3):416–430, 2008.

Robin Burke. Knowledge-based Recommender Systems, In *Encyclopedia of Library and Information Systems*. Marcel Dekker, 2000.

Robin Burke. Hybrid recommender systems: Survey and experiments. *User Modeling and User-Adapted Interaction*, 12(4):331–370, 2002. https://ieeexplore.ieee.org/document/6259846.

Luca Canini, Sergio Benini, and Riccardo Leonardi. Affective recommendation of movies based on selected connotative features. *Circuits and Systems for Video Technology*, IEEE Transactions on Circuits and Systems for Video Technology, 23(4):636–647, 2013.

Ivan Cantador, Martin Szomszor, Harith Alani, Miriam Fernandez, and Pablo Castells. Enriching ontological user profiles with tagging history for multi-domain recommendations. 2008.

Xiaofei Chao, Mark J Huiskes, Tommaso Gritti, and Calina Ciuhu. A framework for robust feature selection for real-time fashion style recommendation. In *Proceedings of the 1st inter-national workshop on Interactive multimedia for consumer electronics*, pages 35–42, 2009.

Guanliang Chen and Li Chen. Recommendation based on contextual opinions. In *User Modeling, Adaptation, and Personalization*, pages 61–73. Springer, 2014.

Mark Claypool, Anuja Gokhale, Tim Miranda, Pavel Murnikov, Dmitry Netes, and Matthew Sartin. Combining content-based and collaborative filters in an online newspaper. In *Proceedings of the ACM SIGIR'99 Workshop on Recommender Systems: Algorithms and Evaluation*, Berkeley, California, 1999. ACM.

Yashar Deldjoo and Reza Ebrahimi Atani. A low-cost infrared-optical head tracking solution for virtual 3d audio environment using the nintendo wii-remote. *Entertainment Computing*, 12:9–27, 2016.

Yashar Deldjoo, Mehdi Elahi, Paolo Cremonesi, Franca Garzotto, Pietro Piazzolla, and Mas-simo Quadrana. Content-based video recommendation system based on stylistic visual features. *Journal on Data Semantics*, pages 1–15, 2016.

Christian Desrosiers and George Karypis. A comprehensive survey of neighborhood-based recommendation methods. In Francesco Ricci, Lior Rokach, Bracha Shapira, and Paul B. Kantor, editors, *Recommender Systems Handbook*, pages 107–144. Springer, 2011.

LLC Timely Development. Netflix prize, 2008. http://www.timelydevelopment.com/demos/NetflixPrize.aspx.

Mehdi Elahi. Adaptive active learning in recommender systems. In *Proceedings of the 19th International Conference on User Modeling, Adaption and Personalization*, pages 414–417, 2011.

Mehdi Elahi. *Empirical Evaluation of Active Learning Strategies in Collaborative Filtering*. PhD thesis, Ph. D. Dissertation. Free University of Bozen-Bolzano, 2014.

Mehdi Elahi and Lianyong Qi. *Fashion Recommender Systems in Cold Start*. 2020.

Mehdi Elahi, Valdemaras Repsys, and Francesco Ricci. Rating elicitation strategies for collaborative filtering. In *Proceedings 12th International Conference on E-Commerce and Web Technologies*, pages 160–171, 2011.

Mehdi Elahi, Francesco Ricci, and Neil Rubens. Adapting to natural rating acquisition with combined active learning strategies. In *ISMIS'12: Proceedings of the 20th international conference on Foundations of Intelligent Systems*, pages 254–263, Berlin, Heidelberg, 2012. Springer-Verlag. ISBN 978-3-642-34623-1.

Mehdi Elahi, Mouzhi Ge, Francesco Ricci, David Massimo, and Shlomo Berkovsky. Interactive food recommendation for groups. In *Poster Proceedings of the 8th ACM Conference on Recommender Systems, RecSys 2014*, Foster City, Silicon Valley, CA, USA, October 6-10, 2014. 2014.

Mehdi Elahi, Yashar Deldjoo, Farshad Bakhshandegan Moghaddam, Leonardo Cella, Stefano Cereda, and Paolo Cremonesi. Exploring the semantic gap for movie recommendations. In *Proceedings of the Eleventh ACM Conference on Recommender Systems*, pages 326–330. ACM, 2017.

Ralph Ewerth, Martin Schwalb, Paul Tessmann, and Bernd Freisleben. Estimation of arbitrary camera motion in MPEG videos. In *Proceedings of the 17th International Conference on Pattern Recognition, 2004. ICPR 2004*. IEEE, 2004. URL: https://doi.org/10.1109/icpr.2004.1334181.

A. Felfernig and R. Burke. Constraint-based recommender systems: Technologies and research issues. In *Proceedings of the 10th International Conference on Electronic Commerce*, ICEC '08, pages 3:1–3:10, New York, NY, USA, 2008. ACM. ISBN 978-1-60558-075-3. URL: http://doi.acm.org/10.1145/1409540.1409544.

Ignacio Fernandez-Tobıas and Ivan Cantador. Exploiting social tags in matrix factorization models for cross-domain collaborative filtering. In *CBRecSys@ RecSys*, pages 34–41, 2014.

Jill Freyne and Shlomo Berkovsky. Intelligent food planning: personalized recipe recommen-dation. In *IUI*, pages 321–324. ACM, 2010.

Jill Freyne and Shlomo Berkovsky. Evaluating recommender systems for supportive technologies. In *User Modeling and Adaptation for Daily Routines*, pages 195–217. Springer, 2013.

Simon Funk. Netflix update: Try this at home, 2006. http://sifter.org/~simon/journal/20061211.html.

Daniel Gallego, Wolfgang Woerndl, and Gabriel Huecas. Evaluating the impact of proactivity in the user experience of a context-aware restaurant recommender for android smartphones. *Journal of Systems Architecture*, 59(9):748–758, 2013.

Seyed Mohssen Ghafari, Shahpar Yakhchi, Amin Beheshti, and Mehmet A. Orgun. Social context-aware trust prediction: Methods for identifying fake news. In *Web Information Systems Engineering - WISE 2018 - 19th International Conference, Dubai, United Arab Emirates, November 12-15, 2018, Proceedings, Part I, volume 11233 of Lecture Notes in Computer Science*, pages 161–177. Springer, 2018.

Mohammad Hammoud, Dania Abed Rabbou, Reza Nouri, Seyed-Mehdi-Reza Beheshti, and Sherif Sakr. DREAM: distributed RDF engine with adaptive query planner and minimal communication. *Proceedings of the VLDB Endowment*, 8(6):654–665, 2015. URL: http://www.vldb.org/pvldb/vol8/p654-Hammoud.pdf.

Negar Hariri, Bamshad Mobasher, and Robin Burke. Context-aware music recommendation based on latenttopic sequential patterns. In *Proceedings of the sixth ACM conference on Recommender systems*, pages 131–138. ACM, 2012.

Naieme Hazrati and Mehdi Elahi. Addressing the new item problem in video recommender systems by incorporation of visual features with restricted boltzmann machines. *Expert Systems*, page e12645, 2020.

Ruining He and Julian McAuley. Ups and downs: Modeling the visual evolution of fashion trends with one-class collaborative filtering. In *proceedings of the 25th international conference on world wide web*, pages 507–517, 2016.

Ruining He, Chen Fang, Zhaowen Wang, and Julian McAuley. Vista: A visually, socially, and temporally-aware model for artistic recommendation. In *Proceedings of the 10th ACM Conference on Recommender Systems*, RecSys '16, pages 309–316, New York, NY, USA, 2016. ACM. ISBN 978-1-4503-4035-9. URL: http://doi.acm.org/10.1145/2959100.2959152.

Timothy Heiderich. Cinematography techniques: The different types of shots in film. *Ontario Mining Assosiation. Recuperado de https://www.oma.on.ca/en/contestpages/resources/free-report-cinematography.pdf*, 2018.

Hirevue; job search engine. https://www.hirevue.com/products/video-interviewing, 2019. Accessed: 2019-09-14.

Weiming Hu, Nianhua Xie, Li Li, Xianglin Zeng, and Stephen Maybank. A survey on visual content-based video indexing and retrieval. *Systems, Man, and Cybernetics, Part C: Applications and Reviews, IEEE Transactions on*, 41(6):797–819, 2011.

Dietmar Jannach, Markus Zanker, Alexander Felfernig, and Gerhard Friedrich. *Recommender Systems: An Introduction*. Cambridge University Press, 2010.

Marius Kaminskas, Francesco Ricci, and Markus Schedl. Location-aware music recommendation using auto-tagging and hybrid matching. In *Proceedings of the 7th ACM conference on Recommender systems*, pages 17–24. ACM, 2013.

Peter Knees, Tim Pohle, Markus Schedl, and Gerhard Widmer. A music search engine built upon audio-based and web-based similarity measures. In *Proceedings of the 30th annual international ACM SIGIR conference on Research and development in information retrieval*, pages 447–454. ACM, 2007.

Yehuda Koren. Factorization meets the neighborhood: A multifaceted collaborative filtering model. In *Proceedings of the 14th ACM SIGKDD International Conference on Knowledge Discovery and Data Mining*, KDD '08, pages 426–434, New York, NY, USA, 2008a. ACM. ISBN 978-1-60558-193-4. URL: http://doi.acm.org/10.1145/1401890.1401944.

Yehuda Koren. Factorization meets the neighborhood: a multifaceted collaborative filtering model. In *KDD '08: Proceeding of the 14th ACM SIGKDD international conference on Knowledge discovery and data mining*, pages 426–434, New York, NY, USA, 2008b. ACM. ISBN 978-1-60558-193-4.

Yehuda Koren and Robert Bell. Advances in collaborative filtering. In Francesco Ricci, Lior Rokach, Bracha Shapira, and Paul Kantor, editors, *Recommender Systems Handbook*, pages 145–186. Springer Verlag, 2011.

Taras Lehinevych, Nikolaos Kokkinis-Ntrenis, Giorgos Siantikos, A Seza Dogruoz, Theodoros Giannakopoulos, and Stasinos Konstantopoulos. Discovering similarities for content-based recommendation and browsing in multimedia collections. In *Signal-Image Technology and Internet-Based Systems (SITIS), 2014 Tenth International Conference on*, pages 237–243. IEEE, 2014.

Qing Li and Byeong Man Kim. *An approach for combining content-based and collaborative filters*. In *Proceedings of the Sixth International Workshop on Information Retrieval with Asian Languages - Volume 11*, AsianIR '03, pages 17–24, Stroudsburg, PA, USA, 2003. Association for Computational Linguistics. URL: http://dx.doi.org/10.3115/1118935. 1118938.

Henry Lieberman and Ted Selker. Out of context: Computer systems that adapt to, and learn from, context. *IBM Systems Journal*, 39(3&4): 617–632, 2000.

Pasquale Lops, Marco De Gemmis, and Giovanni Semeraro. Content-based recommender systems: State of the art and trends. In *Recommender Systems Handbook*, pages 73–105. Springer, 2011.

Yucheng Low, Danny Bickson, Joseph Gonzalez, Carlos Guestrin, Aapo Kyrola, and Joseph M Hellerstein. Distributed graphlab: a framework for machine learning and data mining in the cloud. *Proceedings of the VLDB Endowment*, 5(8):716–727, 2012.

Marcelo Garcia Manzato. gsvd++: Supporting implicit feedback on recommender systems with metadata awareness. In *Proceedings of the 28th Annual ACM Symposium on Applied Computing*, SAC '13, pages 908–913, New York, NY, USA, 2013. ACM. ISBN 978-1-4503-1656-9. URL: http://doi.acm.org/10.1145/2480362.2480536.

Pablo Messina, Vicente Dominquez, Denis Parra, Christoph Trattner, and Alvaro Soto. Exploring content-based artwork recommendation with metadata and visual features. *UMUAI*, 2018.

Raymond J Mooney and Loriene Roy. Content-based book recommending using learning for text categorization. In *Proceedings of the fifth ACM conference on Digital libraries*, pages 195–204. ACM, 2000.

H. R. Naphide and Thomas Huang. A probabilistic framework for semantic video indexing, filtering, and retrieval. *IEEE Transactions on Multimedia*, 3(1):141–151, March 2001. ISSN 1520-9210.

Nagarajan Natarajan, Donghyuk Shin, and Inderjit S Dhillon. Which app will you use next?: collaborative filtering with interactional context. In *Proceedings of the 7th ACM conference on Recommender systems*, pages 201–208. ACM, 2013.

Hai Thanh Nguyen, Thomas Almenningen, Martin Havig, Herman Schistad, Anders Kofod-Petersen, Helge Langseth, and Heri Ramampiaro. Learning to rank for personalised fashion recommender systems via implicit feedback. In *Mining Intelligence and Knowledge Exploration*, pages 51–61. Springer, 2014.

Michael J. Pazzani. A framework for collaborative, content-based and demographic filtering. *Artificial Intelligence Review*, 13(5-6): 393–408, December 1999. ISSN 0269-2821. URL: http://dx.doi.org/10.1023/A:1006544522159.

Michael J. Pazzani and Daniel Billsus. *The Adaptive Web. chapter Content-based Recommendation Systems*, pages 325–341. Springer-Verlag, Berlin, Heidelberg, 2007. ISBN 978-3-540-72078-2. URL: http://dl.acm.org/citation.cfm?id=1768197.1768209.

Person. Definition of fashion, 2019. URL: https://fashion-history.lovetoknow.com/alphabetical-index-fashion-clothing-history/definitionn-fashion.

Hua Quanping. Analysis of collaborative filtering algorithm fused with fashion attributes. *International Journal of u-and e-Service, Science and Technology*, 8(10):159–168, 2015.

Zeeshan Rasheed, Yaser Sheikh, and Mubarak Shah. On the use of computable features for film classification. *Circuits and Systems for Video Technology, IEEE Transactions on*, 15 (1):52–64, 2005.

Al Mamunur Rashid, Istvan Albert, Dan Cosley, Shyong K. Lam, Sean M. McNee, Joseph A. Konstan, and John Riedl. Getting to know you: Learning new user preferences in recommender systems. In *Proceedings of the 2002 International Conference on Intelligent User Interfaces, IUI 2002*, pages 127–134. ACM Press, 2002.

Steffen Rendle. Factorization machines with libfm. *ACM Transactions on Intelligent Systems and Technology (TIST)*, 3(3):57, 2012.

Paul Resnick and Hal R Varian. Recommender systems. *Communications of the ACM*, 40(3): 56–58, 1997.

Francesco Ricci and Quang Nhat Nguyen. Acquiring and revising preferences in a critique-based mobile recommender system. *Intelligent Systems, IEEE*, 22(3):22–29, 2007.

Francesco Ricci, Lior Rokach, and Bracha Shapira. Recommender systems: Introduction and challenges. In *Recommender Systems Handbook*, pages 1–34. Springer US, 2015.

Mohammad Hossein Rimaz, Mehdi Elahi, Farshad Bakhshandegan Moghadam, Christoph Trattner, Reza Hosseini, and Marko Tkalcic. Exploring the power of visual features for the recommendation of movies. In *Proceedings of the 27th ACM Conference on User Modeling, Adaptation and Personalization*, pages 303–308, 2019.

Ralph J. Roberts, Lisa D. Hager, and Christine Heron. Prefrontal cognitive processes: Working memory and inhibition in the antisaccade task. *Journal of Experimental Psychology: General*, 123(4):374–393, 1994. URL: https://doi.org/10.1037/0096-3445.123.4.374.

Sujoy Roy and Sharath Chandra Guntuku. Latent factor representations for cold-start video recommendation. In *Proceedings of the 10th ACM Conference on Recommender Systems*, RecSys '16, pages 99–106, New York, NY, USA, 2016. ACM. ISBN 978-1-4503-4035-9. URL: http://doi.acm.org/10.1145/2959100.2959172.

Neil Rubens, Mehdi Elahi, Masashi Sugiyama, and Dain Kaplan. Active learning in recommender systems. In *Recommender Systems Handbook - chapter 24: Recommending Active Learning*, pages 809–846. Springer US, 2015.

Stefano Savian, Mehdi Elahi, and Tammam Tillo. Optical flow estimation with deep learning, a survey on recent advances. In *Deep Biometrics*, pages 257–287. Springer, 2020.

Andrew I. Schein, Alexandrin Popescul, Lyle H. Ungar, and David M. Pennock. Methods and metrics for cold-start recommendations. In *SIGIR '02: Proceedings of the 25th annual international ACM SIGIR conference on Research and development in information retrieval*, pages 253–260, New York, NY, USA, 2002. ACM. ISBN 1-58113-561-0.

Klaus Seyerlehner, Markus Schedl, Tim Pohle, and Peter Knees. Using block-level features for genre classification, tag classification and music similarity estimation. *Submission to Audio Music Similarity and Retrieval Task of MIREX 2010*, 2010.

Usman Shahbaz, Amin Beheshti, Sadegh Nobari, Qiang Qu, Hye-Young Paik, and Mehregan Mahdavi. irecruit: Towards automating the recruitment process. In *Service Research and Innovation - 7th Australian Symposium, ASSRI 2018, Sydney, NSW, Australia, September 6, 2018, and Wollongong, NSW, Australia, December 14, 2018, Revised Selected Papers*, volume 367 of *Lecture Notes in Business Information Processing*, pages 139–152. Springer, 2018.

Cees G.M. Snoek and Marcel Worring. Multimodal video indexing: A review of the state-of-the-art. *Multimedia Tools and Applications*, 25(1):5–35, Jan 2005. ISSN 1573-7721. URL: https://doi. org/10.1023/B:MTAP.0000046380.27575.a5.

Xiaoyuan Su and Taghi M. Khoshgoftaar. A survey of collaborative filtering techniques. *Advances in Artificial Intelligence*, 2009:4:2–4:2, January 2009. ISSN 1687-7470. URL: http://dx.doi. org/10.1155/2009/421425.

Yap-Peng Tan, D. D. Saur, S. R. Kulkami, and P. J. Ramadge. Rapid estimation of camera motion from compressed video with application to video annotation. *IEEE Transactions on Circuits and Systems for Video Technology*, 10(1):133–146, February 2000. ISSN 1051-8215. URL: https://doi. org/10.1109/76.825867.

Chun-Yuen Teng, Yu-Ru Lin, and Lada A Adamic. Recipe recommendation using ingredient networks. In *Proceedings of the 4th Annual ACM Web Science Conference*, pages 298–307. ACM, 2012.

Michele Trevisiol, Luca Chiarandini, and Ricardo Baeza-Yates. Buon appetito: recommending personalized menus. In *Proceedings of the 25th ACM conference on Hypertext and social media*, pages 327–329. ACM, 2014.

Qingqing Tu and Le Dong. An intelligent personalized fashion recommendation system. In *2010 International Conference on Communications, Circuits and Systems (ICCCAS)*, pages 479–485. IEEE, 2010.

TURI. Graphlab recommender factorization recommender, 2018. URL: https://turi.com/products/ create/docs/generated/graphlab.recommender.factorization_recommender.Factorization Recommender.html.

Hee Lin Wang and Loong-Fah Cheong. Affective understanding in film. *IEEE Transactions on Circuits and Systems for Video Technology*, 16(6):689–704, jun 2006. URL: https://doi.org/10.1109/ tcsvt.2006.873781.

Yuanyuan Wang, Stephen Chi-Fai Chan, and Grace Ngai. Applicability of demographic recommender system to tourist attractions: A case study on trip advisor. In *Proceedings of the The 2012 IEEE/WIC/ACM International Joint Conferences on Web Intelligence and Intelligent Agent Technology - Volume 03*, WI-IAT '12, pages 97–101, Washington, DC, USA, 2012. IEEE Computer Society. ISBN 978-0-7695-4880-7. URL: http://dx.doi.org/10.1109/WI-IAT.2012.133.

Shoujin Wang, Liang Hu, Yan Wang, Longbing Cao, Quan Z Sheng, and Mehmet Orgun. Sequential recommender systems: challenges, progress and prospects. *arXiv preprint arXiv:2001.04830*, 2019.

Robert West, Ryen W White, and Eric Horvitz. From cookies to cooks: Insights on dietary patterns via analysis of web usage logs. In *Proceedings of the 22nd international conference on World Wide Web*, pages 1399–1410. International World Wide Web Conferences Steering Committee, 2013.

Shahpar Yakhchi, Amin Beheshti, Seyed Mohssen Ghafari, and Mehmet Orgun. Enabling the analysis of personality aspects in recommender systems. *arXiv preprint arXiv:2001.04825*, 2020.

Bo Yang, Tao Mei, Xian-Sheng Hua, Linjun Yang, Shi-Qiang Yang, and Mingjing Li. Online video recommendation based on multimodal fusion and relevance feedback. In *Proceedings of the 6th ACM international conference on Image and video retrieval*, pages 73–80. ACM, 2007.

Xiaojian Zhao, Guangda Li, Meng Wang, Jin Yuan, Zheng-Jun Zha, Zhoujun Li, and Tat-Seng Chua. Integrating rich information for video recommendation with multi-task rank aggregation. In *Proceedings of the 19th ACM international conference on Multimedia*, pages 1521–1524. ACM, 2011.

3

Machine Learning for Data Science Applications

Ravindra B. Keskar and Mansi A. Radke

Visvesvaraya National Institute of Technology, Nagpur, Maharashtra, India

CONTENTS

3.1 Introduction

As data is growing exponentially, taking the form of *big data*, data analysis has become extremely crucial from the perspective of understanding the existing patterns in the data, as well as to predict accurately. Machine learning (ML) involves the use of various mathematical and statistical methods (along with the domain expertise and programming skills) to draw useful conclusions and insights from the given data. It is said that a computer program learns when its performance, as measured by some performance metric, improves with experience in the context of a certain task. There are broadly two kinds of important machine learning techniques, namely *supervised* and *unsupervised* machine learning. In a supervised machine learning technique, the system/machine learns from given *input-output* pairs. Examples of supervised learning techniques are *naïve Bayes, support vector machines (SVM), decision trees,* and many others. Supervised learning is a technique that is based on the *inductive learning hypothesis*. As described by John Mitchell [1], the inductive learning hypothesis states, *"Any hypothesis found to approximate the target function well over sufficiently large set of training examples will also approximate the target function well over other unobserved examples."* When the output is a continuous valued function, the task is called as *regression*, and when the output is a discrete valued function, the task is called as *classification*. On the other hand, unsupervised learning techniques work on unlabeled data and explore hidden undetected patterns in the given data, an example being *K-means clustering algorithm*. To reduce the complexity of the machine learning models as well as to improve accuracy, *dimensionality reduction* or *feature selection* methods like *principal component analysis, singular value decomposition, linear discriminant analysis* and others are used.

In this chapter we take an overview of different techniques like *linear regression, decision trees, naïve Bayes, K-means clustering,* and *support vector machines.* We discuss error terms in both, classification as well as regression problems. We also discuss *ensembling, dimensionality reduction,* and some other machine learning methodologies.

3.1.1 Data Science and Machine Learning

Data science typically involves predicting a value based on the inputs given, for example, weather prediction based on meteorological parameters, classification tasks like detecting whether an email is spam or not, recommendations that one gets on Netflix and YouTube in a personalized way, document clustering, anomaly detection to detect errors and frauds, image identification, share-market forecasting, and so on. In all these arenas, various machine learning algorithms do naturally come into play. For example, a model to detect whether an email is spam or not could be modeled as a clustering application. In most of the manufacturing units, sensors are installed and sensor values captured to monitor and predict health parameters of the system. In this case, regression, as well as classification algorithms, can be used; use of artificial neural networks (ANNs) and their variants are very good choices. In banks and financial works, predictive modeling can be done to gauge whether a customer will be a defaulter in loan repayment. This could be modeled as a classification problem, and classification algorithms like decision tree or support vector machine (SVM) can be used. Text classification tasks and NLP applications like *named entity recognition* heavily uses naïve Bayes algorithm. In addition, health care applications like early prediction of a disease for a patient, based on the symptoms (and other details), also entails the use of the naïve Bayes algorithm. Recommender systems recommend to users products that are relevant to them (for example, movies, books, and other products), and it could result in income and financial gains to a company. Data science is heavily transforming the finance sector too, through algorithmic trading and using big data applications. In fields like bioinformatics, protein classification can be done using machine learning algorithms like SVMs. In businesses, it is crucial to predict the demand versus supply values to be ready for the future, which could involve the use of regression.

Principal component analysis (PCA) is used in image compression, facial recognition, and a variety of other applications. In this chapter we take a brief overview of the techniques mentioned here.

3.1.2 Organization of the Chapter

The remainder of this chapter is organized as follows. In Section 3.2, a brief introduction to *linear regression* is given. Section 3.3 explains the details of *decision trees*, followed by Section 3.4 which presents the naïve *Bayes* model used in data science. This is followed by an introduction to *support vector machines* in Section 3.5. Section 3.6 presents an example of an unsupervised learning technique namely *K-means*. Section 3.7 presents the evaluation techniques for the machine learning methods discussed. Section 3.8 throws light on some other learning techniques in brief. Section 3.9 explains the concepts of *meta-learning* and *ensemble methods*. Then, various dimensionality reduction methods are introduced in Section 3.10. Section 3.11 concludes the chapter by listing of some of the latest well-known applications of machine learning in data science.

3.2 Linear Regression Models and Issues

The goal of regression is to predict one or more real target values for a given a data point that has D *attributes* or *features*. In regression problems, the target variable is *continuous*, i.e., *real valued*. The technique of linear regression generalizes the curve fitting and involves real values as inputs as well as output. This section describes the important aspects of linear regression with a brief overview of the topic, that has its detailed exposition in [2].

3.2.1 Linear Regression

The simplest problem of curve fitting in X–Y plane is to predict the value of y given the value of x. The same can be extended to the D-dimensional space. Consider $x = <x_1, x_2, ..., x_D>$ as the D-dimensional input vector (denoting D features) for a data point, x. Without loss of generality, let's assume that a single target variable t is to be predicted. The simplest form of any regression function is a linear function of the D input variables, predicting output variable y, that can be written as:

$$y = f(x, W) = w_0 + w_1 \times x_1 + w_2 \times x_2 + ... + w_D \times x_D \qquad (3.1)$$

where $W = <w_0, w_1, ..., w_D>$ are the D design/model parameters. Here, the function f is linear in both x and W (i.e., with respect to their individual components). Given N data points (or instances or observations) $X = <X_1, X_2, ...X_N>$, and their respective known output values $T = <t_1, t_2, ..., t_N>$, the goal is to arrive at the values for the components of $W = <w_0, w_1, ..., w_D>$ such that the function f has the least error in prediction, the predicted values being $Y = <y_1, y_2, ..., y_N>$. Once the component values of W are determined, then for any given data point X, the function f can be used to make a prediction, with the expectation of an approximately correct result, y. From a probabilistic perspective, the problem is to model predictive distribution $p(t \mid x)$ that denotes certainty of value of t given the value of x. Thus, the goal can be set to minimize the expected value of a loss function that is suitably chosen (based on the context and information available). The loss function or the cost function is a measure of overall loss incurred in prediction due to the choice of a given model for a given dataset. A common choice for the loss function in case of continuous of real-valued variables is the squared-loss function. It can be shown that conditional expectation of *t*—i.e., *p(t | x)* leads to an optimal solution for the squared loss function. The square-loss for the given dataset *X* and assumed (or *arrived-at*) *W*, can be given as:

$$E(W) = \frac{1}{2}\sum_{i=1}^{N}(y_i - t_i)^2 = \frac{1}{2}\sum_{i=1}^{N}(f(X_i, W) - t_i)^2 \qquad (3.2)$$

The term ½ is taken for mathematical convenience. In geometric terms, *y*, the value predicted by function *f*—i.e., *f(x, W)*—represents a vector which is a linear combination of D vectors and hence is part of the hyperplane defined by these D vectors. Using Equation (3.2), the calculated error is always +ve, or is zero when all the predictions exactly match. The square-loss or squared-error is a measure that calculates the sum of squares of (the minimum) distance between each pair of the predicted target *y* and actual target *t*. The predicted target vector *t* need not be part of the same plane as output vector *y*. In other sense, predicted vector *y* is the orthogonal projection of *t* onto the plane defined by vector components of *f(x, W)* and the squared-error measures the square of the Euclidean distance between *y* and *t*. The root mean square (RMS) is defined by [2]:

$$E_{RMS} = \sqrt{2 \times \frac{E(W)}{N}} \qquad (3.3)$$

The term E_{RMS} measures the error in the same units as the target variable *t*, with the use of square root. Also, the division by *N* ensures that different sizes of datasets are compared uniformly. Equation (3.1) is a special and simplest instance of linear regression, wherein the prediction function *f* is linear in both *x* as well as *W*. In general, the model is still considered as *linear* if the function *f* is linear in *W* but nonlinear in *x*. Equation (3.1) can be rewritten [2] as:

$$y = f(x, W) = w_0 + \sum_{i=1}^{D} w_j \times \phi_j(x) \qquad (3.4)$$

where w_0 is a bias parameter that allows for any fixed offset to the function. Each function $\phi_j(x)$ is known as a basis function. In Equation (3.1), the basis function is simply defined as, $\phi_j(x) = x_j$, which is a linear function. Thus, the function *f(x, W)* is linear in both *W* as well as *x*. The function *f(x, W)* can be made nonlinear by choosing a nonlinear basis function $\phi_j(x)$, although it would still be linear in *W*, and hence the model is still called as a linear model. There are various other choices for the basis function to model the nonlinearity in varying measures. One possibility is to set the basis function $\phi_j(x)$ as a polynomial function with respect to the jth component of x, i.e., $\phi_j(x) = x_j^j$. This is a global function and sensitive to the input variable/dimension, in the sense that changes to input variable/component values in one region/dimension can dictate the effects on other dimensions, and hence on the result. In such a situation, input space is divided into different regions, and different basis functions are used per region, thus leading to spline functions. Other choices for basis functions are *Gaussian basis function, sigmoidal basis function,* and *Fourier Basis function.*

3.2.2 Gradient Descent Method

After a specific linear regression model (i.e., the set of basis functions) is chosen, the *gradient descent* technique can be applied to get a good approximation for the weight vector *W*, using the square-loss function given in Equation (3.2). The gradient descent algorithm [3] successively modifies the weight vector such that the error term decreases monotonically. The process can be stopped after a fixed number of iterations or when the *minimal* error is reached (although it may have been stuck in local minima). In either case, naturally the optimality cannot be guaranteed. If the cumulative error (that is the sum of error terms for all of the data observations/instances) is used to update the weight vector, then the algorithm is called as *standard gradient descent* algorithm (or just *gradient descent* algorithm). On the other hand, if the weight vector is updated after evaluating the error term for every data instance/example independently, then the gradient descent algorithm is called as *stochastic gradient descent* (or *incremental* or *sequential* gradient descent) algorithm.

If W^0 is considered as the default initialization of vector *W* at the start of the algorithm, then at the end of i+1 iterations, the new vector W^{i+1} can be represented as:

$$W^{i+1} = W^i - \eta \times \Delta E \qquad (3.5)$$

where the term η is the learning rate (a configurable/design parameter), and ΔE denotes the first differential of the *error function*. If the error function chosen is the squared-error as in Equation (3.2), then the update in the weight variable w^j in each jth dimension independently for k^{th} example by stochastic gradient descent algorithm can be given as:

$$w_j = w_j + \eta \times (t_k - y_k) \times \phi_j(x_j) \qquad (3.6)$$

where t_k and y_k are the target and predicted values for the kth data instance X_k, from the input data instance set $X = <X_1, X_2, ..., X_N>$. Thus, in the stochastic gradient descent algorithm, one iteration through all the instances of the dataset would update the weight vector *N* times. As the updates are taking place *N* times in a single iteration over the data set, the learning rate η can be made very small still approximating the true gradient descent. On the other hand, standard gradient descent can use a larger step size in every weight update, although it may require more computation. In a gradient descent algorithm, typically there is always a danger of the computation getting stuck in local minima, which eventually gets proposed as the solution to the regression problem. But the stochastic gradient descent, having updates for every data instance, can avoid falling in the local minima trough.

3.2.3 Regularization

One of the main issues in any regression model (including neural networks), or for that matter in most of the machine learning algorithms, is the danger of *overfitting* the data. In such cases, even the inherent noise in the data also gets modeled and, as a result, the learning model performs poorly on testing or real-life data. Depending on the machine learning model, different ways are used to avoid the *overfitting*, all of which can be bracketed under a generic term called *regularization*. In case of regression problems, extra terms (to impicitly model *overfitting*) can be added to the error functions themselves, so that the process of regularization is integrated with the gradient descent algorithms. Typically, it is observed that the *overfitting* is accompanied with the increase in the weight vector component values. Thus, one way in which the regularization can be achieved is by adding a penalty term proportional to the square of the current value of the weight vector. Thus, the error term in the Equation (3.2) can be modified [2] using L2 regularization or Ridge regession estimator [4] as:

$$E^R(W) = \frac{1}{2} \sum_{i=1}^{N} \left(f(X_i, W) - t_i \right)^2 + \frac{\lambda}{2} \times |W|^2 \qquad (3.7)$$

Here the term $||W||^2$ denotes the scalar product of the weight vector W with itself, and the coefficient λ determines the relative importance to be given to the second term (i.e., the regularization term) as compared to the sum-of-squares error term appearing as the first term. We need to minimize the new error term E^R, which prevents the values of components of weight vector becoming too large, otherwise the overall error would also increase. In other words, after an initial increase of weights upto a certain level, a weight decay would set in. This should expectedly prevent the learning models from becoming too complex and would be useful when the dataset is of limited size. In a sense, the onus of arriving at an optimal solution now rests also with the determination of the regularization coefficient λ, rather than the determination of only the number and the nature of the basis functions.

3.2.4 Artificial Neural Networks

One of the popular generalizations of regression techniques can be found in *artificial neural networks* (ANNs). Artificial neural networks are multi-layer networks wherein every layer contains many *neurons*. The outputs of neurons of previous layer are connected to the inputs of neurons of the next layer though *weighted edges*. Every neuron first models a linear function (like as given in Equation [3.1]) to create a weighted sum and then applies an activation function like *perceptron* or *sigmoid* or *tanh* or *rectified linear unit* on the sum. The role of activation unit is to model nonlinearity in the data. The objective of ANNs is to come up with weights on edges connecting neurons so that the outputs are faithfully produced at the last layer, given the input attributes at the first layer. To do this, the concept of gradient descent algorithm is used on an error curve similar to the one given in Equation (3.2). The problem becomes a bit complicated due to involvement of multiple layers and many more neurons but is resolved at every neuron level by calculating the error backward through an algorithm named as *backward propagation*. The key idea behind ANNs can be understood by looking at them as a technique for *adaptive curve fitting*. When the weights on the edges are small, the system models a constant or linear curve. As the iterations and weights increase, the system starts modeling complex polynomial curves. Due care can be taken to avoid overfitting; one of the techniques used is weight decay or regularization, as discussed in the previous subsection. In the last few years, there has been a great interest in ANNs and its variants like deep neural networks (DNNs), recurrent neural networks (RNNs), convolutional neural networks (CNNs), long- and short-term memory (LSTM), and so on. The detailed discussion on ANNs and its latest versions is beyond the scope of this chapter.

3.3 Decision Trees

Decision tree learning, which is one of the widely used techniques in classification problems, is based on the inductive learning hypothesis mentioned in Section 3.1. It states that the hypothesis that approximates the target function well on a sufficiently large training dataset is likely to approximate the target function well on a set of unobserved instances too. A decision tree consists of nodes, each of which represents a *feature* or an *attribute*, and the branches arising from it, representing the possible values the feature can take. The leaf nodes are the class values or the target function values. A new instance is classified by starting at the root of the decision tree and then following the branches according to the corresponding values of every attribute on the path successively, until a leaf node (i.e., the target class) is reached. An example of a decision tree is shown in the Figure 3.1. A species X, with characteristics as *cold blooded* and having *no scales on the skin* will be classified as being *amphibian*, while another species Y, which is *not cold blooded* and *lays eggs on land*, will be classified as *not being amphibian*. The decision tree in Figure 3.1 is equivalent to a disjunction of conjunctions to classify *amphibian* class as shown below:

$$\left(cold\ blooded = \text{Yes} \land scales\ on\ skin = \text{No} \right) \lor \left(cold\ blooded = \text{No} \land lays\ eggs\ on = \text{water} \right)$$

Decision tree learning is best suited for discrete valued attributes, that is where the attributes take values from a predefined set. Similarly, the target class label also takes discrete values from a predefined set. Decision trees could be used even when the training data is erroneous or has missing attributes. One of the major decision points in any decision tree algorithm is to decide which attribute to select at a particular node. To take this decision, two measures are required: namely *entropy* and *information gain* at different levels.

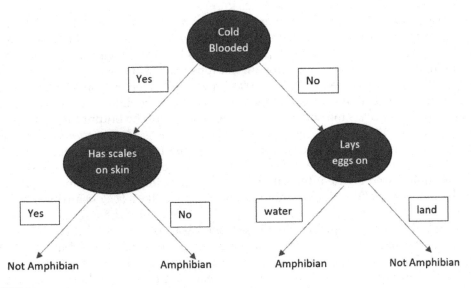

FIGURE 3.1
Example of a Decision Tree

For *c* number of output classes, the entropy *E* is given as:

$$Entropy(D) = \sum_{i=1}^{c} -P_i \log_2 P_i \qquad (3.8)$$

where D is the dataset used and P_i stands for proportion of D belonging to the output class $c = i$. Informally, the term entropy denotes the minimum number of bits required to represent randomness or the information content in the set of data samples D. In case of binary classification, the formula reduces to:

$$Entropy(D) = -P \log_2 P - N \log_2 N \qquad (3.9)$$

where P is the probability of an instance being positive and N is the probability of the instance being negative. The term *information gain* for an attribute A in a dataset D is given by:

$$Gain(D,A) = Entropy(D) - \sum_{v \in Values(A)} |D_v| / |D| * Entropy(D_v) \qquad (3.10)$$

where D_v is the number of samples in D which take value v for attribute A. The term *information gain* denotes the reduction in the system entropy by selecting a particular attribute A at a particular level in the tree. $|D_v| / |D|$ gives us the probability that the value v will appear in the sample for that attribute and the Entropy of D_v gives us the information content in the sub-tree with the root as that particular attribute. Similarly, the gain for all the attributes is calculated, and the attribute with highest gain value is considered as the root of the tree. The process is repeated recursively for every branch at every level and is stopped when the residual entropy reduces to zero.

There are cases where attributes like *date* end up having a very high information gain. This is because in such trees, the number of branches is very high and the tree has a very low depth, sometimes even just a depth of one. Such trees are naturally favored by the algorithm, but their utility is very low for obvious reasons. Hence, to avoid such situation, another measure called as *split information* is used which accounts for how broadly or uniformly the attribute splits the data. In case when the data is noisy or number of data points/instances is too small to be a representative of the output function, decision trees tend to overfit the data. There are techniques like *reduced error pruning* and *rule post pruning* to avoid overfitting. Decision trees can also be tuned for continuous valued attributes. It marks a few candidate threshold values for every such attribute and selects the best threshold based on the information gain. This best threshold can then be used and samples below and above the threshold can be classified like a *boolean* attribute at a node in the decision tree. There are versions of decision trees (algorithms) that handle attributes with differing costs too. In these cases, one basic approach is to divide the gain by the cost of the attribute so that low-cost attributes get selected. These features are handled in C4.5 algorithm [5], which is an improvisation over the basic ID3 decision tree algorithm. The approximate inductive bias of decision trees is that shorter trees are preferred over longer ones. Whether this is a sound basis for generalization beyond the training data or not, it is an instance of an open philosophical question in the literature, known as the *Occam's Razor*.

3.4 Naïve Bayes Model

Naïve Bayes is a probabilistic algorithm that is widely used for classification problems. It is based on the *Bayes rule of probability*. Given that events A and B are independent of each other, the Bayes rule can be stated as given in Equation (3.11).

$$P(A|B) = \frac{P\left(\frac{B}{A}\right) \times P(A)}{P(B)} \tag{3.11}$$

Consider a tuple of features of input data $F:<f_1, f_2, f_3, \ldots f_n>$ and let $f(x)$ be the output or target function that takes one of the values from a predefined finite set V. To predict the output class for this set of features F, we consider the best hypothesis V_{MAP}, which fits the training data.

$$V_{MAP} = argmax_{v_j \in V}(P(v_j|f_1 f_2 \ldots f_n)) \tag{3.12}$$

Applying the *Bayes Rule* given in Equation 3.11, we get:

$$V_{MAP} = argmax_{v_j \in V} P(f_1 f_2 \ldots f_n | v_j) \times P(v_j) / P(f_1 f_2 \ldots f_n) \tag{3.13}$$

We can easily calculate $P(v_j)$. To calculate $P(f_1, f_2, f_3, \ldots f_n | v_j)$, the complexity of the task would blow up. This is because we are required to calculate the probabilities for all combinations of the possible values which all the features can assume (i.e., their *cartesian product*). Every such combination might not even be present in the training data. Hence to simplify, an assumption is made that the features are conditionally independent given the output class value. This is a fair assumption in many situations and leads to the *naïve Bayes* formula given in Equation (3.14).

$$V_{nb} = argmax_{v_j \in V} P(v_j) \prod P(f_i | v_j) \tag{3.14}$$

We estimate the probabilities by counting the number of instances for which a particular attribute is *true* and taking its ratio to the total number of opportunities where it could have been true. However, this would give a poor estimate when the number of instances in the training dataset for which the attribute takes a particular value is very less or close to zero. In this case, the value close to zero being a multiplicative factor, dominates the *naïve Bayes* formula given in Equation (3.14) and makes the value of the multiplication of conditional probabilities $P(f_i | v_j)$ very low (close to *zero*). To avoid this, we use the *m-estimate*, a generalized form of *Laplace Smoothing* (wherein m = 1). Then the term $P(f_i | v_j)$ in Equation (3.14) is estimated using *m-estimate* as follows:

$$P(f_i | v_j) = (n_c + mp) / (n + m) \tag{3.15}$$

where n is the total number of samples, and n_c is total number of samples for which the event is true, that is the attribute f_i takes a particular value v_j. The probability p is the prior estimate of probability of this event. The value of p can be approximated as *1/k* in most cases where k is the number of distinct discrete values the attribute can take. Also, m is a constant denoting the equivalent sample size.

Naïve Bayes has been traditionally used in spam filters and nowadays finds applications heavily in text classification and natural language processing tasks.

3.5 Support Vector Machines

Support vector machines (SVMs) fall under the category of supervised machine learning algorithms. SVMs are widely used in classification, though they can be used for regression too. In SVMs, each instance is represented in an N dimensional space where each dimension is a feature. When we have two input features and a binary classification is to be made, a line is identified which separates the data points into two classes. In case of higher dimensions, that is, when we have more than two input features, we aim to obtain hyperplane separating the classes. The coordinates of the instance in the high dimensional space which are close to the hyperplane and influence it are called as the support vectors. The margin of the classifier is the distance between the decision surfaces/hyperplanes, which pass through support vectors. The margin should be maximized as a smaller value of margin increases the probability of misclassifications. SVM is robust to outliers in case of classification. SVM can cleanly determine a hyperplane when the data is linearly separable. Consider data points with two dimensions which are linearly separable. In this case, the SVM would find the hyperplanes with maximum margin such that they separate the data into the two output classes. A typical hyperplane equation can be given as

$$W^T x + b = 0 \qquad (3.16)$$

Here W^T indicates the orientation of the hyperplane and b indicates the displacement of the hyperplane from the origin. The margin between two separating hyperplanes can then be defined by the following two equations:

$$W^T x + b = 1 \qquad (3.17)$$

$$W^T x + b = -1 \qquad (3.18)$$

The width of the margin is given by $2/\|w\|$, which means that the width is inversely proportional to the length of the normal vector. To maximize the length of the margin, we need to minimise the length of the normal vector which is $\|w\|/2$. Now, consider two points denoted by $[-1,1]^T$ and $[1, -1]^T$, which belong to the positive and negative class respectively. Let's say that $y_1 = 1$ and $y_2 = -1$ are the output class labels. One class is to the left of the hyperplane given by Equation (3.17) and one is to the right of another hyperplane given by Equation (3.18). This is indicated by the inequalities in (3.19) and (3.20).

$$W^T x_1 + b >= 1 \qquad (3.19)$$

$$W^T x_2 + b \le -1 \qquad (3.20)$$

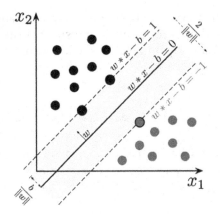

FIGURE 3.2
Support Vector Machines

This implies that we have to solve to minimize the objective function given in Equation (3.21) subject to the constraints given in equation (3.22, 3.23).

$$F(w) = |W|^2 \tag{3.21}$$

$$y_1\left(W^T x_1 + b\right) >= 1 \tag{3.22}$$

$$y_2\left(W^T x_2 + b\right) >= 1 \tag{3.23}$$

Solving these inequalities, we can get the required values of maximum width margin and our separating hyperplanes get defined. The Figure 3.2, as given in [6], shows the separating hyperplanes in binary classification and the corresponding margin. When the data is not separable in the current feature space, it happens that there is no hyperplane separating the data points into the output classes. In such cases, the data points are mapped into a higher dimension and then a separating hyperplane is found. SVM does this through a kernel that transforms a lower dimensional data point into higher dimensional data point such that the data points become separable by a hyperplane in the higher dimensional space. The strong point of SVM is that it works on a smaller number of training samples, even when the number of data samples is less than the number of dimensions. However, it is computationally intensive as the training data increases. Some of the real-life applications of SVMs are face detection, image classification, text categorization, handwriting recognition, and so on.

3.6 K-Means Clustering Algorithm

K-means clustering is a simple unsupervised learning algorithm. It divides the data points into subsets or sub-units such that the data points in the same subset are similar to each other, and those in different subsets differ from each other based on the similarity measure chosen. Here, the algorithm is explained using Euclidean distance as the similarity metric. The value of k in *K-means* indicates the number of distinct clusters to which the data points could belong to, and is an input parameter to the algorithm. The algorithm proceeds as follows:

```
1. Fix the number of clusters as k.
2. Select k points from among the data points randomly as k centroids of
   the k clusters.
3. Keep iterating as long as there is a change in the cluster centroids.
   a. Find the distance of each data point from each centroid.
   b. Associate it with the cluster of the centroid which is closest to
      the data point.
   c. Calculate the new centroid of each cluster by taking the mean on
      each dimension.
```

It can be easily shown that the algorithm converges quickly, and the time complexity of the algorithm is $O(tkmn)$ where t is the number of iterations, n is the number of dimensions, k is number of clusters, and m is the number of elements to be *clustered*. There are k clusters formed. For each point in each cluster, the distance metric from the centroid is calculated. This entails number of multiplications equal to the number of dimensions involved. The process is repeated in each iteration, and there is a total of t iterations. Thus, the complexity of the algorithm is $O(tkmn)$.

K-means is a popular algorithm due to its simplicity and time efficiency. However, it has its own shortcomings. The algorithm, since it begins with a random initialization, may get stuck in a local minimum and may not reach the global minimum at convergence. Hence, the initialization of the k centroids is the crucial step and is repeated several times throughout execution. Then, the initialization, which results in low sum of squared distance between the data points and the respective cluster centroids (i.e., the centroid of the cluster to which they belong), is used. The parameter k is decided empirically by the *elbow method*, wherein we experiment with different values of k and plot the *Within Cluster Sum of Squares* (*WCSS*) for each value of k. The distance of a data point i from the centroid of the cluster to which it belongs is, say, d_i. We take the summation over all d_i; this is done for all points that are considered for clustering. This value is called as the *WCSS*. The curve is plotted for values of k starting with $k = 2, 3, 4, \dots$ and so on. The value of k at which the (diminishing) curve seems to flatten forming an elbow shape is taken as the value of k. This algorithm is used in document clustering, computer vision for image compression, and so on.

3.7 Evaluation of Machine Learning Algorithms

We have seen various machine learning algorithms that fall in the category of supervised and unsupervised algorithms. To infer how good or bad an algorithm performs on known as well as unknown datasets, we need some evaluation metrics and methods. For the process of evaluation, the dataset is divided into two parts. Training data is the part of the dataset from which the machine learns and outputs a model. This model is then tested on the *testing data*, which is not seen by the model, and the results are reported. In cases when we do not have separate training and testing data being provided, we split the training dataset into the required two parts. This data-split is usually ranges from 70–30 to 90–10, where the larger chunk forms the training data and the smaller one is kept aside for testing. In case, if the testing is to be done separately, then the given dataset is split into *training* data and *validation* data. The purpose of validation data is to tune the hyperparameters of the system during the training phase. Though it is ideal to have separate training, testing, and validation data, many times the size of the dataset is very small. In such cases, the data is randomly split (according to the split size chosen) into training and testing data. The process is repeated *k* times, and the performance metric values are averaged out. This is called as *k-fold* cross validation. The specific performance measures used in machine learning algorithms are specific to whether the problem at hand is *regression, classification,* or *clustering,* and are described below.

3.7.1 Regression

This subsection discusses the loss/error and correlation terms in regression which are used for evaluation of regression.

3.7.1.1 Loss and Error Terms in Linear Regression

The expectation E[f] of function f(x) is the average value of some function f(x) under a probability distribution p(x). If probability distribution is discrete, the average is calculated as a weighted sum of the relative probabilities of different values of *x*. On the other hand, if the probability distribution is continuous, the corresponding probability density values are integrated to calculate the expectation. When we want to calculate error in misprediction, a simple assumption is typically made that all kinds of mispredictions (whether in classes in classification problems or values in regression) incur the same cost. This need not be true as different misclassifications (or mispredictions) could inflict varying costs. This fact can be formalized by the term loss function (or cost function), which gives a comprehensive measure for the loss incurred due to different misclassifications, wherein different kinds of errors could be weighed differently. Our goal then is to come up with a model that minimizes the total loss incurred. In practice, one major impediment in calculating such a loss function would be that one doesn't know the true class for data instances. In general, we need to find out the hyperparameters for the machine learning algorithms, which minimizes the loss function on training data.

The absolute error (AE) is defined as the sum of errors in target values and corresponding predicted values, whereas mean absolute error (MAE) denotes the mean of AE. The MAE is useful when outliers (i.e., too high or too low values) are present in the dataset as then the error is not amplified in such cases. It gives a *linear* error value, which averages the weighted individual differences equally. The lower the MAE value, better is the model's performance. The relative absolute error (RAE) is calculated by comparing total absolute error with the error of a naïve model. All of these error terms, AE/MAE/RAE are also known as linear errors or L1 losses.

The sum of squared error (SSE, as in Equation [3.2]), the mean squared error (i.e., mean of the SSE) and the RMSE (as in Equation [3.3]) are squared errors, also known as the L2 losses. The mean squared error (MSE) is the most commonly used metric due to its nice mathematical properties and useful implications. Due to the error being squared, it could be thought of as not being useful when the dataset contains a lot of noise or outliers, as just a few deviations can dominate the error term. Root mean squared error (RMSE) can help to subdue outliers in such cases. But for the same reason, SSE turns out to be the most useful model to detect the outliers or unexpected values in the dataset. In this metric, the lower the value, the better the performance of the model. Like RAE, the *relative squared error* (RSE) is calculated by comparing total squared error with the error of a naïve model. Using the squared error, the equation system is easier to solve, but as mentioned, using the absolute error turns out to be more robust to outliers. Both functions, the absolute as well as the squared error, assume the minimum value when all the predictions are accurate.

In some situations, neither loss function (L1 or L2) gives desirable results. This can happen when MAE (mean) gets closer to median value whereas MSE is skewed towards a significant number of outliers which are far away from the median/mean value. In such situations, target function could be transformed or other loss functions like Huber loss, Log-cosh loss, or Quantile loss.

3.7.1.2 Correlation Terms in Linear Regression

In statistical terms, *variance* provides a measure of the variability of a function f(x) around its mean value whereas the term *bias* provides a measure for *overestimation* (or *underestimation*) in prediction across different datasets. There is a tradeoff associated between *bias* and *variance*. Decrease in the bias results in the increase in the variance and vice versa. The aim of machine learning algorithms is to have low bias as well as low variance. The term *correlation* denotes an association between two quantitative variables. The *Pearson's correlation coefficient* (or just *correlation coefficient*, R) quantifies the strength of the linear association between two quantitative variables. The correlation coefficient R takes a value in the range [−1, +1], each extreme value indicating a perfect correlation. When *increase* (*decrease*) in one variable corresponds to *increase* (*decrease*) in the other variable, a *positive* (*negative*) correlation is said to exist. No association between the variables is indicated by a correlation value close to 0.

The term R-squared (R^2) or squared correlation is also called the coefficient of determination (CoD). The coefficient of determination (R^2) is computed using two sums-of-squares terms, sum of squared error (SSE) and sum of squares total (SST), which is sum of squared difference between the observed value of an output variable and its mean value. In regression model, the proportion of the variance of the dependent variable that can be attributed to the independent variable is denoted by R^2. If sum of squared error (SSE) is zero, then R^2 is 1 and the regression model is said to be *perfect*. R^2 is zero when no variance is explained by regression. The correlation coefficient R explains (the strength of) the relationship between a dependent and independent variable, whereas R^2 explains the extent to which the variance of one variable can be attributed to the variance of the other variable. Other correlation terms used are *Spearman correlation* and *Kendell-Tau* correlation. The *Spearman correlation* (Rho, ρ) evaluates the monotonic relationship between two continuous or ordinal variables, whereas *Kendall rank correlation* (Kendall-τ) is used to test the similarities (*strength* as well as *direction*) in the ordinal data.

3.7.2 Classification

In case of supervised classification algorithms, we have labeled training data. The data could be labeled by a human judge or a domain expert (said to be *labeling by gold standard* or *gold labor*), or it could be an output of a process. The labeled value in such case is called as the actual value and the value output by the algorithm is called as the predicted value. The performance metrics typically used in classification are *precision*, *recall*, *F-measure* (F1 more generally), and *accuracy*.

3.7.2.1 Binary Classification

If there are only two output classes in a classification problem, it is termed as binary classification. Let's assume the two classes denoted as class P and class N. We define the following terms: If the instance belongs to the class P as per the labeling or annotation and predicted value is also P, then it is called as *true positive*. If the instance belongs to the class N as per the annotation and the predicted value is N too, then it is called as *true negative*. If the actual value of an instance is P and the predicted value is N, it is called as a *false negative*. If the actual value of an instance is N and the predicted value is P, it is called as *false positive*. This is shown in Table 3.1, also called as *confusion matrix*. The *precision* of an algorithm is the ratio of correctly labelled data points out of those marked as belonging to the positive class. The term *recall* is defined as the portion of the total number of positive data points in the dataset, which are correctly labeled.

Precision and recall can be given by Equations (3.26) and (3.27) respectively.

$$Precision = (tp)/(tp + fp) \tag{3.26}$$

$$Recall = (tp)/(tp + fn) \tag{3.27}$$

Consider an example of a search engine that returns 10 documents, out of which 7 are relevant. Then the precision of the search engine is said to be 7/10. If there are total 12 relevant documents in the system, then the recall would be 7/12. Precision and recall share the numerator value which is number of true positives. F measure is the weighted harmonic mean of precision and recall. The harmonic mean is closer to the smaller value in case the data is skewed. Hence it gives a more realistic measure than arithmetic mean or geometric mean.

$$F - measure = \frac{(\beta^2 + 1)PR}{\beta^2 P + R} \tag{3.28}$$

In the above Equation (3.28), when $\beta = 0$, F measure is equal to the precision value. When $\beta = \infty$, F measure is equal to the recall value. When $\beta = 1$, precision and recall are given equal importance and it is called as F1 measure or the F1 score. When $\beta < 1$, precision is more important. When $\beta > 1$, recall is more important. Another measure that is less frequently used is the *accuracy*. It is given by the equation:

$$Accuracy = (tp + tn)/(tp + fp + tn + fn) \tag{3.29}$$

TABLE 3.1

Confusion Matrix for Binary Classification

Confusion Matrix for Binary Classification		Actual Values (Annotated Values)	
		Class P	Class N
Predicted Values	Class P	tp	Fp
	Class N	fn	tn

Accuracy indicates the ratio of correctly classified data points to the total number of data points.

3.7.2.2 Multiclass Classification

For multiclass classification problems, the precision and recall need to be calculated on per class basis. Once the calculations per class basis are done, they can be averaged in two ways. Macro averaged measures and micro averaged measures. In the macro averaged precision, recall and F1 score is the arithmetic mean of precison, recall, and F1 score of each class respectively. In micro-averaged measures precision, recall and F1 all have the same value, which is equal to the sum of the diagonal cells in confusion matrix divided by the sum of the non diagonal cells.

3.7.3 Clustering

In case of unsupervised algorithms, the performance metrics are different as there are no labels available while training the data. However, ground truth is needed when evaluating the clustering methods. Test data has some output labels given by human judges. Purity of clustering gives the portion of total number of data instances that are marked correctly, i.e., the predicted value and the actual label given by the human judge matches. The purity of clustering is calculated by the formula:

$$Purity = \frac{1}{n} \sum_{i=1}^{k} \max_j |c_i \cap p_j| \qquad (3.30)$$

where n is the number of data points, k is the number of clusters, c_i is the ith cluster, and p_j is the class to which maximum data points in the ith cluster fall into. However, in the extreme case, if we consider one cluster per data point, the purity measure becomes high. Here, other measures like *normalized mutual information* (NMI) and *rand index* (RI) are also used.

3.8 Some Other Types of Learning Models

Most of the methods that we have seen fall under the category of *inductive learning*, wherein hypotheses are generalized based on the training data. In inductive learning, a certain number of training examples D, possibly containing errors, as well as a space of candidate hypotheses H is given. The objective is to determine a hypothesis which best fits the training data and is generalized well on the unseen dataset. Examples of inductive learning are decision tree, regression, ANN, SVM, KNN, and so on. K-nearest-neighbor (KNN) is an instance-based algorithm that assumes data instances to be points in N-dimensional space (where N is the number of data attributes), and calculates label of a new instance by considering labelling of its K nearest neighbors (where K is the hyperparameter that can be tuned by experiments). On similar lines, in locally weighted regression methods, an explicit local approximation is constructed for each new query instance. Some of the other important learning models are *lazy learning, rule-based learning, analytical learning,* and *reinforcement learning.* Lazy learning avoids forming the hypothesis until the data instance is required to be labeled. In *rule-based learning, first order logic* is used to define rules, whereas *analytical learning* uses prior knowledge and deductive learning techniques. In *reinforcement learning,* probable actions are evaluated based on rewards or punishments. In the recent past, DeepMind [7] software based on reinforcement learning made waves by beating a human player in the game of *alphago* and becoming the strongest player on the chess circuit with just a few hours of training.

3.9 Ensemble Learning with Bagging, Boosting, and Stacking

This section describes ways in which different machine learning models can be combined together to get improved prediction results. The term *ensemble* denotes a group of items viewed as a whole rather than individually. Ensemble learning combines different machine learning models together to improve results. The combination helps to achieve a better prediction as against each model considered separately and also helps to decrease error by decreasing variance or bias. The three most commonly used ensemble meta-methods are *bagging* (decreases variance), *boosting* (decreases bias), and *stacking* (improves predictions). Many ensemble methods use *homogeneous ensembles*—that is, they use a single base learning algorithm to produce base learners. Examples of homogeneous ensembles are *random forests, committee of ANN models,* and so on. When the ensemble methods use learners/models of different types, they are known as *heterogeneous ensembles*. It is assumed that before using any ensemble technique, base learners themselves are designed to be accurate as well as diverse. The ensemble learners can also be divided into *sequential learners* and *parallel learners*. In *sequential learners,* base learners are generated sequentially and hence the dependence between the base learners is exploited. Previously mislabelled examples can be weighed with higher weights thus improving (*boosting*) the overall performance. In *parallel learners,* base learners are generated in parallel (e.g., random forests) and hence the independence between the base learners can be exploited.

3.9.1 Bagging

The term bagging is also known as *bootstrap aggregation*. The variance of a prediction can be reduced by averaging together the multiple predictions. If the dataset is divided into M different subsets (formed randomly by choosing data items with *replacement*), then we can train M different trees/models to compute the ensemble by averaging (for a *regression* problem) as given below. In a classification problem, the same can be done by majority vote.

$$f(x) = \frac{1}{M} \sum_{m=1}^{M} f_m(x) \tag{3.31}$$

When samples are drawn with replacement, it leads to resampling wherein the same samples can be drawn again and again. In this way, if large numbers of smaller samples (of the same size) are drawn, then it is known as bootstrapping. The data subsets thus drawn can be used for training and aggregating different base learners (*estimators*) and this process is known as *bagging*. It is observed that bagging works better with decision trees than KNNs (K-nearest neighbor algorithms). This is because KNNs are less sensitive to the perturbations in the dataset and hence are stable learners. This implies that combining stable learners is less advantageous from the perspective of improvement in accuracy. It is also found that bagging the performance accuracy depends on the number of base estimators. The accuracy increases as the number of base estimators are increased and then flattens afterwards. Thus, adding base estimators beyond a particular number (which needs to be determined by experimentation for the given set of data and models) may increase computational complexity without increasing the accuracy. Random forests (RFs) are sets of randomized decision trees, and are commonly used ensemble learning models which internally use bagging. In addition to bagging, a random (subset of) feature-set can be selected, thus randomizing the trees further. This may increase the bias of the ensemble, but averaging of outputs from less correlated trees may lead to decrease in variance as well, thus potentially resulting into an overall better model.

3.9.2 Boosting

The technique of converting weak learners to strong learners is termed as *boosting*. In bagging, base learners are trained in parallel; whereas in boosting, sequential ensembles are created using base learners and weighted version of the data. In every stage, the *misclassified* examples in the earlier stages are given more weights. The final prediction is produced using individual predictions by weighted voting in classification, or by a weighted average in regression. In AdaBoost, initially all data points are weighed equally. In later stages of boosting, the weights for the misclassified data points are increased, and the weights are decreased for the accurately classified data points. In every round, a weighted error rate ϵ is calculated for each of the base classifiers. Also, the weighting coefficients are used to give a greater weight to more accurate classifiers. Gradient tree boosting is used for both regression and classification problems and builds the model in a sequential way. Let M_n be the model to be generated in the nth round. At every n^{th} stage, let's say a decision tree T_n minimizes a loss function L given the current model M_{n-1}. Then, this decision tree model T_n is combined in a linearly weighted fashion with previous stage model M_{n-1} to generate M_n, the model at the nth stage. One well known implementation of gradient tree boosting is XGBoost (extreme gradient boosting). The classification and regression models differ in terms of the loss function used.

3.9.3 Stacking

Stacking combines multiple estimators first and then builds a meta-classifier (or a meta-regressor) model. The first stage of *stacking* consists of different kinds of learning algorithms leading to heterogeneous ensembles. Essentially, stacking can be thought of as a 2-stage learning procedure. In stacking, the base models are trained in stage-1 using the complete dataset. The outputs of base estimators produced in stage-1 are used in stage-2 as input features to train a meta-model (which produces the *correct* outputs for the given data instances). The stage-2 meta-model in a way combines learnings (outputs) of base learners using a machine learning model itself, and thus implicitly captures interdependencies between base learners to predict a better output.

3.10 Feature Engineering and Dimensionality Reduction

A given data instance X may have many input variables, for example a data instance x can be comprised of input variables, $x_1, x_2, ..., x_D$. These input variables are called as *attributes* or *features*, where D is the number of dimensions of the data. In general, a high number of dimensions D create issues in the prediction (in classification as well as regression) algorithms, as all dimensions are considered equally important. But in reality, only a few attributes may be governing the prediction of output variables, and the prediction may get skewed due to the unnecessary consideration of the irrelevant dimensions/variables. This is known as the *Curse of Dimensionality,* and there are a few approaches that can help mitigate it. One of the ways is to associate variable weights to different dimensions; by making them *compressed* or *elongated* in comparison to other dimensions, we implicitly define the relative importance of the dimensions among themselves. At an extreme, some dimensions can be assigned weight 0 and can be completely eliminated to be considered for a prediction system. This is called as *dimensionality reduction*. The objective of dimensionality reduction is to minimize the number of dimensions without compromising on accuracy. Many times, the accuracy actually improves on reduction of the number of dimensions! It may further help in better calculations of Euclidean distances between two data instances in supervised (e.g., KNN) as well in non-supervised (e.g., K-means) learning algorithms. This may also result in ease or simplification of the hypothesis generalization. In general, dimensionality reduction techniques involve feature selection, linear algebra methods, projection methods, autoencoders, and mutual information-based methods. The dimensionality reduction techniques can also be thought of as feature selection techniques that will maximize accuracy with minimal set of features. These techniques include wrapper methods and filter methods. In wrapper methods, different subsets of input features are used to evaluate the model. The subset of features that enables the model to produce the best performance is chosen. On the other hand, filter methods exploit correlation between a feature and the target variable to select a subset of input features that produces the best performance [8]. Matrix factorization methods like the *Eigen-decomposition* and *singular value decomposition* (SVD) are used to create constituent parts of a dataset, which are then ranked. A subset of these parts is then selected to represent the dataset. The ranking of the components can be done using *principal components analysis,* (PCA). The PCA is defined [2] as *the orthogonal transformation of the data onto a lower dimensional (linear) space (principal subspace)* wherein the components of the principal subspace maximize the variance of the projected data. The number of lower dimensions can be ascertained by evaluating the model with different numbers of input features and then choosing the number of features that provides the best average performance. In manifold learning, high-dimensional data is projected onto low-dimensional space while preserving the notable (including *non-linear*) relationships in the data, e.g., [9] isomap, locally linear embeddings, multidimensional scaling (MDS), laplacian Eignmaps, spectral embedding, Hessian Eignmapping, and so on.

Another interesting approach for dimensionality reduction is that of *autoencoders*. They are obtained by modeling an identity function using a self-supervised learning problem (typically using deep learning neural network model) that reproduces the input *as is*. A neural network layer that has a far fewer dimensions than the number of original input features is called as a *bottleneck layer*. When the data flow passes though this network layer, the data gets compressed to a lower dimensional description. The part of the network model upto the bottleneck layer (inclusive), is called the *encoder*, and the remaining latter part of the network is called the *decoder*. After training, the output from the bottleneck layer can directly be used as the *encoding* of the set of input features which also implies the reduced dimensionality.

Linear discriminant analysis (LDA), a linear supervised machine learning algorithm used for multiclass classification, and can also be used for dimensionality reduction. LDA for multiclass classification uses matrix factorization as a core technique. The LDA calculates a projection of a dataset with the objective of maximum class separability. The components of such a projection forms a reduced input set. The singular value decomposition (SVD) is a linear algebra–based technique that automatically performs the dimensionality reduction. SVD is typically used when the data is sparse; that is when many of the values in the data instances are zeroes.

Mutual information (MI) is an entropy-based term that measures the uncertainty in one variable given the value of another variable. Hence, it can measure how the uncertainty of the target class decreases in presence of a particular feature. The higher the MI score, the corresponding feature is a better feature than that of a low MI score. In classification problems, MI can be calculated between a class label and individual features, and the features can then be arranged in the descending sorted order of mutual information with respect to the output class labels [10]. This sorted order of features can then be used to select top m features that will maximize the MI gain without compromising the accuracy. An optimal number of feature set can also be found out by successively reducing the features from lowest MI to the highest and monitoring the resultant accuracy with the reduced feature set.

3.11 Applications of Machine Learning in Data Science

Machine learning, which finds patterns in data, naturally has a plethora of applications in the field of data science. In this chapter, we have provided an overview of a few of the important machine learning techniques/variants. A few of standad applications were mentioned in the Section 3.1.1. We now conclude this chapter by discussing a few more recent applications, primarily using the techniques discussed in this chapter.

Linear regression is a statistical machine learning technique that has its applications in market research studies and and used ubiquitously everywhere from transportation domain to market survey. A more generalized technique of artificial neural networks (ANNs) has been used in a variety of scenarios from forecasting applications, like predicting the foreign exchange rates to material science research [11, 12].

Random forests are ensemble of decision trees. They are used in many different areas of pattern recognition, including text as well as image domains. Genomic data science is today evolving as a new and independent field. One of the important applications of random forests in the text domain is genomic data analysis [13]. Global climate change, global warming, and other environmental factors are directly affected by the land cover. Hence, studying and classifying the land cover has a direct impact on human lives [14]. Random forests are used in various classification tasks like image classification, land cover classification and classification in ecology [14–16], cancer classification [17], and so on. In addition, random forests are considered to be one of the best algorithms for classifying cartographic and geographic data. At times they have been observed to outperform ensemble techniques like bagging and boosting. Naïve Bayes classifier finds applications in the field of bioinformatics [18]. There are instances of the algorithm being applied to detect insurance claim frauds [19]. It is also used to classify emotions on social media platforms, like Twitter [20].

Support vector machines are used in cheminformatics for drug design and discovery, as well as in pharmaceutical data analysis [21, 22]. They are used to successfully predict the bus arrival time in transportation systems [23]. They are also used to study the diffusion of solar radiation in air polluted regions [24]. Stock price forecasting is another application of SVMs [25]. Recently the evolution of malwares has been studied using support vector machines [26]. In recent works, the outliers in IOT data are being detected using SVMs [27]. Image segmentation is an important aspect of image processing as it separates out the object of interest from an image, which can further be processed. Clustering techniques are heavily used in image segmentation [28, 29].

In today's world of chatbot applications like Alexa and Siri, speech recognition is fast becoming an important aspect of *hands-free computing*. Hidden Markov model (HMM), a statistical machine learning technique, is at the heart of most of the automatic speech recognition systems [30].

Data science being an integral part of human life today, we cannot imagine our life without data science and data science cannot be effective without machine learning techniques!

Bibliography

1. Tom M. Mitchel, *Machine Learning*, McGraw-Hill, New York, 1997.
2. Christopher M. Bishop, *Pattern Recognition and Machine Learning*. New York: Springer, 2009.
3. Haskell B. Curry, " The Method of Steepest Descent for Non-linear Minimization Problems". *Quarterly of Applied Mathematics* 2 (3): 258–261, 1944.
4. A.E. Hoerl and R. Kennard, "Ridge regression: Biased estimation for nonorthogonal problems". *Technometrics*, 12:55–67, 1970.
5. John Quinlan, *C4. 5: Programs for Machine Learning*. Elsevier, 2014.
6. Support Vector Machines, Wikipedia https://en.wikipedia.org/wiki/Support_vector_machine
7. Deepmind https://deepmind.com/
8. Machine Learning Mastery https://machinelearningmastery.com
9. Ethem Alpaydin, *Introduction to Machine Learning*, MIT Press, 2014.
10. Roberto Battiti, 2009, "Using Mutual Information for Selecting Features in Supervised Neural Netlearning." *IEEE Transactions on Neural Networks*, 5 (4): 537–550, 1994.
11. Wei Huang, Kin Keung Lai, Yoshiteru Nakamori, and Shouyang Wang, "Forecasting foreign exchange rates with artificial neural networks: A review." *International Journal of Information Technology & Decision Making*, 3 (01): 145–165, 2004.
12. W. Sha and K. L. Edwards, "The use of artificial neural networks in materials sciencebased research." *Materials & Design*, 28 (6): 1747–1752, 2007.
13. Xi Chen and Hemant Ishwaran, "Random forests for genomic data analysis." *Genomics*, 99 (6): 323–329, 2012.
14. D. RichardCutler, Thomas C. Edwards Jr, Karen H. Beard, Adele Cutler, Kyle T. Hess, Jacob Gibson, and Joshua J. Lawler, "Random forests for classification in ecology." *Ecology*, 88 (11): 2783–2792, (2007).
15. Anna Bosch, Andrew Zisserman, and Xavier Munoz, "Image classification using random forests and ferns." In *2007 IEEE 11th international conference on computer vision*, IEEE (2007), 1–8.

16. Pall Oskar Gislason, Jon Atli Benediktsson, and Johannes R. Sveinsson, "Random forests for land cover classification." *Pattern Recognition Letters*, 27 (4): 294–300, (2006).

17. Alexander Statnikov, Lily Wang, and Constantin F. Aliferis, "A comprehensive comparison of random forests and support vector machines for microarray-based cancer classification." *BMC Bioinformatics*, 9 (1): 319, (2008).

18. Yoichi Murakami and Kenji Mizuguchi, "Applying the Naïve Bayes classifier with kernel density estimation to the prediction of protein–protein interaction sites." *Bioinformatics*, 26(15): 1841–1848, (2010).

19. Stijn Viaene, Richard A. Derrig, and Guido Dedene, "A case study of applying boosting Naive Bayes to claim fraud diagnosis." *IEEE Transactions on Knowledge and Data Engineering*, 16 (5): 612–620, (2004).

20. Liza Wikarsa and Sherly Novianti Thahir, "*A text mining application of emotion classifications of Twitter's users using Naive Bayes method.*" In *2015 1st International Conference on Wireless and Telematics* (ICWT), IEEE (2015), 1–6.

21. Essam H. Houssein, Mosa E. Hosney, Diego Oliva, Waleed M. Mohamed, and M. Hassaballah. "A novel hybrid Harris hawks' optimization and support vector machines for drug design and discovery." *Computers & Chemical Engineering*, 113, (2020).

22. Robert Burbidge, Trotter Matthew, B. Buxton, and Sl Holden. "Drug design by machine learning: support vector machines for pharmaceutical data analysis." *Computers & Chemistry*, 26 (1): 5–14, (2001).

23. Bin, Yu, Yang Zhongzhen, and Yao Baozhen, "Bus arrival time prediction using support vector machines." *Journal of Intelligent Transportation Systems*, 10,(4): 151–158, (2006).

24. Junliang Fan, Lifeng Wu, Xin Ma, Hanmi Zhou, and Fucang Zhang, "Hybrid support vector machines with heuristic algorithms for prediction of daily diffuse solar radiation in air-polluted regions." *Renewable Energy*, 145, 2034–2045, (2020).

25. Pai Ping-Feng, and Chih-Sheng Lin, "A hybrid ARIMA and support vector machines model in stock price forecasting." *Omega*, 33, (6): 497–505, (2005).

26. Mayuri Wadkar, Fabio Di Troia, and Mark Stamp, "Detecting malware evolution using support vector machines." *Expert Systems with Applications*, 143, (2020).

27. Imran Razzak, Khurram Zafar, Muhammad Imran, and Guandong Xu, "Randomized nonlinear one-class support vector machines with bounded loss function to detect of outliers for large scale IoT data." *Future Generation Computer Systems*, 112: 715–723, (2020).

28. H. P. Ng, S. H. Ong, K. W. C. Foong, P. S. Goh, and W. L. Nowinski, "*Medical image segmentation using k-means clustering and improved watershed algorithm.*" *Southwest symposium on image analysis and interpretation*, IEEE, 2006 61–65.

29. Nameirakpam Dhanachandra, Khumanthem Manglem, and Yambem Jina Chanu, "Image segmentation using K-means clustering algorithm and subtractive clustering algorithm." *Procedia Computer Science*, 54: 764–771, (2015).

30. M. Gales and S. Young, "The Application of Hidden Markov Models in Speech Recognition", *Foundations and Trends in Signal Processing*, 3: 195–304, (2007).

4

Classification and Detection of Citrus Diseases Using Deep Learning

Alok Negi and Krishan Kumar

National Institute of Technology, Uttarakhand, India

CONTENTS

4.1 Introduction

Agriculture is the very first climate change that helped humanity to advance and develop. It is really important to take care of plants. Plant diseases are the key reasons for the fall in agricultural development quantity and quality [1]. Environmental food safety has been an increasingly important subject of research. That is because food is a fundamental human requirement, and its proper availability must be assured to satisfy human needs. A sequence of plant diseases like citrus canker has caused annual losses of hundreds of billions. The citrus plant is the primary type of the *Rutaceae* family, which is the most popular agricultural crop in a global context.

Citrus is an important crop that has been grown as a source of food for centuries because of its nutritious fruit as well as economic, environmental, and other associated advantages, and its main products involve fresh fruit and refined juice that is a commodity trade around the world. In contrast, citrus industry by-products, such as pectin and basic essential oil, are extensively used in many industries (skincare products, sanitation, therapeutic, etc.), which enhances this crop's economic relevance, as associated fruit and vegetable diets are closely correlated with various health benefits and reduce diseases [2].

Citrus fruit provides a diverse range of proteins, minerals, and vitamins, including limonoids, flavonoids, and carotenoids that signify balanced biological activity. Due to its abundance in vitamin C as well as other essential nutrients, citrus is a popular plant cultivated primarily in the world's coastal regions. Some diseases, along with cancer, atherosclerosis, and inflammation, are exacerbated inside living organisms by free radicals and lipid peroxidation. Thanks to the vast volume of natural antioxidants within plant products, this threat can be minimized by an acceptable dietary routine containing a significant portion of fresh fruits and vegetables [3].

The fruits contain numerous biologically active compounds, including nutrients and non-nutrients for which positive health benefits have been asserted. Citrus flavonoids have a wide variety of biological properties including antibacterial, antibiotic, ant insulin, coronary anticancer, analgesic, anti-inflammatory, antianxiety, and still other benefits, including vitamins C, carotenoids, potassium, dietary fibers, selenium, folic acid, and a diverse variety of phytochemicals [4]. As a result, epidemiological research findings have shown that the use of citrus fruit inside a diversity of human cancers seems to be protective. The level of ingestion of citrus fruit is much more closely connected to reducing the risk than the consumption of vitamin C. This indicates that citrus fruits provide only one but multiple prevention agents for the chemo cancer. Citrus species belong to the broad family of *Rutaceae*, comprising 130 genera within seven subgenera, with several significant producers of fruit as well as essential oil as seen in Table 4.1.

In this chapter, we propose a CNN model for classification and detection of citrus diseases; the model employs two-stage classifier learning. Our dataset includes images of both citrus fruits, and collectively safe and unhealthy leaves. The targeted diseases in the datasets are blackspot, canker, scab, greening, and melanose, as shown in Figure 4.1. For detection of citrus disease, we first build a binary CNN-based classifier for recognizing fruit or leaf abstract category, and then build multi-class CNN model for recognizing individual targeted disease on that category. The proposed work is useful to monitor citrus disease because the crop yield losses can be reduced and unnecessary fungicide application, a major component of environmental emissions and a primary component of spending, can be prevented. The control of citrus disease in groves planned for processing and the demand for fresh fruit must be taken into account.

The rest of the chapter is structured as follows: Section 4.2 describes some basic deep learning methods. Section 4.3 describes the related work in the field of plant diseases, and

TABLE 4.1

Citrus Classification

Classification Class	Details
Kingdom	*Plantae*
Class	*Magnoliopsida*
Division	*Plantae*
Order	*Sapindales*
Sub class	*Rosidae*
Genus	*Citrus*
Family	*Rutaceae*

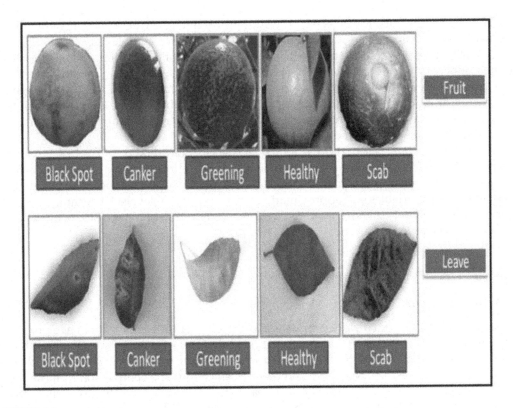

FIGURE 4.1
Sample Images of Dataset

proposed work is given in Section 4.4. Result and analysis are discussed in Section 4.5, and Section 4.6 describes the conclusion followed by references.

4.2 Deep Learning Methods

Deep learning (DL) has become a key factor in a wider category of machine learning techniques, focused on learning representations of the data. An object (for example, an image) can be expressed in various ways, such as a set of pixel intensities for every pixel, or just as a series of edges, regions with specific shape and so on, in a much more abstract manner. Some models promote the learning of behaviors from instances (visual recognition). These are some of the abilities of DL to substitute handcrafted features to optimization techniques for semi-supervised or unsupervised machine learning and the abstraction of hierarchical feature maps [5]. Numerous fundamental learning systems have been extended to areas along with artificial neural networks, deep neural convolution networks, deep assumption networks, and recurring neural networks. DL can be classified as a subcategory of machine learning techniques, and has a multi-layered cascade of nonlinear processing elements to extract and convert features. The data from the preceding layer is used as feedback for each subsequent layer. The algorithms can be controlled or unmonitored, and implementations include network analysis and evaluation.

DL is a concept that encompasses a specific approach to constructing and training neural networks. It has enabled many high-accurate systems for complex application [6–8]. Neural nets have operated ever since the 1950s. One of of the fundamental characteristics of neural networks that have kept the research community working on them is that they are going to be trained. It is fairly easy to demonstrate on a limited scale that you can generate a set of input variables and predicted outputs, and then go through the computational cycle to take the values from initial random quantities to increasingly better numbers that generate more precise predictions.

DL techniques are based on distributed existence interpretations. The fundamental principle behind decentralized simulations is that the correlations of factors in layers arranged within them produce observational data. DL incorporates the expectation that certain layers of variables suit approximation or compositional levels. DL techniques have further improved performance for classification and detection of plant diseases on several benchmark datasets.

4.3 Related Work

Iqbal et al. [2] carried out a survey on several categories for the methods of image processing that related to the detection and recognition of diseases of citrus plants. A comprehensive taxonomy among citrus plant leaves diseases includes four main steps: pre-processing, extraction of features, segmentation, and then classification. The comparison analysis provides efficiency, benefits, and drawbacks of each step in the process. The researchers concluded throughout the study that pre-processing strategies help to increase the precision of segmentation. but also characterized that K-means is one of the most prevalent technologies for segmentation of samples of infected plants. In comparison, the feature vectors are most popular for infection interpretation in the image processing with SVM and NN. Therefore, efforts are required to incorporate a simple, reliable, and automated method used on the unaffected leaves of citrus for disease detection. Information from the survey showed that the use of automatic methods for identifying and classifying citrus plant diseases is in its primary stage. Therefore, novel and new technologies are required to completely automate the procedures of classification and recognition.

Loey et al. [9] reviewed the application of DL to recognize plant diseases and analyzed the overall effectiveness of the application. It has already been identified throughout the survey that DL has brought an immense evolution as it enabled a substantially improved degree of accuracy and also a greater scope in respect of plants and categorized diseases. Several comparisons taken among DL with traditional approaches and these comparisons demonstrated that DL consistently outperforms conventional machine learning approaches and usage of current state-of-the-art methods alongside transfer learning strategies lead to increased performance and better classification accuracy. It has also been explained that DL enables the advancement of precision farming and intelligent agricultural automation for the development of food and agriculture industries.

Yang et al. [10] implemented Parametric Exponential Nonlinear Unit (PENLU) to enhance the performance of neural network frameworks that displaced the activated function of neural networks and strengthened the neural network generalization ability. Regional urban navel orange lesion images were chosen as a reference, and ResNet preparation was enhanced to acquire the model. Overall, the model identification rate introduced 100%, and the prediction accuracy of the output sample was 98.86%. Compared to other similar technologies, the findings have great benefits. The importance of research showed that under some conditions, the suggested Parametric Exponential Nonlinear Unit increased the performance of the deep learning model and obtained better precision at really low cost. The experimental methodology applied and provided a new concept for potential strategies for the identification of plant diseases. In general, these approaches introduced a unique detection method for identifying navel orange lesions throughout the southern province of Jiangxi, and played a supporting role in the development on navel orange research. Finally, a comprehensive plant disease image collection was created, along with the images of navel orange foliage and other images of plant foliage similar to navel orange foliage.

Mari et al. [11] presented an automated identification and classification for citrus diseases by integrating a set of four main processes, respectively data pre-processing, segmentation, feature extraction, then classification. To improve image quality, pre-processing is performed. Therefore, an Otsu-based segmentation procedure was implemented, accompanied by inception with a feature extractor based on ResNetv2. Consequently, a random forest (RF) classifier has been used to classify the various types of citrus diseases. A thorough testing of the developed model mainly occurs on the Citrus Image Gallery dataset samples, and the simulated outcomes illustrated that the proposed model is successful in detecting and classifying excellence diseases with a best accuracy of 99.13%.

Sun et al. [12] developed a method for generating complete and scarce crop lesion leaf images with a particular shape and synthesizing a complete plant lesion leaf image to enhance the precision of the classification process recognition. The authors recommended a framework based on binary generator to address the question of how a generative adversarial network (GAN) induced a lesion image with a particular shape using the edge-smoothing-through-image-pyramid methodology to help overcome a particular challenge that occurs when synthesizing a complete and total lesion leaf image: when synthetic edge pixels appear distinct and the system output size is fixed, but real exact size of the lesion unpredictable. The approach addressed the problem where several plant lesions attributable to very similar patterns were hard to access, and so the lesion and leaf details were merged to correctly classify the associated disease, which allowed the DL platform to have sparse training of data. Particularly, in comparison with the performance of recognition by human experts and AlexNet, it was seen that the proposed approach significantly extended the plant lesion datasets and enhanced a classification network's accuracy of recognition.

Ngugi et al. [13] focused on the usage of RGB images and the relatively low cost and high availability of digital RGB cameras. DL methods have overtaken deeper classifiers, including hand-crafted features, and all these approaches are capable of incredible high accuracy with the identification of pathogens and diseases. The authors also described the significance in enhancing the accuracy rate of large datasets with significant uncertainty, transfer learning, data augmentation, and visual analytics of a CNN feature map. A comprehensive comparison of results of ten state-of-the-art models of CNN architectures was performed on the plant leaf disease recognition and classification. The efficiency analysis of CNN architectures, ResNet-101, DenseNet201, and Inceptionv3 stated that the most appropriate methods to be used in typical computing applications reported better-fit architectures for mobile and embedded devices as compared to Shuffle Net and Squeeze Net, which quantified seven performance metrics.

Sunny et al. [14] proposed detection of canker in citrus using the Contrast Limited Adaptive Histogram Equalization method, which enhances the quality of image. Gavhale et al. [15] presented image processing for early diseases detection on plant using the inspection of leaf feature and SVM for classification. Mokhtar et.al [16] introduced Gabor wavelet change, and SVM for classification and identification of tomato diseases. Mitkal et al. [17] proposed techniques for detection of diseases from sugarcane leaf using linear, non-linear and multiclass SVM.

4.4 Proposed Work

In agriculture, plant disease is mainly responsible for production decreases that cause economic loss. Citrus is used in plants worldwide as a significant source of nutrients such as vitamin C. In this study, we suggest a two-level model for classification and recognition of citrus diseases using deep learning, as shown in Figure 4.2. In the dataset, the target disease is canker, black spot, greening, scab, and melanose. The objectives of the proposed work are as follows:

- Breaking down the multi-class problem into simpler problem units to achieve better performance. So, training of the classifier is conducted via a two-stage process.
- In the first stage or coarse level, a binary CNN model for abstract class (fruits or leaves) recognition is trained.
- In the second stage or fine level, the CNN model is trained for classifying individual target disease.
- Finally, accuracy-curve and loss-curve based analysis is performed for both levels.

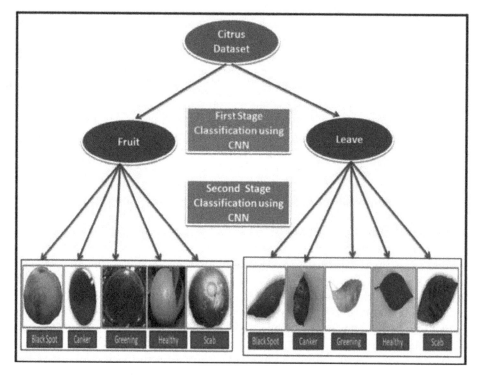

FIGURE 4.2
Block Diagram of the Proposed Work

4.4.1 CNN Architecture

CNN [18] model takes an input, processes it, and classifies it under the certain class, as shown in Figure 4.3. The input layer holds the pixel information of the image in many types of ANN. The convolution layer is a major aspect of the CNN model, which extracts features and calculates the output of neurons linked to local input regions by measuring the gradient magnitude between respective weights as well as the region associated to the input volume. In order to add translation invariance to minor shifts and transformation distortions, and to reduce the amount of subsequent trainable parameters, a pooling layer provides a standard down sampling process along the spatial dimensionality, which decreases the in-plane dimensionality of the function maps. Max pooling extracts patterns from the maps of the input function, produces each feature patches' maximum value, and removes all the other values. The biggest benefit of CNN compared to other models is its ability to automatically recognize the significant features without any oversight by a human. CNN is also effective in terms of computing. Special convolution and pooling operations are used, and parameter sharing is carried out. This allows any machine to run CNN models, making them uniformly attractive.

The following are some concepts that are used in CNN:

- Sequential: Sequential () provides training and inference features on this model.
- Convolution layer: Convolution layer is the first layer and is sometimes called the feature extraction layer because the image features are extracted inside this layer. This layer has a mathematical operation that takes two inputs, such as a kernel or a filter and image matrix.
- Pooling layer: After convolution, the pooling layer is used to reduce the input image spatial volume. It is employed between two layers of convolution. If we apply FC without applying pooling or max pooling after the convo layer, then it will be computationally expensive. Thus, the max pooling is the only way to reduce the input image's spatial volume. Down samples the representation of the inputs by taking the maximum value for each dimension along the features axis over the window defined by pool size.

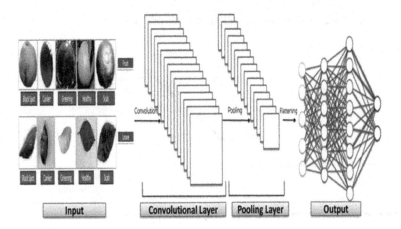

FIGURE 4.3
CNN Architecture

- Flatten: Flattening is performed to create a feature vector for the output of the convolution layers, and it does not affect the batch size.
- Dense: Regular densely connected NN layer.
- Activation function: If we do not specify anything, there will be no activation (i.e., "linear" activation: a(x) = x). ReLU activation function is a non-linear operation of the rectified linear unit for which the output is given as max (0, x).
- Add: Adds a layer instance on top of the layer stack.
- Compile: Configures the model for training.
- Optimizer: Class Adam that implements the Adam algorithm.
- Loss: Binary cross entropy calculates the cross-entropy loss between predicted labels and true labels.
- Metrics: "accuracy": Calculates how often predictions match labels.
- Strides: Stride is defined as the number of pixels shifted over the input matrix.
- Padding: Padding concept is used when filters do not fit the image perfectly.

4.4.2 CNN Architecture for First Stage Classification

In the first stage or coarse level, a binary CNN model for abstract class (fruits or leaves) recognition is trained. In this model, six convolution layers are implemented using 32, 32, 64, 64, 128, and 128 filters respectively, with size 3 × 3. Relu activation function is used, and the output of Relu is measured by $f(x) = \max (0, x)$, as shown in Figure 4.4.

The model used three maxpooling layers with stride 2, followed by flatten layer. Then three dense layers are constructed, in which the first and second dense layers used relu activation function with 128 hidden nodes. Finally, a third dense layer with two hidden nodes is used for the output using softmax activation function. Softmax has the ability to handle multiple classes, so it is used on output layer for classifying inputs into multiple classes. Layered architecture for this classification is shown in Figure 4.5.

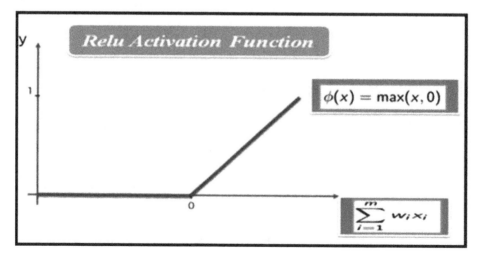

FIGURE 4.4
Relu Activation Function

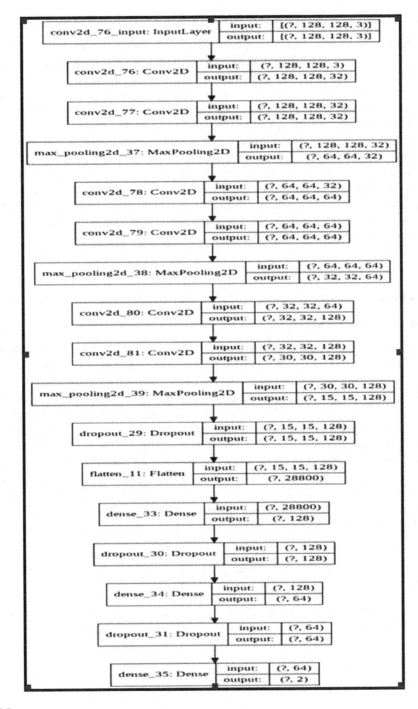

FIGURE 4.5
CNN Layered Architecture for First Stage Binary Classification

4.4.3 CNN Architecture for Second Stage Classification

In the second stage or fine level, the CNN model is trained to classify individual target diseases for fruits and leaves. Fruit class contains black spot, fruits canker, fruits greening, fruits healthy, and fruits scab subclasses, while leaves classes contain leaves black spot, leaves canker, leaves greening, leaves healthy, and leaves melanos subclasses. So the multi-class problems are divided into simpler problem units to achieve better performance and training of the classifier, and training is conducted via a two-stage process.

In this model, four convolution layers are implemented using 16, 32, 64, and 128 filters respectively with size 3 × 3, and Relu is used as an activation function which is measured by $f(x) = \max(0,x)$. The model uses four maxpooling layers with stride 2, followed by flatten layer. Then two dense layers are constructed in which the first dense layer uses Relu activation function with 128 hidden nodes. Finally, a second dense layer with five hidden nodes is used for the output using softmax activation function. Layered architecture for this classification is shown in Figure 4.6.

4.5 Result and Analysis

The models are trained on 6th Generation Intel Core i5, 2.30 GHz CPU, 12 GB RAM, and 2 GB AMD Radeon R5 M330 graphics engine support on Windows 10 OS for this work. For stage classification, accuracy curve and loss curve analysis are carried out.

The batch size hyperparameter determines the number of samples to work through prior to updating the parameters of the internal model. Batch size 32 and 8 are used for first-stage classification and second-stage classification respectively in the proposed work to provide a reliable enough approximation of what would be the gradient of the full dataset. The weight parameters are modified by optimizers to minimize the loss function, so we used Adam optimizer for first stage and fruit diseases multiclass classification of second stage while rmsprop is used for second stage leaf diseases multiclass classification.

Accuracy is one criterion for testing models of classification. This is the fraction of predictions that our model has been accurate depicting.

$$Accuracy = \frac{\text{Number of Correct Predictions}}{\text{Total Number of predictions made}} \tag{4.1}$$

The accuracy can also be measured for binary classification in terms of positives and negatives as follows:

$$Accuracy = \frac{(TP + TN)}{(TP + TN + FP + FN)} \tag{4.2}$$

Where TP, FP, TN, and FN denote true positives, false positives, true negatives, and false negatives respectively.

Binary cross entropy is a loss function that is used in binary classification tasks, while logarithmic loss or log loss works for penalizing incorrect classifications that fit well for

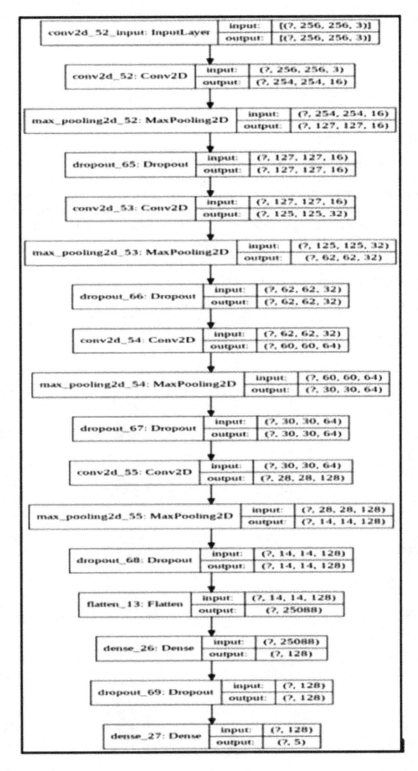

FIGURE 4.6
CNN Layered Architecture for Second Stage Multiclass Classification

multi-class classifications. If there are N samples of the groups M, then the Log Loss is determined as follows:

$$Logarithmic\ Loss = \frac{-1}{N}\sum_{i=1}^{N}\sum_{j=1}^{M}y_{ij}*\log(p)_{ij} \qquad (4.3)$$

4.5.1 Dataset Description

The dataset includes images of safe and unhealthy citrus fruits and leaves that could be used to protect plants from diseases by using advanced computer vision techniques for researchers. The targeted disease in the datasets is canker, black spot, greening, scab, and melanose. The dataset includes 759 images of both citrus fruits and both safe and unhealthy images of citrus leaves. Images have 256 * 256 dimensions, with a resolution of 72 dpi. Sample images of the dataset are shown in Figure 4.7.

4.5.2 Data Pre-Processing and Augmentation

Large input shape significantly affects model output due to more computation time to extract the function, so input size is resized to $128 \times 128 \times 3$ for the first-stage classification and $256 \times 256 \times 3$ for second-stage classification.

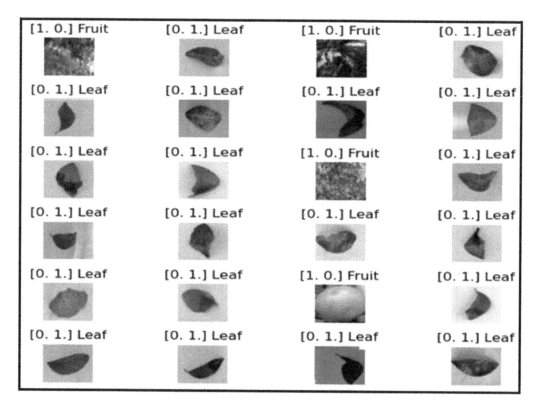

FIGURE 4.7
Sample Images from Dataset (with Labels)

Data augmentation is a way of producing further data from our current collection of training. This way, we increase the size of the training set artificially, reducing overfitting. Proposed work uses the image data generator class on training and test set for data augmentation. A random transformation of images using data augmentation for first-stage binary classification and second-stage multiclass classification are plotted in Figure 4.8, Figure 4.9, and Figure 4.10, respectively. The parameter used for data augmentation for proposed work is below:

- Rotation: 15
- Shear: 0.2
- Rescale: 1/255
- Zoom: 0.2
- Horizontal Flip: True
- Height Shift: 0.1
- Width Shift: 0.1

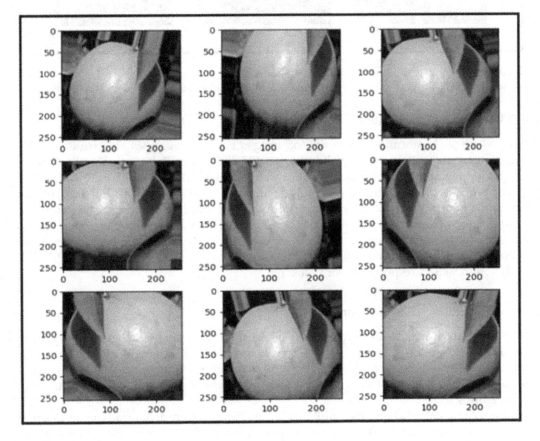

FIGURE 4.8
Random Transformations of Image using Data Augmentation for First-Stage Binary Classification

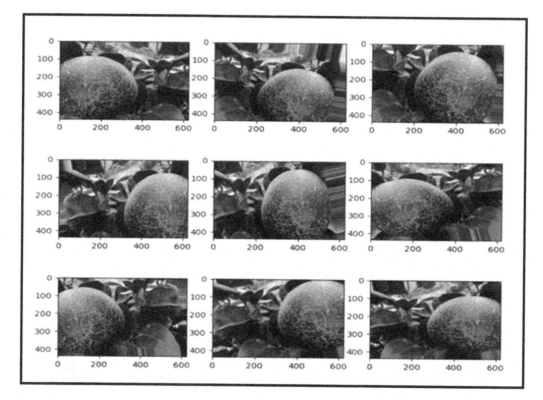

FIGURE 4.9
Random Transformations of Fruit Image using Data Augmentation for Second-Stage Multi-Class Classification

4.5.3 First-Stage Classification

For first-stage classification, there are 645 images in the training set (127 fruits and 518 leaves), and 114 images in the validation set (23 fruits and 91 leaves). Distributions of images in the training and validation sets are shown in Figure 4.11 and Figure 4.12.

The proposed work recorded a training accuracy of 99.53%with logarithm loss 0.01 and validation accuracy of 91.23% with logarithm loss 0.40 in only 30 epochs. The model has 3,981,922 total parameters, out of which 3,981,922 are trainable parameters; there are no nontrainable parameters. Figure 4.13 and Figure 4.14 display the accuracy curve and loss curve for the first-stage classification. Precision, recall, F1 score are recorded 97.65%, 91.21%, and 94.32% respectively for first stage.

4.5.4 Second-Stage Classification

For second-stage leaf diseases multi-class classification, there are 546 images in the training set (153 black spot, 147 canker, 183 greening images, 52 healthy, and 11 melanose) and 63 images in the validation set (18 black spot, 16 canker, 21 greening images, 6 healthy, and 2 melanose). Distributions of images in training and validation sets are shown in Figure 4.15 and Figure 4.16.

The second-state leaf diseases multi-class classification recorded a training accuracy of 87.00% with logarithm loss 0.38 and validation accuracy of 71.43% with logarithm loss 0.90 in 30 epochs. The model has 3,309,477 total parameters, out of which 3,309,477 are trainable

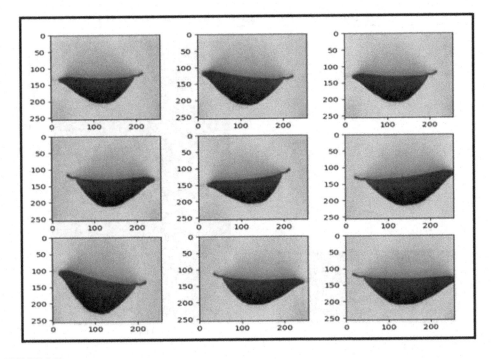

FIGURE 4.10
Random Transformations of Leave Image using Data Augmentation for Second-Stage Multi-Class Classification

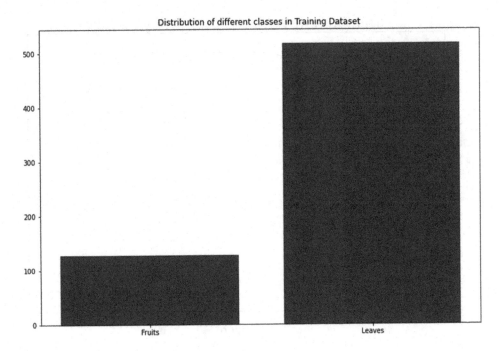

FIGURE 4.11
Distribution of Images in Training Set for First-Stage Binary Classification

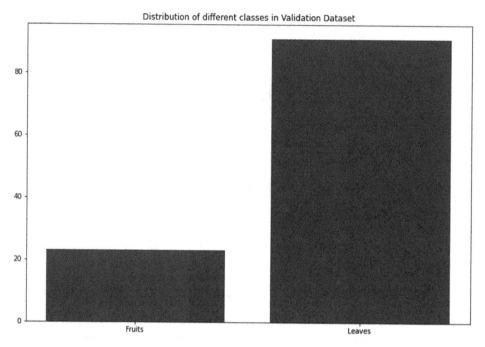

FIGURE 4.12
Distribution of Images in validation Set for First-Stage Binary Classification

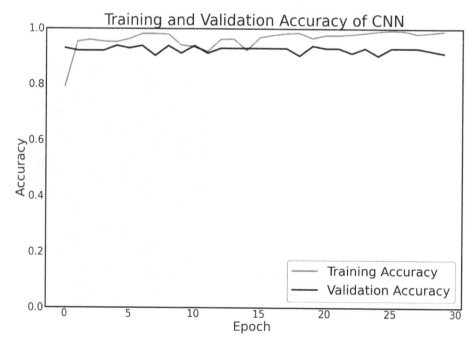

FIGURE 4.13
Accuracy Curve for First-Stage Classification

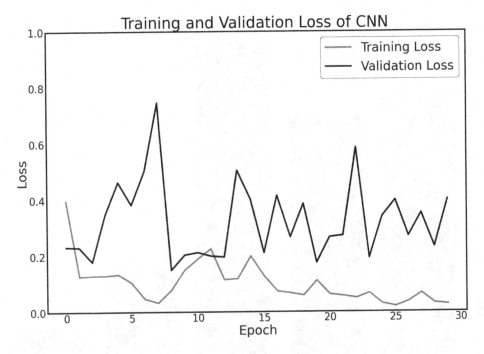

FIGURE 4.14
Loss Curve for First-Stage Classification

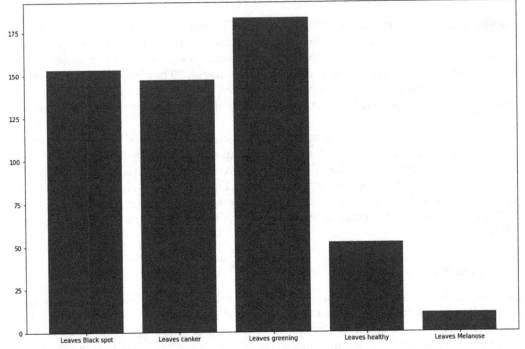

FIGURE 4.15
Distribution of Images in Training Set for Second-Stage Leaf Diseases Classification

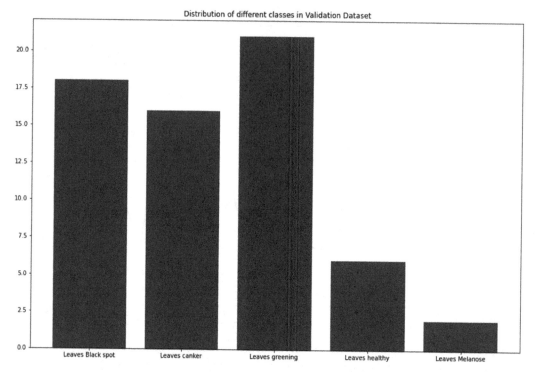

FIGURE 4.16

Distribution of Images in Validation Set for Second-Stage Leaf Diseases Classification

parameters; there are no nontrainable parameters. Figure 4.17 and Figure 4.18 display the accuracy curve and loss curve for the multiclass classification of leaf diseases.

For second-stage fruit diseases multi-class classification, there are 138 images in the training set (17 black spot, 74 canker, 14 greening images, 20 healthy, and 13 scab) and 16 images in the validation set (2 black spot, 8 canker, 2 greening images, 2 healthy, and 2 scab). Distributions of images in the training and validation set are plotted in Figure 4.19 and Figure 4.20.

The second-stage fruit diseases multi-class classification recorded training accuracy of 65.94% with logarithm loss 0.91 and validation accuracy of 62.50% with logarithm loss 1.09 in 30 epochs. The model has 3,309,477 total parameters, out of which 3,309,477 are trainable parameters; there are no nontrainable parameter.s Figure 4.21 and Figure 4.22 display the accuracy curve and loss curve for the multiclass classification of fruit diseases.

Table 4.2 describes the comparison table for the overall experiments of the proposed work.

4.5.5 Limitations

For this work, an existing dataset is used from the internet that is imbalanced and smaller in size. Due to less training of the model, the second-stage disease multiclass classification recorded less accuracy and loss as compared to the first stage. Unabalance data are not handled in this work, while augmentation is used to increase the size of the dataset in some instances. This dataset does not have a validation set, so it was divided into a training set

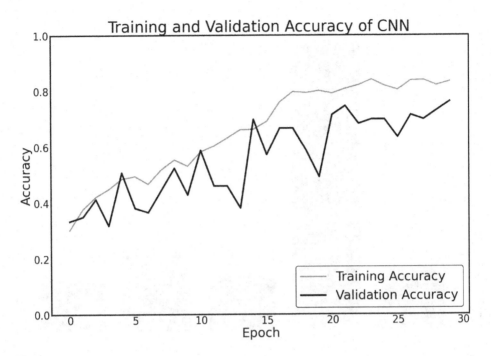

FIGURE 4.17
Accuracy Curve for Multiclass Classification of Leaf Diseases

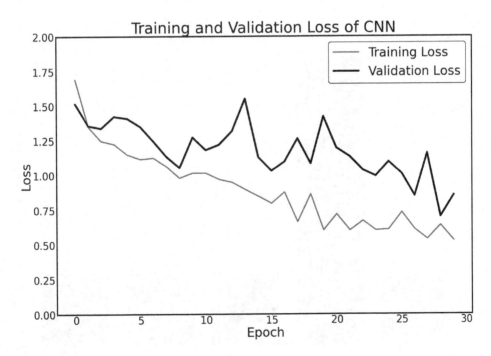

FIGURE 4.18
Loss Curve for Multiclass Classification of Leaf Diseases

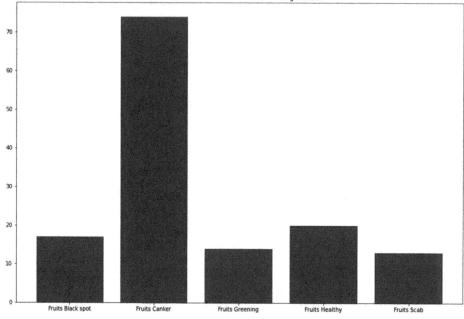

FIGURE 4.19
Distribution of Images in Training Set for Second-Stage Fruit Disease Classification

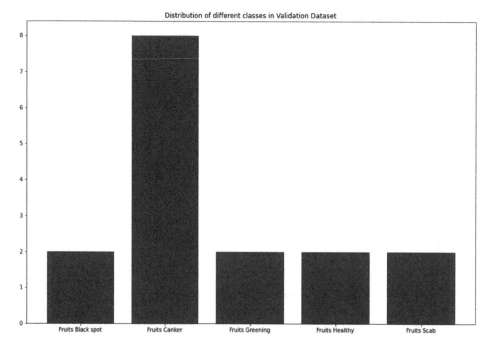

FIGURE 4.20
Distribution of Images in Validation Set for Second-Stage Fruit Disease Classification

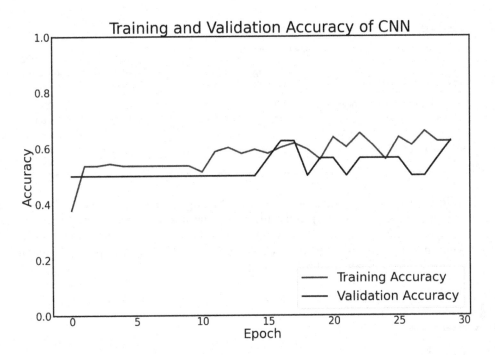

FIGURE 4.21
Accuracy Curve for Multiclass Classification of Fruit Diseases

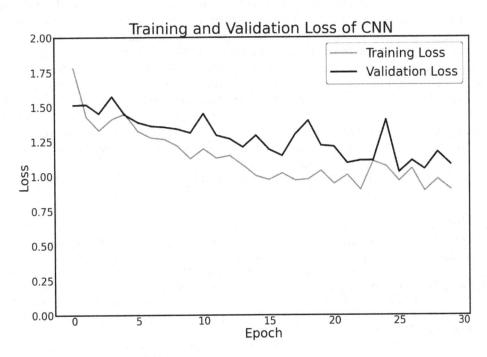

FIGURE 4.22
Loss Curve for Multiclass Classification of Fruit Diseases

TABLE 4.2

Accuracy and Loss Curve Analysis (In Percent)

Experiment Description	Training Accuracy	Training Loss	Validation Accuracy	Validation Loss
First-Stage Binary Classification	99.53	0.01	91.23	0.40
Second-Stage Leaf Disease Classification	87.00	0.38	71.43	0.90
Second-Stage Fruit Disease Classification	65.94	0.91	62.50	1.09

and a validation set for the assessment. Instead of using two different stages, all ten classes can be taken together to make it purely multiclass classification and comparison with two level or stage classification. Further, it was not possible to run more experiments using different known architectures other than CNN like VGG, ResNet, Inception, Efficient Net, and others due to smaller size of this dataset.

4.6 Conclusion

Deep learning techniques in smart farming have many possibilities in the process of automatic or computer vision plant disease detection and classification. We established extensive deep learning models for the detection of citrus disease through CNN-based fruit and leaf images. First, a CNN classifier has been used to distinguish input images into two classes: fruits and leaves. In the second phase, two CNN classifiers have been trained for recognition of separated diseases within fruit and leaves. Our research findings showed how the deep-learning approach is capable of consistently detecting citrus diseases. Our work recorded validation accuracy of 91.23% with logarithm loss 0.40 for first-stage classification, while in the second stage we achieved a validation accuracy of 71.43% with logarithm loss 0.90 and validation accuracy of 62.50% with logarithm loss 1.09 are recorded in only 30 epochs for leaves and fruits diseases classification respectively. In the future, this divide-and-conquer approach can be applied on larger dataset using different advanced convolutional neural network models for better analysis.

References

1. Chohan, Murk, Adil Khan, Rozina Chohan, Saif Hassan Katpar, and Muhammad Saleem Mahar. "Plant Disease Detection Using Deep Learning." *International Journal of Recent Technology and Engineering* 9 (2020): 909–914. doi: 10.35940/ijrte.A2139.059120.
2. Iqbal, Zahid, Muhammad Attique Khan, Muhammad Sharif, Jamal Hussain Shah, Muhammad Habib ur Rehman, and Kashif Javed. "An Automated Detection and Classification of Citrus Plant Diseases Using Image Processing Techniques: A Review." *Computers and Electronics in Agriculture* 153 (2018): 12–32.
3. Sidana, J., V. Saini, S. Dahiya, P. Nain, and S. Bala. "A Review on Citrus-"The Boon of Nature"" *International Journal of Pharmaceutical Sciences Review and Research* 18 (2) (2013): 20–27.
4. Silpa M, Suresh Joghee, and Hamsalakshmi. "A Phytochemical Study on Eupatorium Glandulosum". *Asian Journal of Pharmaceutical and Clinical Research* 13 (1) (2019): 77–80.

5. Benuwa, Ben Bright, Yong Zhao Zhan, Benjamin Ghansah, Dickson KeddyWornyo, and Frank BanasekaKataka. "A Review of Deep Machine Learning." *International Journal of Engineering Research in Africa* 24 (2016): 124–136. Trans Tech Publications Ltd.

6. Kumar, Krishan, and Deepti D. Shrimankar. "Deep Event Learning Boost-Up Approach: Delta." *Multimedia Tools and Applications* 77 (20) (2018): 26635–26655.

7. Kumar, Krishan. "EVS-DK: Event Video Skimming Using Deep Keyframe." *Journal of Visual Communication and Image Representation* 58 (2019): 345–352.

8. Kumar, Krishan, Anurag Kumar, and Ayush Bahuguna. "D-CAD: Deep and crowded anomaly detection." In *Proceedings of the 7th International Conference on Computer and Communication Technology,* (2017), pp. 100–105.

9. Loey, Mohamed, Ahmed ElSawy, and Mohamed Afify. "Deep Learning in Plant Diseases Detection for Agricultural Crops: A Survey." *International Journal of Service Science, Management, Engineering, and Technology (IJSSMET)* 11(2) (2020): 41–58.

10. Yang, Guoliang, Nan Xu, and Zhiyang Hong. "Identification of Navel Orange Lesions by non-linear Deep Learning Algorithm." *EngenhariaAgrícola* 38 (5) (2018): 783–796.

11. Mari, Kamarasan & Senthilkumar, C. "A Novel Citrus Disease Detection and Classification Using Deep Learning-Based Inception Resnet V2 Model." *ADALYA Journal* 9 (2020): 1008–1034.

12. Sun, Rongcheng, Min Zhang, Kun Yang, and Ji Liu. "Data Enhancement for Plant Disease Classification Using Generated Lesions." *Applied Sciences* 10 (2) (2020): 466.

13. Ngugi, Lawrence C., Moataz Abelwahab, and Mohammed Abo-Zahhad. "Recent Advances in Image Processing Techniques for Automated Leaf Pest and Disease Recognition-A Review." *Information Processing in Agriculture* 8 (2020): 27–51.

14. Sunny, S., and Gandhi, M. I. "An Efficient Citrus Cancer Detection Method Based on Contrast Limited Adaptive Histogram Equalization Enhancement". *International Journal of Applied Engineering Research*, 13 (1): (2018) 809–815.

15. Gavhale, Kiran R., Ujwalla Gawande, and Kamal O. Hajari. "*Unhealthy region of citrus leaf detection using image processing techniques.*" In *International Conference for Convergence for Technology-2014,* (2014), pp. 1–6. IEEE,.

16. Mokhtar, Usama, Mona AS Ali, Aboul Ella Hassenian, and Hesham Hefny. "*Tomato leaves diseases detection approach based on support vector machines.*" In *2015 11th International Computer Engineering Conference (ICENCO).* IEEE, (2015), pp. 246–250..

17. Mitkal, Prajakta, Priyanka Pawar, Mira Nagane, Priyanka Bhosale, Mira Padwal, and Priti Nagane. "Leaf Disease Detection and Prevention Using Image Processing Using Matlab." *International Journal of Recent Trends in Engineering & Research (IJRTER)* 2 (2016): 26–30.

18. Yamashita, R., Nishio, M., Do, R. K. G., and Togashi, K. Convolutional Neural Networks: An Overview and Application in Radiology. *Insights Into Imaging,* 9(4) (2018): 611–629.

5

Credibility Assessment of Healthcare Related Social Media Data

Monika Choudhary

Department of CSE, MNIT Jaipur, India
Department of CSE, IGDTUW, Delhi, India

Satyendra Singh Chouhan and Emmanuel S. Pilli

Department of CSE, MNIT Jaipur, India

CONTENTS

5.1 Introduction

In this digital era, online platforms are heavily used to share user views, opinions, and information. Social networking applications like Twitter and Facebook, websites (e.g., Medical News Today, WebMD, *The Times*, *The New York Times*), blogs, and online review portals (e.g., Amazon, TripAdvisor) engage a large number of users. As the content on these platforms is created by the user and instantly shared with the online community without any moderation, the quality and trustworthiness of the content is highly questionable.

Pew Research Center published a report in October 2019 that revealed that 55% of US adults get their news from social media either "often" or "sometimes" [1]. As such, the credibility of widely consumed information becomes highly significant. As online social platforms are neutral toward the credibility of information, we can say that they transmit both information and misinformation. This is quite different from what used to happen in traditional mediums of information delivery where the authorized gatekeepers would verify the content before sharing. The volume and impact of user-generated content has increased with the increase in penetration of social media in recent years.

5.1.1 User-Generated Content (UGC)

User-generated content (UGC) is content like text, images, and videos created and posted by users on online platforms. The online platforms include social media, websites, review forums, and so on. The content is created by the users and for the users. In other words, users are both content creators and content consumers. Some of the key advantages of sharing user-generated content over various online platforms are easy and quick reachability, social awareness, resource of knowledge, and learning. But the spread of misinformation through social media can be critical. We shall see such examples in the next section.

5.1.2 Impact of User-Generated Content

User-generated content has a significant impact on the masses. But this content can be noisy, unreliable, and may contain large amounts of spam and misinformation introduced by creators or contributors themselves. For example, in the US presidential election of 2016, WTOE 5 News published a news story that claimed that Pope Francis endorsed Trump for president (Figure 5.1), but it was later found that the news story was almost entirely fabricated despite engaging a large number of users [2].

FIGURE 5.1
Fake Facebook Post [2]

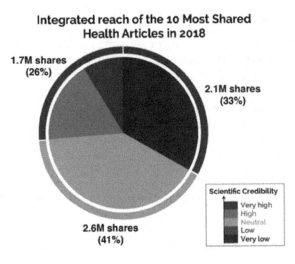

FIGURE 5.2
Credibility of Health Articles [4]

In the healthcare domain, misinformation from websites and health forums can lead to hazardous repercussions because they are usually checked by a large number of users in order to figure out symptoms of diseases, know about active pharmaceutical ingredients, their potential side effects, seek consultation from health care providers, and so on [3]. A group of scientists collaborated and assessed the credibility of health articles published in media to examine the 100 most popular health articles of 2018 (published by premier media agencies like Daily Mail, CNN, and so on). They concluded that out of the top 10 shared articles, three quarters were misleading or included some false information, as shown in Figure 5.2 [4].

Recent events have shown that false information and hoaxes can create a sense of panic among people as it spreads faster compared to the truth because false information seems surprising, and hence gets more retweets and public attention. People also tend to believe tweets without verifying. In the year 2020, COVID-19 spread in large parts of the world, affecting several countries. People found it difficult to reach out to reliable sources for proper information and knowledge [5]. Instead, they turned to social media websites like Twitter and several other online platforms for information. In such a situation, incorrect information can lead to anxiety among people, resulting in drastic consequences. Not only that, there are tweets about vaccines, immunization, medicine, and many more. Some of the example tweets that demonstrate this are shown below.

Tweet 1: *"Turmeric in milk .... Best & perfect medicine for #Coronavid19 #coronavirusinindia #CoronaVirusUpdate"*
Tweet 2: *"crazy part is that once temperatures hit 26–27 degrees CoronaVirus won't survive"*
Tweet 3: *"No religion forbids vaccination"*

Tweet 3 is perhaps the most ignorant statement that's ever been made. Religion is what people choose to believe in or NOT believe in.

Therefore, it is clearly evident that sharing misleading and fake information can greatly scrape public trust and confidence on online information. As the users are not always able to judge the correctness of information shared online, there should be mechanisms for them to know whether they are coming across true or fake information.

5.1.3 Credibility Assessment of Social Media Data

Credibility implies the concept of eliciting or showing confidence. It can be related to trustworthiness and truthfulness. Truthfulness is related to correctness, and hence must be backed by facts. Any individual or source of information is trustworthy if we have faith and confidence in that individual/source of information. Trust can be classified into several categories, like individual, relational, and so on. It is crucial to determine the trust and credibility of the content posted by users. This will not only enhance individual understanding, but will also prevent the spread of false and fabricated content on social media.

5.1.4 Credibility Metrics

Various credibility metrics can be used to determine content credibility. Some of the most commonly used credibility metrics are discussed here:

1. *Assertives*: Verbs such as "claim" are considered to be more credible because they tell us the user is talking about facts in the statement.
2. *Factives:* Factive verbs (e.g., "indicate") decrease the credibility, as the user tries to put the claim on something about which he is not sure.
3. *Implicatives*: Words like "complicit" define that the user is in some external pressure to write the above.
4. *Report verbs:* The verbs (e.g., "argue") are used to report what someone said more accurately, rather than using just say and tell.
5. *Discourse markers:* Strong modals like "would," "could," and "if" are considered less credible as they raise doubts over the statement.
6. *Subjectivity and bias:* Statements that are subjective and include the sentiments and opinions of a single person are not considered credible.
7. *Question:* Questions in the tweet are considered less credible.
8. *Authority's statements*: Statements made by any government authority or news channels are considered credible.
9. *Individuals statement*: Statements made by individuals are considered less credible compared to group statements.

This research focuses upon the health-related content posted on social media (specifically on Twitter), and tries to classify it as fake or real with the help of the deep-learning based model. The presented model is also compared with the baseline models for efficacy and analysis. In the rest of the chapter, the presented approach is explained in detail with implementation details and results. Extensive literature review has been done to arrive at the presented model as shown in the next section.

5.2 Literature Review

Over the last few years, social media has been used to disseminate misinformation in the form of rumors, misinformation, and fake news. Several researchers have addressed the challenge of trustworthiness of content posted on online platforms. This section presents the research work related to credibility assessment of online information.

5.2.1 Classification of Credibility Assessment of UGC

After doing an extensive literature survey, the credibility assessment of user-generated content is classified based on different scenarios. It is generally assessed at either or all three levels, i.e., the post level, topic level, and user level. The techniques and methods used at each level can differ depending upon various factors like the underlying model, datasets, amount of human intervention and participation required, and so on.

- *Post level:* The main goal at post level is to examine the content of the post to determine the credibility score and overall trustworthiness of the post. The various post level features studied in literature are summarized in Table 5.1.

- *Topic level:* Events are usually the topics that are trending on social media. Topic becomes trending if a large number of users are posting, commenting, and reposting about that topic during a particular time interval. This generally happens when a high-impact event occurs and thousands of posts are created in a short span of time. Various topic level features used by researchers are listed in Table 5.2.

- *User level:* User level credibility assessment is primarily based upon features related to details of user profile or account. The information related to count of posts, reposts,

TABLE 5.1

Post Level Features Used in Literature

Serial No.	Feature	Type
1.	No. of Characters & Words	Int
2.	No. of Question Marks	Int
3.	No. of Responses & Republishing	Int
4.	No. of #,@ Links, Emojis	Int
5.	No. of Verbs & Nouns	Int
6.	No. of Affirmative & Critical Phrases	Int
7.	No. of URLs, Images, Videos & Metadata	Int
8.	No. of Duplications in a post	Int
9.	Time	Str
..	many more	..

TABLE 5.2

Topic Level Features Used in Literature

Serial No.	Feature	Type
1.	No. of Responses & Republishing	Int
2.	No. of #, @ Links, Emojis	Int
3.	No. of Verbs & Nouns	Int
4.	No. of Affirmative & Critical phrases	Int
5.	No. of URLs, Images, Videos & Metadata	Int
6.	No. of Duplicate Posts	Int
7.	Time	Str
8.	Geographic Location	Str
..	many more	..

friends, and followers can be helpful in determining trusted versus fake user accounts.

5.2.2 Credibility Assessment Approaches

From the literature, the approaches used for credibility assessment can be broadly categorized into automation-based and manual approaches as discussed in Table 5.3.

- *Automated approaches:* As we discussed in the previous section, digital data is created and diffused in an online network at a very high rate. So given the nature and amount of data streaming, automatic assessment of online content is crucial. The automated approaches include supervised and unsupervised machine learning, graph-based approaches, and techniques working on weighted algorithms. Summary literature reviews of automated approaches are given in Tables 5.4 and 5.5.

- *Manual approaches:* Manual approaches are highly accurate, but given the amount of data that is generated on online platforms it becomes infeasible to apply manual approach for credibility assessment at large scale. Thus, manual approaches are highly precise, but cost and time prohibitive. Manual methods can be broadly classified into voting, perception-based methods, and manual verification. Table 5.6 shows the summary of related work in manual approaches.

5.2.3 Credibility Assessment Platforms

The various platforms where credibility assessment plays a key role are:

- *Social media:* It includes interactive Web 2.0 applications that publish data generated through online interactions. The most popular social media examples are Facebook, Youtube, Twitter, Whatsapp, and so on. Networks formed through social media called online social networks (OSN) change the way groups of people interact and communicate with each other.

TABLE 5.3

User Level Features Used in Literature

Serial No.	Feature	Type
1.	Profile Picture	Y/N
2.	Age	Int
3.	Sex	Str
4.	Ideological Affirmation	Str
5.	No. of Followers & Friends	Int
6.	No. of Posts	Int
7.	No. of Republishes	Int
8.	Geographic Location	Str
..	many more	..

TABLE 5.4

A Comparison Between Various Machine Learning–Based Approaches

S.N	Author and Publication Year	Topic Level	Post Level	User Level	Platform	Approach
1.	Abbasi and Liu, 2013 [6]	–	–	√	US Senate Official Websites	Credrank and K-means
2.	Lamba et al., 2013 [7]	√	√	–	Twitter	Naive Bayes and J48 decision tree
3.	Boididou et al., 2014 [8]	–	√	√	Twitter	Naive Bayes, J48 decision tree, Random Forest
4.	Li et al., 2014 [9]	–	√	√	Trip Advisor, Expedia, Mturk	SVM
5.	Finn et al., 2015 [10]	–	√	–	Twitter	Naive Bayes and decision tree
6.	Thandar and Usanavasin, 2015 [11]	√	-	√	Flickr, Stack Overflow	SVM
7.	Saikaew and Noyunsan, 2015 [12]	–	√	–	Facebook	SVM
8.	Sarna and Bhatia., 2017 [13]	-	√	√	Twitter	Naive Bayes, SVM, and KNN
9.	Gupta et al., 2018 [14]	√	√	-	Facebook	Logistic regression, Naive Bayes, SVM, and Random Forest
10.	Jo et al., 2019 [15]	–	√	–	Blogs	Random Forest, Logistic Regression, SVM, and Multi-Layer Perceptron

TABLE 5.5

A Comparison Between Various Graph-Based Approaches

S.N	Author and Publication Year	Topic	Post	User	Platform	Approach
1.	Ratkiewicz et al., 2011 [16]	√	√	–	Twitter	Google-based profile-of-mood-states
2.	Nguyen et al., 2012 [17]	–	√	–	Epinion, Facebook	Ranking and optimization based algorithms
3.	Ulicny and Kokar, 2012 [18]	–	√	–	Twitter	RDF graph and Tunkrank
4.	Mckelvey and Menczer, 2013 [19]	√	√	–	Twitter	Trustworthiness score
5.	Pasternack and Roth, 2013 [20]	–	√	–	Twitter	Credibility propagation and latent
6.	Samadi et al., 2016 [21]	–	√	√	Website claims	graph, joint source credibility assessment and Probabilistic soft logic
7.	O'Brien et al., 2019 [22]	√	√	√	Twitter	Graph Estimator Model, Iterative classification

- *Websites:* Websites can be categorized into various domains depending upon their content, such as healthcare (Eg.WebMD, Practo, Everyday Health), trade e-commerce (Eg. Ally Invest, Amazon, flipkart), news (Eg. CNN, the Times), *and* Wikipedia.
- *Review forums*: Online product reviews are important information sources for consumers choosing a product. These reviews may also be spam or fake. Some of the common review platforms are TripAdvisor, Yelp, and others..

TABLE 5.6

A Comparison Between Various Human-Based Approaches

S. N	Author and Publication Year	Topic level	Post level	User level	Platform	Approach
1.	Westerman et al., 2012 [23]	–	√	√	Twitter	ANOVA
2.	O'Donovan et al., 2012 [24]	√	√	√	Twitter	Amazon MTurk and distribution Analysis
3.	Kwon et al., 013 [25]	√	-	–	Twitter	Interclass correlation coeff
4.	Edwards et al., 2014 [26]	–	√	–	Twitter	ANOVA
5.	Zubiaga et al., 2014 [27]	√	√	–	Twitter	Statistical Methods
6.	Shariff et al., 2014 [28]	√	√	√	Twitter	CrowdFlower and Association rule mining
7.	Kang et al.,2015 [29]	–	√	√	Twitter, Reddit	Statistical Analysis
8.	Johnson et al., 2015 [30]	–	√	–	Twitter	Amazon MTurk
9.	Go et al., 2016 [31]	–	√	–	Website	Statistical Methods
10.	Alrubian et al., 2017 [32]	√	√	√	Twitter	User Sentiment

In the next section, we discuss a method for finding the credibility of user-generated medical and health-related tweets. We also intend to determine the trustworthiness of their authors by exploiting linguistic features. Multiple models were used against several comparison methods, on online health-related tweets. The presented work uses a hybrid model with concatenation of Bidirectional encoder representation using transformers (BERT) and convolutional neural network (CNN) to learn user trustworthiness by using linguistic features of the tweet. This method can reliably extract noncredible statements.

5.3 Credibility Assessment of Healthcare Related Tweets

The credibility assessment of healthcare related tweets is done following a modular approach. There are two main parts: part I is used for creating an automated labeling technique based on a semi-supervised approach. And Part II is the classification using a deep learning approach. The overall methodology is shown in Figure 5.3.

5.3.1 Data Acquisition and Labeling Using Semi-Supervised Approach (Part I)

In order to deal with the real problem, it is necessary to work with real-time data. Various fake claims and news are found all over the internet in the form of social media content, reviews, and on various websites. We took the social media platform Twitter, and found various health- and medicine–related noncredible tweets. The challenge of short texts is the lack of context and the ambiguity that may arise due to it.

Web scraping (also known as web data extraction) is a technique to extract large amounts of online data from various websites. This extracted data can be stored on local systems for processing and further use. Data on most of the sites is not available to be directly downloaded. Manually copy-and-pasting a large amount of data is a very tedious

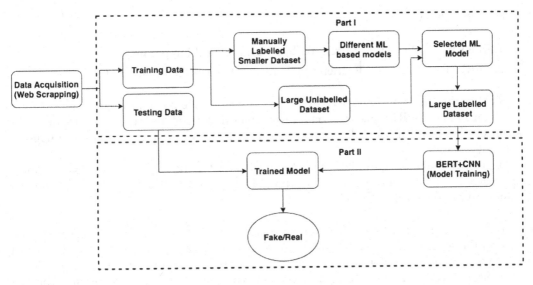

FIGURE 5.3
Overall Methodology of Credibility Assessment

job. Web scraping is a technique that automates this process and saves time and effort. We used a custom-built web scraping technique for Twitter that involves using the Twitter API. Using basic Python libraries (NLTK), we preprocess the data and remove any special symbols or links.

For **labeling** the data, we use the *semi-supervised* approach. Semi-supervised learning combines both supervised and unsupervised learning. In a situation where we make use of semi-supervised learning, we have both labeled and unlabeled data. Suppose we would like to train a model with a large number of datasets, and labeling all the data manually is not possible. It is possible to label some portion of the data ourselves and use that portion to train our model. We use our model to predict on the remaining unlabeled portion of data after training the model on the labeled portion of the dataset. We take each piece of unlabeled data and label it according to the individual outputs that were predicted for them.

For that, we "manually" labeled the smaller dataset, which we further used to label the bigger dataset. We labeled 1500 tuples with a team of 5 members labeling the tweets as credible (1) or non-credible (0) on the basis of a credibility matrix (Section 5.1.4).

We performed experiments using six machine learning algorithms on the small manually labeled dataset. The results of the experiments are discussed in the results section. From the evaluation, we selected a best performing model for labeling the remaining unlabeled instances in the dataset.

5.3.2 Tweet Text Embedding (Part II)

We use BERT for text tokenizing and embedding purposes. BERT is pre-trained on a large corpus of unlabeled text, including Wikipedia and a huge book corpus (800 million words). It is deep bidirectional unsupervised language representation that is pre-trained using a large set of corpus [33].

BERT has two variants:

1. BERT base: 12 layers, 12 attention head, and 110 million parameters.
2. BERT large: 24 layers, 16 attention heads, and 240 million parameters.

BERT is mainly used for language modeling; however ,we have used only the encoding mechanism here. BERT makes use of a transformer that reads the entire sentence of words at once. This characteristic allows the model to gain an in-depth sense of language or context.

Almost all the seq2seq models predict the next word in the sequence using a directional approach. But this limits our context learning. Instead of this, BERT use two strategies for achieving bidirectional approach:

- *Masked LM:* In masked LM, before feeding the words to the encoder, 15% of the words of the sentence are masked with [MASKED]. The task is to predict the masked word with the help of other non-masked words, based on the context. First, the words are embedded to convert string into vectors. Then, the encoder performs its function. The result is passed to a classification layer. The output vectors are multiplied with the embedding matrix and then transformed into vocabulary. At last, it calculates the probability of various words with the help of softmax function. The word with the highest probability is predicted as the masked word.

- *Next sentence prediction:* The model receives pair of inputs to predict whether the next sentence is a subsequent part of the original sentence. During the training process, we give half of the inputs as a pair while the second sentence is the subsequent sentence in the original sentence; for the other half, a random sentence from the data is chosen as the second sentence.

As BERT is deeply bidirectional and achieves a deeper sense of context, it can give good results in classification of text for credibility because credibility is not word specific; instead, it is a sentence-specific assessment. The labeled data is given as an input to BERT to generate word vectors, and these word vectors are fed into CNN model for classification purposea.

For experimental analysis we also used BERT as Tokenizer, i.e., we used BERT to generate tokens only, which are given as input to CNN model.

In both cases, we are using the base version of BERT with 12 layers. In the next segment we will describe the internal functioning of how BERT can be used as tokenizer and embedder.

1. BERT as a tokenizer: Data preprocessing is one of the most important tasks for dealing with datasets as it can help in getting cleaner and more manageable data. For processing long strings of data, it needs to be broken down into smaller pieces. Tokenization is the process of tokenizing or splitting long strings of data into tokens. Token is the smallest unit value processed. BERT can be used as a tokenizer, which can further increase the efficiency of the model.
   Example of tokenization: - String - "India is my country."
   After Tokenization - ["India","is","my","country","."].
   BERT uses the wordPiece Tokenizer which consists of -30522 words

Dealing with words combining with known words, each one corresponds to an ID; so from stings we get numbers usable by computer. Various models can be found on TensorFlow hub, and we used the model *-bert_en_cased_L-12_H-768_A-12*. Here, L (stack of encoder), H (Hidden size), and A (Attention Heads) are used in this model. It is a lighter model, which is easy to train. Here fine-tuning of the model won't be performed as only the tokenizer of the BERT layer will be used. The complete vocabulary file and information regarding lower casing the words will all be available in the BERT layer.

2. BERT as an embedder. For a computer, words are a combination of characters, which in turn have numerical representation. The idea is that computers and algorithms are more comfortable dealing with numbers (vectors) rather than strings or characters that have no sense of meaning to it, or doing math and complex modeling, which is really hard to deal with. With embedding we can have vector representation of each word and to make a model more powerful by having connection between the words and fetch meaning out of it. We have various encoding such as:

- **One hot encoding**: Having a vocabulary of 1,00,000 words, vector representation of each word will be a vector of size 1,00,000 with "zeros" at all the positions except "one" at the position of the word itself. This way, we have a unique representation for each of the 1,00,000 words. But there is no relation between words (vectors) in this type of embedding, which conveys no information or meaning.

- **Word embedding**: Smaller size vectors are required for embedding. So we add constraints to information so that it has less liberty and forces our system to create relations, links, or even meaning. Word embedding lets us perform mathematical operations on words and provide relation between them.

5.3.3 CNN for Text Classification (Part II)

Convolutional neural network is an artificial neural network that has so far been most popularly used for analyzing images. Apart from image analysis, it can also be used for other data analysis and classification purposes as well.

The hidden layers of CNN, called convolutional layers, are able to detect patterns in images. Each convolutional layer has a specific number of filters that are used to detect varying underlying patterns.

CNN for NLP: Instead of taking image pixels as input matrix, the inputs for most NLP tasks are taken as sentences that are represented in matrix form. Each word is converted to a vector form and is represented in each of the rows of the matrix. These vectors are called word embeddings, which are low-dimensional representations. For example, our "image," which we will use for input for a 10-word sentence using 100-dimensional embedding, would be a 10×100 matrix. We used BERT to represent sentences as a word vectors (sentence matrix). We have adopted the Kim CNN Model [34] for classification purposes.

Convolution and maxpooling: Suppose we have two sentences: "Cat sitting there" and "Represented as shown in Figure 5.4." For each word in the two sentences, we have a row that represents a word embedding for a certain length. To analyze the 2-grams here, we can apply a convolutional filter as shown in Figure 5.4. The sentence "Lion resting here" has similar values to "Deer sitting here," and hence convolving them with the same convolutional filter produces a high activation. It can be extended to 3-grams, 4-grams, and so on.

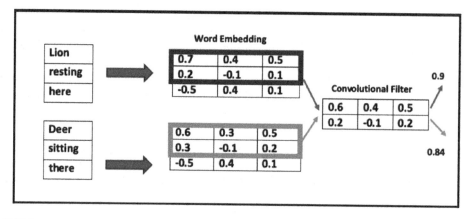

FIGURE 5.4
Representation of Words Using Word Embeddings and Applying Convolution Filter to Input Matrix

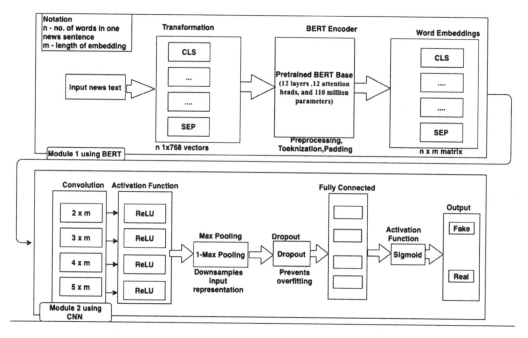

FIGURE 5.5
BERT and CNN Based Classification Model (part II)

You need multiple filters to track the meaning of different n-grams. These are called 1D convolution because we slide the window only in one direction, contrary to the image where we slide the window in both the directions. The one direction that we slide the window is actually the time. Taking the maximum activation (0.7) that we get going through the whole text and then taking that value as the result of the convolution is called maximum pooling over time. In images we have maximum pooling; in text we have it over time.

The overall architecture for part II is shown in Figure 5.5. The input matrix has different words. The next six matrices are the feature detectors. Here we can see three window sizes: 2, 3, and 4, each of which has 2 filters or feature detectors. The feature detectors have the same width as the embedding size of the model. Every feature detector generates a feature map. Next, the maximum of each of the feature maps is taken. This process can also be called the 1-max pooling. This means that we only want to know if the feature has been detected. Then we concatenate everything and apply a dense layer at the end to perform the classification tasks. Here, we assume binary classification, and hence we depict two output states. For detailed description and mathematical analysis, readers can refer to [32].

5.4 Experiments and Results

For validation of proposed methodology, we have performed experiments on the generated dataset. Our final dataset includes around 43000 instances (tweets). The implementations were done using Python using various machine learning and deep learning libraries, such as: Sci-Kit learn, Numpy, Pandas, Keras, and so on. The experimental environment was a computer equipped with 1.80 GHz Dual-Core Intel core i5 and 8 GB DDR3 RAM, running a MacOS 10.15.3, 64-bit processor. The performance evaluation of the model is done by using various performance metrics such as accuracy, precision, recall, F1-score, specificity, MCC (Mathew's correlation coefficient), and G-mean. The description of the performance matrices is given in Table 5.7.

The overall experiment has two parts as discussed below.

1. *Automated labeling of dataset (part I):* 1500 instances out of 43000 tweets are manually labeled based on the credibility matrices shown in Section 5.1.4. Next, we experimented with six different machine learning algorithms: logistic regression, K-nearest neighbor, SVM (support vector machine), Naïve Bayes, decision tree, and random forest. The experimental results are shown in Table 5.8.

   From the results we observe that:

   - The performance on KNN and Naïve Bayes is poor in comparison to all the other algorithms on the manually labeled dataset.

   - Logistic regression and random forest are the two best-performing algorithms, with accuracies of 0.72 and 0.68 respectively.

   - Overall, logistic regression performs better than the other algorithms and, therefore, it is selected as a final model to label the remaining unlabeled dataset.

TABLE 5.7

Description of Performance Metrics

Performance metrics	Formula
Accuracy	$(TP+TN)/(TP+TN+FP+FN)$
Precision	$TP/(TP+FP)$
Recall	$TP/(TP+FN)$
F1-score	$(2*Precision*Recall)/(Precision+Recall)$
MCC (Mathew's correlation coefficient)	$(TP*TN - FP*FN)/\sqrt{(TP+FP)(TP+FN)(TN+FP)(TN+FN)}$
Specificity	$TN/(TP+FN)$
G-mean	$\sqrt{(Recall*Specificity)}$

TABLE 5.8

Performance Comparisons of Various Machine Learning Algorithms

Algorithms	Accuracy	Precision	Recall	F1-score	Specificity	MCC	G-mean
Logistic regression	0.72	0.75	0.74	0.74	0.60	0.34	0.67
KNN	0.63	0.66	0.43	0.52	0.68	0.11	0.54
SVM	0.7	0.75	0.75	0.75	0.58	0.33	0.66
Naïve Bayes	0.61	0.72	0.48	0.57	0.68	0.16	0.57
Decision tree	0.62	0.70	0.68	0.69	0.51	0.19	0.59
Random forest	0.68	0.74	0.70	0.72	0.60	0.29	0.65

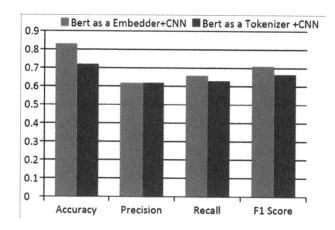

FIGURE 5.6

Performance Evaluation of Bert Embedder with CNN and Bert Tokenizer with CNN

2. *Credibility Assessment using BERT and CNN model.* After labeling the dataset, we performed experiments on the full dataset using the BERT +CNN model. In the experiments, we have used two variations of BERT: BERT as an embedder and BERT as a tokenizer. For classification purposes we have used convolutional neural networks. Figure 5.6 shows the results of the two above-mentioned variations. From the figure, we observe that BERT with embedder and CNN perform better in comparison with the other versions. The overall accuracy achieved is 83%, which shows the effectiveness of the proposed approach with respect to the credibility assessment of healthcare-related tweets.

5.5 Conclusion

In conclusion, we can say that our model with BERT as an embedder and CNN as classifier gives 83% efficiency. With the capability of bidirectional flow, the model has a good understanding of the sentence and helps with the credibility results. We can also conclude that deep learning approaches perform better than manually trained and handcrafted baselines techniques with the help of automatically learnt feature representations from BERT. This is also backed by the fact that credibility is not word specific; instead, it is sentence-specific assessment.

This model can further be deployed as a website or an Android application for checking the credibility of tweets related to health data. This can help people find tweets that are trustworthy. If the people use such websites to check credibility before re-tweeting or before believing information, it can reduce rumors at a certain level and limit the spread of wrong information around the world. A possible extension of this work could be a multimodal system that takes multiple types of data (images along with text) into consideration.

References

1. Ospina, E. 2019. *The rise of social media.* https://ourworldindata.org/rise-of-social-media. (accessed March 5, 2020)
2. Bharat, K. 2017. *How to detect fake news in Real-Time.* https://medium.com/newco/how-to-detect-fake-news-in-real-time-9fdae0197bfd. (accessed March 12, 2020)
3. Zhan, G. 2019. Online forum authenticity: big data analytics in healthcare. *In Proceedings of the 2019 11th International Conference on Machine Learning and Computing*: 290–294.
4. Teoh, F. 2018. *The most popular health articles of 2018, a scientific credibility review.* https://health-feedback.org/the-most-popular-health-articles-of-2018-a-scientific-credibility-review/. (accessed March 12, 2020)
5. Al-Rakhami M. S. and A. M. Al-Amri. 2020. Lies kill, facts save: detecting COVID-19 misinformation on twitter. *IEEE Access*, vol. 8:155961–155970.
6. Abbasi M.-A. and H. Liu. 2013. Measuring user credibility in social media. *Social Computing, Behavioral-Cultural Modeling and Prediction*, vol 7812: 441–448.
7. Gupta, A., H. Lamba, P. Kumaraguru and A. Joshi. 2013. Faking sandy: characterizing and identifying fake images on twitter during hurricane sandy. *Proceedings of the 22nd International Conference on World Wide Web.* 729–736.
8. Boididou, C., S. Papadopoulos, Y. Kompatsiaris, S. Schifferes, and N. Newman. 2014. Challenges of computational verification in social multimedia. *Proceedings of the 23rd International Conference on World Wide Web*, 743–748.
9. Li, J., M. Ott, C. Cardie, and E. Hovy. 2014. Towards a general rule for identifying deceptive opinion spam. *Proceedings of the 52nd Annual Meeting of the Association for Computational Linguistics*, no.1: 1566–1576.
10. Finn, S., P. T. Metaxas, and E. Mustafaraj. 2015. *Spread and skepticism: Metrics of propagation on twitter.* Proceedings of the ACM Web Science Conference, 1–2.
11. Thandar, M. and S. Usanavasin. 2015. Measuring opinion credibility in twitter. *Recent Advances in Information and Communication Technology*, vol. 361: 205–214.
12. Saikaew, K. and C. Noyunsan. 2015. Features for measuring credibility on facebook information. *International Scholarly and Scientific Research & Innovation*, vol. 9, no. 1:74–177.
13. Sarna, G., and M. Bhatia. 2017. Content based approach to find the credibility of user in social networks: an application of cyberbullying. *International Journal Of Machine Learning and Cybernetics*, vol. 8, no. 2: 677–689.
14. Gupta, S., S. Sachdeva, P. Dewan and P. Kumaraguru. 2018. Cbi: improving credibility of user-generated content on facebook. *International Conference on Big Data Analytics*, 170–187.
15. Jo, Y., M. Kim and K. Han. 2019. How do humans assess the credibility on web blogs: Qualifying and verifying human factors with machine learning. *Proceedings of the 2019 CHI Conference on Human Factors in Computing Systems*, 674:1–12 http://library.usc.edu.ph/ACM/CHI2019/1proc/paper674.pdf
16. Ratkiewicz, J., M. Conover and M. Meiss, et al. 2011. Truthy: mapping the spread of astroturf in microblog streams. *Proceedings of the 20th international conference companion on World wide web*, 249–252.

17. Nguyen, D. T., N. P. Nguyen and M. T. Thai. 2012. Sources of misinformation in online social networks: who to suspect? *MILCOM 2012–2012 IEEE Military Communications Conference*, 1–6.
18. Ulicny, B. and M. M. Kokar. 2011. Automating military intelligence confidence assessments for twitter messages. *Proceedings of the 14th International Conference on Information Fusion*, 1–8.
19. McKelvey, K. R. and F. Menczer. 2013. Truthy: enabling the study of online social networks. *Proceedings of the International Conference on Computer Supported Cooperative Work Companion*, 23–26.
20. Pasternack, J. and D. Roth. 2013. Latent credibility analysis. *Proceedings of the 22nd International Conference on World Wide Web*, 1009–1020.
21. Samadi, M., P. Talukdar, M. Veloso, and M. Blum. 2016. Claimeval: integrated and flexible framework for claim evaluation using credibility of sources. *Proceedings of the 13th AAAI Conference on Artificial Intelligence*, 215–222.
22. O'Brien, K., O. Simek, and F. Waugh. 2019. Collective classification for social media credibility mestimation. *Proceedings of the 52nd Hawaii International Conference on System Sciences*, 2235–2243.
23. Westerman, D., P. R. Spence and B. Van Der Heide. 2012. A social network as information: The effect of system generated reports of connectedness on credibility on twitter. *Computers in Human Behavior*, vol. 28, no. 1:99–206.
24. ODonovan, J., B. Kang, G. Meyer, T. Hollerer and S. Adalii. 2012. Credibility in context: an analysis of feature distributions in twitter. *Proceedings of the International Conference on Social Computing*, 293–301.
25. Kwon, S., M. Cha, K. Jung, W. Chen, and Y. Wang . 2013. Aspects of rumor spreading on a microblog network. *Proceedings of the International Conference on Social Informatics*, 299–308.
26. Edwards, C., A. Edwards, P. R. Spence, and A. K. Shelton. 2014. Is that a bot running the social media feed? testing the differences in perceptions of communication quality for a human agent and a bot agent on twitter, *Computers in Human Behavior*, vol. 33, 372–376.
27. Zubiaga, A. and H. Ji. 2014. Tweet, but verify: epistemic study of information verification on twitter. *Social Network Analysis and Mining*, vol. 4, no. 1:163.
28. Shariff, S. M., X. Zhang, and M. Sanderson. 2014. User perception of information credibility of news on twitter. *European Conference on Information Retrieval*, 513–518.
29. Kang, B., T. Hollerer, and J. O'Donovan. 2015. Believe it or not? analyzing information credibility in microblogs. *Proceedings of the IEEE/ACM International Conference on Advances in Social Networks Analysis and Mining*, 611–616.
30. Johnso, T. J. and B. K. Kaye. 2015. Reasons to believe: Influence of credibility on motivations for using social networks. *Computers in Human Behavior*, vol. 50, 544–555.
31. Go, E., K. H. You, E. Jung, and H. Shim. 2016. Why do we use different types of websites and assign them different levels of credibility? structural relations among users' motives, types of websites, information credibility, and trust in the press. *Computers in Human Behavior*, vol. 54, 231–239.
32. Alrubaian, M., M. Al-Qurishi, M. Al-Rakhami, M. M. Hassan and A. Alamri. 2017. Reputation-based credibility analysis of twitter social network users. *Concurrency and Computation: Practice and Experience*, vol. 29, no. 7: 1–3.
33. Devlin, J., M.-W. Chang, K. Lee and K. Toutanova, 2018. *Bert: Pre-training of deep bidirectional transformers for language understanding*, https://arxiv.org/pdf/1810.04805.pdf
34. Kim, Y. 2014. Convolutional neural networks for sentence classification. *Proceedings of the 2014 Conference on Empirical Methods in Natural Language Processing*, 1746–1751. https://www.aclweb.org/anthology/D14-1181.pdf

6

Filtering and Spectral Analysis of Time Series Data: A Signal Processing Perspective and Illustrative Application to Stock Market Index Movement Forecasting

Jigarkumar H. Shah and Rutvij H. Jhaveri

Pandit Deendayal Petroleum University, Gandhinagar, Gujarat, India

CONTENTS

6.1 Introduction

Linear digital filters and adaptive filters are very common in most digital signal processing applications. Time-series analysis and linear prediction have found that auto-regressive moving average, auto-regressive integrated moving average, and seasonal auto-regressive integrated moving average models are extremely useful in prediction and forecasting from past data. They are abbreviated as ARMA, ARIMA, and SARIMA models respectively. A prediction stratgegy provides a possible result of future occurrence, while a forecast strategy provides a quantitative result of future occurrence. Forecast is based on a calculation or an estimation that uses historical data combined with recent trends. Quantitative forecast implies time series and future, while prediction does not. Researchers in econometrics and data scientists often use time-series modeling for quantitative forecasting. These parametric time-series analysis methods are analogous to linear filtering concepts of DSP. A digital filter is basically classified as finite impulse response (FIR) and infinite impulse response (IIR) filter. The design and analysis of these filters is carried out in frequency domains with the use of spectral (Fourier) domain tools and optimization methods. However, linear filters are not useful in handling in-band interference, additive white noise, or time varying fluctuations in input due to randomness and spectral overlap associated with such disturbances. The adaptive filters are addressing these problems. The adaptive filters consist of FIR digital filters (due to guaranteed stability) and adaptive algorithms such as least mean square (LMS) and its variants. The architecture of adaptive filters consists of feedback loop and hence the stability, convergence rate, and computation load are concerned parameters when implemented practically. The time-series analysis that is used by researchers in econometrics is also used by researchers in DSP for parametric power spectrum estimation and designing adaptive filters. The econometircs researchers mostly use auto-correlation (ACF) and partial auto-correlation functions (PACF) for time-series modeling and forecasting, while the DSP researchers mostly use them in spectral or transformed domain by applying concept of power spectral density and frequency response transfer functions.

Methods and algorithms in spectral domain are much more matured and developed in the digital signal processing field. Therefore, the econometric sector can take advantage of this development for improved results [1]. As per results presented in [2], there exists some fine structures in stock time-series data; DSP can provide more powerful analytical tools than traditional economic research indicates. The only difficulty in this correlation is that the input-output relationship is governed by time invariant physical laws in digital signal processing, while in the financial sector application it is mostly data driven and sometimes also driven by time varying and instantaneous events [3]. For highly accurate forecasts in financial applications, a machine learning or deep learning–based model is required. However, for some applications, such as short-term stock market index movement, forecasting the time-series model can be used due to simplicity of its implementation [4].

6.2 Overview of Digital Filtering Concepts of DSP

A digital filter is an example of linear time invariant (LTI) discrete time system, and it is designed to pass a certain band of frequencies and to stop other frequencies contained in input signal. The input signal is processed as per filter characteristics and produced at the output. In a block diagram form, it is represented in Figure 6.1 with $x(n)$ representing

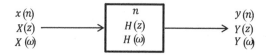

FIGURE 6.1
Block Diagram Representation of a Digital Filter in Time, **Z**, and Frequency Domain

discrete time input signal and $y(n)$ representing output signal. Here, n represents sample index (discrete time index), and theoretically it can take any integer value. A discrete time signal can also be called sequence of numbers, and is actually time-series data. A digital filter is completely characterized by its unit impulse response sequence $h(n)$ as it is LTI system [5]. Here, the discrete time and digital signal are the same. In practice, a digital signal is a quantized version of discrete time signal and subjected to finite precision effects due to quantization error. To simplify, analysis quantization errors are neglected, but it can be modeled in final implementation.

6.2.1 Time Domain Representations

The input-ouptut relation for the digital filter is given by convolution operation in natural (time) domain. It is modeled as $y(n) = x(n) * h(n)$ or $y(n) = h(n) * x(n)$ where the convolution sum is a commutative operation. Here $*$ sign denotes convolution sum operation. The mathematical operation for it is given by Equation (6.1). In this equation, k represents a dummy variable.

$$y(n) = x(n) * h(n) = \sum_{k=-\infty}^{\infty} x(k) h(n-k) \ OR \ y(n) = h(n) * x(n) = \sum_{k=-\infty}^{\infty} h(k) x(n-k) \quad (6.1)$$

Equation (6.1) defines the time domain representation of a digital filter. The evaluation of a convolution sum involves four-signal processing operations includingfolding, shifting, multiplication, and addition. Further, the length of the unit impulse response specifies the type of the digital filter. If length of $h(n)$ is finite—let it be $M + 1$—then it is called $M + 1$-tap FIR filter. On the other hand, if the length of $h(n)$ is infinite, then it is called IIR filter. Theoretically, $h(n)$ can exists for n ranging any value from $-\infty$ to ∞. But the filter is physically realizable only if $h(n) = 0$ for $n < 0$. Such a filter is called a causal filter. The causal FIR and IIR digital filters are described by Equations (6.2) and (6.3), respectively [5].

$$y(n) = h(n) * x(n) = \sum_{k=0}^{M} h(k) x(n-k) \quad (6.2)$$

$$y(n) = h(n) * x(n) = \sum_{k=0}^{\infty} h(k) x(n-k) \quad (6.3)$$

Another time domain representation of a digital filter is difference equation representation. For a causal FIR filter, the present ouput $y(n)$ depends only upon present input $x(n)$ and past or delayed M inputs given by $x(n - 1)$, $x(n - 2)$, ..., $x(n - M)$. As the digital filter is an LTI system, the output of the FIR filter is a linear combination of present input and past M inputs. Such a relation is called linear constant coefficient difference equation (LCCDE) representation. It is given by Equation (6.4) for FIR digital filters.

$$y(n) = b_0 x(n) + b_1 x(n-1) + \ldots + b_{M-1} x(n-M)) = \sum_{k=0}^{M} b_k x(n-k) \quad (6.4)$$

Here, $\{b_k\}; k = 0, 1, \ldots, M$ represents constant coefficients. Compare Equations 6.2 and 6.4:

$$h(k) = \{b_k\}; k = 0, 1, \ldots, M \qquad (6.5)$$

For a causal IIR filter, the present ouput $y(n)$ depends upon present input $x(n)$, past M inputs, and also on past N outputs given by $y(n-1)$, $x(n-2)$, $\ldots$, $y(n-N)$. The LCCDE representation of an IIR filter is given by Equation (6.6).

$$
\begin{aligned}
y(n) &= b_0 x(n) + b_1 x(n-1) + \ldots b_M x(n-M)) - a_1 x(n-1) + \ldots - a_N x(n-N)) \\
&= \sum_{k=0}^{M} b_k x(n-k) - \sum_{k=1}^{N} a_k y(n-k)
\end{aligned}
\qquad (6.6)
$$

Here, $\{b_k\}; k = 0, 1, \ldots , M$ and $\{a_k\}; k = 0, 1, \ldots , N$ represent two sets of constant co-efficients with $a_0 = 1$. N also represents the order of the IIR filter, which is a very important parameter. The LCCDE can be solved to obtain $h(n)$ using various methods [5]. From Equations (6.4) and (6.6), it is apparent that the IIR filters involve feedback and their implementation involves mandatory recursion, while the FIR filters can be implemented without invovling feedback or recursion. Another important practical aspect of the digital filter is its stability. For stablility of LTI system, its unit impulse response $h(n)$ must be absolutely summable, that is to say:

$$\sum_{k=-\infty}^{\infty} |h(k)| < \infty \qquad (6.7)$$

From this stability condition it is obvious that FIR filters are always stable, but IIR filters are not always stable, and their stability needs to be investigated [5].

6.2.2 Z-Domain Representation

The time domain representation of discrete time LTI system has very little use in finding the unit impulse response, stability, and response to arbitrary inputs. Z-transform is a mathematical tool used to transform the domain of discrete time signal and system, and obtain representation of system in terms of its system transfer function and pole-zero form. For any discrete time signal, $x(n)$ its Z-transform $X(z)$ is defined by Equation (6.8). Here z is a complex variable. It is necessary to specify the Z-transform along with its region of convergence (ROC) where magnitude of $X(z)$ is finite, i.e., $| X(z) | < \infty$. The signal in Z-domain is represented in complex Z-plane.

$$X(z) = \sum_{n=-\infty}^{\infty} x(n) z^{-n}; z = re^{j\omega} \qquad (6.8)$$

The digital filter in Z-domain is represented in Figure 6.1, and the relationship between input and output is given by multiplication:

$$Y(z) = H(z) X(z). \qquad (6.9)$$

Here $H(z)$ represents system transfer function which is actually Z-transform of unit impulse response $h(n)$. For practical IIR filters, the system transfer function is available in rational form given by Equation (6.10). Here z^{-1} is also called unit delay operator as z^{-1} in Z-domain corresponds to one sample delayed signal $x(n-1)$ in time domain.

$$H(z) = \frac{B(z)}{A(z)} = \frac{\displaystyle\sum_{k=0}^{M} b_k z^{-k}}{1 + \displaystyle\sum_{k=1}^{N} a_k z^{-k}} \tag{6.10}$$

The M roots of numerator $B(z)$ are called zeros $(z_1, z_2, ..., z_M)$, and the N roots of the denominator $A(z)$ are called poles $(p_1, p_2, ..., p_N)$ of the system transfer function $H(z)$. The system transfer function can be expressed in pole-zero form as given in Equation (6.11).

$$H(z) = \frac{K(z-z_1)(z-z_2)......(z-z_M)}{(z-p_1)(z-p_2).....(z-p_N)} \tag{6.11}$$

Here K represents constant gain. The pole locations are responsible for the system causality and stability. For a causal and stable system, the poles must be located inside the unit circle in complex Z-plane or, in other words, the magnitude of poles must be less than one. The zeros can be located at any place in complex Z-plane, but their locations are also important in the design of an inverse system. As IIR digital filters in general involve both poles and zeros, they are called pole-zero systems. It is possible that an IIR digital filter can have all zeros located at origin (i.e. at $z = 0$), and poles are located at nonorigin locations. Such an IIR filter is called an all-pole filter. The zeros or poles located at origin are called trivial zeros or poles, while others are called nontrivial. For an FIR filter, the system transfer function has denominator polynomial $A(z) = 1$ and hence it contains M trivial poles and M nontrivial zeros. Therefore, an FIR filter is also called an all zero filter, and it is always stable [5]. Equation (6.12) specifies system transfer function for FIR filter.

$$H(z) = \frac{B(z)}{1} = \sum_{k=0}^{M} b_k z^{-k} = \frac{K(z-z_1)(z-z_2)......(z-z_M)}{z^M} \tag{6.12}$$

Figure 6.2 (a) and (b) shows Z-plane representation examples of a stable IIR digital filter and an IIR digital filter with pole on unit circle (just unstable) respectively obtained using MATLAB®. In this figure, a small circle (o) denotes zero and a cross sign (x) denotes pole. Also, it should be noted that for a general IIR digital filter, if all poles and zeros lie inside the $|z| = 1$ circle, the filter belongs to minimum phase system; it is possible to find a causal and stable inverse $(1/H(z))$ for such system. Therefore, the causal FIR digital filter is also to be designed in such ways that its zeros are also within the unit circle if its inverse is desired.

6.2.3 Frequency Domain Representation

Frequency domain representation of discrete time LTI system, and particulary that of digital filter, is very useful in communication and signal processing, and it is facilitated by using Fourier analysis. However, this analysis is applicable only to stable systems and bounded signals. Some liberty can be taken in Fourier analysis to represent the discrete

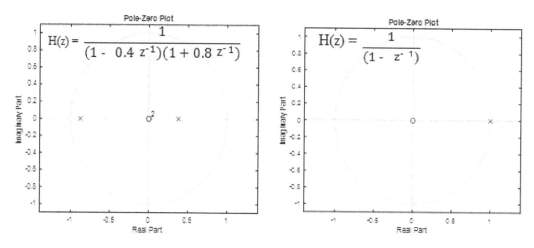

FIGURE 6.2
Pole-Zero Plots of IIR Filter System Transfer Functions: (a) Stable System (b) System with Pole on Unit Circle

time systems or signals having poles on unit circle (just unstable or sometimes called marginally stable). For a bounded discrete time signal, $x(n)$ the discrete time Fourier transform (DTFT) designated as $X(\omega)$ and it is given by Equation (6.13). It is the frequency domain or Fourier domain or spectral domain representation of a signal.

$$X(\omega) = \sum_{n=-\infty}^{\infty} x(n) e^{-j\omega n} \tag{6.13}$$

Here, ω is a frequency variable, and it is a continuous variable representing the normalized frequency; it is also sometimes called digital frequency. For finite energy sequence $x(n)$ (having poles inside unit circle), the DTFT is its Z-transform evaluated on $|z| = 1$ circle, i.e., by substituting $z = e^{j\omega}$ in Equation (6.8). The function $X(\omega)$ possesses an important property of periodicity. It is a periodic function with period 2π, and hence it is required to know this representation over only any 2π interval. The interval $[0, 2\pi)$ or $[-\pi, \pi)$ is called principal interval, and the DTFT is usually specified within this interval. Furhter, $X(\omega)$ is a complex function and its magnitude $|X(\omega)|$ is called magnitude or amplitude response and angle is called phase response $\theta_x(\omega)$. For any real valued sequence $x(n)$, the amplitude response plot is always symmetric and the phase response plot is always anti-symmetric function.

$$X(-\omega) = X^*(\omega); |X(-\omega)| = |X(\omega)| \text{ and } \theta_x(-\omega) = -\theta_x(\omega) \tag{6.14}$$

The magnitude square of DTFT is called energy spectral density of signal $S_{XX}(\omega)$. Its integration over a period represents total energy of a signal (E_x). This relationship is given by Equation (6.15), and it is called Parseval's theorem [5].

$$E_x = \sum_{n=-\infty}^{\infty} |x(n)|^2 = \int_{-\pi}^{\pi} S_{xx}(\omega) d\omega = \int_{-\pi}^{\pi} |X(\omega)|^2 d\omega \tag{6.15}$$

An important concept in digital signal processing is time cross-correlation and time autocorrelation. They are used to measure similarity of one reference signal with one or more target signals. For deterministic (a signal whose amplitude at any time index can be computed with complete confidence) and finite energy signals, $x(n)$ and $y(n)$ the time cross correlation sequence $r_{xy}(l)$ is given by Equation (6.16). In this equation, the variable l referes to correlation lag and takes any integer value; it is not time-index. The time cross correlation between $y(n)$ and $x(n)$ is flipped version of $r_{xy}(l)$

$$r_{xy}(l) = \sum_{n=-\infty}^{\infty} x(n)y(n-l) = \sum_{n=-\infty}^{\infty} x(n+l)y(n) = x(l)*y(-l) ; r_{yx}(l) = r_{xy}(-l) \qquad (6.16)$$

The time auto correlation sequence of signal $x(n)$ is given by Equation (6.17), and it is an even function of lag parameter l.

$$r_{xx}(l) = \sum_{n=-\infty}^{\infty} x(n)x(n-l) = \sum_{n=-\infty}^{\infty} x(n+l)x(n) = x(l)*x(-l) ; r_{xx}(l) = r_{xx}(-l) \qquad (6.17)$$

It is interesting to note that the frequency domain representation of the time autocorrelation sequence is energy spectral density. That means the DTFT of a time autocorrelation sequence is energy spectral density.

$$S_{xx}(\omega) = \sum_{l=-\infty}^{\infty} r_{xx}(l)e^{-j\omega l} \qquad (6.18)$$

The time autocorrelation at zero lag ($l = 0$) represents energy of the signal, and it is the highest value in time correlation sequence. In practice, instead of using absolute value of correlation coefceints, the normalized value is preferred so that all correlation coefficients will remain in the range [−1,1]. The nornamlized time autocorrection sequence is obtained by dividing the correlation sequence by energy of the signal. It is given in Equation (6.19).

$$\rho_{xx}(l) = \frac{r_{xx}(l)}{E_x} = \frac{r_{xx}(l)}{r_{xx}(0)} \qquad (6.19)$$

The digital filter in frequency domain is represented by a block diagram in Figure 6.1. Here, the relationship between input and output is given by Equation (6.20).

$$Y(\omega) = X(\omega)H(\omega) \qquad (6.20)$$

Here, $H(\omega)$ denotes frequency response functions, and it is a DTFT of unit impulse response $h(n)$. This relationship is applied under assumption that the digital filter is a stable system [5]. In terms of time correlation sequences and energy spectral densities the representation is as given by Equation (6.21) and (6.22) respectively [5].

$$r_{yy}(l) = r_{hh}(l) * r_{xx}(l) \qquad (6.21)$$

$$S_{yy}(\omega) = |H(\omega)|^2 S_{xx}(\omega) \qquad (6.22)$$

The linear digital filter has very interesting property called the Eigen value property. Using this property, it is inferred that a pure sinusoidal signal applied to linear digital filter produces a pure sinusoidal signal at the same frequency, but the amplitude and phase may differ. The amplitude at the output is scaled by amplitude of frequency response function at the frequency of sinusoid, and the phase is shifted by the angle of the frequency response function at the frequency of sinusoidal signal. This can also be extended to a sum of any number of pure sinusoids.

Up to this point, basic background of digital filter analysis is explained. Here, the signals are considered deterministic. But in real practice, the signals are random in nature and have stochastics characteristics. The next section illustrates the digital filter analysis equations with stochastic signals.

6.3 Digital Linear Filtering Analysis with Stochastic Signals

A random or stochastic sequence (time series) is a member of an ensemble (infinite collection) of discrete-time sequences that is characterized by probability density or distribution function (PDF). Speech, noise, quantization error, and so on are all examples. The amplitude of a stochastic signal at a particular sample time is estimated by an underlying probability distribution scheme. That means $x(n)$ is value taken by some random variable X_n. Random variables (R.V.) are described by their statistical properties like mean (expected value), variance, and so on. An R.V. that is a function of time is called a random process or stochastic process, and it is a collection of an infinite number of R.V.s. Random process is a family of random variables. In statistical signal analysis, we must make certain assumptions about the random process, and hence about the underlying random signal. A strict stationary random process does not change its statistical characteristics, i.e., a PDF with respect to time that has a great analytical importance. A process may not be strictly stationary, yet it may have a mean value and an ensemble autocorrelation function that are independent of time origin; such a process is called weakly stationary process or a wide sense stationary (WSS) process. A truly stationary process can never occur in real life as truly stationary process starts at $-\infty$ time and goes on forever. Practical random processes always have finite duration, but can be considered stationary for the time interval of interest. Also, the use of stationarity model allows use of manageable mathematical models [6].

Let the input $x(n)$ and output $y(n)$ be a member of WSS random process, corresponding R.V.s are X_n and Y_n respectively taking real values, and let $h(n)$ represent a stable digital filter. Let the mean or expected values of X_n and Y_n are m_{Xn} ($E[X_n]$) and m_{Yn} ($E[Y_n]$) respectively, and their variances are $\sigma_{Xn}^2 \left(E\left[(X_n - m_{Xn})^2 \right] \right)$ and $\sigma_{Yn}^2 \left(E\left[(Y_n - m_{Yn})^2 \right] \right)$ respectively.

Let the average power (mean square value) of R.V.s X_n and Y_n be P_{Xn} ($E[X_n^2]$) and P_{Yn} ($E[Y_n^2]$) respectively. The relationships between these quantities are specified in equation (6.23).

$$\sigma_{Xn}^2 = E\left[X_n^2 \right] - m_{Xn}^2 = P_{Xn} - m_{Xn}^2 ; \sigma_{Yn}^2 = E\left[Y_n^2 \right] - m_{Yn}^2 = P_{Yn} - m_{Yn}^2 \qquad (6.23)$$

If the WSS stochastics signal $x(n)$ is passed through a digital filter with unit impulse response $h(n)$ and corresponding frequency response function $H(\omega)$, the output $y(n)$ is specified by its expected value and variance as given by Equation (6.24).

$$E[Y_n] = \left(\sum_{k=-\infty}^{\infty} h(k)\right) E[X_n] = |H(0)| E[X_n]; \sigma_{Y_n}^2 = |H(0)|^2 \sigma_{X_n}^2 \qquad (6.24)$$

The Fourier transform of stochastic signals can't be determined, but the Fourier transform of their ensemble autocorrelation sequence often exists. The effect of a filter on the ensemble autocorrelation sequence describes the signal processing operation carried out by the filter. For WSS random process, the ensemble autocorrection sequence depends on lag parameter *l* only and not on time origin. Random signals are always treated as power signals (i.e., they have ∞ energy but finite average power). Hence, for random signals the concept of energy spectral density is replaced with the analogus term called power spectral density (PSD). The PSD is DTFT of corresponding ensemble autocorrelation sequence [6]. Let $\gamma_{XX}(l)$ and $\gamma_{YY}(l)$ be the ensemble autocorrelation sequences of $x(n)$ and $y(n)$ respectively, and $\Gamma_{xx}(\omega)$ and $\Gamma_{yy}(\omega)$ be corresponding PSDs, then the relationships are specified by Equation (6.25) and (6.26), considering the WSS model.

$$\gamma_{yy}(l) = E[X_n X_{n+l}] = r_{hh}(l) * \gamma_{xx}(l) \qquad (6.25)$$

$$\Gamma_{yy}(\omega) = DTFT\{\gamma_{yy}(l)\} = |H(\omega)|^2 \Gamma_{xx}(\omega) \qquad (6.26)$$

The ensemble autocorrelation sequence is always the even function of *l* and corresponding PSD is always the even function of ω. The ensemble autocorrelation at zero lag ($l = 0$) represents average power of random signal. A special case that is of most use in the analysis is zero mean white noise random process $w(n)$. The zero mean white noise has zero expected value and uniform PSD, which is equal to its variance. Its autocorrelation function is impulse signal with magnitude equal to its variance, and the average power of zero mean white noise process is equal to its variance value [6]. This is given in Equation (6.27).

$$\gamma_{ww}(l) = \sigma_{Wn}^2 \delta(l); \Gamma_{ww}(\omega) = \sigma_{Wn}^2; P_{Wn} = \gamma_{ww}(0) = \sigma_{Wn}^2 \qquad (6.27)$$

Here, $\delta(l)$ represents unit impulse signal, which has unit magnitude at $l = 0$ and zero magnitude for $l \neq 0$. For a white noise process, if passed through a digital fitler $H(\omega)$, output is colored noise process. Its PSD is given by Equation (6.28).

$$\Gamma_{yy}(\omega) = \sigma_{Wn}^2 |H(\omega)|^2 \qquad (6.28)$$

In practice, normalized autocorrelation sequences are used, which can be obtained from corresponding autocorrelation sequence after dividing it by autocorrelation at zero lag as given in Equation (6.19). Finally, it is important to note ensemble cross-correlation sequence and cross PSD. For two WSS random processes $x(n)$ and $y(n)$, ensemble cross-correlation between them is denoted by $\gamma_{xy}(l)$ and corresponding cross PSD is denoted by $\Gamma_{xy}(\omega)$. Their properties are described by Equations (6.29) and (6.30).

$$\gamma_{xy}(l) = E[X_n Y_{n+l}] = \gamma_{yx}(-l) \qquad (6.29)$$

$$\Gamma_{xy}(\omega) = DTFT\{\gamma_{xy}(l)\} = \Gamma_{yx}(-\omega) \qquad (6.30)$$

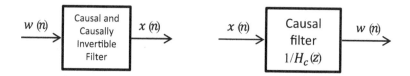

FIGURE 6.3
Wold Representation of a WSS Random Process (a) Innovation Filter (b) Whitening Filter

Two random processes are said to be uncorrelated if their ensemble cross correlation sequence is equal to the product of their means; that is, $\gamma_{xy}(l) = E[X_n]E[Y_{n+l}] = E[X_n]E[Y_n]$ and they are said to be orthogonal (or incoherent) if $\gamma_{xy}(l) = 0$ [6].

The Z-domain representations corresponding to equations (6.26), (6.28), and (6.30) are given by Equations (6.31), (6.32), and (6.33) respectively.

$$\Gamma_{yy}(z) = H(z)H(z^{-1})\Gamma_{xx}(z) \tag{6.31}$$

$$\Gamma_{yy}(z) = \sigma_{Wn}^2 H(z)H(z^{-1}) \tag{6.32}$$

$$\Gamma_{xy}(z) = \Gamma_{yx}(z^{-1}) \tag{6.33}$$

For any general WSS random process $x(n)$, its PSD function can be factorized or decomposed into three components. This statement is called spectral factorization theorem and is stated in Equation (6.34) and (6.35) in Z-domain and frequency domain respectively.

$$\Gamma_{xx}(z) = \sigma_{Wn}^2 H_c(z)H_c(z^{-1}) \tag{6.34}$$

$$\Gamma_{xx}(\omega) = \sigma_{Wn}^2 |H_c(\omega)|^2 \tag{6.35}$$

Here, $H_c(z)$ represents a causal digital filter called innovation filter and its inverse $1/H_c(z)$ is called whitening filter. Equation (6.34) demonstrates that a WSS random process $x(n)$ can be represented as the output of a causal filter $H_c(z)$ excited by a white noise process $w(n)$ having variance σ_{Wn}^2. By placing the condition that the filter is causally invertible (i.e., a minimum phase system), a WSS random process $x(n)$ can be represented as the input of the inverse filter $1/H_c(z)$, which produces a random process $w(n)$, white noise, also called innovation process. This concept is very important and is shown in block diagram form in Figure 6.3. This is also called Wold representation [7].

6.4 Time-Series Analysis from Signal Processing Perspective

From this section, the way of looking at the input random signal $x(n)$ is changed and now it is viewed as a time series of some random data. Time-series data is like a random signal and can be thought as a realization of a stochastic process. Stationary time-series (WSS) data shows no orderly change in mean and variance and no periodicity. This means it has no trend and seasonality. The properties of one section of data are much like the properties of the other sections of the data. From the signal processing analogy, WSS time series is generated by innovation filter with a white noise as its input. This causal linear filter $H_c(z)$ can be modeled in three different ways: (a) all-zero FIR filter, (b) all-pole IIR filter, and (c) pole-zero IIR filter. This filter corresponds to three different linear time-series models, namely (a) moving average, (b) auto regressive, and (c) auto regressive moving average, respectively; these are also abbreviated as MA, AR, and ARMA, respectively. Corresponding $H_c(z)$ and LCCDE representations are given in Equation (6.36), (6.37), and (6.38) respectively. From this point onward, the intersection of digital signal processing field and time-series data analysis field starts. Here $q + 1$ specifies the FIR filter tap length and p specifies IIR filter order which corresponds to MA (q) and AR (p) time-series models respectively.

$$\text{All zero FIR Filter: } H_c(z) = \frac{X(z)}{W(z)} = \sum_{k=0}^{q} b_k z^{-k};$$

$$\text{MA}(q) \text{ Time Series Model: } x(n) = \sum_{k=0}^{q} b_k w(n-k)$$

$$(6.36)$$

$$\text{All pole IIR Filter: } H_c(z) = \frac{X(z)}{W(z)} = \frac{1}{1 + \sum_{k=1}^{p} a_k z^{-k}};$$

$$\text{AR}(q) \text{ Time Series Model: } x(n) = w(n) - \sum_{k=1}^{p} a_k x(n-k)$$

$$(6.37)$$

$$\text{Pole-zero IIR Filter: } H_c(z) = \frac{X(z)}{W(z)} = \frac{\sum_{k=0}^{q} b_k z^{-k}}{1 + \sum_{k=1}^{p} a_k z^{-k}};$$

$$\text{ARMA}(p,q) \text{ Time Series Model: } x(n) = \sum_{k=0}^{q} b_k w(n-k) - \sum_{k=1}^{p} a_k x(n-k)$$

$$(6.38)$$

The relationship between autocorrelation sequence of $x(n)$ and the filter parameters (time-series coefficients) is specified by Yule-Walker equations, given by Equation (6.39) for AR (p) time series model [7].

$$\gamma_{xx}(l) = \sigma_{Wn}^2 \delta(l) - \sum_{k=1}^{p} a_k \gamma_{xx}(l-k); l \geq 0; \gamma_{xx}(-l) = \gamma_{xx}(l) \qquad (6.39)$$

For MA (q) time-series model, the relationship is given by Equation (6.40) [7].

$$\gamma_{xx}(l) = \begin{cases} \sigma_{Wn}^2 \sum_{k=0}^{q-l} b_k b_{k+l}; 0 \leq l \leq q \\ 0; l > q \end{cases}; \gamma_{xx}(-l) = \gamma_{xx}(l) \qquad (6.40)$$

For ARMA (p,q) models, the autocorrelation sequence is actually a superposition of that of the MA (q) and AR (p) model. ARMA (p,q) is a more economical model compared to MA (p) and AR (q) models, as it requires small number of model parameter sets ($\{a_k, b_k\}$) to represent stationary random data adequately. This is called parsimony of parameters in model building. This concept is analogus to digital filter design in digital signal processing, where the filter can be designed with lesser number of coefficients for given specifications using pole-zero IIR model instead of using only all-zeros FIR model or only all-poles IIR model. The ARMA (p,q) model governing equation is given by Equation (6.41).

$$\gamma_{xx}(l) = \begin{cases} \sigma_{Wn}^2 \sum_{k=0}^{q-l} h(k) b_{k+l} - \sum_{k=1}^{p} a_k \gamma_{xx}(l-k); 0 \le l \le q \\ \\ -\sum_{k=1}^{p} a_k \gamma_{xx}(l-k); l > q \\ \\ \gamma_{xx}(-l) \end{cases} \tag{6.41}$$

However, the above-mentioned modeling exercise works only if the time series-data are stationary. But most of the practical data are non-stationary. Operations such as differencing may make data stationary. Also, operation such as logarithm is required before time series modeling and forecasting to stabilize the variance of a series. Two such models for nonstationary data are ARIMA and seasonal ARMA (SARMA). In ARIMA models, the difference data $x(n) - x(n-1)$ is modeled as an ARMA model. If the time-series data contains a seasonal fluctuation term a SARMA model is useful. The signal after differencing by a step equal to the seasonal period (s) the data $x(n) - x(n-s)$, becomes stationary and the ARMA model can be fitted to the resulting data [8]. This is considered in subsequent sections.

6.5 Time-Series Models

From this section onward, the notations used are per standard time-series analysis. The signal processing researcher and data science researcher are now having a convergence. The discrete time random sequence $x(n)$ is replaced by the random variable X_n and so on. The coefficients $\{a_k\}$ are replaced with $\{-\varnothing_k\}$. With this, the AR (p) model of time series is given by Equation (6.42). The mean m_{Xn} of X_n in (6.42) is assumed to be zero here. If it is not zero, replace X_n by $X_n - m_{Xn}$ and X_{n-k} by $X_{n-k} - m_{Xn}$ and obtain Equation (6.43).

$$X_n = W_n + \sum_{k=1}^{p} \varnothing_k X_{n-k} \tag{6.42}$$

$$X_n = \alpha + W_n + \sum_{k=0}^{p} \varnothing_k X_{n-k}; \text{ where } \alpha = m_{Xn}\left(1 - \sum_{k=1}^{p} \varnothing_k\right) \tag{6.43}$$

Also, in time-series analysis, instead of using Z-transform–based transfer function, a backshift-operator (B)—based polynomial is used, which is defined as $B^k X_n = X_{n-k}$ and is analogus to Z-transform operator given by relationship $B = z^{-1}$. The representation using this notation is given in Equation (6.44).

$$X_n = \alpha + W_n + \sum_{k=1}^{p} \phi_k B^k X_n; \ i.e. \ \emptyset(B) X_n = \alpha + W_n; \ where \ \emptyset(B) = 1 - \sum_{k=1}^{p} \phi_k B^k \quad (6.44)$$

The MA (q) model of time series is given by Equation (6.45). Here, the coefficients $\{b_k\}$ are replaced with $\{\theta_k\}$. Using the backshift-operator notation the representation is given by Equation (6.46):

$$X_n - m_{Xn} = \sum_{k=0}^{q} \theta_k W_{n-k} \quad (6.45)$$

$$X_n = m_{Xn} + \theta(B) W_n; \ where \ \theta(B) = \sum_{k=0}^{q} \theta_k B^k \quad (6.46)$$

The ARMA (p,q) model of time series is given by Equation (6.47) and corresponding representation using backshift operator is given by Equation (6.48) [8]. Here $\emptyset(B)$ and $\theta(B)$ are polynomials in backshift operator B.

$$X_n = \alpha + \sum_{k=0}^{q} \theta_k W_{n-k} + \sum_{k=1}^{p} \phi_k X_{n-k} \quad (6.47)$$

$$\emptyset(B) X_n = \alpha + \theta(B) W_n \quad (6.48)$$

The concept of stability of linear digital filtering is analogus to the concept of stationarity in time-series data analysis. An MA (q) model is stationary always, as corresponding FIR filter is always stable. Also, it is possible to get its stationary inverse process, which is AR (∞) process under the condition that all the roots of $\theta(B)$ must lie outside the unity circle in complex B-plane. (Recall the analogy with minimum phase and invertibility in digital filter, and the also the analogy $B \leftrightarrow z^{-1}$.) For a stationary AR (p) model, the corresponding IIR filter must be stable i.e., the poles must be within the unity circle in Z-plane. Therefore, in context of an AR (p) model, the process is stationary if all the roots of $\emptyset(B)$ lie exterior to the unity circle in complex B-plane. Also, the inverse of stationary AR (p) model is MA (q) process, and it is always stationary. The AR (p) model itself is equivalent to some MA (∞) model. The causality is embedded in both the filter and corresponding time-series models because of nondependency on future values. An ARMA (p, q) model is causal, stationary, and invertible if roots of both the polynomials are outside the unity circle in complex B-plane. ARMA (p, q) can be expressed as MA (∞) or AR (∞).

The normalized autocorrelation function for both AR (p) and MA (q) time-series models are specified in Equations (6.49) and (6.50), respectively. They are analogus to Equations (6.39) and (6.40). Equation (6.49) represents Yule-Walker equations, which can also be written in matrix form. In the literature of time series analysis $\gamma_{xx}(l)$ is called autocovariance function and $\rho_{xx}(l)$ is called autocorrelation function (ACF) [8, 9].

$$\rho_{xx}(l) = \frac{\gamma_{xx}(l)}{\gamma_{xx}(0)} = \sum_{k=1}^{p} \varnothing_k \rho_{xx}(l-k); l > 0; \rho_{xx}(0) = 1; \rho_{xx}(-l) = \rho_{xx}(l) \text{ and}$$

$$\sigma_{Wn}^2 = \gamma_{xx}(0)\left[1 - \sum_{k=1}^{p} \varnothing_k \rho_{xx}(k)\right]$$

(6.49)

$$\rho_{xx}(l) = \frac{\gamma_{xx}(l)}{\gamma_{xx}(0)} = \begin{cases} \dfrac{\sum_{k=0}^{q-l} \theta_k \theta_{k+l}}{\sum_{k=0}^{q} \theta_k^2} ; 0 < l \leq q \\ 0; l > q \end{cases} ; \rho_{xx}(0) = 1; \rho_{xx}(-l) = \rho_{xx}(l)$$

(6.50)

The relationship in Equation (6.49) is linear, while that in Equation (6.50) is non-linear. Thus, fitting the MA (*q*) model is difficult compared to an AR (*p*) model. Also, efficient simultaneous linear equation solution algorithms are readily available, and hence the AR (*p*) model is preferred over the MA (*q*) model. (Again an analogy with digital filter: IIR filters are preferred over FIR filters due to efficient implementations.) To estimate the parameters of AR (*p*) model parameters ($\{\varnothing_k\}$), a prior knowledge of ACF is required. In practice they are estimated from given time-series data and Yule-Walker equations are solved iteratively to get the whole parameter set. Following are the steps to estimate the AR (*p*) model parameters ($\{\varnothing_k\}$) from given time-series data.

- Assume stationarity in advance and AR process order *p* (a priori assumption).
- Estimate ACF $\rho_{xx}(l)$ from given time-series data using sample ACF.
- Get *p* simultaneous linear equation from Equation (6.49). This set of equations is called Yule-Walker equations.
- Solve these equations using efficient algorithms available; for example, Levinson-Durbin algorithm.
- Obtain the estimation of variance of σ_{Wn}^2 using Equation (6.49) and estimated ACF.
- This gives the AR (*p*) parameters and now the model is ready for prediction or forecasting.

6.5.1 Partial ACF (PACF)

Empirical results show that ACF provides an estimate of the order of the dependence when the process is MA. ACF of MA (*q*) process cuts off after lag *q*. But ACF of AR (*p*) process tails off. Hence, the partial autocorrelation function (PACF) is used for AR (*p*) process and it cuts off after lag *p*. The PACF for MA (*q*) process behaves like ACF for AR (*p*) process. It decides whether to include the pth term in ACF, depending on the correlation at lag *p* that has not been accounted for in a model with *p* − 1 coefficients. The basic idea is to find the correlation between random variables X_n and X_{n-k} after accounting for or "partialling out" the linear effects of the intervening random variables. It is based on linear regression principle. The formula and details of mathematics is avoided here. The basic formula for PACF coefficients is mentioned in Equation (6.51). The PACF can be computed iteratively from the ACF using Levinson-Durbin algorithm. For ARMA (*p, q*) models, ACF suggests an order of moving average process (*q*) and PACF suggests order of autoregressive process (*p*). The ACF and the PACF are used to determine the orders of the underlying MA and AR processes, respectively. Box-Jenkins methodology uses analysis of ACF and PACF to ascertain appropriate time-series models [9].

$$\phi_{hh} = corr\left[x_{n+h} - \widehat{x_{n+h}}, x_n - \widehat{x_n} \right] \tag{6.51}$$

6.5.2 Akaike Information Criterion (AIC)

An important issue in time-series modeling is deciding which model will describe the process better and which generated the underlying data. Only ACF or PACF won't be enough to judge the quality of a model or to decide the proper values for p and q and the other quantities for the ARIMA and SARIMA models (to be described in next sub-sections). Out of different ways available to judge the quality of a time-series model most common way is to use Akaike information criterion (AIC). The AIC tries to help assessing the relative quality of several competing models by giving credit for models that reduce the error sum of squares and at the same time by building in a penalty for models, which bring in too many parameters. Different authors and software packages use varying forms of the AIC. The basic form is given by Equation (6.52). A model with low AIC value is preferred [9].

$$AIC = -2\log\left(maximum\ likelihood\right) + 2\left(number\ of\ parameters\ in\ the\ model\right) \tag{6.52}$$

6.5.3 Auto-Regressive Integrated Moving Average (ARIMA) Model

In many practical situations, time series is composed of two components: a zero-mean stationary component as well as nonstationary trend component. For example, a random walk process: $X_n = X_{n-1} + W_n$. To remove trend from the non-stationary time-series data, a difference operator $\nabla = 1 - B$ is used. Equation (6.53) illustrates the use of this operator.

$$\nabla X_n = X_n - X_{n-1} = (1 - B) X_n \tag{6.53}$$

In general, a process X_n is ARIMA of order (p, d, q) if $Y_n = \nabla^d X_n = (1 - B)^d X_n$ is ARMA (p, q). Over-differencing may introduce dependence, and ACF might also suggests differencing is needed. The polynomial for representation of ARIMA (p, d, q) model is given by Equation (6.54). The term $\emptyset(B)(1 - B)^d$ has one unit root with a multiplicity of d. As a result, ACF will decay slowly. This actually corresponds to just unstable (marginally stable) digital filters. The ACF will help in finding correct value of d and then on differenced time series ACF and PACF are used to find q and p respectively as in ARMA model. In some cases, a difference of log ∇ log (X_n) is used depending upon nature of the time-series data. The Ljung–Box–Pierce Q-statistic is also used to determine the significant ACF coefficients.

$$\emptyset(B)\nabla^d X_n = \theta(B)W_n \ \text{OR} \ \emptyset(B)(1-B)^d X_n = \theta(B)W_n \tag{6.54}$$

If $\nabla^d X_n$ has mean value $m_{\nabla dXn}$ the ARIMA model is given by Equation (6.55) [9].

$$\emptyset(B)\nabla^d X_n = \alpha + \theta(B)W_n; \alpha = m_{\nabla dXn}\left(1 - \sum_{k=1}^{p} \phi_k\right) \tag{6.55}$$

6.5.4 Seasonal ARMA (SARMA) and Seasonal ARIMA (SARIMA) Models

Data might contain seasonal periodic component in addition to correlation with recent lags. It repeats every s observation. For a time series of monthly observations, X_n might depend on annual lags: $X_{n-12}, X_{n-24}, \ldots$. A pure seasonal ARMA model SARMA $(P,Q)_s$ has the form given by Equation (6.56).

$$\Phi_p\left(B^s\right)X_n = \Theta_q\left(B^s\right)W_n; \Phi_p\left(B^s\right) = \left(1 - \sum_{k=1}^{P}\Phi_k B^{ks}\right); \Theta_q\left(B^s\right) = \left(1 + \sum_{k=1}^{Q}\Theta_k B^{ks}\right) \quad (6.56)$$

Just like pure ARMA processes, for the SARMA process to be stationary and invertible, the complex roots of the polynomials $\Phi_p(B^s)$ and $\Theta_q(B^s)$ must be outside the unit circle in complex B-plane. Seasonal ARIMA process (SARIMA) is written as SARIMA (p,d,q,P,D,Q,s), and it is given by Equation (6.57).

$$\Phi_p\left(B^s\right)\varnothing(B)\left(1 - B^s\right)^D\left(1 - B\right)^d X_n = \Theta_q\left(B^s\right)\theta(B)W_n \quad (6.57)$$

It has two parts: seasonal parts $(P,D,Q)_s$ and nonseasonal partz (p,d,q). Here, D is order of seasonal differencing (i.e., power of $(1 - B^s)$). The seasonality part in time series is analogus to "comb filtering" in digital signal processing. The ACF and PACF of stationary ARIMA process show peaks at every s lag but damping out as lag index increases. In ACF of ARIMA process, the adjacent spikes show the nonseasonal MA order (q) and spikes around seasonal lags show seasonal MA order (Q). In PACF the adjacent spikes show the nonseasonal AR order (p) and the spikes around seasonal lags show seasonal AR order (P) [9].

6.6 Time-Series Modeling Using Spectal Analysis and Optimum Filtering

Up to now the time series is viewed as a time sample indexed sequence of random variables, and the analysis is done in the time domain. There is, however, an alternate but very different viewpoint that explains a time series as a summation of sinusoids of different amplitudes, frequencies, and phases. This is termed as analysis in the spectral domain, or the Fourier domain. The Fourier transform provides spectral representation of time series. The estimation of the strength of the sinusoid at particular frequency is referred to as spectrum estimation. That's why it is also called spectral analysis.

From the discussion in section 6.2.3 and 6.3, the power spectral density (PSD) of ARMA (p,q) process is given by Equation (6.58).

$$S_{xx}\left(\omega\right) = \sigma_{Wn}^2 \frac{\left|\theta\left(e^{-j\omega}\right)\right|^2}{\left|\phi\left(e^{-j\omega}\right)\right|} \quad (6.58)$$

A method called parametric spectral estimation adapted from the digital signal processing is quite handy in estimating the PSD of ARMA (p, q) process from given time-series data. Such an estimator is called a parametric spectral estimator [8, 9]. Let $G(\omega)$ be the power spectral density of a stationary process, then, given $\varepsilon > 0$, there exists an ARMA (p, q) time series X_n with the PSD $S_{xx}(\omega)$ such that

$$|G(\omega) - S_{xx}(\omega)| < \varepsilon \text{ for } \omega \in [-\pi, \pi) \qquad (6.59)$$

where the order (p, q) is determined by one of the model selection criteria, such as AIC.

In some time-series analysis, filtering of data is required to infer some paramters such as trend, seasonality, and others. Digital filter design techniques can be used to realize various frequency response plots depending on requirement and then passing the time-series data to the digital filter can produce the desired results. The concept of optimum Wiener filter and derived adaptive filtering algorithms from this basic concept are extensively used in DSP for designing a time-varying digital filter. The prime aim of such filters is to remove the uncorrelated additive noise from signal. Such filters usually require two signals at the input; one is corrupted (or primary) signal due to additive noise and the second one is reference (or secondary) signal, which has some correlation with the noise actually added in the signal. Sometimes the reference signal is derived from the primary signal using some signal extraction techniques. Such adaptive filtering algorithms can also become very useful in adapting forecasting after time-series modeling or adaptively modeling the time series data.

6.7 Linear Prediction and Time-Series Modeling

In prediction the goal is to predict future values of a signal, $x(n + m)$, $m = 1, 2, \ldots\ldots$ based on the past data collected upto the present $\{x(n), x(n - 1), \ldots\ldots, x(n - p)\}$. The predictor that tries to minimize the mean square prediction error is called minimum mean square error (MMSE) predictor. The predicted value at instant $n + m$ is written as $\widehat{x(n+m)}$. The MSE is given by $E\left[\left(x(n+m) - \widehat{x(n+m)}\right)^2\right]$. The simplest predictor is a linear predictor. The linear

prediction coding (LPC) in various forms is used in DSP for speech signal compression and coding [7]. The linear predictor can be considered a digital filter, with its output is prediction error and input the time series data. The aim is to whiten the prediction error, and it is actually a whitening filter. This filter performs the action depicted by block diagram in Figure 6.5(b). The implementation of this filter can be done using causal and stable all zero FIR filter or pole-zero IIR filter. The linear prediction with MMSE requires that the coefficients of prediction error filter should be such that the output is zero mean white noise, and hence the prediction error is uncorrelated random sequence. This can be achieved by solving again the Equation (6.39) if all zero FIR filter is used as a linear predictor. The efficient algorithm like Levinson-Durbin [7] is quite handy in solving these equaitons. In this case the underlying process is AR (p). If pole-zero FIR filter is used as a linear predictor, then the underlying process is ARMA (p,q) and Equation (6.41) is required to solve to get the best prediction error filter coefficients [9]. Hence, the task of linear prediction is the same as AR (p) or ARMA (p,q) modeling. Thus, the time-series modeling and linear prediction are the same thing, and have an awesome analogy with the linear prediction error filter in digital signal processing [11]. Also, while using Equations (6.39) and (6.41) for practical applications, proper normalization is required.

6.8 Forecasting Trends and Seasonality

The Holt-Winters method, also called triple exponential smoothing, is very common in practice for designing short-term forecasting models. It includes exponential smoothing of level, trend, and seasonality (with period s). Three optimized parameters for particular time series are required to obtain, designated as α, β, γ, and they corresponds to level, trend, and seasonality respectively [10]. Considering additive and multiplicative seasonality, the forecasting of time-series data at m steps ahead is given by Equation (6.60) and (6.61), respectively.

$$\widehat{x(n+m)} = level(n) + m.trend(n) + seasonal(n+m-s) \tag{6.60}$$

$$\widehat{x(n+m)} = \left(level(n) + m.trend(n)\right).seasonal(n+m-s) \tag{6.61}$$

The update for level, trend, and sesonal parameters are given by equaitons (6.62), (6.63), and (6.64) respectively.

$$level(n) = \alpha\left(x(n) - seasonal(n-s)\right) + (1-\alpha)\left(level(n-1) + trend(n-1)\right) \tag{6.62}$$

$$trend(n) = \beta\left(level(n) - level(n-1)\right) + (1-\beta)trend(n-1) \tag{6.63}$$

$$seasonal(n) = \gamma\left(x(n) - level(n)\right) + (1-\gamma)seasonal(n-s)$$

The initialization is given by Equation (6.62). The seasonal operation is modulo s.

$$level(0) = x(0), trend(0) = x(1) - x(0), seasonal(0) = x(0) \tag{6.64}$$

6.9 Steps for Modeling ARMA (p, q) Stochastic Process

Given the autocorrelation sequences ACF and PACF, we can find the model parameters of ARMA (p,q) process or equivalently linear prediction coefficients. The ACF and PACF are estimated from given stationary time-series data. Following are the steps for building an ARMA (p,q) model from given stationary random time-series data, which are similar to designing prediction error filter.

i. Transformations to achieve stationary time series using ARIMA and/or SARIMA modeling.

ii. Finding parameters (p,q) using ACF, PACF and AIC.

iii. Estimate model parameter sets $(\{\theta_k, \varnothing_k\})$ from ACF. In some cases, a maximum likelihood (ML) estimator can also be used (this is beyond the scope of discussion here).

iv. Check for plausibility: (a) If residual white noise, i.e., shows no autocorrelation, then stop, select new values of (p,q), and repeat steps (ii–iv). The investigation of ACF of the residuals and the Ljung-Box test is useful for this check. (b) If the model delivers sensible forecasts, then accept it; else repeat steps (i–iv) with different strategy.

6.10 Adaptive Filters for Forecasting

Classical statistical approach employs regression and correlation methods. These methods have some constraints such as stationarity, correlation within the data, linear structure, model-based probability distribution, and so on. In real-life financial series, these conditions are not satisfied. As such, the statistical approach alone leads to poor forecasting capability. Recently an interest is found to develop more accurate prediction models based on adaptive filters, which are better suited for real-time purpose. Such a forecasting model consists of mainly two components: (i) Adaptive filter structure: linear combiner (FIR filter structure), multi-layer perceptron (MLP), functional link artificial neural network (FLANN) [12], cascaded FLANN (CFLANN) structure, and so on. (ii) Adaptive learning algorithms, divided into two categories: (a) derivative based: least mean square (LMS) and its variants, recursive least square (RLS), Kalman filter, back propagation (BP); and (b) derivative free: evolutionary and nature–inspired algorithms such genetic algorithms, simulated annealing, and others. Proper combination of the adaptive filter structure and the learning algorithm is important so that the rate of convergence is fast, training time is less, computational complexity is low, and prediction accuracy is high.

A basic block diagram of adaptive filter using L-tap FIR filter structure and LMS update algorithm is shown in Figure 6.4. The input signal X_k here is in vector (frame) form with length L and the unit impulse response coefficients (weight) vector W_k of the FIR filter is of the length L. It can be written as $X_k = [x_k \, x_{k-1} \ldots\ldots x_{k-L+1}]^T$ and $W_k = [w_{0k} \, w_{1k} \ldots\ldots w_{(L-1)k}]^T$. The LMS adaptive algorithm is an iterative algorithm, and it is used to update the weight vector of the FIR filter at the end of every iteration. The update depends on the error signal $e_k = d_k - y_k$. The output of the FIR filter is given by $y_k = X_k^T W_k = W_k^T X_k$. The signal d_k is called desired signal or training signal, which is very important for correct updation. The LMS weight update rule is given by Equation (6.65).

$$W_k(n+1) = W_k(n) + 2\mu e_k(n) X_k^T; 0 \leq \eta \leq 1 \tag{6.65}$$

Here, μ represents learning rate parameter. This procedure is iterated until the threshold value is attained by mean square error (MSE).

In addition to adaptive filtering algorithms, hybrid approaches like use of ARIMA time-series modeling and Wavelet transform along with nature-inspired optimization algorithms and can give some fruitful results at the cost of increased computation.

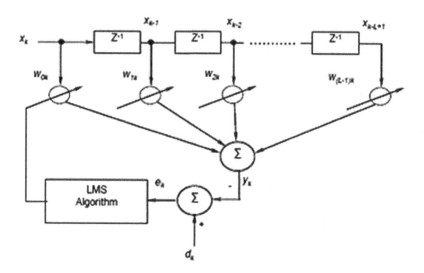

FIGURE 6.4
Adaptive Filter using FIR Filter Structure and LMS Algorithm

6.11 Steps for Forecasting Model Development

Following are the general and simplified steps for forecasting model development [12, 13].

  i. Pre-processing of input data:

   a. The time-series data adjusted with zero mean, normalized values (usually between 0 and 1), logarithm of data for variance stabilization, and so on.

   b. Input features are normalized to lie between 0 and 1.

   c. A set containing input features corresponding to a particular period (day, week, month, and so on.). This set is called an input pattern.

   d. Computing input patterns from the past time-series data.

   e. For training the model, a majority of the patterns (70 to 75%) is used.

   f. To test the trained model performance, the remaining patterns (25 to 30%) are used.

   g. For forecasting, the trained and tested model is used.

 ii. Model training:

   a. The initial weights of the model can be set to zero or some known and special values.

   b. The output is computed after applying the first input pattern.

   c. The output is compared with the desired output (reference value), and the error is calculated by subtracting output and reference value.

   d. The change in weight vector is calculated using an adaptive algorithm such as LMS.

   e. The change in weight vector is obtained with all other input training patterns.

   f. The average weight vector change is obtained.

g. The updated weight vector is obtained by adding the average weight vector change to the original value.

h. The above mentiond steps constitute one experiment cycle.

i. The above experiment cyle is iterated several times.

j. In each experiment cycle the MSE value is calculated.

k. A plot of numbers of experiment cycle versus corresponding MSE is obtained, which are called the training or learning curves of the model.

l. When the MSE becomes less than or equal to required tolerance, the learning process completed.

m. The final values of weights are then locked, and they represent the model parameters.

iii. Model testing:

a. The model testing is done with the leftover known input patterns.

b. The output is obtained with the leftover known pattern is applied as input to the model.

c. The obtained output is called predicted output, and it is compared with the expected known output.

d. Prediction performance is evaluated by % of prediction error (PER) defined as PER = ((True value–Predicted value)/True value)*100.

6.12 Illustrative Application

To illustrate the concepts cited in the above sections, a time-series modeling of National Stock Exchange (NSE)'s NIFTY50 index daily closing price is considered. The daily closing price of NIFTY50 for the period 01-04-2007 to 30-06-2020 is downloaded from [14] and stored in a single .csv file along with a date stamp. This time-series data are imported into MATLAB® using import data utility and stored as a table in the MATLAB® workspace. The table is then stored in a .mat file in a working directory. Care should be taken for proper labeling of data columns at all stages. In this example, the date column is labled as "Date," and the daily closing price is labeled as "Close." The size of the data is 3279. The time series is plotted in Figure 6.5 (pane 1). Visual inspection recommends that the time series is not stationary, the variance is fluctuating, and there is a time-varying trend (sometimes up and sometimes down). Also, no proper seasonality is seen. Such time-series data are very difficult to model. It is required to perform objective tests for stationarity (stability in terms of signal processing). The KPSS test can do this [15]. The results support the visual inspection.

The logarithm of time series is taken to stabilize the variance to some extent. Also, the difference of resulting time series is taken (one sample less than original series), and the stationarity test is conducted again on resulted time series. The differenced time series data passes the stationarity test and suggests the need of ARIMA model with parameter $d = 1$ to handle the non-stationarity in original time series. The plots are shown in Figure 6.5 (panes 2 and 3). The next step is to obtain ACF and PACF of the logarithm of original time series and to decide the parameters p and q.

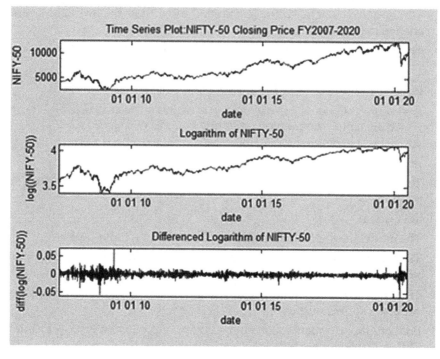

FIGURE 6.5
Plot of NIFTY 50 Daily Closing Price in Different Forms

The results in Figure 6.6(a) suggest ACF decay very slowly, and hence the value of q cannot be decided. Looking at PACF, the value of $p = 12$ may be sufficient. For simplicity q is taken to 1. Therefore, the time-series model here is ARIMA (12,1,1). Other values can also be taken and tried. Now, the coefficients and other model parameters can be estimated by doing the model fitting to the time-series data. The AIC value of the fitted model can be computed then, and AIC values of different suitable ARIMA (p,d,q) models can be compared; the model with least AIC value will be selected.

Then, the fitting check is carried out for final fitted model. This can help identify areas of model shortfall and also suggest ways for improving the model. Residual diagnostic plot is a useful way to assess deviations from model assumptions. Residuals are checked for normality and residual autocorrelation. If residual ACF and PACF give a significant result, there is a need to improve the model fit by adding AR or MA terms. For checking the predictive performance, total available data are divided into training and validation set. The training data is used to fit the model, and then the fitted model is used to forecast over the period provided by validation set. By comparing true remaining observations with forecasted values, the predictive performance of the model can be assessed. Prediction mean square error (PMSE) indicates numerical measure of the predictive performance. The testing data are separately stored and taken here as NIFTY50 closing values from 01-07-2020 to 14-08-2020 (33 data).

Figure 6.6(b) illustrates forecasting capability of the fitted model within a95% confidence interval. Finally the PMSE is 6.6745e-04 which indicates some mean square error in prediction. To further enhance the accuracy of forecasting, adaptive algorithms can be used in along with the time series data modeling.

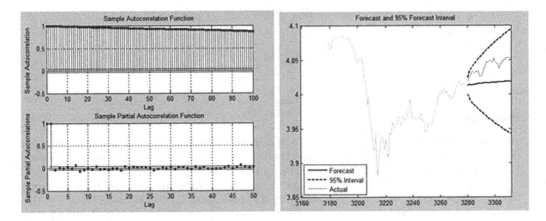

FIGURE 6.6
(a) Plot of ACF and PACF of NIFTY50 Time Series (b) Plot of Residual Diagnosis Checks

6.13 Conclusion and Future Scopes

This chapter has described the concepts of digital filtering used in the field of DSP. The filtering concepts are better understood in the spectral domain rather than in the time domain. The description of digital filters with stochastic input signal involves the auto-correlation and spectral density terms. Also, the linear prediction filters involve these terms in their description. The time-series data analysis and modeling can be viewed as an analysis and design of digital filter and hence an obvious analogy exists between them. An effort is made here to describe the time-series analysis from the signal processing point-of-view. So, the researchers working in DSP domain can be attracted to time-series data analysis and modeling. The time-series data modeling and analysis are usually carried out in time domain; while digital filter analysis and design are usually carried out in spectral domain. The spectral domain description of time series analysis is also presented here in brief that can also inspire DSP researchers to contribute more in-time series analysis and modeling by applying the spectral domain concepts. Also, the forecasting models used in time-series data are usually forecasting future data based on level, trend, and seasonality embedded in past data, but lack adaptivity. An adaptive filtering concept using LMS algorithm is presented here in brief. The DSP researchers can contribute more by applying principles of adaptive signal processing to the time-series forecasting by making the series paramenters adaptive. This chapter has tried to present a roadmap for systematic incorporation of well-developed DSP concepts to the modeling and forecasting using time-series analysis. The chapter ended with an illustrative application of time-series analysis in forecasting the NSE NIFTY50 index movement using ARIMA modeling. The simulation results are encouraging and with the possible future involvement of spectral domain and adaptive filtering concepts in time-series analysis and forecasting, the results can be improved further. A future scope can be use of adaptive filtering structure with special ANN, as mentioned in this chapter, for improved modeling and forecasting. There are many other open research questions, such as improvement in prediction error using spectral domain time-series analysis and modeling, application of Discrete Wavelet Transform in time series data forecasting, and use of variants of evolutionary and nature inspired optimization algorithms, which may be of interest to many researchers. The practical results and data forecasting procedures described in this paper can be used as a seed point for more advanced researches.

References

1. Thad B. Welch, Cameron H. G. Wright, and Michael G. Morrow. 2009. *"The DSP of money."* In *Proc. IEEE International Conference on Acoustics, Speech, and Signal Processing 2009, Taipei, Taiwan, 19-24 April 2009*: 2309–2312. IEEE Signal Processing Society.
2. A. W. Lo, H. Mamaysky, and J. Wang. 2000. "Foundations of Technical Analysis: Computational Algorithms, Statistical Inference, and Empirical Implementation." *The Journal of Finance*, vol. 55, no. 4, Aug. 2000: 1705–1765.
3. Xiao-Ping (Steven) Zhang and Fang Wang. 2017. "Signal Processing for Finance, Economics, and Marketing; Concepts, framework, and big data applications." *IEEE Signal Processiessing Magazine*, May 2017: 14–35.
4. Sheikh Mohammad Idrees, M. Afshar Alam, and Parul Agarwal. 2019. "A Prediction Approach for Stock Market Volatility Based on Time Series Data." *IEEE Access*, vol. 7, 2019: 17287–17298.
5. Jigar H. Shah, and Jay M. Joshi. 2011. *"Digital Signal Processing: Principles and Implementations."* New Delhi: Laxmi Publications, University Science Press.
6. B.P. Lathi and Zhi Ding. 2010. *"Modern Digital and Analog Communication Systems."* New York: Oxford University Press.
7. J.G. Proakis and Dimitris G, Manolakis. 2006. *"Digital Signal Processing: Principles, Algorithms and Applications."* Noida: Pearson Education.
8. Klaus Neusser. 2016. *"Time Series Econometrics."* AG Switzerland: Springer International Publishing.
9. Robert H. Shumway and David S. Stoffer. 2016. *"Time Series Analysis and its Applications With R Examples."* AG Switzerland: Springer International Publishing.
10. Min Wen, Ping Li, Lingfei Zhang and Yan Chen. 2019. "Stock Market Trend Prediction Using Higher-Order Information of Time Series." *IEEE Access*, vol. 7, Feb. 2019: 28299–28308.
11. Yiyong Feng and Deniel P. Palomar. 2015. "A Signal Processing Perspective on Financial Engineering." *Foundations and Trends® in Signal Processing*, vol. 9, 2015: 1–231.
12. Ritanjali Majhi, G. Panda and G. Sahoo. 2009. "Efficient Prediction of Exchange Rates using Low Complexity Artificial Neural Network Models." *Expert Systems with Applications, Elsevier.* vol. 36, 2009: 181–189.
13. R. Majhi, S. Mishra, B. Majhi, G. Panda and M. Rout. 2009. "Efficient sales forecasting using PSO based adaptive ARMA model." In *Proc. World Congress on Nature & Biologically Inspired Computing (NaBIC)*, Coimbatore, India, 9–11 December 2009: 1333–1337. IEEE.
14. NSE historical data. 2020. https://www1.nseindia.com/products/content/equities/indices/historical_index_data.htm
15. MATLAB Econometrics Toolbox Documentation. 2020. https://in.mathworks.com/help/econ/

7

Data Science in Education

Meera S Datta and Vijay V Mandke

NIIT University, India

CONTENTS

7.1 Introduction

In the field of education, the learning experience is regulated in terms of deductively arrived elements of the lecture, tutorial, or practical in higher education, or through classroom-lab experience in other educational settings, including the corporate world. Advances in technology have impacted education with the emergence of technology-enhanced learning, e-learning, and online learning, including massive open online course (MOOCs), leading to a manifold increase in educational data available for research. Current technologies, such as artificial intelligence (AI), machine learning, internet of things (IoT) and cloud computing will see an exponential rise in educational data. Educational data mining (EDM) and learning analytics (LA) are being increasingly adopted by educational institutions to extract insights from educational data to improve student and institutional performance.

While there is a large body of educational research work in the pedagogy and assessment domains, content is still presumed to be predetermined and remains more or less static; delivery is predominantly didactic, while assessments rarely address readiness for the next phase after completion of the current program of study.

The ineffectiveness of the lecture method of instruction has been conclusively shown by Freeman et al. (2014) and Weiman (2014). A meta-analysis of 225 studies (Freeman et al., 2014) revealed that there was a measurable improvement in student performance in examinations, as well as concept inventories when active learning was adopted. The failure rates were also lower than under the lecture method. They go on to say that the debate now should be which of the active learning methods yield better student performance, and not whether active learning is better or not than the lecture method. The effectiveness of peer instruction and strategies to adopt peer instruction in classrooms has been shown by Mazur (1997). Classroom-based pedagogies, in particular cooperative and problem-based learning, have been demonstrated by Smith et al. (2005). Peer-assisted learning and small group learning as effective strategies for large class learning have been demonstrated by Omer et al. (2008). The key message from these studies indicates that student engagement in learning is vital to enhance learning outcomes.

The rationale for our approach has also been derived from how and when humans learn. Ronni Hendel-Giller et al. (2010) introduce the concept of the "social brain" and cite numerous studies that show a brain needs interaction with other brains to grow, and that one of the primary ways it learns is through imitation. Several researchers have put forth certain core principles to organize learning. Anderson (2009) puts forth the three presences that need to be brought into learning to make teaching effective: teaching, cognitive, and social presences. Aurobindo (1956) puts forth three principles of education: "Nothing can be taught," with implications for the role of the teacher who is now a guide and not an "instructor" or a "taskmaster"; "The mind has to be consulted in its own learning," implying the uniqueness of each human brain and hence the individual learner; "Work from the near to the far, from that which is to that which shall be," implying the local and global nature of knowledge and hence the context of learning has to move from here and now to global and future times in "ever widening circles." Bender and Waller (2011) propose a new differentiated instruction based on brain science research findings. They strongly advocate instruction based on "brain-compatible research," which addresses the unique needs of each student in contrast to whole class instruction that is normally taught the way teachers plan instruction. They claim that this is different from differentiated instruction, which was based primarily on multiple intelligences theory and learning styles preferences.

We also observe two distinct phases in education brought upon by the COVID-19 pandemic: the pre–COVID-19 and the post–COVID-19 phases. While the pre–COVID-19 phase was predominated by face-to-face classroom instruction, the post–COVID-19 phase relies on online means due to physical distance restrictions imposed by the pandemic. But more importantly, the COVID-19 pandemic has brought to focus the importance of engagement at the *futurefront*—the place where maximum change occurs, and hence maximum information is available to lead to maximum learning. This implies that attempting to replicate pre–COVID-19 practices in the online mode will not yield the desired results if current technology, online learning, and e-learning and data science practices do not address the two key differences: unequal distribution of resources and physical non-proximity of learners.

Based on the above, we propose a new framework for learning that uses an information-processing–based approach and relies on realistic project-based learning with projects drawn from the industry in contrast to contrived projects for learner engagement. We put forth the following as part of the framework: a *connectomnal* teaching-learning organization that builds a network of learners, teachers, parents, and industry professionals; a contextualized, constructively conflicting, internal regulating teaching-learning interplay in contrast to mere decontextualized, destructively conflicting, external regulation mode; teacher-extended professionality satisfying learners (unexpected learners included) with teachers actively engaged in identifying and organizing realistic projects horizontally and vertically, spanning multiple courses across academic years.

This chapter briefly traces and identifies limitations in prevalent educational systems, gives the necessary current view of the data science and learning analytics domain from the perspective of the educational systems, examines framework and features of SMART educational systems proposed in literature as applicable to learning in the Digital Age, and describes relevant socioeconomic and technical challenges in adopting learning analytics in educational systems. To overcome the technical challenges and drawbacks in the above incumbent view, it describes a new framework and model that can inform EDM and LA. The proposed framework has been used in realizing a research-based pedagogic innovation for learning futures to achieve IoT competency.

7.2 Tracing and Identifying Limitations in Current Educational Systems

The education model that pervades the world today can be traced back to the Industrial Era and had its beginnings with the Industrial Revolution. The Industrial Revolution spawned the factory system which needed labor to operate machines first and foremost, as well as perform related work associated with mechanized production. In addition to technical skills, attitudes and behaviors to conform to the factory system—punctuality, obedience, and adherence to rules, to name a few—were also needed. Factory owners took interest in education even to the extent of funding educational institutions. The funding was in part only as there was a perceived distinction between specific skills needed for a factory and generic skills that could be taken across factories. Educational institutions organized their teaching to create a workforce that met the needs of the factory system and relied on classroom lectures and practical work with emphasis on skill acquisition (Mokyr, 2001).

Factories began to look for better practices—in the areas of production process, products and machines—in response to consumer demand for better products. The factories themselves invested in evolving better practices, leading to an increase in knowledge and knowhow. This now required specialized labor. The education system evolved into higher education, in particular for technical and engineering fields, in order to meet the needs and provided specialized knowledge and skills in the required domain areas of value to the factories (Mokyr, 2001).

Simultaneously, educational institutions began to be regulated by government bodies and together the content, pedagogy, and assessment, as well as degree granting, was decided by the perceived needs of the industrial society.

The advent of ICT (Information and Communication Technology) led to a knowledge explosion, which required working with knowledge instead of materials—harnessing and managing existing knowledge and the creation of new knowledge. There was a growing alienation of industry and educational institutions, which were increasingly managed by governments, with the role of educational institutions limited to existing-knowledge transmission and degree-granting. Knowledge creation was observed in those higher educational institutions that worked closely with industry, as was seen in the California region with the University-Industry collaboration leading to the emergence of Silicon Valley. Bombay College of Pharmacy is another notable example.

Prevalent practices in most educational institutions continue to adhere to those that met the needs of the Industrial Era successfully, but were inadequate in the Knowledge Era. (Harris 2002.) traces the genesis and evolution of the credit system that has become the basis for granting degrees and diplomas. The report espouses that while the credit system that uses time as a basis helps in managing the fiscal aspects of education, an outcomes-based approach is needed rather than the time spent. This tracks with brain science research that points out that every brain is unique, which implies that time spent and a rigid academic calendar using the lecture-tutorial-practical mode can hardly be the only basis for academic achievement. Roy-Singh (1991) identified several lacunae in prevalent educational systems, in particular in Asia, and attempted to propose several guiding principles and frameworks. Knowledge explosion may have led to specializations as a mechanism to handle ever-expanding knowledge, but problem-solving necessarily involves drawing from multiple disciplines to arrive at a solution, thus bringing out a need for synthesis and collaboration. It also talks about how educational institutions were separated from the very society into which the student is expected to enter. It examines the foundations of a "knowledge-based society that derives from human potential" and hence "is an open society because it relies on how humans think and create," with "creativity and inventiveness" being at its core. It goes on to state that "past models and experiences do not respond to this core." It lays the framework for educational institutions by stating that the role of an educational institution is three-fold" knowledge generators, centers of innovation, and service centers for their communities.

Singh (2014) and Maitra (2016) trace the historical development of education and technical education in India respectively, and describe the several committees constituted, reports produced, and fiscal aspects debated by governments. Salmon (2019) traces briefly the historical development of education in the West, and how education has evolved from Education 1.0 to Education 3.0 in response to technological advances throughout the Industry Revolution 1.0 – 3.0—although the evolution has not been uniform, with universities still struggling with technologies and pedagogies. With Industry 4.0 becoming a reality, it proposes what can constitute Education 4.0: a "complex view of higher education as an adaptive system" and "universities to have their own vision and work towards realizing it." This would imply learners will become aware of their learning capabilities and motivations, and become "creators of knowledge artifacts," rather than consumers of knowledge.

From the above discussions, the authors have identified the following key issues in the current education system:

- Lack of individualization
- No content innovation
- Scalability of sameness instead of scalability of variability
- No realistic industry linkage with higher education
- Missing seamless tertiary-secondary-primary school connects

We now examine the role being played by data science and learning analytics in educational systems.

7.3 Data Science and Learning Analytics: Recent Educational System View

While the term data acience has been in existence in academia since the 1960s, its usage has seen a rapid growth with its adoption by the tech industry. The tech industry claims to have coined the term in 2018, showing the chasm between academia and industry with respect to new knowledge creation. The distinction the tech industry brought to data science was to include data wrangling, or the ability to "bring structure to large quantities of formless data and make analysis possible."

While the initial definitions of data science appeared to overlap with the definitions of the domain of statistics, it became increasingly clear that the scope of the domain of data science went beyond the mathematical underpinnings provided by statistics. Data science also did not fit neatly into the computer science domain where the emphasis was on proving and improving algorithm efficiency using mathematics. It was also recognized that data science needed a multiple set of knowledge, skills, and expertise that was perhaps difficult for one individual to possess. Another observation was that several domains, such astrophysics and geonomics, were relying heavily on data analysis to make sense of the vast amounts of data generated using much of the techniques under the discipline of data science, but did not use the term, perhaps viewing from tools and techniques perspective rather than a discipline in itself. Providing the above reasoning, Irizarry (2020) attempts to provide a definition of data science as follows: "data science is an umbrella term to describe the entire complex and multistep processes used to extract value from data." It puts forth three distinct areas: backend data science, frontend data science, and software tools development. The backend data science deals with data storage and efficient computing, while the frontend data science deals with the analysis of data, including prediction and software tools development deals with creation of specialized tools. Hadoop and TensorFlow are some examples of software tools that facilitate data science. An underlying assumption here is that having knowledge in the domain of data science is being put to use is implicit.

The National Academies of Sciences, Engineering, and Medicine (2018) discusses the need to elucidate the discipline of data science to address the growing need for data scientists by industry and government to handle and derive meaning from the vast quantity of data originated primarily due to digitalization. While giving shape to the data science discipline, in particular as an undergraduate course of study, it proposes two relevant and novel suggestions: prospective data scientists undergoing a program of study in data science should work with real data in the form of projects by connecting with industry and government that generate this data, and data scientists should undertake a "Data Scientist Oath" similar to the Hippocrates Oath taken by physicians to address the issue of ethics in the field given several instances of highly visible research work resulting in erroneous findings as well as legal implications of data access. There are also suggestions on how data science should be taught, since the discipline itself will be continuously impacted by rapidly evolving technologies and tools and fresh problem-solving approaches.

Bienkowski and others (2012) draw a parallel between data mining and analytics used in industry to derive business intelligence by analyzing consumer data to aid decision making and EDM and LA used in education to improve student learning experience by analyzing student data and inform educational decision-making. While there is no clear distinction between EDM and LA, broadly, EDM deals with discovering patterns, developing algorithms, and creating models while LA applies algorithms and models in educational settings and systems. A third domain is visual data analytics, which deals with graphical representation of data that becomes amenable to interpretation by humans.

While both deal with data, data itself can structured or unstructured. Data, such as age, marks scored, and so on, that can be stored in relational databases and can be handled computationally is called *structured data*, while data such as images and voice files that carry semantic information that can be understood by humans is called *unstructured data*. For a computer to handle such data, it has to be supplemented with additional information by humans.

With human endeavors becoming increasingly technology driven and going online, the quantity of data generated has increased exponentially giving rise to big data—datasets requiring new database technologies to store and manipulate data characterized by the three Vs: volume, velocity, and variety. In education, online learning, adaptive learning, computer-supported collaborative learning, and other learning management systems and learning content management systems (LMS and LCMS) generate rich big data with respect to learners, learning, learning design, and learning environments in the form of clicks and traces.

While data science deals with transforming data into actionable insights, machine learning deals with programs and algorithms that learn from big data and produce actionable insights including predictive and prescriptive actions. It includes both data analysis and production environment stages.

Klašnja-Milićević and others (2017) proposes a general platform for big data analytics for higher education institutions that includes suggested learner and institutional data to be captured so the possible useful feedback can be generated. It also puts forth an architectural framework for setting up a big data analytics research systems in higher education institutions. The application architecture drawn from the authors' experience rests on current database technology, Hadoop, to store unstructured data drawn from LMSes, social media, and weblogs.

While it is important to draw insights and perform trend analysis to aid educational decision-making from learner data such as grades, attendance, class behavior, online behavior – clicks, time spent on a module, viewing a video, listening to an audio clip, and course completion time, it is equally important to align EDM and LA with prevalent learning theories and develop frameworks to capture in-depth and comprehensive data about learners, learning, and learning environments. The same is addressed in Saqr (2018), Viberg et al. (2020), and Grunspan et al. (2014); all three discuss collaborative learning, self-regulation, and engagement and measures therein that can provide both the theoretical underpinnings as well as data for learning analytics. In the context of online learning engagement, content becomes important. In computer-supported collaborative learning, engagement with other learners becomes a critical factor for effective learning. Further online learning demands learners exhibit a high degree of self-regulation, especially in asynchronous online learning and blended learning.

A framework for self-regulation is provided in Winne (2017). The authors elaborate on the four recursive phases that take place as a learner undertakes a learning task. In phase 1, the learner surveys resources and constraints the learner predicts may affect the progress of the learning task. In phase 2, the learner sets goals and plans for attaining the goals. In phase 3, the learner carries out the plans formulated to complete the learning task. In phase 4, the learner steps back, surveys progress on phases 1–3, and takes action. During the course of executing a learning task, learners leave "traces," such as clicking a hyperlink, highlighting sentences, or annotating figures. The authors propose that the traces form input data to learning analytics systems and can be used to draw inferences. Saqr (2018) describes in detail how self-regulation and engagement, viewed as social activities, were "operationalized" by identifying relevant learner data as well as data that the learner generated during the learning task. Winne (2017) concludes that learning analytics research was conducted to "measure rather than to support SRL," and hence there is a need to actively nurture self-regulated learning in online learners by suitably exploiting learning analytics.

We believe that all students should be encouraged to "manage their resources." The view that we adopt about self-regulation is as follows (Mandke 2013):

- Good learners are self-regulated.
- Being self-regulated means that a learner has appropriate knowledge, a repertoire of strategies to perform tasks, and the motivational will to do so.
- Self-regulation relates to ability, skill, and motivation, and a willingness to manage one's own limited cognitive resources in the most strategic way possible.
- Helping students (or workers) to become more strategic, to identify important information (i.e., learning in a process-centric manner), and to use prior information/knowledge is an essential part of good teaching (working) environment.

In Saqr (2018) we see a social network snalysis (SNA) being used as a tool to measure and monitor collaborative learning. The author elaborates on how social network analysis is informed by learning theories such as constructivism and connectivism, and its visual analysis and mathematical indicators such as centrality measures makes it an apt tool in the computer supported collaborative learning. Social network analysis provides a visual representation of interaction amongst learners and teachers that is easy to interpret, and the authors report a research experiment where interventions were taken based on SNA visualizations and relevant interaction indicators. The National Academies of Sciences, Engineering, and Medicine (2018) applies social network analysis in a classroom setting, wherein the social interaction data has been collected using surveys and the same mapped using social network analysis tools.

Dashboards provide a convenient way of displaying the analysis information from LA and EDM to students, teachers, and administrators so that actions can be taken. Examples of dashboards can be seen in Bienkowski et al. (2012).

In Winne (2017) we see learning analytics dashboards being used for academic advising. Based on their research experiment, the authors report that dashboards enabled expert advisers to handle more low achievers in less time, and inexperienced advisers were able to make informed decisions in times comparable to experienced advisers.

Dashboards also form a significant component in educational recommender systems. Recommender systems used extensively in platform economy are based on big data and aim to predict users product and service preferences based on previous choices, feedback on products and services, and feedback to other users. The system relies on two filtering methods: collaborative and content filtering methods. Educational recommender systems aim to personalize a student's learning experience by recommending learning resources and activities. Abdi et al. (2020) observe that existing educational recommender systems take a "black-box" approach with learners not being aware of the basis of learning resources recommended. The "black-box" approach might lead to trust issues with learners not in agreement with the recommendations. Further, from current education perspective, the reigns of learning should rest in the hands of the learners which is possible by keeping "openness" as a core principle of learning. They suggest complementing an ERS with open learning models wherein the parameters that go to form a model of the learner are made available to learners and instructors through visualizations. They report that the results of their randomized control trial, while indicating that there was an overall positive effect on student engagement and perception of effectiveness of the system, also showed that there were cases of falling engagement and perception of fairness of the combined system.

Lastly, applying EDM and LA can be a daunting task to instructors who have to grapple with technologies, as well as be involved in identifying and gathering relevant learner data. Eyman and Dilek (2020) conduct a literature review to identify the most commonly reported factors that influence prediction of students academic achievement and grades the five factors identified in decreasing order of influence. The study provides a set of guidelines with a six-stage framework to follow for implementing EDM techniques for improved student achievement.

We move on to look at smart learning, a concept that has been proposed to address learning in the digital age and relies on current digital age technologies such as AI, IoT, machine learning, and data analytics.

7.4 Learning in the Digital Age: Framework and Features of a SMART Educational System

While there is no clear-cut definition or a single understanding of the term "smart" in the educational context reported in literature or industry on one hand, several countries—Malaysia, Singapore, Australia, South Korea, to name a few—have undertaken large-scale national level "smart school" projects to leverage technology and pedagogy into their national and political agenda with a few projects being described in Zhu et al. (2016). The goal of such smart learning projects is to equip its people with twenty-first century skills and create a workforce for the digital economy.

Martín et al. (2019) reports the literature review of research work being carried out in smart education. From their study, though limited, it can be observed research interest in smart learning is increasing. Further, IoT pertaining to education has received the maximum attention of researchers from amongst various technologies. The authors have also suggested the following areas for further research: connectivity (speed issues), security (data privacy), prediction systems, and data visualization. All four issues are pertinent when IoT technology is applied in learning environments.

Smart education, smart learning, and smart learning environments can be viewed from technology or pedagogy perspectives, but a fusion of the two is necessary to cause improvement in learning as can be seen in Shoikova et al. (2017) and Hoel and Mason (2018). In Hoel and Mason (2018), the authors have conducted their review study from the perspective of identifying conceptual frameworks for evolving standards for smart learning environments. They have proposed two models: a model to depict the flow of learning processes relevant in a smart learning environment and a model that is indicative of the level of smartness in the smart learning environment. Through their analysis, they claim that these models will inform ITLET (IT for Learning Education and Training, a term coined and used in Subcommittee 36 of ISO/IEC Joint Technical Committee 1) standardization agenda.

To improve performance of learning in smart education, the authors in Zhu et al. (2016) have proposed four instructional strategies to address needs at different levels: "class-based differentiated instruction, group-based collaborative learning, individual-based personalized learning, and mass-based generative learning." They also propose the following ten features, which they state are key to smart education. While location aware, context aware, and socially aware pertain to the learner, interoperability, seamless connection, and whole record (learning path data for mining) characterize technology. Adaptability, ubiquitous, natural interaction, and high engagement characterize the instructional environment.

We put forth our observations of learning environments, including smart learning environments, and state that content is predetermined and remains fixed; assessment rarely addresses the readiness in the learner's journey—be it joining the workforce, research by way of discovery, higher education aiming at higher order complex thinking or creating value to the corporate organization.

Further, there is enough body of research and data—particularly advances in brain science—to show that each learner is distinct and unique, and hence requires a teaching-learning method tailored to his/her learning characteristics, motivations, and beliefs. Another observation is that several studies done under the realm of future of work report that the world of work, which absorbs most of the learners coming out of higher education institutions, finds their knowledge and skills inadequate. A similar observation is reported for learners entering higher education from schools. Even within schools, a similar phenomenon is observed: primary school children are not meeting the standards of secondary levels.

In our view, past studies and techniques used in education systems as reported in literature can be classified into two types: standalone in the past and statically connected in the recent past and present. We propose a type: networked dynamically, for learner benefit and improved experience futures. Key features of the three types are shown in Table 7.1.

TABLE 7.1

Proposed Classification of Studies and Techniques Reported in Literature

Standalone	Statically Connected	Networked Dynamically
Executing main lessons delivery plan	Adapting main lessons delivery plan in response to failure to achieve a milestone	Evolving main lessons plan in response to an event
Information is given, no ambiguity	Finite choice of information, no ambiguity	Information complex and unknown, infinite choice, ambiguous, uncertain
Decontextualized content teaching	Decontextualized content teaching	Contextualized and individual situation-based content learning
Cognitive elements of memory, problem-solving and critical thinking	Cognitive elements of memory, problem-solving and critical thinking	Metacognitive elements of learning goal, strategy, regulation, self-efficacy and belief
Theoretical, structured, linear learning	Project-based experiential learning (no information origination)	Value-creating project-based experiential learning with information origination
Focus on quality and efficiency	Focus on quality and efficiency	Focus on quality, efficiency and effectiveness leading to integrity learning
Collective learning	Collective learning with finite variations	Individualized and collaborative learning using convergence technologies for learner benefit and improved experience futures

A recent phenomenon reported in literature is digital transformation. Digital transformation refers to the changes occurring in our society due to infusion of digital technologies. This infusion has impacted the way industry operates giving rise to the platform economy. Digital organizations scale faster, create more value, and do business differently. These organizations rely on data science and data analytics to generate business intelligence that can be acted upon in real time using machine learning and deep learning algorithms. Development in digital technologies has also led to rapid emergence of online, computer-supported collaborative learning and blended learning systems, as well as mobile learning with mobility affordances.

The pandemic due to COVID-19 has led to stringent requirements of maintaining physical distances between human beings, altering the way humans have been conducting their lives and businesses. This has seen an acceleration in digital transformation with education at all levels moving from classroom to online. While this scenario may not be expected to continue indefinitely, the benefits of online learning will encourage educational institutions and organizations to adopt a blended form of learning. Online learning and remote working will put demands on collaborative modes of learning and working.

We take an informational view of learning and state that currently a feed-forward system of design, as shown in Figure 7.1, is used wherein content is predetermined, learning activity is restricted to deductive strategies such as internships, industry guest faculty lectures, and assessments are done with the intent to find out if predetermined content is mastered. The linear flow from content to learning activity to assessment does not consider the requirements of the external environment.

The deductive model of the teaching-learning process, as illustrated in Figure 7.2, lays emphasis on "decontextualized content teaching," wherein learning occurs by leveraging the pure cognitive elements of memory, problem-solving, and critical thinking alone seem inadequate to meet the requirements of changing and complex needs of learners and workplaces.

Feed-Forward Instruction Design
(FFID) Framework

FIGURE 7.1
Feed-Forward Instruction Design Framework

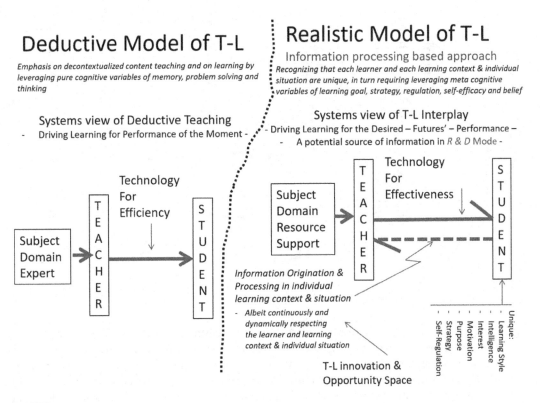

FIGURE 7.2
Illustrating the deductive and realistic models of teaching-learning

But industry and society as a whole are changing rapidly due to digital technologies, which is putting a reverse pressure on the education system to change their educational objectives and models, in particular content reformation.

What is needed is a realistic model of teaching-learning. Figure 7.2 gives a systems view of the two models of teaching-learning. The realistic model is based on feed-backward design and information processing approach, which recognizes that each learner and learning context is unique and learning occurs by leveraging the metacognitive elements of goal, strategy, self-regulation, self-efficacy, belief, and requirements' information complexity. The realistic model of education necessarily uses convergence technologies and attendant data generated to improve student learning experience and learning outcomes. The realistic feed-backward design has to have the capability to capture environmental data on a continuous basis, analyze, and act upon it by modifying the content, pedagogy, and delivery, and all of this is in real time. Insistently adhering to information processing

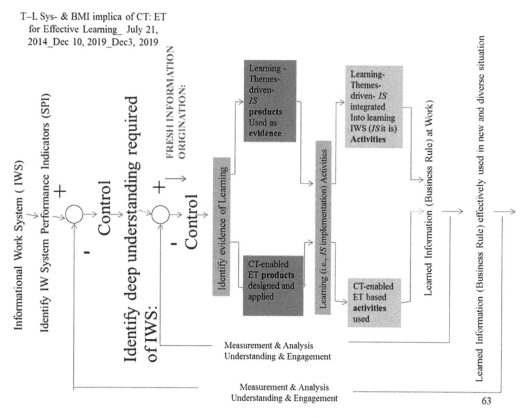

FIGURE 7.3
Process Flow for Feed-Backward Instructional Design (FBID)

approach this leads to laying out transformative, clear guidelines and requirements of data science, data mining, and learning analytics for smart educational systems.

Our framework for smart learning rests on the seven cognitive themes for education as stated by Bruning et al. (2014). Our model for smart learning environment takes into account students' stated educational goals, realistic industry connect that aids in achieving the goals, process-centric feed-backward instructional design (FBID; Figure 7.3) that factors both the global and the local needs (Mandke 2013), and additive curriculum structure that provides a mechanism for students to chart their own learning path to achieve their stated goals with self-monitoring and self-assessment by collaboratively engaging in executing realistic industry projects.

We next examine the challenges, technical, social, and economic, that arise in implementing EDM and LA into educational systems.

7.5 Socioeconomic and Technical Challenges in Adopting Learning Analytics in Educational Systems

There are technical challenges, data privacy and ownership issues as well as cost associated with data collection, storage and software required to mine and analyze the data, with the software itself undergoing continuous change. The inclusion of IoT technologies for ubiquitous sensing in learning environments gathering momentum, the quantity and characteristics of educational data will see an exponential growth drawing a strain on the AI and machine learning algorithms that that data science relies on. This section will discuss at length the technology limitations and proposes a way forward.

Bienkowski et al. (2012) briefly describe a few challenges likely to be faced during the process of adopting and integrating learning analytics into the educational system. In the context of cost associated with storage and making sense of data, identifying pertinent questions whose answers impact learning the most and aligning the questions with what data to collect is critical. Since information about learners and learning is complex, standards for data collection and storage is necessary to ensure no relevant data gets missed and different software can operate upon the data. EDM and LA also put additional demands on institutional human resources. While EDM and LA technologies can act on data, the data itself has to be collected, cleaned, and prepared in formats as required by database technologies. This entails significant human effort that leads to educational institutions allotting dedicated human resources. Further, the data itself has to be presented in an easily digestible form to stakeholders—students, teachers, administrators, governance—which would again need human intervention to configure the EDM and LA software to generate appropriate reports. There will always exist a tradeoff between privacy and personalization. The decision to store data on internal servers or on third-party servers of LA software providers, especially in the context of cloud computing, will entail additional steps to be taken for ensuring data security and privacy. Gursoy et al. (2017) discuss at length prevalent privacy protection methods and provides implementations of privacy-preserving learning analytics from two perspectives: anonymization of data and providing access to non-anonymized data through a privacy-preserving interface that serve as proofs of concepts.

Disparity in basic infrastructure can make it difficult to implement LA uniformly. Take the case of India; while there are several issues impacting implementation of LA, two issues are considered here (Ghosh, 2019; World Economic Forum, 2019). There is a rural-urban divide with respect to access to internet, as well as IT infrastructure in schools and colleges that can hamper effective LA implementation. Further, while 80% of the jobs are in the informal economy, only 20% are in the formal economy. This has an implication for the training sector engaged in reskilling and upskilling as a different nature of data unlike formal education data will be needed to be identified and analyzed for drawing insights.

7.6 Technology Limitations

In *The Economist* (11 June 2020; Thompson et al., 2020), we see various limitations being expressed about AI, machine learning, and deep learning, a machine learning method that has been responsible for much of the successes seen in areas of pattern recognition, speech recognition, and autonomous vehicles. The limitations can be summarized as follows:

- Despite being trained on very large data sets, machine learning algorithms still cannot handle the unexpected like humans can.

- Computer power used to train AI systems is accelerating, and it is becoming economically, technically, and environmentally unsustainable.

- Businesses are not finding investments in AI profitable or value creating.

Sutton (2019), based on the experiences of applying AI that relies on "human knowledge" and AI that uses searching and learning algorithms in the domain of gaming and speech recognition, opines that given the success of searching and learning algorithms, "we have to learn the bitter lesson that building in how we think we think does not work in the long run."

However, as AI begins to pervade much of human endeavors, there is a growing concern that machines may take over, more so if humans delegate decision-making entirely to machines, as has been seen with self-driving cars. Hannah Fry opines that while there is no doubt that AI can perform assigned tasks better than humans, the output itself may not be reliable if the underlying data is "biased" (*The Economist*, 8 April 2018).

The above contradictions, as well as observations regarding technology limitations, brings about a requirement to think about how open systems work. In an open system design, local and contextual information must be taken into consideration and become part of the database. One has to think of the system as a "system to be" rather than as a "system in being." A "system to be"' is a connectonmal system that facilitates integrating cognition with emotion.

The above suggests that putting together (Mokyr, 2001) how an open system thinks and (Harris, 2002) how everything works in long term is what gives maximal performance. And for this "togetherness" to happen, the system must be in a connectomnal mode and design in a feed-backward instructional design (FBID) mode. This instructional information processing approach can inform the instructional model for the domain of IoT as well as framework for IoT based EDM and LA.

7.7 Description of a Research-based Pedagogic Innovation for Learning Futures and Underlying Model for IoLT (Internet of Learning Things)–Driven EDM and LA

A proposed multidisciplinary project in *IoT Competency for Sustainability* capacity building, namely *Project IoT-Industry Linked Additive Green Curriculum (IoT-ILAGC) Development: Internationalized Higher Education in IoT Competency for Ecosystem- and Capacity-Sustainability*, is described. It is based on a proposal developed for Erasmus+ (Mandke, 2019), and our earlier experience implementing an international curriculum in nanoelectronics funded by Erasmus+ (NIIT University, 2016)

7.7.1 IoT: What's in It?

Internet of things (IoT) is an enabler of a future hyper-connected system, which individuals, groups, organizations, and business design implement to reduce risks they experience from environmental—external as well as internal—complexities and uncertainties.

In concrete terms, it is an end-to-end information processing set of interdependent sensors, actuators, smart objects, data communications, and interface technologies, which together allow (system) information—external as well as internal—to be collected, tracked, and processed across local and global network infrastructures. IoT makes workable the realistic model of teaching-learning, while e-learning is sufficient for the deductive model of teaching-learning.

7.7.2 IoT: What It Means to India?: GOI (Government of India) Planning for IoT Expansion in India

Given current global developments, GOI is implementing its plan of developing 100 smart cities and has also launched the Digital India Program (Meit, 2015). These together, have the following objectives:

- A massive expansion of IoT in a short time.
- Use IoT to automate solutions to problems faced by various industries like agriculture, health services, energy, security, disaster management, etc.
- Pursue smart city aspects of: smart parking, intelligent transport system, tele-care, women's safety, smart grids, smart urban lighting, waste management, smart city maintenance, digital-signage, water management.
- Transforming India into "digital empowered society and knowledge economy," which will act as a catalyst to boost the development of the IoT industry in the country.

7.7.3 GOI Planning for IoT Capacity Building in India

To achieve above objectives, from 2015 GOI has proposed IoT capacity building initiatives through creation of an IoT Education and Awareness program in the country to develop skill sets for IoT at all levels. In addition, the creation of an industry-academia platform to set up test beds and labs for IoT design, development, and testing is also proposed. This will help academia to share research-based specialized knowledge with industry. The academia will also get more conversant with the recent developments in industry.

7.7.4 IoT: What It Means to Countries Outside of India, EU as a Representative Group of Countries

Kearney (2015) states that for the EU, adopting IoT would result in an increase in GDP growth by 7 percentage points by 2025. The report says that this is due to value expected to be derived from three sources (Mokyr, 2001). *Increased productivity*: Analysis of real-time as well as historical data to coordinate connected remote objects will enable businesses to act earlier and at a lower cost (Harris, 2002). *Increased consumer purchasing power*: IoT-enabled objects will result in significant energy savings for end users as well as increase durability of products themselves and (Roy-Singh, 1991). *Freed-up time for individuals*: People will be freed from performance of repetitive tasks and the time released can be used to perform economically productive tasks. In addition, IoT will impact healthcare positively bringing health gains to people thus leading to a "multiplier" effect.

7.7.5 Proposed Project Framework: Industry Linked Additive Green Curriculum (ILAGC)

The opportunity of delivering (i) survivalist competitive advantage and (ii) sustainability by way of continuity planning constitutes the basis of the Learning-Information Work

(L-IW) integrating Pedagogic Integration Mechanism (PIM) activities for IoT system design processes futures.

Briefly, capacity building has to play an important role in defining the targets and executing the processes for achieving a sustainable future. More importantly, the process of education cannot remain detached from the real world. Therefore, the desired performance, as the outcome of the capacity building, must include the agility to cope up with the real-world information processing and decision-making scenarios.

In this regard, IoT-based systems and devices have much to offer. A broad composition for a typical IoT system would be the devices for collecting the real-world data, processing the data using AI and machine learning algorithms, and finally providing a human readable output. The applicability of IoT systems enables huge end-customer benefits in various application areas. At the same time, the implementation of an IoT system requires a different level of skill set to be developed amongst the students, which enhances their job prospects by enabling them to cater the real time data processing requirements of an end customer in a variety of ways. These interlinked situations constitute a challenge for the conventional university systems to innovate on the curriculum design in order to deliver much desired survivalist competitive-advantage based customer demands, as well as the demands of a sustainable future.

The proposed innovative curriculum is designed for capacity building systems and processes for future survivalist jobs via *Additive Curriculum* and for sustainable entities such as green environment via *Green Curriculum*, making it an Industry Linked Additive Green Curriculum (ILAGC).

7.7.6 Shift from Internet of Things to Internet of Learning Things

Traditionally, IoT is seen as a seamless internet enabled connected network of "embedded objects/devices, with identifiers, in which machine to machine (M2M) communication without any human intervention is aimed at using standard and interoperable communication protocols." But this view of IoT has a challenge. To give one significant context and individual situation— significant that human safety, particularly, is—from, say, the domain of smart connected car, on March 18, 2018, Uber, the ride-sharing company, was testing a vehicle in autonomous mode. It was traveling within the speed limit. One Ms. Herzberg, who was wheeling a bicycle, stepped suddenly into the car's path as seen in the recorded video later on. A human safety driver in the vehicle did not take manual control as the collision was not anticipated. More investigations are underway, but Uber suspended its autonomous vehicle testing in the meanwhile (*The Economist*, 22 March 2018).

A vehicle in an autonomous mode (AV) —a seamless internet-enabled connected network, which constitutes IoT—represents a complex system. Our work in integrity learning systems (Mandke, 2017) researches complex system failures by positioning latent failures (opportunities) models as learning errors (variabilities). In this context, one relevant finding is that a complex system is a potential source of information, and that a system's failure—which then is an information error, i.e., a learning error in the context of the failure setting—occurs due to consequences of interdependent, evolving, and conflicting trivial system environmental factors (system external and internal) that come together (as schemata) at the instant (moment) of the failure. The challenge is to incorporate design processes so that system learns about the latent failures in waiting to formalize adverse event (AE) that is evolving and controls the system performance by diffusing latent failures as well as the rise and occurrence of AE.

Our work informs that, going beyond the incumbent view of IoT, the above calls for restructuring this incumbent task-centric, restricted designability view of IoT into that of a process-centric, complex, extended designability, networked system view by reconstituting it (the incumbent, task-centric view) as composed of things, design (of objects, concepts, insights), people (training), behavior, norms and procedures, standards, policy, financial mechanisms, and the relations (informational functions) and interactions (informational interfaces) —rather interplays—among them. This calls for a shift from IoT to IoLT.

7.8 Emerging Insights Leading to Genesis of ILAGC

The ILAGC framework and model arose out of the following emerging insights.

7.8.1 Emerging Insight I: Rise of CT, Professional Competitiveness, and Emerging Requirement to Recast Curriculum Implementation to Prepare Students for *Learning Skills Futures*

Given the twenty-first century reality of convergence technology (CT) (Internet included) and with CT tools continually getting more miniaturized, faster, more efficient, and cheaper, every going day the world is having more of them and for survival—*learning that it requires*—individual, group, and business are routinely networking and evolving their structures to be decentralized and distributed, develop ecosystem focused performance indicators, and design processes for them, which in turn are automized *using* CT (Internet included)-enabled information delivery system. For professional competitiveness, this is requiring the workforce at all levels to transform into learning engineers by acquiring new knowledge and information processing competencies for driving newly emerging work processes and in respect of them motivating the self for the value creating performance enhancement and sustenance.

(*FICCI, NASSCOM, EY Report*, 2017) abundantly reinforces the above insight. Specifically, the publication analyzes that, under the impact of globalization, demographics, and Industry 4.0, in India by 2022 (i) 9% of professionals will be employed in new jobs roles that do not exist as of today, and (ii) 37% of professionals will be deployed in jobs that have drastically modified skill sets. Among many others, its surveys indicate the need for an "IoT Developer."

Understandably, *this* entirety of the capacity building requirements (all levels of Professions/Employment/Job Skills Futures'—Work Skill Futures' *for short*—that it addresses) *is* posing before institutions, academia, and teachers, *hitherto*, not addressed challenge; namely, *using* CT (I\internet included) as information delivery system to leverage extended instructional processes and recast external relationships of education and training, curriculum design and implementation so as to prepare students for learning skills of Work Wide Work Long (3WL), i.e., (for) learning skills futures.

7.8.2 Emerging Insight II: Requirement to Recast External Relationships of Curriculum Design and Implementation Necessitates Curriculum Emphasizing *Industry Connect and Environment Linkages*

While the need to recast external relationships of the curriculum is clear, what factors inform this recast are changes in industry and environment. Recast of external relationships of the curriculum emphasizing industry connect is achieved by integration of value creating experiential learning processes (which link classroom learning with industry work on the future front) into pure cognitive variables based traditional classroom learning. This type of recast emphasizes training the student for professions/employment/job skill futures abilities.

Recasting of external relationships of the curriculum emphasizing environment linkages derives its design strength from following logic. Environment means the surroundings in which individual, group, institution, business exist and perform. It includes every form of object—living and non-living thing—internal and in the ecosystem of the organization. The major environmental issue is environmental pollution—air, water, noise, soil. Sensitizing society to activities causing damage environment and measures to mitigate will also inform the domain of "smart environment."

The above proposition is valid and applicable for campus environments of educational institutions as well leading to smart campus which is an innovative application in the paradigm of *using* CT (internet, wireless sensory networks, cloud computing, and consumer electronics included). The concept of constructing a "smart campus" implies that the institution will adopt CT, mobile technologies, and social media to implement networked advanced information processing technologies to automatically monitor and control every facility on campus. Integrating teaching-learning instead of value adding from a traditionally practiced linear value chain, the teaching-learning (T-L) environment is transformed into value network (information flow digital) emphasizing value creation for classroom learning, in particular, and academics administration, in general, and *that* the energy consumed at all levels is minimized.

Understandably, the above once again calls for integration of teaching-learning processes, but now with processes of prospective, i.e., smart campus construction, operation and maintenance activities; in turn, this time, recasting external relationships of curriculum emphasizing environment linkages and creating value for academics.

7.8.3 Emerging Insight III: With the Rise of CT and Requirement for Industry Connect Emphasizing Curriculum, It Is the Processes of Learning That Are Changing

Specifically, cognitive science literature informs that, with speed of information processing increasing and with exponentially growing information—given the twenty-first century reality of the external relationships recasting convergence technology (internet included)—the codified knowledge orthodoxies are increasingly finding difficult to organize; makes both for teacher and student impossible and it is not useful to focus on "taking as much information as possible."

Within this framework and within the confines of the knowledge area of learning engineering (LE) that draws on cognitive science, systems engineering, and CT-enabled educational technology (ET), our LE research recognizes that instead a focus on teaching-design and learning-outcomes by way of contextual and individual situation of learning, which is always at sharp-end of learning to decide on (i) customer and his/her survivalist and sustenance benefits; (ii) for it determining desired (not actual) performance improvement processes; (iii) and, in the context a focus on learning to network, learning to undertake T-L interplay, learning to implement processing centric T-L through learning to think, learning to learn, learning to collaborate, and learning to regulate, learning to implement metacognitive learning processes, and learning to integrate *value creating experiential learning* into instruction becomes significant.

Further, these learning outcomes should operate on information and learning processes so as to deliver value creating knowledge progression as demanded by future desired work performance and employability skills.

For future skills it is required is to move on from the incumbent subtractive curriculum to additive curriculum, under which learning takes place only and only if knowledge is constructed and processed in a new way to deliver benefits and value creation to customer.

7.8.4 Emerging Insight IV: Change in Learning Processes Is Leading to the Construct of Additive Curriculum

In formal education, a curriculum is the planned engagement of students with instructional content, materials, resources, and processes and activities for assessing the attainment of educational objectives. Specifically, the planned engagement outlines the skills, performances, attitudes, and values students are expected to learn from program pursuing. In the process, it makes declarative statements of desired study outcomes, descriptions of materials, and the planned sequence that will be used to help students attain the outcomes.

Within the above framework, a subtractive curriculum is a process by which teachers teach and students learn by semester-to-semester cutting, i.e., delivering and completing, respectively, contents and learning outcomes from a well-defined course structure, and similarly structured course packages, under a pre-determined program structure. Traditionally, the subtractive curriculum content is delivered by lecture and practical method using chalk and blackboard and laboratory, but is most typically done using e-learning technologies. Given this, subtractive curriculum specifies students by collective (and not unique) learning requirements.

With the rise of twenty-first century CT, as explained above, this incumbent, proven curriculum, which sees learners' learning requirements as a collective, is under stress on account of both learner as well as teacher; the codified knowledge orthodoxies increasingly finding difficult to organize. This is because it is becoming—both for teacher and student—impossible and not useful to focus on "taking as much information as possible."

At a more basic level, the stress is because cognitive science, advances in brain science, systems engineering, and educational technology (ET) literature inform that it *is* when students make meaning and sense of what they are being taught in classes that they (students) experience improved learning experience, which is the cause and consequence of *all* learning. Drawing on *this* research and (in contrast to the subtractive curriculum's collective view of learners learning requirements) recognizing that (i) learners' brains are unique; (ii) all brains are not equal because context and because individual situation and ability influence learning; (iii) the brain is changed by information origination and processing experience; and (recognizing *that*) (iv) learning takes place when brain connects new information to old information. This clear in part due to 2013 NU's ET discipline learning engineering (LE) research, which has put in place a hybrid combination with traditional lectures and practical methods designed for various industry connections and environment linkages, driving brain-aligned project-based learning (PBL) and implementing innovative pedagogic initiatives (PI) [PI-PBLs for short] in classroom/laboratory instruction *using* convergence-technology-(CT)-enabled ET (*ET*). The brain aligned PI-PBL's being constructed *endogenous* to the context & individual situation of learning and not exogenous as in case of subtractive curriculum).

Specifically, the feed-backward form of instruction, as illustrated in Figure 7.3 in this case, starts with (a) determining end deliverables desired, i.e., futures; (b) followed by analyzing and measuring, for the purpose, performance future requirements; (c) leading to obtaining the gap between the desired, i.e., requirements in the future and the actual, i.e., of the moment requirements; (d) further leading to originating information to reduce this gap—this originated information comprising already known information (in this case learning is nil), linearly predicted information (in this case learning is small), and prospective, i.e., future and non-linearly predicted information (in this case learning is huge); (e) followed by designing/constructing brain-aligned (learning-themes driven) instructional engagements to originate this information using ET as information delivery system; (f) further followed by implementing learning activities using ET as information delivery system so as to implement the designed/constructed engagements; and to finally (g) undertake informational work (IW), i.e., business work. This leads to the delivery of productive economic activity (PEA), which is leveraged through processes of sustainable continuity planning.

Against this, we propose an *additive curriculum model*, which evolves out of the brain aligned PI-PBLs (Pedagogic Innovation-Project Based Learning), and is a process, which:

- First, is entirely implemented *using* convergence technology (internet included) – driven brain-aligned educational technology (ET) as information delivery system;
- Second, the process at the start necessarily identifies a customer to be served/ addressed, when the customer may be a student/worker, teacher/work-supervisor, employer, institution, industry, community, or the society, as the case may be;
- Third, (for the identified customer) further identifies desired benefit(s) to be delivered at the process end (or intermittently); and (for it),
- Fourth, the desired final (or intermittent) value creation(s) and, in the context, the required knowledge progression stages.

Based on this and for the objective(s) of delivering desired final (intermittent) benefit(s) and improved experience(s) to customer(s), the additive curriculum model process, then:

- Fifth, through-the-semesters-identified-courses requires teachers (in their roles as mentor/guide) to plan student engagements for learning by pedagogically linking classroom-industry as a part of assessment and (requires) students in research-and-discovery-mode of learning to construct, i.e., deliver and complete, in semester-to-semester layers the planned engagements with digitally driven instructional content, materials, resources, and processes and activities for assessment of the attainment of flexible learning objectives such that the pre-designated benefits are demonstratively delivered to participating and contributing industry.

7.8.5 Summarizing: ILAGC: IoLT Curriculum Design in Brief

It may be observed that in the purview of additive curriculum as well as green curriculum, feed-backward instruction design (FBID) approach needs to be employed. In case of additive curriculum, which leverages survivalist competitive advantage under an FBID approach, the project involves designing the stages in the format of yearly curriculum advancement in the courses. The necessary progression requirement on yearly or semester basis is decided to deliver intermediate work outcomes at appropriate semester and year points and end-work performance of direct interest to collaborating industry at the end of the degree program.

Understandably, this pedagogic process will include defining the problem statement, identification of the courses, content development, and so on. Similar would be the case with green curriculum, too. For example, the content for achieving and managing a green campus requires setting up the sensors network for monitoring the soil moisture content, nutrition content, humidity, temperature of the environment, and so on. The data collected through various sensors needs further processing to be consumed by a human operator or to be provided to automated control systems forming a feedback loop. The design, implementation and operation of such a system involves topics covered or additional topics to be covered in multiple courses, such as say Fundamentals of Electronics Engineering, Instrumentation and Control, Sensing Technologies, Big Data Analysis, AI, Machine Learning, Database Management Systems, and so on.

Finally, the curriculum engages the students in real-world problem solving and exposes them to specific challenges. The approach of delivery to the end customer enhances the skills of students as well as of the teacher, enabling improvement in teaching-learning system performance. The essential qualities required for professional development of a student is enhanced with a higher order interdisciplinary knowledge creation within the system. The real-world deliverable amplifies the impact of the curriculum enabling a method for future design of education.

The evaluation and assessment are also an important part of any curriculum. Since, this curriculum is developed as certificates with industry linkages, industry partners will play an important role in evaluation and assessment. The benchmarks for the assigning grades and so on are developed within the university framework. The course content is delivered using ICT and digitally available online for the interested audience. It will also be available for improvement and modifications via an open-source policy.

7.8.6 How Does Designing Realistic T-L Systems Through Feed-Backward Instruction Design Framework Inform Data Science and Analytics?

As incumbent data mining and analytics have addressed automation of predictably smart instruction and business work processes, value stream stake holders can now commit available information processing resources for smart, further data mining and analytics that it calls, higher-order complex thinking making competitive and continuity planning – survivalist's opportunity, safety, and sustainability delivering. So the new challenge for data science, data mining, and analytics involves deriving meaning and sense of realistically integrating instruction process and business process using educational technology, including internet-enabled convergence technology, as information delivery system deliver amazing benefit and experience to the learner.

7.9 Conclusion

The chapter traced the forces that shape education, discussed the domain of datasScience as is being applied to education currently, along with the tools and technologies for discovering patterns, gaining insights from these patterns, predictions based on the patterns and modeling learners' knowledge, skills, behavior, and experience including user profiling. It also dwelled upon visual data analytics that deal with the creation of meaningful dashboards for learners, teachers, academic leaders, and education administrators. It identified the shortcomings in incumbent education system based on research and proposed the new framework of additive curriculum using feed-backward instructional design approach that can inform the domain of data science as applicable to education and calls for a shift from internet of things (IoT) to internet of learning things (IoLT).

References

Abdi, Solmaz, Khosravi Hassan, Sadiq Shazia and Gasevic, Dragan. 2020. *Complementing Educational Recommender Systems with Open Learner Models.* In *Proceedings of the Tenth International Conference on Learning Analytics & Knowledge (LAK '20).* Association for Computing Machinery, New York, NY, USA, 360–365. doi: doi:10.1145/3375462.3375520

Anderson, Terry. 2009. *Towards a Theory of Online Learning. Book Chapter in The Theory and Practice of Online Learning* (2nd ed.). AU Press, Canada.

Aurobindo, Sri and the Mother. 1956. *Sri Aurobindo and the Mother on Education.* Sri Aurobindo Ashram Press, Pondicherry.

Bender, William N. and Waller, Laura. 2011. The New Differentiated Instruction: Changing The Way Teachers Teach. Book Chapter in The Teaching Revolution: RTI, Technology, and Differentiation Transform Teaching for the 21st Century, Corwin.

Bienkowski, Marie, Mingyu Feng, Barbara Means. 2012. Enhancing Teaching and Learning Through Educational Data Mining and Learning Analytics: An Issue Brief.; Center for Technology in Learning SRI International. U.S. Department of Education, Office of Educational Technology.

Bruning, R.H., Schraw, G.J., Norby, M.M. and Ronning, R.R. 2014. *Cognitive Psychology and Instruction.* 4th. Pearson.

Eyman, Alyahyan and Dilek, Düştegör. 2020. Predicting academic success in higher education: literature review and best practices. *International Journal of Educational Technology in Higher Education* 17, 3. doi:10.1186/s41239-020-0177-7

FICCI, NASSCOM, EY Report. 2017. Future of Jobs in India – A 2022 Perspective. http://ficci.in/spdocument/22951/FICCI-NASSCOM-EY-Report_Future-of-Jobs.pdf (last accessed September 2020)

Freeman, Scott, Eddy, Sarah L., McDonough, Miles, Smith, Michelle K., Okoroafor, Nnadozie, Jordt, Hannah and Wenderoth, Mary Pat. June 2014. Active learning increases student performance in science, engineering, and mathematics. *PNAS* 111 (23): 8410–8415.

Future of Consumption in Fast-Growth Consumer Markets: INDIA. 2019. A report by the World Economic Forum's System Initiative on Shaping the Future of Consumption Prepared in collaboration with Bain & Company.

Ghosh, Mayuri. 2019. The three biggest challenges for India's future. World Economic Forum Annual Meeting. https://www.weforum.org/agenda/2019/01/India-biggest-future-three-challenges-consumption/ (accessed September 25 2020)

Grunspan, D. Z., Wiggins, B. L., and Goodreau, S. M. 2014. Understanding classrooms through social network analysis: a primer for social network analysis in education research. *CBE Life Sciences Education*, 13(2), 167–179. doi:10.1187/cbe.13-08-0162

Gursoy, M. E., Inan, A., Nergiz M. E. and Saygin Y. 2017. Privacy-preserving learning analytics: challenges and techniques. *IEEE Transactions on Learning Technologies*, 10, (1), pp. 68–81. doi: 10.1109/TLT.2016.2607747.

Harris, John. 2002. *Brief History of American Academic Credit System: A Recipe for Incoherence in Student Learning.* https://eric.ed.gov/?id=ED470030

Hendel-Giller, Ronni, Hollenbach, Cindy, D. Marshall, Kathy Oughton, Tamra Pickthorn, M. W. Schilling and Giulietta Versiglia. 2010. *The Neuroscience of Learning: A New Paradigm for Corporate Education.* The Martiz Institute White Paper

Hoel, T. and Mason, J. 2018. Standards for smart education – towards a development framework. *Smart Learning Environment* 5, 3 doi:10.1186/s40561-018-0052-3.

Irizarry, R. A. 2020. The role of academia in data science education. *Harvard Data Science Review*, 2(1). doi:10.1162/99608f92.dd363929

Kearney A. T. 2015. The Internet of Things- A New Path to European Prosperity, *Whitepaper.* https://iofthings.org/whitepaper/the-internet-of-things-a-new-path-to-european-prosperity/ (last accessed September 2020)

Klašnja-Milićević, Aleksandra, Ivanović, Mirjana and Budimac, Zoran. 2017. Data science in education: big data and learning analytics. *Computer Applications in Engineering Education*, 25: 1066–1078. doi:10.1002/cae.21844

Maitra, Subir. 2016. An investigation into the quality of technical education in India. PhD diss., University of Calcutta. http://hdl.handle.net/10603/185731 https://shodhganga.inflibnet.ac.in/handle/10603/185731

Mandke, Vijay. 2013. Feed-Backward-Instructional-Design-(FBID)- Framework for Networked-ET-System automated Cognitive-themes- and Business-Information-Flow-Themes- driven and Multiple-Intelligences-integrated Information Processing: Beyond e-Learning based ET: Networked ET System Development. Lecture # 14: Topics in Integrity Learning Systems. Educational Technology Area, NIIT University.

Mandke, Vijay. 2017. *Integrity Learning System – Course Handout*. NIIT University

Mandke, Vijay. 2019. A Project Proposal for Erasmus+ – IoT based Industry Linked Additive Green Curriculum (IoT-ILAGC) Development: Internationalized Higher Education in IoT Competency for Ecosystem and Capacity Sustainability in Asian Universities. Proposal developed for Erasmus+. NIIT University.

Martín Adrián C, Alario-Hoyos, Carlos and Kloos, Carlos D. 2019. Smart Education: A Review and Future Research Directions. 13th International Conference on Ubiquitous Computing and Ambient Intelligence UCAmI, Proceedings 31, (1): 57. doi:10.3390/proceedings2019031057.

Mazur, E. 1997. *Peer Instruction: A User's Manual*. Delhi, India: Prentice Hall. ISBN 0-13-565441-6

Meit Y. 2015. Draft Policy on Internet of Things. Ministry of Electronics & Information Technology, Government of India. https://www.meity.gov.in/writereaddata/files/Revised-Draft-IoT-Policy%20%281%29_0.pdf (accessed November 04 2020).

Mokyr, Joel. 2001. The rise and fall of the factory system: technology, firms, and households since the industrial revolution. *Carnegie-Rochester Conference Series on Public Policy*, 55, 1: 1–45, ISSN 0167-2231. doi:10.1016/S0167-2231(01)00050-1.

National Academies of Sciences, Engineering and Medicine. 2018. Envisioning the Data Science Discipline: The Undergraduate Perspective: Interim Report. The National Academies Press. doi: 10.17226/24886.

NIIT University. 2016. International Nanoelectronics Project @ NU – Industry Connect Based Course Planning Approach. Erasmus+ Project. https://www.niituniversity.in/academics/relevant-links/partnerships/research/

Omer, S., Hickson, G., Taché, S., Blind, R., Masters, S., Loeser, H., Souza, K., Mkony, C., Debas, H. and O'Sullivan, P. 2008, Applying innovative educational principles when classes grow and resources are limited. *Biochemistry and Molecular Biology Education*, 36: 387–394. doi:10.1002/bmb.20210

Open Future – Algorithms should take into account, not ignore, human failings. 8 April 2018. https://www.economist.com/open-future/2019/04/08/algorithms-should-take-into-account-not-ignore-human-failings (accessed October 17 2020).

Roy-Singh, Raja. 1991. *Education for the twenty-first century: Asia-Pacific perspective*. UNESCO, 93 p. Asia and the Pacific Programme of Educational Innovation for Development, Bangkok

Salmon, G. 2019. May the fourth be with you: creating education 4.0 *Journal of Learning for Development*, 6(1), 95–115.

Saqr, Mohammed. 2018. Using Learning Analytics to Understand and Support Collaborative Learning. PhD Diss., Stockholm University, Faculty of Social Sciences, Department of Computer and Systems Sciences. ORCID iD: 0000-0001-5881-3109. (http://su.diva-portal.org/smash/record.jsf?pid=diva2%3A1245435&dswid=7643)

Shoikova, Elena, Nikolov, Roumen and Kovatcheva, Eugenia. 2017 Conceptualising of smart education. *Electrotechnica & Electronica*, 3–4.

Singh, Jaswant. 2014. Right to education in India _ an evaluative study with special reference to the implementation aspects of right to education act 2009 in Mandi District of Himachal Pradesh. PhD diss., Himachal Pradesh University. http://hdl.handle.net/10603/127683 https://shodhganga.inflibnet.ac.in/handle/10603/127683

Smith, K. A., Sheppard, S. D., Johnson, D. W. and Johnson, R. T. 2005. Pedagogies of engagement: classroom-based practices. *Journal of Engineering Education*, 94: 87–101. doi:10.1002/j.2168-9830.2005.tb00831.x

Sutton, Rich. 13 March 2019. The Bitter Lesson. http://incompleteideas.net/IncIdeas/BitterLesson.html (accessed October 17 2020)

Thompson, Neil C., Greenwald, Kristjan, Lee, Keeheon and Manso, Gabriel F. 2020. The Computational Limits of Deep Learning. https://arxiv.org/pdf/2007.05558.pdf (accessed October 17 2020)

Viberg, Olga, Khalil, Mohammad, and Baars, Martine. 2020. Self-regulated learning and learning analytics in online learning environments: A Review of Empirical Research. 10.1145/3375462.3375483.

Weiman, E. Carl. June 2014. Large-scale comparison of science teaching methods sends clear message. *Commentary. PNAS* 111 (23). http://www.pnas.org/content/111/23/8319

Winne, P.. 2017. Learning Analytics for Self-Regulated Learning. In Lang, C., Siemens, G., Wise, A. F., and Gaevic, D., editors, *The Handbook of Learning Analytics*, pages 241–249, 1 edition. Society for Learning Analytics Research (SoLAR), Alberta, Canada.

Zhu, Z., Yu, M. and Riezebos, P. 2016. A research framework of smart education. *Smart Learning Environment* 3, 4. doi:10.1186/s40561-016-0026-2

8

Spectral Characteristics and Behavioral Analysis of Deep Brain Stimulation by the Nature-Inspired Algorithms

V. Kakulapati

Sreenidhi Institue of Science and Technology, Hyderabad, India

Sheri Mahender Reddy

Otto-Friedrich university of Bamberg, Bamberg, Germany

CONTENTS

8.1 Introduction

Deep brain stimulation (DBS) is a procedure to implant a system that delivers electric impulses to body activity areas in the brain. Electrodes are placed deep within the brain and then connected to a pacemaker. DBS is an attempt to construct a working brain or brain-machine model, though the transmission of neuronal signals on this scale's networks cannot be replicated at the moment, even if one uses the most efficient supercomputers possible.

DBS treatment focuses on both correct neurosurgical goals and the systemic optimization of interventions to produce significant clinical effects. The development of DBS arrays with electrodes separated along and around the DBS lead is a recent move forward to enhance targeting. However, increasing the number of different electrodes raises the technical difficulty of effectively maximizing stimulus parameters. DBS's therapeutic effectiveness depends not only on the successful implantation of one or more electrode leads into deep brain locations, but also on specifying conditions for stimulation to reduce symptoms without causing adverse effects. DBS's design tends to lead with electrolytes spread both along and around the cell's dart is a new investigation which could resolve both aspects of the design [1].

DBS decreased neuronal function and diminished the target nucleus's output due to the likenesses between the result of applying a high-frequency stimulus and the lesion of the same brain region. This was confirmed by test results indicating a decreased neuronal activation at the stimulus site, likely by triggering receptor projections in the target region [2, 3]. In contrast, the downstream neuronal activity of one of the most crucial target nuclei used to treat Parkinson's symptoms increased during high-frequency stimulation: subthalamic nuclei [4]. This is reflected in a subsequent regeneration or down-regulation of neuronal function based upon whether the transmission was either excitatory or inhibitory from the target nucleus to the corresponding nuclear [5, 6]. The investigator's anticipate that the treatment will be used by other neurodegenerative disease types, including Alzheimer's.

Alzheimer's disease (AD) is the utmost prevalent neurosurgical disorder of AD and is characterized by decades of decreased memory and cognitive performance. Even though significant evolution has been completed over the last three decades in understanding AD's histological, genetic, and radiographic characteristics, therapeutics have accomplished little. Present diagnosis methods attempt to improve acetylcholine supply, reverse biological and metabolic changes, or remove or avoid amyloids and tau deposition. DBS has been able to affect the operation of primary limbic circuits in AD.

The symptoms of Alzheimer's are an indication of physicians and clinicians' opinions that these symptoms constitute important DA components and substantially affect both patients and caregivers [7]. Known neuropsychiatric symptoms like apathy, depression, aggressiveness, anxiety, sleep disturbances, and psychosis are the main symptoms of AD present in many degrees throughout the disease [8]. In the initial prodromic stage of insignificant perceptive dysfunction, basic neuropsychiatry and behavioral disorders can also have predictive effects. Maybe in the elderly, the incidence of AD increases twofold [9].

In order to illumine pathogenesis illnesses or prognostic awareness of the symptoms, as mentioned earlier, the main neuropsychiatric and behavioral symptoms of AD will be examined. Dementia is a result of numerous mechanisms, including aberrant amyloid therapy [10]. Due to apolipoprotein E deficiency alleles, changes in lipid metabolism [11], hyperphosphorylation of the tau [12], misfolding of protein [13], vascular dysfunction pressure is seen [14]. There have been important neuropsychiatric effects and pathogens mechanisms, oxidative stress, and functions controlled by many AD-associated genes [15]. Such receptors can influence neural networks that overlap and cause the imbalance of illness and the diversity of neurodevelopmental disorders. The analysis of disorder is done using:

- The use of perturbation theory–stacked automotive encoders to design calculations and Spektral functions.
- Hippocampus structure surface meshes created from segmented MRI.
- The surface correspondence point-to-point is formed by spectral equivalence among populations (NC, AD, EMCI, LMCI).

The relations are modeled as graphs in a spectral type, matching method and the separate breakdown of these graphs to enable one to compare related characteristics. The coordinates of vertex are used to form feature descriptors until the matched surfaces are formed. Then, a nonlinear, low-dimensional embedding of the structure features is accomplished by the variational autoencoder (VAE). At the same time, a multilayer perceptron (MLP) classification is equipped to model class nonlinear decision borders.

The second process in work determines how to use facts from the first method to draw interpretation through the artificial neural network (ANN), which is simultaneously a typical nonlinear conclusion restricted boundary of the early stage of feature extraction between groups. This method can be comparable to the factual consolidation and the validity of the expert's theory. ANN-based methodologies provide computers with the highest computer output in a reasonable time to process a high quantity of information. The excellent use of ANN in resolving medical problems increases the efficiency and quality of healthcare very effectively. Furthermore, ANN's intrinsic solidity and adaptability to various involvement and productivity relationships promote their usage of decision-making in the healthcare field [16].

When evaluating and analyzing images of MRI in the brain to identify tumors or blocks in the brain, we show that the spectral characteristics of patient brain pictures are restored. Swarm intelligence models are called natural swarm-based computational models. To date, many swarm intelligence models have been suggested by literature and applied successfully to several real-life applications based on various wild swarm systems. To optimize brain image functionality, use the Swarm optimization in this analysis. The study shows that after preproduction extraction and ANN classification, objective diagnosis is significantly increased, and the probability of developing a diagnostic system with the help of computers is established.

8.2 Related Work

Cognitive abilities are based on the action of a wide variety of spatial scales, ranging from the nanometer scales of atoms and molecules to the entire organism meter scales [17]. Although a single gas molecule is not substituted with one another, the gas's general behavior is not changed. Changes in a DNA molecule, as with Huntington's disease, can change the brain drastically. Mechanical models can serve as "conveys between various levels of understanding," such as in the Huxley model, in which the characteristics of molecules incorporated in the cell membrane describe axonal action-potential propagation.

The incidence of AD worldwide has risen considerably as the health hazard increases in life expectancy [18]. This is distinguished by neurofibrillary envelopes of nerves, changes of synaptic communication, and mortality in neuro parenchyma nerves [19]. At present, sluggish or reverse AD progression is not feasible therapy. Also, neurodegeneration's underlying development cannot be stopped by any medications developed today to treat AD symptoms [20]. Several non-pharmaceutical techniques, including DBS [21], are currently being tested [22].

Various Alzheimer DBS targets were established, including immediate pre-fornix areas, entorhinal cortex (EC), and Meynert nucleus basalis (NBM). Many investigations have shown that DBS can induce metabolic effects through physiological networks in the memory pathway and influence the aspects of memory functionality.

Six NBM stimulation patients with AD were further stimulated in a combined 4-week, double-blind, 11-month, open-label investigation [23]. Four out of six patients reacted to the treatment at 12 months. The authors reported. However, a Phase 2 randomized, DBS double-blind fornix analysis in insignificant AD did not establish any substantial distinction in the 12-month primary cognitive result measurement between active and flawless stimulation. This research has shown statistically significant associations between patient age and clinical outcomes and show a trend towards better memory and metabolism for patients over 65 years at 12 months. An assessment of which DBS patients would respond and not is an active study field. In reality, the mutables that affect outcomes include essential neuroanatomic substrates, surgical procedure, lead location, choice of the target group, and outcome calculation. DBS clinical research may also face inherent challenges.

The advantages of DBS are well known as well as proven therapy for treating movement disorders that are medically refractory, as is the case with dementia disease [24], simple tremor [25], and dystonia [26]. Tourette syndrome also has a low prevalence and a relatively low level of severe complication [27], obesity, and chronical illnesses, such as neurological or psychiatric conditions like depression [28].

Present cognitive simulations and neural networks are primarily biophysical input variables and consider the neurons' electrophysiology, for example the processing of dendritic input, the ionic basis of the electrical excitability exegetic input processes such as the DBS signal [29, 30]. Conversely, certain models neglect neuronally and biophysically transcriptional data, representing the neural cycle of phenomena like synchronization [31] as a phase network of oscillators. Biophysical considerations like rapid and enduring temporal dependency in thwarting behavior, for example refractory and explosive, are not considered in these techniques. They do offer insight into the network's dynamic and are additional convenient for regulating strategy over biophysical models. In conclusion, a strictly data-driven approach has been adopted by several researchers to model only the timeframe among data-carrying activities captured in neuronal networking rather than prototypical the biophysical processes leading to spike generation. The key events are the abrupt spikes in the "action potentials" [32] neuronal transmembrane voltage. Modulate both superficial (for example external stimulus, DBS signal) and inherent (for example the proprietary neuron) and adjacent neuron antiquity, influences, and capture temporal dependency in neuronal activity.

In patients with neurosurgical epilepsy [33], stimulation was applied in entorhinal encoding and post-for-nix stimulation [34]. An alternative strategy is to perform minor adaptive experiments that may routinely change multiple treatment variables. Stimulation protocols are used because, even in the few memory tests performed to date, significant variability can be seen. For example, a 50 HZ stimulation was applied unilaterally for 5 seconds, one-sided theta-burst stimulation was used for long periods (20 minutes or more), and continuous bilateral stimulation was applied at 130 Hz [35]. Additional new therapies should also be used to allow more accurate neuronal circuit modulation in disease models. A recent study has shown that directly optogenetic stimulation of hippocampum memory engram cells in early AD transgenic mouse models results in memory recovery [36].

Therefore, in the clinical sense, quantitative EEG analyses may be helpful. For example, decreases in dominant and secondary strength and intensifications in frequencies are well known to be linked to brain impairment and intellectual disabilities [37]. Scientific investigations have shown that AD is known pre-symptomatically as mild cognitive impairment (MCI), and clinical symptoms remain subtle when neuronal degeneration occurs. Therefore, early comport cognitive and pharmacological interventions that may improve illness, based on clinical evidence, should not be conducted on their own [38]. Nevertheless, comprehensive literature indicates that such medications cause electroencephalographic readings to be changed, which summarizes various pharmacological drugs' expected results from recent studies [39]. Specifically, neuronic hyperexcitability or drowsiness may be triggered by medicines that affect the nervous system and, such as psycholeptics and psychoanalytic, EEG habits may change [40].

Nevertheless, it was proved that the remaining EEG behavior could predict potential cognitive declines or dementia conversion in highly reliable MCI subjects [41]. Moreover, spectral analyses to differentiate AD against other dementias are suggested from recent studies [42]. The research uses several EEG indications, for instance, supernatural strength, accuracy, and frequencies, which in many studies were regarded as useful markers of group classification [43]. Though, the additional EEG functions inestigated that the huge samples, often not easily obtained, are required. Besides, several EEG studies with QEEG analysis differs in validation, size of sample, techniques, derived characteristics, and methods [44] for classification.

8.3 About Brain Simulation of Alzheimer's Disease

The nervous system is a complicated neural structure. There are many space neural areas in this network that can be studied in various ways: conducting a systematic analysis, investigating these brain regions' functional connectivity, and identifying the connectivity of these functions to structural connectivity [45]. Researchers explore fMRI use to perform spatiotemporal analysis to create connexions between various neural regions of different mental states.

AD is a complicated persistent brain disorder that causes several clinical phenomena and has implications for multiple brain systems. Increasingly more brain areas and intellectual disabilities are impaired as the disease progresses. Cognitive impairment and the incremental impairment of everyday life tasks contribute to a rise in patient dependence. AD-related neuropsychiatric symptoms (NPS) appear to adopt a more extreme path of time, which they share with cognitive and functional deterioration. However, more significant variability is observed in behavioral changes and evolution patterns than the decline in cognition and function. Furthermore, as calculated using the mini-mental state test (MMSE) or the Alzheimer's Disease Evaluation Scale (ADAS-Cog), there is an ambiguous association between NPS and cognitive impairment (Figure 8.1).

8.3.1 Perceptual Variations Over Life

AD is marked by a decrease in interacting directly active intellect and preservation, and an increase to late-life crystallized mind. Dimensions of psychiatric disorders start at an early age, but the incidence of disability varies greatly among the individuals.

8.3.2 Cognitive Domains Differently Decline

The efficiency of cognitive abilities metrics such as intellectual dealing out speeds, employed remembrance, recalling, and preservation of aesthetic and oral knowledge (culture and remembering). Specifically, memory of the Visuospace and thinking in individual adults between the ages of 20–30 years [59–60] are beginning to decrease.

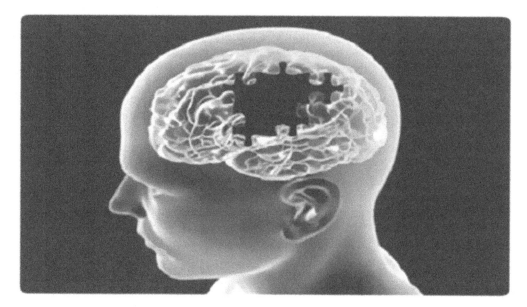

FIGURE 8.1
The Alzheimer's Disease Patient Brain Sample

These neurological issues can influence ingenuity, logical thought, and new ability to solve problems.

This transition can impact the acceleration and performance of new knowledge processing and storage; it can translate into a reduced rate of learning and measured processing of memories and knowledge.

8.3.3 Preserved Intelligence Results

By means of age, the build-up and acquisition of greater information will boost output in crystallized intelligence measurements.

Better crystallized intelligence displays enhanced or stable outcomes in experiments of particular procedures, such as learned skills, semantic information, world data, reading, and vocabulary between the ages of 50 and 70. These cognitive levels continue to rely on the efficient retrieval of stored procedures and records; data storage loss is not considered a natural part of mental maturity (Figure 8.2).

8.3.4 Symptoms

Perceptual symptoms include: deterioration of mind, concentration problems and learning, uncertainty during the night period, illusion, dizziness, oblivion, composition, inconsistency, trouble focused, incapacity to build new memories, incapacity to math, or to identify common stuff.

8.3.4.1 Conduct

This includes hostility, anger, difficulties in self-care, restlessness, nonsensical use of one's own vocabulary, shifts of personality, restlessness, inadequate discipline, or running and roaming. Mood: anger, resentment, general frustration, depression or swings in mood.

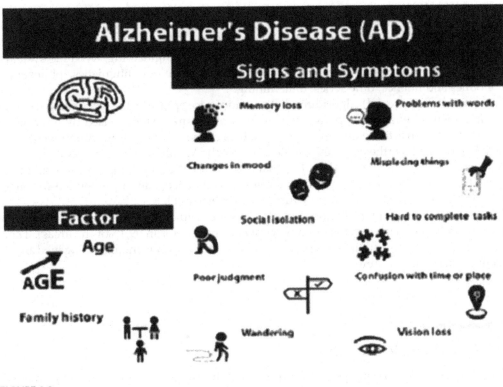

FIGURE 8.2
Alzheimer's Disease Symptoms

8.3.4.2 Emotional

Examaples are hopelessness, illusion, or mistrust.

8.3.4.3 Communal

In this symptom, an individual cannot mix muscle movements, pain, or poor appetite.

Behavioral method to patients and carers in general, including context generalization; routines; maintaining a secure, calm, and coherent atmosphere for carers; using techniques like calming engagement, a redirection to pleasurable and environment-friendly activities and reassurance, offering only knowledge that is needed in a way that the patient will appreciate.

8.4 Methodology

Most suffer from mild forgetfulness or delays in memory that are part of the natural cognitive decline. It is also difficult for us all to recall a word or the name of someone. However, people with Alzheimer's or another dementia are gradually symptomatic and severe.

The ANN [46] is inherited from the organic nervous system and stimulates the human brain behavior. It applies different learning processes that are suitable for problems in real life. The neural network has multidivisional applications covering IT, artificial intelligence, mathematics, the theory of approximation, optimization, engineering, dynamic systems, mathematical engineering, neurobiology, cognitive psychology, linguistics, philosophy, economics and finance, time series, data mining.

Swam Intelligence (SI) algorithms better choose to optimize the evaluation process within a method wrapper approach for a subset of features. Models used by wrapper to determine the consistency and representative bias of the ML algorithms are prevented by the FS method. Nevertheless, they also need to use the ML algorithm to assess the selected function subsets' consistency. Thus, the goal is to decide the increasing subset of all possible features provides the best predictive output when used with a predefined ML algorithm to optimize the FS procedure within a wrapper model.

The brain's independent regions' spectral profiles typically consist of more than one continuum (more than one cluster conveys spectral behavior in 99,1% of the areas). There is a minimum of one peak in any spectrum. Each brain region is therefore engaged in different modes of the continuum.

8.5 Implementation Results

For evaluation and the analysis of the proposed approach on a popular brain imaging dataset of AD from Kaggle, the dataset should be cleaned to delete redundant records from dataset preprocessing. In Alzheimer's disease, apathy and depression are the most common types of NPS. Although there are various methods for diagnosing geropsychiatric disease and assessing the severity and progression of depression care, these tests remain imperfect. Numerous therapies are still used in AD patients for depression, in pharmacological and non-pharmacological situations.

Some preprocessing and transformation to ensure that the data is predictable. We utilized 10 attributes, namely age, gender, and financial stability, as input to our model. Moreover, the class function was the expected class based on the input features. The following Table 8.1 displays the associated data set disorder. The result was the AD assessment score, provided the feature sequence as the input, which contained implied information required for evaluation. We made the argument that we have an AD with a feature sequence function of a set of tokens.

The useful tool for the diagonalization of Alzheimer's disease is artificial neural network approaches and discriminatory approaches. The results of our study show that artificial neural networks can discriminate against healthy controls against AD patients. The finally developed ANN with multiple information, including epidemiological and neuropsychological parameters and biomarkers, has achieved high diagnostic accuracy and performance. It can be used as a cheap instrument for the diagnosis and testing of AD. In conclusion, a predator-prey particle swarm optimization was proposed to train the classifier's weights and biases (Figures 8.3–8.15, and Table 8.2).

TABLE 8.1

Feature Evaluation

Feature	ID	Age	Sex	Family history	Financial stability	Medical history	Marital status	Education
ID	1	0.3318154	-0.005198153	-0.03199349	0.16521626	0.0427083	0.1178248	0.20464144
Age	0.3318154	1	0.140252281	0.0993212	0.30820715	0.10816534	0.2321324	0.58315382
Sex	-0.00519815	0.1402523	1	0.35832086	0.10109016	-0.19390934	0.1349206	0.13101041
Family history	-0.03199349	0.0993212	0.358320864	1	0.32652253	-0.32490713	-0.1381164	0.09177079
Financial stability	0.165216257	0.3082071	0.101090164	0.32652253	1	-0.08555839	-0.130294	0.45859087
Medical history	0.0427083	0.1081653	-0.193909341	-0.32490713	-0.08555839	1	0.342193	0.02510527
Marital status	0.117824803	0.2321324	0.134920635	-0.13811641	-0.13029399	0.34219296	1	0.2550336
Education	0.204641435	0.5831538	0.131010413	0.09177079	0.45859087	0.02510527	0.2550336	1

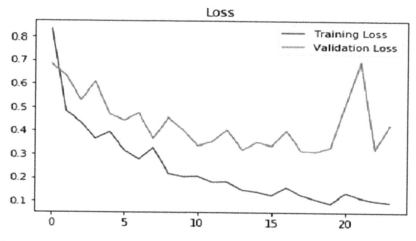

FIGURE 8.3
Dataset Training Loss Values

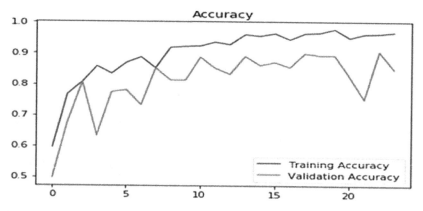

FIGURE 8.4
Training and Accuracy versus Validation Accuracy

	Validation Set	Test Set
Accuracy	91%	89%
F1 score	0.91	0.88

Number of examples: 2065
Percentage of positive examples: 52.542, number of positive examples: 1085
Percentage of negative examples: 47.457, number of negative examples: 900

8.6 Conclusion

Significant progress was made with system methods in considering and augmenting DBS in recent years. Many models at various detail levels and complexity have led to the high frequency medicinal merit, frequent DBS by isolating potentials. The analysis of new, sporadic, and low-frequency DBS programs was also assisted by computer models. In all

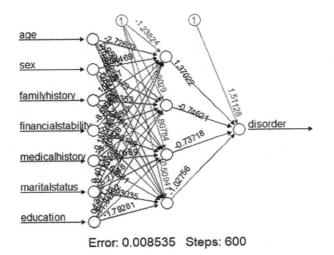

Error: 0.008535   Steps: 600

FIGURE 8.5
Alzheimer's Disease Disorder Based on Different Contexts

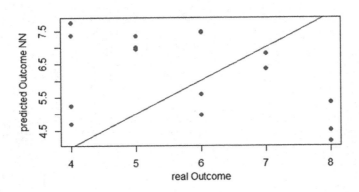

FIGURE 8.6
Predicted Outcome of Neural Network

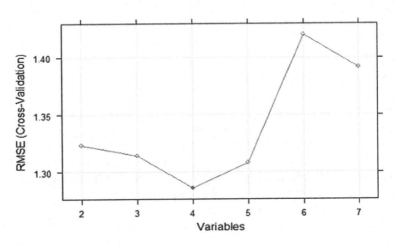

FIGURE 8.7
The Disorder Feature Cross-Validation

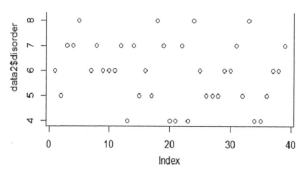

FIGURE 8.8
The Alzheimer's Disease Disorder Index

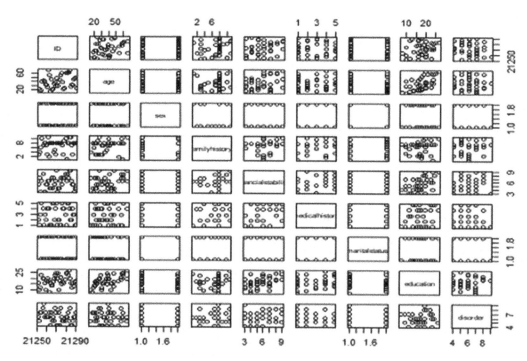

FIGURE 8.9
The Alzheimer's Disease Disorder Based on Feature Selection

dimensions, artificial neural networks have shown very drastic progress. Artificial neural networks can no longer be represented as a black box or incomprehensible as rule extraction is overcome by qualified ANN. ANN can merge with other technologies and can deliver specific results on its own. These supported models can enable clinicians to determine the most successful DBS location and program and establish quantitative criteria for preparing the most suitable DBS activity for AD patients. Swarm intelligence will optimize the area and features of DBS. The presence of multiple neuropsychiatric symptoms demonstrates heterogeneity in neurodegeneration progressions through neural systems. Generations have specific symptoms or clusters of symptoms, but none seem to display apparent, detailed effects. Overall cognitive decline and noncognitive symptoms are present in AD patients and not memory alone. It is also difficult to assess whether memory

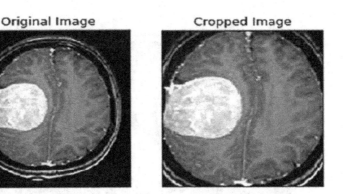

FIGURE 8.10
Brain Images in Original and Cropped

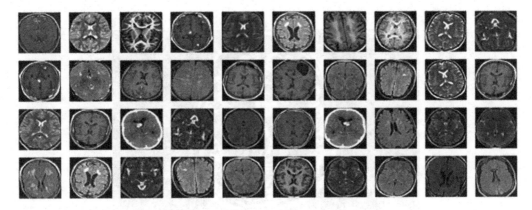

FIGURE 8.11
Brain Images in Different Angles

Accuracy of the best model on the testing data:
Test loss: 0.3339
Test Accuracy=88.7%
F1 Score for the best model on the testing data:
F1 score: 88.3%
Swarm intelligence

enhancement increases the quality of life. Furthermore, DBS does not prevent neurodegenerations in AD, it should be noted. In particular, patient classes, symptoms are alleviated briefly.

8.7 Future Enhancement

In the future, the accuracy of the classification will be enhanced by new information, including multimodal recognition of Alzheimer's. DBS is recognized as an invasive multi-risk procedure that may cause injury, inflammation, and possible behavioral changes. It

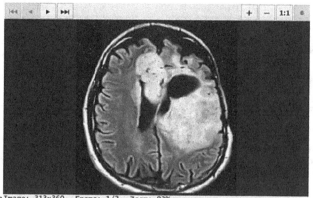

FIGURE 8.12
Image with Noise

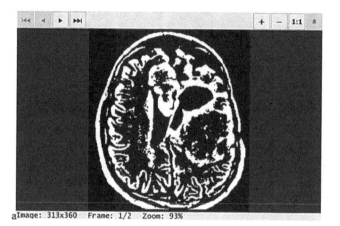

FIGURE 8.13
Adaptive Thresholding

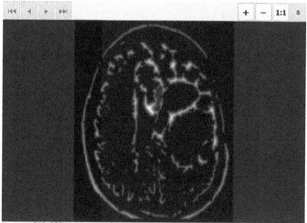

FIGURE 8.14
Recognizing Characteristics

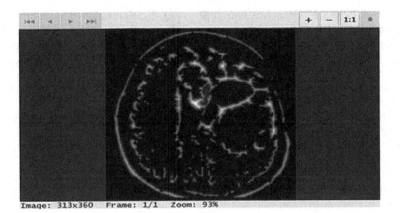

FIGURE 8.15
Normalized

Found 253 images belonging to 2 classes.
Found 253 images belonging to 2 classes.
Found 239 images belonging to 2 classes.

TABLE 8.2

Rank of Importance of Variables for Depression Disorder and Feature Selection

Variables	RMSE	Rsquared	MAE	RMSESD	RsquaredSD	MAESD	Selected
1	1.323	0.3479	1.18	0.3171	0.3155	0.3049	
2	1.315	0.4401	1.173	0.3411	0.3608	0.318	
3	1.286	0.3622	1.127	0.365	0.3387	0.3225	*
4	1.308	0.3981	1.134	0.3314	0.3074	0.2934	
5	1.42	0.3286	1.239	0.3365	0.3063	0.2971	
6	1.391	0.3098	1.207	0.3418	0.2247	0.2949	

may also predict risk assessment of Alzheimer's deep brain stimulation and its consequences. As new ensemble approaches for behavioral analysis of AD patients have been introduced, a more robust clinical decision-making recommendation framework has been placed.

References

1. Connolly A T, et al., Classification of pallidal oscillations with increasing parkinsonian severity. *Journal of Neurophysiology*. 2015; 114: 209–218
2. Benazzouz A, et al., Effect of high-frequency stimulation of the subthalamic nucleus on the neuronal activities of the substantia nigra pars reticulata and ventrolateral nucleus of the thalamus in the rat. *Neuroscience*. 2000; 99:289–295.
3. Dostrovsky JO, et al., Micro stimulation-induced inhibition of neuronal firing in human globus pallidus. *Journal of Neurophysiology*. 2000; 84:570–574. [PubMed: 10899228] 22. Welter M-L. et al., Effects of high-frequency stimulation on subthalamic neuronal activity in parkinsonian patients. Arch Neurol. 2004; 61:89–96.

4. Hashimoto T, Elder CM, Okun MS, Patrick SK, Vitek JL. Stimulation of the subthalamic nucleus changes the firing pattern of pallidal neurons. *The Journal of Neuroscience*. 2003; 23:1916–1923.

5. Anderson ME, et al., Effects of high-frequency stimulation in the internal globus pallidus on the activity of thalamic neurons in the awake monkey. *Journal of Neurophysiology*. 2003; 89:1150–1160.

6. Montgomery EB Jr. Effects of GPi stimulation on human thalamic neuronal activity. *Clinical Neurophysiology*. 2006; 117:2691–2702.

7. Geda Y. E., et al., Neuropsychiatric symptoms in Alzheimer's disease: past progress and anticipation of the future. *Alzheimer's & Dementia*. 2013; 9(5): 602–608.

8. Lozano A. M., et al., A phase II study of fornix deep brain stimulation in mild Alzheimer's disease. *Journal of Alzheimer's Disease*. 2016; 54: 777–787.

9. Barnes D. E., et al., Midlife vs late-life depressive symptoms and risk of dementia: differential effects for Alzheimer disease and vascular dementia. *Archives of General Psychiatry*. 2012; 69(5): 493–498.

10. Gilbert B. J.. The role of amyloid β in the pathogenesis of Alzheimer's disease. *Journal of Clinical Pathology*. 2013; 66(5): 362–366.

11. Liu C., et al., Apolipoprotein e and Alzheimer disease: risk, mechanisms and therapy. *Nature Reviews Neurology*. 2013; 9(2): 106–118.

12. Cornejo V. H., et al., The unfolded protein response in Alzheimer's disease. *Seminars in Immunopathology*. 2013; 35(3): 277–292.

13. Kelleher R. J., et al., Evidence of endothelial dysfunction in the development of Alzheimer's disease: is Alzheimer's a vascular disorder? *The American Journal of Cardiovascular Disease*. 2013; 3(4): 197–226.

14. Caldeira G. L., et al., Impaired transcription in Alzheimer's disease: key role in mitochondrial dysfunction and oxidative stress. *Journal of Alzheimer's Disease*. 34(1): 115–131.

15. Sopova K., et al., Dysregulation of neurotrophic and haematopoietic growth factors in Alzheimer's disease: from pathophysiology to novel treatment strategies. *Current Alzheimer Research*. 2014; 11(1): 27–39.

16. Ibrahim et al., On the application of artificial neural networks in analysing and classifying the human chromosomes. *Journal of Computer Science*. 2006; 2(1): 72–75.

17. Gusella, J., et al., A polymorphic DNA marker genetically linked to Huntington's disease. *Nature*. 1983; 306: 234–238.

18. Morris GP, et al., Inconsistencies and controversies surrounding the amyloid hypothesis of Alzheimer's disease. *Acta Neuropathologica Communications*. 2014; 2: 135.

19. Assoc A. Alzheimer's association report 2015 Alzheimer's disease facts and figures. *Alzheimers Dement*. 2015; 11: 332–384.

20. Corbett A, et al., New and emerging treatments for Alzheimer's disease. *Expert Review of Neurotherapeutics*. 2012; 12: 535–543.

21. Viana JNM, et al., Currents of memory: recent progress, translational challenges, and ethical considerations in fornix deep brain stimulation trials for Alzheimer's disease. *Neurobiology of Aging*. 2017; 56: 202–210.

22. Sharma A, et al., Efficacy and safety of deep brain stimulation as an adjunct to pharmacotherapy for the treatment of Parkinson disease. *Annals of Pharmacotherapy*. 2012; 46: 248–254.

23. Kuhn J, et al., Deep brain stimulation of the nucleus basalis of Meynert in Alzheimer's dementia. *Molecular Psychiatry*. 2015; 20: 353–360.

24. Holslag JAH, et al., Deep brain stimulation for essential tremor: a comparison of targets. *World Neurosurgery*. 2018; 110: e580–e584.

25. Ruvalcaba Y. Effectiveness of bilateral deep-brain stimulation on dystonia: response to the latest meta-analysis. *European Journal of Neurology*. 2017; 24: e35.

26. Zhou C, et al., A systematic review and meta-analysis of deep brain stimulation in treatment-resistant depression. *Progress in Neuro-Psychopharmacology & Biological Psychiatry*. 2018; 82: 224–232.

27. Hollingworth M, et al., Single electrode deep brain stimulation with dual targeting at dual frequency for the treatment of chronic pain: a case series and review of the literature. *Brain Sciences*. 2017.

28. Nangunoori RK, et al., Deep brain stimulation for obesity: from a theoretical framework to practical application. *Neural Plasticity*. 2016; 2016: 7971460.

29. Rubin JE, et al., High frequency stimulation of the subthalamic nucleus eliminates pathological thalamic rhythmicity in a computational model. *Journal of Computational Neuroscience*. 2004; 16: 211–235.

30. Santaniello et al., Basal Ganglia Modeling in Healthy and Parkinson's Disease State. II. Network-based Multi-Units Simulation. 2007 American Control Conference; 2007; 4095–4100.

31. Ermentrout GB, Kopell N. Multiple pulse interactions and averaging in systems of coupled neural oscillators. *Journal of Mathematical Biology*. 1991; 29:195–217.

32. Brodal P. *The central nervous system*. 5. New York, NY, United States of America: Oxford University Press; 2016.

33. Suthana N, et al., Memory enhancement and deep-brain stimulation of the entorhinal area. *The New England Journal of Medicine*. 2012; 366: 502–510.

34. Miller JP, et al., Visual-spatial memory may be enhanced with theta burst deep brain stimulation of the fornix: A preliminary investigation with four cases. *Brain*. 2015; 138: 1833–1842.

35. Laxton AW, et al., A phase I trial of deep brain stimulation of memory circuits in Alzheimer's disease. *Annals of Neurology*. 2010; 68: 521–534.

36. Roy TS, et al., Memory retrieval by activating engram cells in mouse models of early Alzheimer's disease. *Nature*. 2016; 531: 508–512.

37. Babiloni C, et al., Intra-hemispheric functional coupling of alpha rhythms is related to golfer's performance: a coherence EEG study. *International Journal of Psychophysiology*. (2011) 82(3): 260–268. doi: 10.1016/j.ijpsycho.2011.09.008.

38. Cichocki A, et al., EEG filtering based on blind source separation (BSS) for early detection of Alzheimer's disease. *Clinical Neurophysiology*. 2005; 116(3): 729–737. doi: 10.1016/j.clinph.2004.09.017.

39. Schomer DL, et al., *Electroencephalography. Basic Principles, Clinical Applications, and Related Fields*. Philadelphia: Wolters Kluwer/Lippincott Williams & Wilkins Health; (2011).

40. Bauer G, Bauer R. Electroencephalography. In: Niedermeyer E, Schomer DL, Silva FHLD, editors. *Niedermeyer's Electroencephalography. Chapter 43: EEG, Drug Effect, and Central Nervous System Poisoning*. Philadelphia: Wolters Kluwer/Lippincott Williams & Wilkins Health; (2011).

41. Rossini PM, et al., Clinical neurophysiology of aging brain: from normal aging to neurodegeneration. *Progress in Neurobiology*. 2007; 83(6): 375–400. doi: 10.1016/j.pneurobio.2007.07.010

42. Klassen BT, et al., Quantitative EEG as a predictive biomarker for Parkinson disease dementia. *Neurology*. 2011; 77(2): 118–124. doi: 10.1212/WNL.0b013e318224af8d.

43. Fraga FJ, et al., Characterizing Alzheimer's disease severity via resting-awake EEG amplitude modulation analysis. *PLoS One*. 2013; 8(8): e72240. doi: 10.1371/journal.pone.0072240

44. Dauwels J, et al., *Diagnosis of Alzheimer's disease from EEG signals: where are we standing? Current Alzheimer Research*. 7(6); 2010: 487–505.

45. van den Heuvel, et al., Exploring the brain network: a review on resting-state FMRI functional connectivity. *European Neuropsychopharmacology*. 2010; 20(8); 519–534.

46. Ahmet Yardimic. Soft computing in medicine. *Applied Soft Computing*. 2009; 9:1029–1043.

9

Visual Question-Answering System Using Integrated Models of Image Captioning and BERT

Lavika Goel

Malaviya National Institute of Technology, Jaipur, Rajasthan, India

Mohit Dhawan, Rachit Rathore, Satyansh Rai, Aaryan Kapoor and Yashvardhan Sharma

BITS Pilani, Pilani, Rajasthan, India

CONTENTS

9.1 Introduction

Visual question answering (VQA) is a very popular and very important research field [1–2]. Being able to look at an image and ask questions to our computers can be useful to people in numerous ways. A visually impaired person can move about more independently by simply asking questions about his neighborhood, whereabouts, and so on [1–4]. Another major practical implication of VQA is human-computer interaction in order to get visual content: a person in a foreign country can explore the place just by inquiring what his eyes can see, a kid can ask various questions from the model to learn how to call an object by its name, or a person can inquire about outside weather even while staying inside [5–9]. We can understand VQA as a combination of two systems: image processing and question answering (Q&A). The later part (Q&A) is a very in-depth field of study and research itself. The system (BERT) that generates answers based on textual information has evolved a lot and currently achieve up to 89% accuracy [10, 11–17]. The task left to VQA is to generate textual information that can describe the image, thus producing better results than raw systems. These systems rely on various fields of computer vision, namely object detection, classification, and comparison of detected data with the worldly knowledge. We employ four state-of-the-art image captioning models to generate direct textual information describing the image. The image captioning models identify the most significant parts of the image and generate a caption describing the image. Our goal is to develop a visual question-answering system using the BERT model for question answering and four state-of-the-art methods of image captioning, namely BUTD captioning, show-and-tell models, Microsoft's Captionbot, and a show, attend and tell model to develop the image captions [8, 9, 11, 12, 24]. The aim is to examine the relative accuracy of various image captioning models along with BERT as a base for question answering on the task of visual question answering, and discuss the future scope of VQA performance at the aid of image-captioning models. In examples below, there is an input image along with an input question, and the model is supposed to answer the question based on image context (Table 9.1).

We can see few examples here:

Example 1:

Q: What sport is being played?
A: Football

Example 2:

Q: How many giraffes are there?
A: Two

9.2 Related Work

TABLE 9.1

Overview of Recent Work in Visual Question-Answering Systems in Past Years

Model	Characteristics	Language tasks	Accuracy	Rank	Year
Oscar	Oscar is based on aligning text with objects detected in images rather than using brute force to match them automatically.	Visual Question Answering on VQA v2 test-dev	73.82	1	2020
MCAN+VC	Relies on causal intervention: $P(Y\mid do(X))$ rather than using the conventional likelihood: $P(Y\mid X)$, which helps the model to make sense.	Visual Question Answering on VQA v2 test-std	71.49	5	2020
		Visual Question Answering on VQA v2 test-dev	71.21	5	
UNITER (Large)	UNITER proposes a UNiversal Image-TExt Representation, rather than joint text-image multimodal embedding.	Visual Question Answering on VQA v2 test-std	73.4	1	2019
		Visual Question Answering on VQA v2 test-dev	73.24	2	
X-101 grid features + MCAN	Leverages grid-based feature learning, and performs at better speed with same accuracy as the state of art.	Visual Question Answering on VQA v2 test-std	72.71	2	2019
		Visual Question Answering on VQA v2 test-dev	72.59	3	
MuRel	Proposes MuRel cell, capable of defining visual schemes better than attention maps.	Visual Question Answering on VQA v2 test-std	68.4	13	2019
		Visual Question Answering on VQA v2 test-dev	68.03	14	
BLOCK	The concept is based on block-superdiagonal tensor decomposition. The model uses block term ranks.	Visual Question Answering on VQA v2 test-std	67.9	15	2019
		Visual Question Answering on VQA v2 test-dev	67.58	15	
BAN2-CTI	Model uses a trilinear interaction model along with knowledge distillation (novel approach).	Visual Question Answering on VQA v2 test-dev	67.4	17	2019
BAN+ Glove+ Counter	BAN uses bilinear interactions between two groups of input channels. Joint representations for each channel are extracted using its low-rank bilinear pooling.	Visual Question Answering on VQA v2 test-std	70.4	9	2018
		Visual Question Answering on VQA v2 test-dev	70.04	9	
DMN	The model employs DMN as a baseline and uses another visual module to convert images into feature embeddings.	Visual Question Answering on VQA v2 test-dev	68.09	13	2018
		Visual Question Answering on VQA v2 test-std	68.4	14	
BUTD (Bottom-Up, Top-Down Attention)	Combination of top-down and bottom-up mechanisms, bottom-up is based on Faster RCNN.	Visual Question Answering on VQA v2 test-std	70.34	10	2017
Image features from bottom-up attention	Uses faster RCNN for image feature identification and CNN-based pretrained output classifier.	Visual Question Answering on VQA v2 test-std	70.3	11	2017
		Visual Question Answering on VQA v2 test-dev	69.87	11	2017

(Continued)

TABLE 9.1

Continued

Model	Characteristics	Language tasks	Accuracy	Rank	Year
MUTAN	Tucker-based decomposition scheme to efficiently parameterize textual and visual representations.	Visual Question Answering on VQA v2 test-std	67.4	16	2017
		Visual Question Answering on VQA v2 test-dev	67.42	16	2017
N2NMN	Based on ResNet-152 and policy search to dynamically create attention-based neural modules	Visual Question Answering on VQA v2 test-dev	64.9	19	2017

9.3 Datasets

There are numerous datasets for the task of visual answering. Here we describe the most frequently tested dataset, the VQA and COCO-QA dataset [12–25].

1. **Toronto COCO-QA Dataset [20]:** This dataset consists of 123,287 images from the coco dataset and 78,736 training question-answer pairs, along with 38,948 testing images [18]. The questions mainly consist of four types, i.e., object, number, color, or location with one-word answers. This is a relatively easy dataset. Some sample questions can be found in Figure 9.1.

2. **VQA Dataset [19]:** This dataset deals with the binary classification of data (i.e., questions with yes/no answers) and counting problems (How many giraffes?), amongst others. Some of the questions store the answer, as shown below. It is the most commonly used datasets and has been considered standard to test results for some time.

DAQUAR 1553
What is there in front of the sofa?
Ground truth: table

COCOQA 5078
How many leftover donuts is the red bicycle holding?
Ground truth: three

FIGURE 9.1
Sample Images and Questions for Toronto COCO-QA.
{Source: Adapted from [18]}

What color are her eyes?
What is the mustache made of?

How many slices of pizza are there?
Is this a vegetarian pizza?

FIGURE 9.2
Sample questions from VQA.
{Source: Adapted from [4]}

It has over 260,000 images with at least 3 questions per image. It also provides answers that are correct, as well as those that seem correct but are actually not. Some sample questions can be found in Figure 9.2.

9.4 Problem Statement

Designing a visual question-answering system to develop insights over an image and answer questions based on it.

9.4.1 Proposed Solution

The goal is to get abstract information from an image and answer the corresponding question given to us. The problem can be divided into two parts:

1. Extraction of relevant information from an image.
2. Answering a given question based on the information generated from the image.

We employ state-of-the-art models for both the tasks individually by modifying BERT's output and input hidden layers to employ it for context-based question answering. For the job of extracting information from images, we use four state-of-the-art models for image captioning. Extraction of relevant information from the image and its representation in terms of natural language is known as image captioning [21, 23–27]. We use four models, namely BUTD (bottom-up and top-down attention), show-and-tell model, Microsoft's Captionbot, and the show, attend, and tell model. The aim is to define and test the combination of different image-captioning algorithms and question-answering models to model an image as the context for question answering. BUTD, show and tell, and show, attend, and tell are all state-of-the-art methods on the MS COCO captions task [2]. While they have very different architectures, all the models are able to achieve similar accuracies on the task. The above image captioning models generate the most appropriate one-line caption for an image; this caption is then passed into the BERT question-answering system. BERT uses image captions as its context to answer the question.

a. BERT + BUTD

b. BERT + show-and-tell model

c. BERT + Captionbot

d. BERT + show, attend, and tell

9.5 Methodology

We started by training four models that are used to generate a sentence for images. These are the state-of-the-art models for image captioning. After this, we trained the BERT model for a question-answering system. Finally, four combined models were generated for visual question answering.

9.5.1 BUTD Captioning (Pythia)

Generally, just top-down attention methods are used by people for image captioning. Here, a combination of bottom-up and top-down methods of the visual attention are used in combination. This was done to get better outcomes. Faster R-CNN's were used to implement bottom-up. This was done because Faster R-CNN provides a very natural way of executing bottom-up.

A combination of a network that helps the system be aware of the network using proposals is made by Regional Proposals Network (RPN) for regions. Region generation proposals are done using selective search in Fast R-CNN, which costs much more than RPN. This is because Object Detection Network splits up the work with RPN. So, basically RPN tries to find the maximum number of objects it can detect and returns those boxes. These boxes are called anchors. Faster R-CNN works majorly using these anchors. Generally, 9 boxes are chosen at various positions of the image with varying sizes. Figure 9.3 suggests 9 anchors at the position (320, 320) of the photo at the waist (600, 800).

Here, yellow is referring to scale of 128 × 128, red refers to scale of 256 × 256, and green refers to scale of 512 × 512. The three different boxes in each color have sides in the ratio 1:2, 1:1, and 2:1, between height and width. Let's consider a case where all 9 anchors have a stride 16; we can attain a total of 1989 locations. If we select a position with each stride of 16, there will be 1,989 (39 × 51) positions for each block and hence a total of 17901 (9 × 1989) boxes. These boxes provide a wide coverage of the image for all possible image sizes.

This is the default system. We can choose whatever box sizes we need and what should be their stride. The above configuration has proven to work well for COCO and Pascal VOC Dataset.

After RPN has processed the image, it returns a set of a few anchors that it proposes for the classifier to work on. This helps us distinguish between foreground and background. This can speed up the work of regressors and classifiers, as they need to focus more on these boxes only. The complete architecture of the Faster R-CNN can be found in Figure 9.4, while the RPN is explained in Figure 9.5.

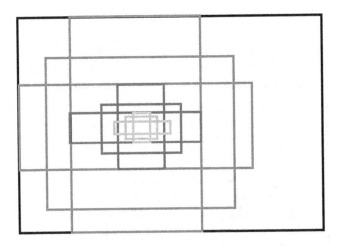

FIGURE 9.3
9 Anchors in Faster R-CNN

9.5.1.1 The Classifier of Background and Foreground

This task is divided into two subtasks:

1. We start by creating a dataset for our classifier. The dataset must have labeled the position's foreground as "ground truth." So, whatever boxes overlap less with "ground truth" are labeled as background, and the ones that coincide more are labeled as foreground.
2. Now, the features of anchors need to be decided. These include the size of stride, number of anchors (2 labels per anchor, making the number of features as twice the number of anchors), the activation function to be used, and so on.

9.5.1.2 The Regressor of Bounding Box

We must pass only the anchors labeled as foreground to the regressors [1, 3, 6, 28–32]. This is because we have values available to compare our outputs with the value of ground truth. Hence, we cannot, in any case, use background images. The number of positions that we get back defines the depth of our feature map (number of anchors times number of positions).

The smooth-L1 type of loss for position (x ,y) of the top-left box is leveraged, and also the height's(h) and width's(w) logarithm.

$$L_{loc}\left(t^u, v\right) = \sum_{i \in \{x, y, w, h\}} Smooth\, L_1\left(t_i^u - v_i\right), \tag{9.1}$$

in which,

$$Smooth\, L_1\left(x\right) = \begin{cases} 0.5x^2, if\, |x| < 1 \\ |x| - 0.5\, otherwise \end{cases} \tag{9.2}$$

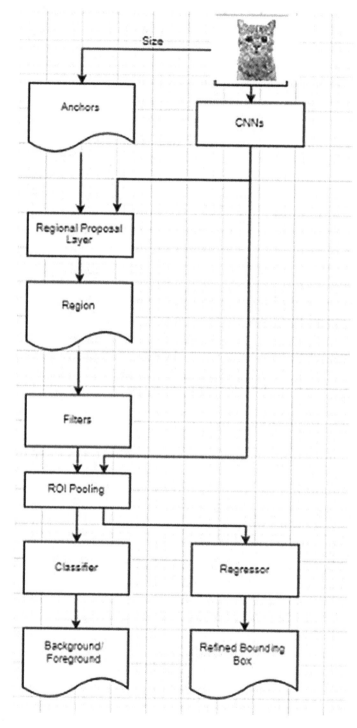

FIGURE 9.4
The Architecture of Faster R-CNN

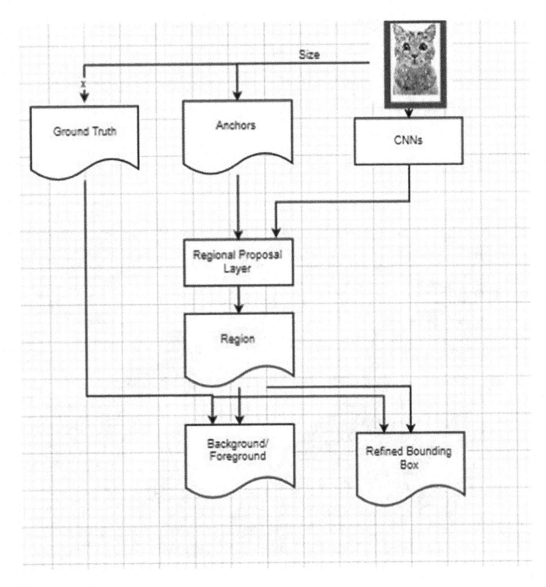

FIGURE 9.5
Region Proposal Network in Training

9.5.1.3 ROI Pooling

RPN returns a set of varying sizes of boxes that it feels are part of the foreground. We cannot directly pass these results to a CNN. Here is where ROI (region of interest) pooling comes into play. This reduces our image (i.e., feature maps) into numerous feature maps of the same size. The number of feature maps generated is a parameter that we decide. After that, max pooling can be applied on each individual feature map. The output received can be used for various purposes according to our needs.

We used the pre-trained model for Pythia (BUTD) model available online, and used it to caption 80,000 plus images from VQA Dataset. The code for captioning is provided below [7].

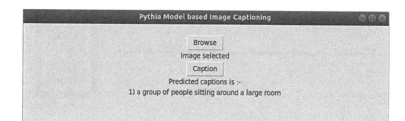

FIGURE 9.6
Caption from Pythia

FIGURE 9.7
Image Used for Caption Generation

The optimal parameters for Pythia were found to be:
Image size: 448 × 448
Channel_mean = [0.485, 0.456, 0.406]
Channel_std = [0.229, 0.224, 0.225]
In Figure 9.6, we see the caption generated for Figure 9.7 by Pythia:
All the captions generated in this section will be for Figure 9.7.

9.5.2 Show and Tell: A Neural Image Caption Generator

The show-and-tell model was developed by researchers at Google. It tries to describe images with the help of machine learning models. Description is part of the problem seen in Natural Language Processing, whereas making sense of the image is at the heart of computer vision. This image-captioning model uses both these techniques (with already existing state-of-the-art models) to develop a generative model. It uses probability to decide if the caption generated fits the image and tries to maximize the probability. After input is provided in the form of images, it tries to make a sequence of words using a dictionary (taking words that fit the image). The probability function $P(S|I)$ is the probability of S (a sequence of words) being the description, given I is the image. A combination of encoder and decoder networks are used, where encoder is a CNN and decoder is an RNN [31–37]. A sentence is input to the encoder, which encodes it into a fixed-size vector. This vector is then given to decoder as input and this decoder outputs the final sentence.[11]

9.5.3 CaptionBot

CaptionBot.ai is an online tool developed by Microsoft Cognitive Services. It is machine learning technology that identifies and captions our photos. The image uploaded on the tool is analyzed at their servers, a caption is generated, and the image is then deleted from their servers (to ensure privacy). It is powered by three APIs, namely Computer Vision API, Emotion API, and Bing Image API. All of these APIs are services provided by Microsoft.[12]

We built a wrapper class in Python that sends an image to the Microsoft server, and then we wait for the response. Then we extracted the result from their website, processed the text, and stored it.

9.5.3.1 Computer Vision API

Computer Vision API works on images and can be used to get a lot of information. Some of these tasks are text extraction, adding discoverability of the data, and so on. No machine learning expertise is required to work with it [1, 3–6, 34–40]. Landmarks can be identified and printed, handwritten words can be read, and popular brand names recognized by the API with the help of visual data processing. Over 10,000 objects and over 20 languages can be recognized by it.

The API can help discover if any content is mature, and restrictions can be put up accordingly. Thumbnails can be generated for a bigger image to store and access data more efficiently. It can even be used to check the contents of an image to categorize it or even write its description.[13]

9.5.3.2 Emotion API

The Microsoft Cognitive Services Emotion API returns a box enclosing a face. Along with the box, it can also be used to detect emotions of all the people in the images (marked by the box). It also works well for videos. It basically captures the video after some time gaps and then runs on it like it works on an image. It is capable of detecting six emotions, namely surprise, happiness, anger, contempt, sadness, and disgust. This API can be used in various languages including Python or, if required, can called directly by any terminal.[14]

9.5.3.3 Bing Image API

The Bing Image Search API allows you to use Bing's photograph search abilities in your application. Snapshots similar to those available at bing.com/images can be obtained with the help of this API. The latest version v7 can be used to search for images on the Internet.

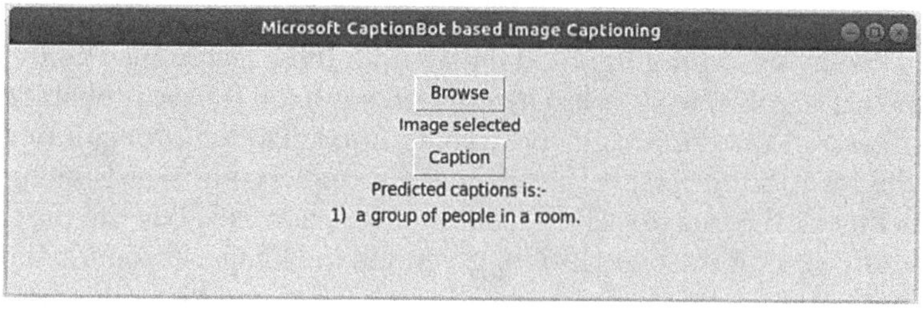

FIGURE 9.8
Caption from Captionbot

Not only for use on images, it also works well for image URLs, image metadata, and information about the website that has the image. API v7 also allows us to use factors like brightness, contrast, and color scheme to filter images or sort. Queries can be raised to the API about a specific described image, and it only returns images that follow this description.[15]

In Figure 9.8, we see the caption generated for Figure 9.7 by CaptionBot.

9.5.4 Show, Attend, and Tell: Neural Image Caption Generation with Visual Attention

Show, Attend, and Tell [24] uses the attention mechanism to generate image captions and to learn to describe an image. The model has to be trained in a deterministic manner by using a technique of standard backpropagation and by maximization of a variational lower bound stochastically. The CNN-LSTM network is used for generating image captions. The lower convolutional layers are used for extracting features, unlike the previous work, which uses the final fully connected (FC) layer thereby capturing multiple objects inside an image. Thus, image representation is done by different features at different locations.

9.5.4.1 Model Details

The model consists of an encoder (CNN) for extracting image features and a decoder (LSTM) for generating sequence of the caption one word at every time. The approach to caption generation attempts to incorporate two variants of attention mechanisms: "soft" and "hard" attention mechanisms.

In Figure 9.9, step 2 features are captured at lower layers of convolutional network. Then at step 3, feature sampling is done and fed to LSTM, which generates a word correspondingly. This step (3) is repeated K number of times in order to generate a caption of K words.

In Figure 9.10, as each word is generated, the model's attention changes over time and the most relevant part of an image is reflected. Both soft and hard attention generate the same caption in this case.

9.5.4.1.1 Encoder (CNN)

The model takes an input as a raw image and generates its caption, which is denoted by y, now

$$y = \{y_1, \ldots, y_c\}, y_i \in R^K \tag{9.3}$$

where K represents vocabulary size and C represents length of caption, hence y is an encoded sequence of 1 to K words. The model uses a convolutional neural network (CNN)

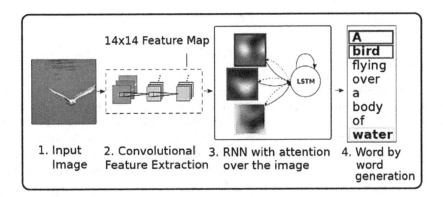

FIGURE 9.9
Learning the Model in Steps
{Source: Adapted from [24]}

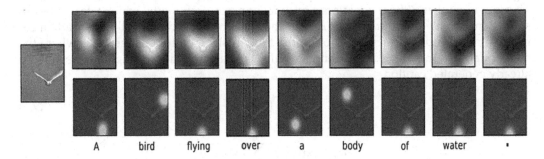

FIGURE 9.10
Model Soft Attention (Top Row) and Hard Attention (Bottom Row).
{Source: Adapted from [24]}

for extracting a set of feature vectors/annotation vectors. The extractor results in D-dimensional L vectors represented by a, each of which is representing any part of the given image.

$$a = \{a_1, \ldots, a_L\}, a_i \in R^D \tag{9.4}$$

Features from lower layer of CNN are extracted by the model to get a similarity between image portions and annotation vectors. This helps the corresponding decoder to select a subset of all annotation vectors to focus selectively on certain locations of the image.

9.5.4.1.2 Decoder (LSTM Network)

The LSTM network now generates one of the words at every time-step constraint on a context vector and generates an overall caption. The LSTM parameters are based on

$$\begin{bmatrix} i_t \\ f_t \\ o_t \\ g_t \end{bmatrix} = \begin{bmatrix} \sigma \\ \sigma \\ \sigma \\ \tanh \end{bmatrix} T_{D+m+n,n} \begin{bmatrix} E_{y_{t-1}} \\ h_{t-1} \\ \hat{z}_t \end{bmatrix} \tag{9.5}$$

$$c_t = f_t \odot c_{t-1} + i_t \odot g_t \tag{9.6}$$

$$h_t = o_t \odot \tanh(c_t) \tag{9.7}$$

Here, i_t, o_t are the input and output state respectively; c_t, f_t, h_t are memory, forget, hidden state of the LSTM correspondingly. Here, σ represent the logistic sigmoid activation function and $\odot$ represents the element wise multiplication. The context vector $\hat{z} \in R^D$ helps to capture the visual information with respect to the input at particular location. A φ represents the mechanism that computes $\hat{z}_t$ with input as annotation vectors (a_i), where $i = 1$, ..., L are the extracted features from an image at varied locations. A positive weight α_i (where $\alpha_i > 0$) is generated by mechanism φ for every i location. These weights are considered either as the probability factor such that to focus on next word production, this location i is the correct place for focus (which is the "hard" attention mechanism but stochastic), or considered to be the relative importance given to location i in blending all the a_i's together. The attention model f_{att} computes the weight α_i for every annotation vector a_i. This is evident that , "the model uses a multilayer perceptron model which takes into consideration the previous hidden state h_{t-1}." It should also be noted that as the RNN advances in producing output sequences through the hidden state. Output sequence is where the network always moves next and generates the feature vector depending on the sequence already generated caption

$$e_{ti} = f_{att}(a_i, h_{t-1}) \tag{9.8}$$

$$\alpha_{ti} = \exp(e_{ti}) / \sum_{k=1}^{L} \exp(e_{tk}) \tag{9.9}$$

After the calculation of weights (having sum = 1), the context vector $\hat{z}_t$ is computed by

$$\hat{z}_t = \varphi(\{a_i\}, \{\alpha_i\})$$

where φ represents the function, which gives a single vector as an output with inputs as a set of feature vectors and their respective weights.

The probability of the output word is calculated using state of LSTM, the context vectors, and the previously generated word, as follows:

$$p\left(y_t | a, y_1^{t-1}\right) \propto \exp\left(L_o\left(Ey_{t-1} + L_h h_t + L_z \hat{z}_t\right)\right) \tag{9.10}$$

Where $L_o \in R^{K \times m}$, $L_h \in R^{m \times n}$, $L_z \in R^{m \times D}$ and E are learned parameters that are randomly initialized.

9.5.4.2 Learning Stochastic "Hard" versus Deterministic "Soft" Attention

There exist two alternate mechanisms for the attention model f_{att}: stochastic hard attention and deterministic soft attention.

9.5.4.2.1 Stochastic "Hard" Attention

The variable s_t decides the location of the image where the model focuses its attention while generating the tth word. $s_{t,i}$ represents the one-hot variable; it is equal to 1 if i is the ith image location, and it is used for extracting visual features. Locations of attentions are used as intermediate latent variables, and a Multinoulli distribution is assigned, which is parametrized by α_i, and $\hat{z}_t$ as a random variable:

$$p\left(s_{t,i} = 1 \middle| s_{j<t}, a\right) = \alpha_{ti} \tag{9.11}$$

$$\hat{z}_t = \sum_i s_{t,i} a_i \tag{9.12}$$

A new L_s function is defined as a lower variational bound on the marginal log-likelihood; that is, $\log p(y \mid a)$ where y is observed sequence of words and a are features of the image. By optimizing L_s, the learning algorithm for the parameter W of the model are derived. It is a "function dependent on features a and their locations s, that is, $f(s, a)$, which maximizes the probability of caption of the image y." Such that:

$$L_s = \sum_s p\left(s \middle| a\right) \log p\left(y \middle| s, a\right) \le \log p\left(y \middle| a\right) \tag{9.13}$$

Hard decisions are made at every point, such that, $\varphi(\{a_i\}, \{\alpha_i\})\varphi(\{a_i\}, \{\alpha_i\})$ function outputs a_i at every point based upon the Multinouilli distribution on time.

9.5.4.2.2 Deterministic "Soft" Attention

Learning of the stochastic attention requires that the location of attention s_t is sampled every time, or we can directly take the expectation of context vector $\hat{z}_t$ as follows:

$$E_{p(s_t|a)}\left[\hat{z}_t\right] = \sum_{i=1}^{L} \alpha_{t,i} a_i \tag{9.14}$$

and establish a deterministic attention model by computing weighted feature vector of soft attention.

$$\varphi\left(\{a_i\}, \{\alpha_i\}\right) = \sum_{i=1}^{L} \alpha_{t,i} a_i \tag{9.15}$$

It means to feed a soft-weighted context vector α into the system. Under this deterministic attention, the entire model is smooth and differentiable, so by using standard back-propagation the learning is trivial end-to-end.

9.5.4.3 Implementation

The code for show, attend, and tell is available online, which is the Python 3 version of the original implementation of the paper by its authors and uses the soft deterministic

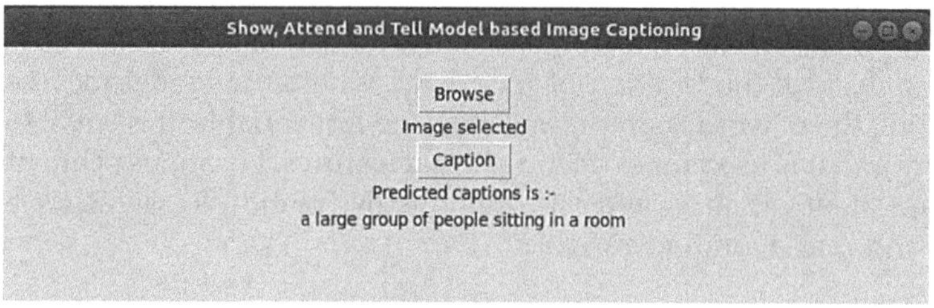

FIGURE 9.11
Caption from Show, Attend, and Tell Model

attention mechanism to generate models. [26, 27] We used the pre-trained model as a part of *torchvision* module of PyTorch, which is trained on MSCOCO dataset. [25]

In the Figure 9.11, we see the caption generated for Figure 9.7 by show, attend, and tell model.

9.5.5 BERT: Bidirectional Encoder Representations from Transformers

BERT was introduced by researchers in Google AI. It was a state-of-the-art model in the field of NLP. BERT uses an attention mechanism, Transformer, that learns the contextual relations between words (or sub-words) in a text. [21] Transformers work differently from other directional models as those models read the text input in a sequential fashion (left-to-right or right-to-left), whereas the transformers read the entire sequence at once. Thus, transformers are called bi-directional, although it's better to call them non-directional. This makes BERT unique due to its ability to learn the context of word based on its surrounding words. The BERT paper describes how to adapt it for question answering. The PyTorch implementation of BERT from HuggingFace includes that. [16] For question answering, the last hidden layer of BERT is taken and fed into a dense layer SoftMax to calculate the distributions of the sentence from its start to end. Special token probabilities, which are added to the head of the input text sequence, give its probability of being answerable or not [17] (Figure 9.12).

We use the pre-trained model of BERT (BERT-large-uncased-whole-word-masking) and then fine-tune it for the question answering by using the training scripts provided by HuggingFace.

9.6 Experimental Results

The combination of the models yields insightful results where the question is being answered directly on the basis of the image. We give the same question for Figure 9.13 to all three combinations and try to see the results. The following is a GUI extension of each of the combination models.

Figure 9.14 shows the results to the question, "What is the man riding the wave on?" by the BERT+BUTD, BERT+show and tell, BERT+CaptionBot, and BERT+show, attend, and tell models; all the models provide the same answers due to the simplicity of the image. The same trend is followed for most images.

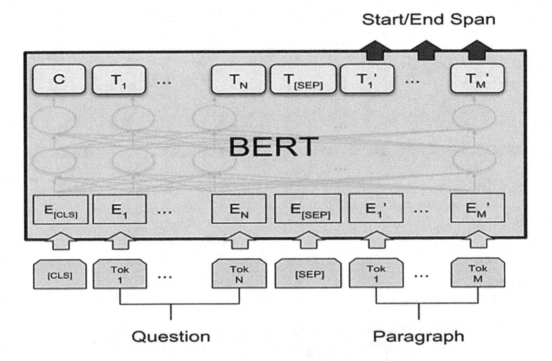

FIGURE 9.12
BERT Model Being Used for Question Answering (From: Adapted from [17])

FIGURE 9.13
Sample Image 1 for Visual Question Answering

Figure 9.16 shows an example where CaptionBot fails to perform on Figure 9.15, but other models perform well. One of the major reasons is because the figure has multiple objects, along with shadows (darker regions), making it difficult for CaptionBot to work well on it. However, it works very well on searchable things, for example famous people.

The results obtained are pretty accurate at answering questions about the images that involve activity being conducted. Also, it is observed that when a single object is present, all models are able to detect it and focus on it properly for captions, and hence the answers generated. Different models work better for better case scenarios. If an image contains Albert Einstein, the BERT + BUTD, BERT + show-and-tell model, and BERT + show, attend,

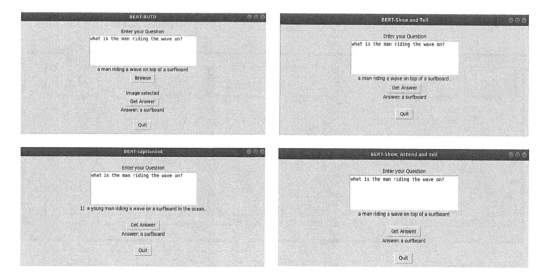

FIGURE 9.14:
Output for Image 1 on All the Model Combinations.

FIGURE 9.15:
Sample Image 2 for Visual Question Answering

and tell model will only caption it as for any other man. On the other hand, the caption generated by BERT + CaptionBot will caption the image with respect to Albert Einstein. Opposite to this, if there are different fruits in an image, BERT + CaptionBot is more likely to answer it as if the image contains generalized fruits, while the other models are more likely to answer for individual fruits. Because CaptionBot uses Bing Search API, it has been trained on images available in Bing Image results. So it uses that huge dataset to identify more specific details about the image by running reverse image search. This is possible as it runs completely on the cloud (i.e., on Microsoft's own servers). The reverse image search can prove to be useful to get keywords about the image that are used to form sentences. An advantage of using the show, attend, and tell model is that it is able to generate near perfect captions for an image that has a lot of different objects, and it is able to identify and properly caption those because of its visual attention mechanism.

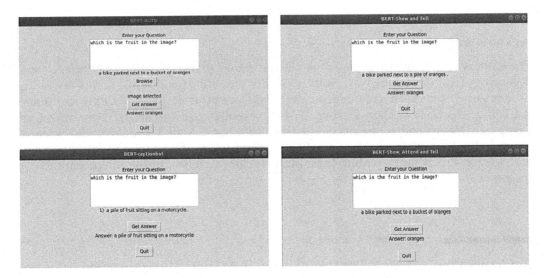

FIGURE 9.16:
Output for Image 2 on All the Model Combinations

9.7 Conclusion

We have created four graphical user interfaces (GUI) for our models. A different GUI is developed for combinations of BERT + BUTD, BERT + CaptionBot, BERT + show and tell, BERT + show, attend, and tell, only BUTD, only show and tell, only CaptionBot, only show, attend, and tell, and only BERT. The first four models take input in the form of images and a question on that image. They return the caption generated for the image, as well as the answer to the input question. The next four models could be used only for image captioning. The last model can take textual context and a question as input, and returns the answer. Combined models are able to achieve significant progress in terms of answering basic data questions over an image. Thus, a combination of two state-of-the-art technologies in different fields trained over different datasets are able to perform very well over tasks like color identification, object classification, and basic numeric questions over natural images. CaptionBot has the added advantage of classifying famous personalities, but doesn't perform very well over complex images.

To improve the work and to get better results in the future, the following things were noticed and are suggested. Since both models have been trained on different datasets, retraining of the combined architecture on the VQA/COCO training data may help in increasing the overall accuracy and establish the model as a whole. Internal changes to the captioning models generate more general, longer captions that contain more information about the scene depicted in the image, and can also help to obtain more vivid information about the image; the larger the details of the image, the larger will be the scope of answering questions accurately and mimic human performance. The input layer of BERT can be changed to use the encodings generated by the captioning models directly instead of encodings of the context-generated image caption. This will give features of image as an input instead of concise information about the image. Use of attention mechanism inside image captioning can help to generate better captions and better feature maps for an image that may directly be used by BERT to answer questions.

Acknowledgments

The authors would like to convey their sincere thanks to the Department of Science and Technology (ICPS Division), New Delhi, India, for providing financial assistance under the Data Science (DS) Research of Interdisciplinary Cyber Physical Systems (ICPS) Programme [DST/ICPS/CLUSTER/Data Science/2018/Proposal-16:(T-856)] at the Department of Computer Science and Information Systems, Birla Institute of Technology and Science, Pilani, India. The authors are also thankful to the authorities of Birla Institute of Technology and Science, Pilani, for providing basic infrastructure facilities during the preparation of the paper.

References

1. Javier, *"Introduction to Visual Question Answering: Tryolabs Blog,"* Introduction to Visual Question Answering | *Tryolabs Blog*, 01-Mar-2018. [Online]. Available: https://tryolabs.com/blog/2018/03/01/introduction-to-visual-question-answering/. [Accessed: 02-Dec-2019].
2. Franky, "Deep Learning and Visual Question Answering," *Medium*, 21-May-2018. [Online]. Available: https://towardsdatascience.com/deep-learning-and-visual-question-answering-c8c8093941bc. [Accessed: 02-Dec-2019].
3. Lu, Jiasen, Jianwei Yang, Dhruv Batra, and Devi Parikh. "Hierarchical question-image co-attention for visual question answering." In *Advances in neural information processing systems*, pp. 289–297. 2016.
4. Antol, Stanislaw, Aishwarya Agrawal et al. *"Vqa: Visual Question Answering."* In *Proceedings of the IEEE international conference on computer vision*, pp. 2425–2433. 2015.
5. Xiong, Caiming, Stephen Merity, and Richard Socher. *"Dynamic Memory Networks For Visual And Textual Question Answering."* In *International Conference on Machine Learning*, pp. 2397–2406. 2016.
6. Fukui, Akira, Dong Huk Park et al. "Multimodal compact bilinear pooling for visual question answering and visual grounding." *arXiv preprint arXiv:1606.01847* (2016).
7. "Google Colaboratory," *Google*. [Online]. Available: https://colab.research.google.com/drive/1vzrxDYB0vxtuUy8KCaGxm--nDCJvyBSg. [Accessed: 02-Dec-2019].
8. "Pythia's Documentation," *Pythia's Documentation - Pythia 0.3 documentation*. [Online]. Available: https://learnpythia.readthedocs.io/en/latest/. [Accessed: 02-Dec-2019].
9. Singh, Amanpreet, Vivek Natarajan et al. *"Pythia-a Platform For Vision & Language Research."* In *SysML Workshop, NeurIPS 2019*. 2018.
10. freeCodeCamp.org, "Building an image caption generator with Deep Learning in Tensorflow," *freeCodeCamp.org*, 28-Mar-2018. [Online]. Available: https://www.freecodecamp.org/news/building-an-image-caption-generator-with-deep-learning-in-tensorflow-a142722e9b1f/. [Accessed: 02-Dec-2019].
11. Vinyals, Oriol, Alexander Toshev, Samy Bengio, and Dumitru Erhan. *"Show and Tell: A Neural Image Caption Generator."* In *Proceedings of the IEEE conference on computer vision and pattern recognition*, pp. 3156–3164. 2015.
12. "For pictures worth the thousand words," *CaptionBot*. [Online]. Available: https://www.captionbot.ai/. [Accessed: 02-Dec-2019].
13. "Image Processing with the Computer Vision API: Microsoft Azure," *Image Processing with the Computer Vision API | Microsoft Azure*. [Online]. Available: https://azure.microsoft.com/en-in/services/cognitive-services/computer-vision/. [Accessed: 02-Dec-2019].

14. "Cognitive Services-APIs for AI Developers: Microsoft Azure," *-APIs for AI Developers | Microsoft Azure*. [Online]. Available: https://azure.microsoft.com/en-in/services/cognitive-services/. [Accessed: 02-Dec-2019].

15. "Bing Image Search API: Microsoft Azure," *API | Microsoft Azure*. [Online]. Available: https://azure.microsoft.com/en-in/services/cognitive-services/bing-image-search-api/. [Accessed: 02-Dec-2019].

16. Huggingface, "huggingface/transformers," *GitHub*, 29-Nov-2019. [Online]. Available: https://github.com/huggingface/pytorch-pretrained-BERT. [Accessed: 02-Dec-2019].

17. Devlin, Jacob, Ming-Wei Chang, Kenton Lee, and Kristina Toutanova. "Bert: Pre-training of deep bidirectional transformers for language understanding." *arXiv preprint arXiv:1810.04805* (2018).

18. Ren, Mengye, Ryan Kiros, and Richard Zemel. "Exploring models and data for image question answering." In *Advances in neural information processing systems*, pp. 2953–2961. 2015.

19. "Announcing the VQA Challenge 2018!," *Visual Question Answering*. [Online]. Available: https://visualqa.org/. [Accessed: 02-Dec-2019].

20. *Toronto COCO-QA Dataset*. [Online]. Available: http://www.cs.toronto.edu/~mren/research/imageqa/data/cocoqa/. [Accessed: 02-Dec-2019].

21. R. Horev, "BERT Explained: State-of-the-art language model for NLP," *Medium*, 17-Nov-2018. [Online].Available:https://towardsdatascience.com/bert-explained-state-of-the-art-language-model-for-nlp-f8b21a9b6270. [Accessed: 02-Dec-2019].

22. Hu, Ronghang, Jacob Andreas et al. "*Learning to Reason: End-to-End Module Networks For Visual Question Answering*." In *Proceedings of the IEEE International Conference on Computer Vision*, pp. 804–813. 2017.

23. Noh, Hyeonwoo, and Bohyung Han. "Training recurrent answering units with joint loss minimization for vqa." *arXiv preprint arXiv:1606.03647* (2016).

24. Xu, Kelvin, Jimmy Ba et al. "*Show, Attend And Tell: Neural Image Caption Generation With Visual Attention*." In *International Conference on Machine Learning*, pp. 2048–2057. 2015.

25. Lin, Tsung-Yi, Michael Maire et al. "*Microsoft coco: Common objects in context*." In *European Conference on Computer Vision*, pp. 740–755. Springer, Cham, 2014.

26. Sagar Vinodababu, "Show, Attend, and Tell | a PyTorch Tutorial to Image Captioning." *GitHub*. [Online]. Available: https://github.com/sgrvinod/a-PyTorch-Tutorial-to-Image-Captioning. [Accessed: 5-March-2020].

27. Kelvin Xu, "arctic-captions.", *GitHub*. [Online]. Available: https://github.com/kelvinxu/arctic-captions. [Accessed: 5-March-2020].

28. Hu, Ronghang, Jacob Andreas, Marcus Rohrbach, Trevor Darrell, and Kate Saenko. "*Learning to Reason: End-to-End Module Networks for Visual Question Answering*." 2017 IEEE International Conference on Computer Vision (ICCV), 2017. doi:10.1109/iccv.2017.93.

29. Fukui, Akira, Dong H. Park, Daylen Yang, Anna Rohrbach, Trevor Darrell, and Marcus Rohrbach. "*Multimodal Compact Bilinear Pooling for Visual Question Answering and Visual Grounding*." Proceedings of the 2016 Conference on Empirical Methods in Natural Language Processing, 2016. doi:10.18653/v1/d16-1044.

30. Ben-younes, Hedi, Remi Cadene, Matthieu Cord, and Nicolas Thome. "*MUTAN: Multimodal Tucker Fusion for Visual Question Answering*." 2017 IEEE International Conference on Computer Vision (ICCV), 2017. doi:10.1109/iccv.2017.285.

31. Teney, Damien, Peter Anderson, Xiaodong He, and Anton V. Hengel. "*Tips and Tricks for Visual Question Answering: Learnings from the 2017 Challenge*." 2018 IEEE/CVF Conference on Computer Vision and Pattern Recognition, 2018. doi:10.1109/cvpr.2018.00444.

32. Anderson, Peter, Xiaodong He, Chris Buehler, Damien Teney, Mark Johnson, Stephen Gould, and Lei Zhang. "*Bottom-Up and Top-Down Attention for Image Captioning and Visual Question Answering*." 2018 IEEE/CVF Conference on Computer Vision and Pattern Recognition, 2018. doi:10.1109/cvpr.2018.00636.

33. Jin-Hwa Kim, Jaehyun Jun, Byoung-Tak Zhang. "Bilinear Attention Networks", NIPS 2018, arXiv:1805.07932

34. Do, Tuong, Huy Tran, Thanh-Toan Do, Erman Tjiputra, and Quang Tran. *"Compact Trilinear Interaction for Visual Question Answering."* *2019 IEEE/CVF International Conference on Computer Vision (ICCV)*, 2019. doi:10.1109/iccv.2019.00048.

35. Ben-younes, Hedi, Remi Cadene, Nicolas Thome, and Matthieu Cord. *"BLOCK: Bilinear Superdiagonal Fusion for Visual Question Answering and Visual Relationship Detection."* *Proceedings of the AAAI Conference on Artificial Intelligence* 33 (2019), 8102–8109. doi:10.1609/aaai.v33i01.33018102.

36. Cadene, Remi, Hedi Ben-younes, Matthieu Cord, and Nicolas Thome. *"MUREL: Multimodal Relational Reasoning for Visual Question Answering."* *2019 IEEE/CVF Conference on Computer Vision and Pattern Recognition (CVPR)*, 2019. doi:10.1109/cvpr.2019.00209.

37. Jiang, Huaizu, Ishan Misra, Marcus Rohrbach, Erik Learned-Miller, and Xinlei Chen. *"In Defense of Grid Features for Visual Question Answering."* *2020 IEEE/CVF Conference on Computer Vision and Pattern Recognition (CVPR)*, 2020. doi:10.1109/cvpr42600.2020.01028.

38. Chen, Yen-Chun, Linjie Li, Licheng Yu, Ahmed El Kholy, Faisal Ahmed, Zhe Gan, Yu Cheng, and Jingjing Liu. *"UNITER: UNiversal Image-TExt Representation Learning."* *Computer Vision – ECCV 2020*, 2020, 104–120. doi:10.1007/978-3-030-58577-8_7.

39. Wang, Tan, Jianqiang Huang, Hanwang Zhang, and Qianru Sun. *"Visual Commonsense R-CNN."* *2020 IEEE/CVF Conference on Computer Vision and Pattern Recognition (CVPR)*, 2020. doi:10.1109/cvpr42600.2020.01077.

40. Li, Xiujun, Xi Yin, Chunyuan Li, Pengchuan Zhang, Xiaowei Hu, Lei Zhang, Lijuan Wang, et al. "Oscar: Object-Semantics Aligned Pre-training for Vision-Language Tasks." *Computer Vision – ECCV 2020*, 2020, 121–137. doi:10.1007/978-3-030-58577-8_8.

10

Deep Neural Networks for Recommender Systems

Ajay Dhruv
Thadomal Shahani Engineering College, Mumbai, India

Meenakshi S Arya
SRM Institute of Science and Technology, Chennai, India

J.W. Bakal
SSJCOE, Mumbai, India

CONTENTS

10.1 Overview of Recommender Systems

Let us go back a few decades to when the concept of a supermarket was restricted to larger cities, and the general public relied on the small stores locally run by a family or a group of people. Whenever you walked into the store, by virtue of knowing you personally as well as your buying preferences, the shopkeeper would keep taking stuff out to show you until eventually you would not get what you had in your mind. This qualifies as simplest kind of content filtering. A decade later with the boom of supermarkets, everything has been placed in these stores in a manner such that you can catch a glimpse of everything available and accordingly fill up your shopping cart. This was a typical scenario when computer technology was growing as per the traditional Moore's law. [1]

However, around the year 2005, technological changes caused the slackening of Moore's law, and the universal computer as proposed by Alan Turing was not improving exponentially (as described in Moore's law) in connection with the speed and energy efficiency. Hardware developments and the processing speeds of devices started escalating at a much faster pace than was expected. The GPUs crunched data at an extremely fast pace, the data storage migrated to cloud, and the availability of the Internet at all places resulted in the fourth revolution, which is popularly termed as Industry 4.0. The advent of Artificial Intelligence changed the complete landscape.

Businesses, as well as their clients, started getting online to increase the base (for businesses) and accessibility and availability (for customers). The availability of user feedback and profiles in multiple systems providing a glimpse into their varied tastes and interests has enabled these businesses to leverage this information to design better user models and thereby focus on personalized selling rather than just selling. Intelligent algorithms run at the backend to try to extract information out of customer browsing behavior and online activity, as well as correlate and associate different customers to understand buying patterns so as to recommend products.

The growth of web services and the availability of multiple options to the customer is the biggest driving factor for recommendation systems. The customer's mindset has changed from, "What do I want to buy, eat, or listen to?" to "What all can you provide me?" If the business cannot show the customer what tempts him, the customer might be lost completely. Thus, it has become imperative for these services to understand the customer so that the loyalty of the customer can be retained, and the customer keeps returning back to get value for his money. Today the amount of data generated daily online is estimated to be roughly around 2.5 quintillion bytes, [2] and it is growing at an equivalent pace with every passing day. According to a study by McKinsey, [3] recommendation algorithms are responsible for nearly 75 percent of the content being viewed by customers on Netflix and around 35 percent of the products being purchased by customers on Amazon.

This brings us to a very important fact that a recommender system isn't only an extravagant algorithm but a software that seeks to predict customer preferences, thereby bringing the complete e-shop to their doorstep. It's also about harnessing the information provided by the data in order to understand users. The long-drawn debate between the importance of whether data or powereful algorithms is the driving factor is still going on. Both have their cons; powerful algorithms require sophisticated hardware and lots of it. More data creates other challenges, like how to access it fast. [4] The recommender systems are needed for: [5]

- converting visitors into customers,
- getting personalized recommendations to the users,
- helping users to take correct decisions in their online transactions,
- redefining the users web browsing experience,
- preventing customer attrition,
- increasing sales, and
- pushing up company revenues.

In addition to this, it is essential to understand the concept of an e-business from the perspective of a recommendation system. Let us take an example of Netflix. Netflix and its 14 libraries in different countries have more than 6000 to 7000 movies, series, and shows available in their network. For a user to know about all these titles is close to impossible; here, the recommendation systems are a big blessing as they recommend to you the top 10 titles with respect to your last seen titles (content-filtering), as well as the titles which other people who have viewed the same title have viewed (collaborative filtering).[6]

10.2 Jargon Associated with Recommender Systems

10.2.1 Domain

Today everything is sold online, from food to movies to clothes to beauty care products—and all provide recommendations to the customer. The kind of content that a recommender system will work upon is referred to as its *domain of recommendation*. Take for example Kindle; the domain is books, but the domain of a recommender system may vary from movies (Netflix), groceries (Amazon), music (Spotify), travel (Trivago), e-learning (Udemy/Coursera), and any other product that can be recommended. The knowledge of the domain plays a significant role as it determines the permissible error in the recommender system. Recommending an incorrect movie (in a movie recommender system) will not have the same catastrophic implication as recommending a specific drug to treat a deadly disease (in a drug recommender system), as the latter can cost somebody their life. The domain also sets the feasibility of repetitive recommendation, i.e., whether the same thing can be recommended more than once.

10.2.2 Goal

As discussed earlier, the main objective of a recommender systems is to retain users by providing them with the requisite information in a manner so as to ensure that they will favor the recommended item. These recommendations are based on the system learning through the former user interaction with the data source. Let's revisit the example of Netflix with its 14 libraries and enormous amounts of content. The ultimate aim is to make customers pay for the subscription and remain hooked month after month by customizing the home screen with content they want to watch. Netflix views its worth though the amount of content viewed. Anyone not having a Netflix account is lured by advertisements, which are furthermore curated to suit the user's preferences so as to convert them from casual customers to permanent customers. The second major goal of recommender systems is to build loyalty, and hence more and more data needs to be analyzed per user to offer super-personalized recommendations of the products.[7]

10.2.3 Context

The context may also be considered as the habitat of a recommendation system. It includes the devices, the platforms, the mood, the nature, the time, or any similar factor, which will be a catalyst in determining how will the user responds to the recommendation.

10.2.4 Personalization

When the phrase "data is the new oil" is used, it has its roots deep into the systems that want to utilize and tap every bit of information about their user to give them the best possible e-commerce experience. Customer browsing behavior and history are a vital part of recommendation systems because they enable systems to model the users and thus personalize items or services for each customer's needs. Recommending an item is based on the popularity of the items (the more popular an item, the more recommendations it gets) whereas personalization is based on individual taste (which may or may not be the most popular). Recommendation is a generic form of personalization, e.g., when you buy a book on Amazon and it recommends other books of the same genre or related to your purchase, it is recommendation. Recommending a book that you have wanted to buy as a birthday gift for your spouse one week prior to his or her birthday is personalization. Personalization is the most data-intensive exercise, as the data pertaining to a person helps you understand them more.

10.2.5 Data

A recommender system seeks to guess and predict the preferences of user content regarding all the utilities or services available online. The suggestions are given or recommended based on user's recent interests by drawing inferences from data usage history. To gain an understanding about the preferences of a customer, a recommender system generally employs data sources that provide an explicit feedback received from diverse evaluation metrics. Depending on the business goals, a system can work based on various types of data like clicks, past records, and so on. The data used for training a model to make recommendations can be split into several categories.

10.2.6 Algorithm

In the subsequent sections, a number of algorithms used for generating recommendations will be discussed.

10.3 Building a Deep Neural Network

Let us consider an example of a binary classification problem. Out of the given dataset, the goal is to forecast or predict whether the given image is a sunflower or not. The applied function should give output as 1 for a sunflower picture and 0 for any other kind of image. The task, however, becomes challenging whenever the classification is a *multi-classification* problem (more than 2 classes need to be predicted). The simplest definition of a neuron is that it is a function. The function comprises of an input, some weights, a bias, and an activation function.

$$y_i = \sigma\left(\sum_{i=1}^{n} w_i x_i + b\right) \qquad (10.1)$$

where w_i refers to the weight assigned to each input node, x_i refers to the value of the input node, and b refers to the bias of the node under consideration. The bias adds on to the neural network an additional parameter to tune with an aim to improve the fit. The bias can be initialized to 0.

A neural network is a network of such neurons wired in a manner that they give the desired output. While constructing a neural network, one of the primary steps is to find an appropriate activation function (σ). The activation function is a very essential parameter that helps to decide which neurons will be allowed to fire the neurons at the next stage and which ones will not be allowed to.

From Equation (10.1), let $u = \left(\sum_{i=1}^{n} w_i x_i + b\right)$. The activation function to be applied can be chosen from the family of activation functions like the

$$\text{tanh activation function}\left(g(u) = \frac{1 - e^{-2u}}{1 + e^{-2u}}\right) \tag{10.2}$$

$$\text{sigmoid activation function}\left(g(u) = \frac{1}{1 + e^{-\lambda u}}\right) \tag{10.3}$$

$$\text{relu activation function}\left(g(u) = \max(u, 0)\right) \tag{10.4}$$

Once an appropriate activation function is chosen, the next step is to describe a function that will be applied for **forward propagation** and **backpropagation**. In forward propagation, we move from input node to output node in one direction and a succession of calculations are performed to make a prediction and to calculate the **cost.** The cost function is calculated as follows:

$$C_i = \left(y - y_i\right)^2 \tag{10.5}$$

where y is the expected value and y_i is the predicted value.

For the network to predict/classify values well, the cost function needs to minimized. The process of backpropagation is used for the same computation of the partial derivatives.

Let us consider a single layered neural network with two layers:

$$u_2 = w_2 x_1 + b_1 \tag{10.6}$$

$$x_2 = \sigma(u_2) \tag{10.7}$$

where x_2 is the predicted value. Let the actual value be x, then the cost function is given by:

$$C = \left(x - x_2\right)^2 \tag{10.8}$$

Upon careful consideration of the same, it can be seen that the cost function is derived from the predicted and the actual value, which in turn is derived from the activation function, and the activation function itself is derived from the weight and the bias. Thus, backpropagation uses the partial derivatives to calculate the effect of changing (tuning) these parameters so as to reduce the cost.

$$\frac{\delta C}{\delta w} = \frac{\delta u}{\delta w} \cdot \frac{\delta x_2}{\delta u} \cdot \frac{\delta C}{\delta x_2} \tag{10.9}$$

It helps to investigate the effect on cost function while changing the bias and the weights. This will be essentially beneficial during the optimization stage to minimize the cost function.

The forward propagation and backpropagation need to be repeated to update the parameters for minimizing the cost function. The learning rate is basically the size of δ (step size) that the algorithm sets for tuning the hyperparameters. This is done using **gradient descent and is a very challenging task.** Gradient descent mainly facilitates in finding out the local minima so as to reduce the cost. The significance of learning rate is extremely pronounced as a small learning rate will cause the algorithm to reach the local minima in a large amount of time whereas a large learning rate might cause it to overshoot the local minima thus never reaching the global minimum thereby causing the gradient descent to oscillate endlessly.

Once the cost function is reduced below an acceptable value, the prediction is done. Generally, at the terminal layer of a neural network, instead of the regular activation functions, the SoftMax activation function is used for multi-class separation. However, for binary classifications, sigmoid activation function can be used, which will output a value between 0 and 1. The prediction can be done by setting the value more than 0.7 as a positive example (it is a sunflower) or a false example (not a sunflower). The efficiency of the network is finally evaluated using various error related metrics.

10.4 Deep Neural Network Architectures

Deep learning is a subset of machine learning that deals with supervised, unsupervised, or semi-supervised algorithms that are inspired by the architecture and functioning of the human brain. These algorithms are emulated in the form of computer programs and a complex network of artificial neurons is created to duplicate the architecture and is called functioning of the human brain. These networks are called **artificial neural networks**.

A deep learning network comprises of two main phases: training and generating predictions. In the training phase the data is labeled to determine its characteristics. The system compares these characteristics and memorizes them to make correct decisions when it comes across similar data in the process. During the prediction phase, the deep learning model derives conclusions and labels new unknown data using previous knowledge.

Deep neural networks are extensively used in image processing, speech recognition, natural language processing, health care, self-driving cars, fraud detection, and many more fields. The term "deep" in deep neural networks simply means "multiple layers" in the network architecture. They have lots of advantages:

- Easier feature selection and learning
- Works best with unstructured data
- Learning with minimal guidelines
- Accurate results

Two important architectures in the context of deep neural networks are recurrent neural networks (RNN) and convolutional neural networks (CNN).

10.4.1 Recurrent Neural Networks (RNN)

The recurrent neural network (RNN) is a specialized kind of neural network model that is more applicable for sequential data. Standard feed-forward neural networks cannot handle sequential data, e.g., for the task of recognizing whether the pattern of words is name of a person. This is mainly because:

1. Input and output can be of different lengths, e.g., translation from Dutch to English language.
2. Simple neural networks do not share features across the network (Figure 10.1).

Learning process of an RNN includes two aspects: forward propagation and backpropagation. Forward propagation is the process of the flow of information from the input layer to the output layer. The RNN first takes input as x_0, i.e., first input and provides the output y_0. For the second step, it not only takes x_1 as input, but also uses activation from previous step. There are some parameters that guide the connection from x_0 to the hidden layer denoted by W_i, horizontal connections are governed by W_r and output predictions W_y.

This process is mathematically represented as:

$$h^{(t)} = g_h\left(w_i x^{(t)} + w_r h^{(t-1)} + b_h\right) \tag{10.10}$$

$$y^{(t)} = g_y\left(w_y h^{(t)} + b_y\right) \tag{10.11}$$

where,
  g_h, g_y = activation functions
  $x^{(t)}$ = input at time t
  w_i, w_r = weight matrix
  b_h = bias

In RNN training, backpropagation is applied for every time stamp. It is commonly known as backpropagation through time. For backpropagation, the total loss needs to be calculated using the following equation:

$$L\left(\hat{y}, y\right) = \sum_{t=1}^{T} L(t)\left(\hat{y}(t), y(t)\right) \tag{10.12}$$

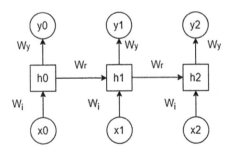

FIGURE 10.1
Recurrent Neural Network Architecture

TABLE 10.1

RNN Architecture Types

Type of RNN	Example
Many-to-many	Name recognition
Many-to-one	Movie review classification
One-to-many	Single word translation
One-to-many	Music generation

L = Total loss, $L^{(t)}$ = Loss at time t

$\hat{y}(t)$ = Output predicted at time t, $y^{(t)}$ = Actual Output at time t

The types of RNN are shown in Table 10.1.

One drawback of RNN is that it only uses the previous information that is information presented earlier in the sequence, but at times there is information after in the sequence that may help in prediction. Bharadhwaj, Park, and Li (2020) leveraged the temporal features of recurrent neural network (RNN) and generative adversarial network (GAN), individually, to improve the significance of recommended items. Two datasets on food and movie recommendations were used, and the results indicated that the proposed model outperformed the other baseline models regardless of user behavior and compactness of training data.

10.4.2 Convolutional Neural Network (CNN)

When subjected to image data (predominantly two-dimensioanl), neural network models are tweaked and enhanced to form a specialized kind of neural network called a convolutional neural network (CNN). These CNNs can be used with multidimensional data (Figure 10.2).

The convolutional layer is at the center of the network, thus its name. This layer performs the convolution operation that involves the multiplication of a set of weights with the input. This convolution operation multiplies an array of input data and a 2D array of weights, called a filter. The main purpose of the convolution layer is to extract features, which may be as simple as detecting edges in the image.

The convolution layer in CNNs is followed by a max-pooling layer, which performs the primary function of reducing the dimensionality without causing a loss of the image quality. Max-pooling is basically a process of sub-sampling and significantly reduces the

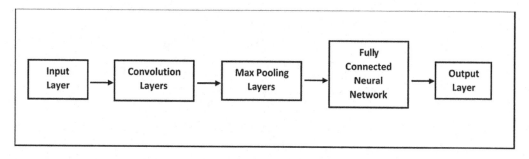

FIGURE 10.2

Convolutional Neural Network Architecture

dimension of the image. Post processing, the image is flattened and passed through the dense layers as in a regular neural network. The SoftMax activation function is applied at the output layer so as to get probabilistic distribution of the likelihood of each output class.

ConvNet requires lower pre-processing, and in last few years convolutional neural networks (CNN) have dominated other algorithms, especially for machine vision tasks and medical imaging. The layers needed to implement CNN are convolutional layer, max pooling layer, flatten layer, and dense layer. The main functionality of CNN is implemented using convolution layer. CNN makes use of multiple conv2D layers and max pooling layers in sequence. A dense layer is required at the terminating point to output the results.

10.5 Recommendation Using Deep Neural Networks

Deep learning has proven enormous benefits in recommending products/items ranging across news articles, restaurants, cuisines, garments, and even the health care sector. [9] As compared to traditional machine learning approaches, recommender systems built using deep neural networks have the ability to perform feature engineering on their own and ensure faster learning. Also, deep learning minimizes the role of a human domain expert, which is not the case in machine learning. A detailed review of recent research advances made on deep learning-based recommender systems is present in multiple papers. [1,10,11] The study outlines an overview of deep learning-based recommendation models, an insight into various dimensions of the deep learning like models utilized in recommender systems, and remedies for the hurdles of recommender systems. A wide-ranging summary of the state-of-the-art as well as the current trends in the domain, along with new perspectives, are described in detail. Today many researchers are developing recommender systems using DNNs. Due to the availability of various tools, pre-trained models, and ease of tuning the hyperparameters, DNNs are assisting the construction of powerful recommender systems. Some of the systems under practice are:

- System to predict an outfit recommendation based on user characteristics and preferences.
- Help assistant systems for recommending the right course for your career.
- Recommending books, novels, music, and movies to users.

A framework for movie recommender systems is proposed in Taheri and Irajian (2018) that allows various heterogeneous inputs ranging from user and item communities and feedback for improving the performance of the recommender system. Deep learning has gained fame across many fields like natural language processing, multimedia file processing, satellite imagery, and most importantly recommender systems. Some of the examples where deep neural networks are used for recommender systems are organized as follows:

- A multi-layer perceptron-based recommendation can be thought of as a bi-interaction method between user choices and items. The matrix factorization works by decomposing the rating matrix into low-dimensional user/item hidden factors. To model a

two-way interaction between users and items such as movies, shows, and so on, neural collaborative filtering constructs a dual neural network. The study, [13] proposes a multi-trans matrix factorization (MTMF) model to arrest the temporal dynamics in data. A personalized time weight is introduced to combine the forgetting curve and item similarity, thereby reducing the influence of outdated information and thus retaining the influence of users' stable preferences. The proposed technique showed promising results when applied on the historical MovieLens dataset vis-à-vis the existing temporal recommendation methods.

- A two-stage recommendation model, i.e., candidate generation and candidate ranking, can be developed using deep neural networks for recommending YouTube videos.

- Collaborative filtering can be used for user-item embeddings and are learned via increasing the distance between users and their poor rated items and minimizing the distance among the users and their preferred products. This work [14] combines the pros of the user based KNN algorithm and item-based algorithm. The authors through experiment analysis on the MovieLens dataset proved that an ensemble based KNN algorithm gives improved recommendation quality.

- CNN is basically a feed-forward neural network with convolution layers and pooling operations and it is extremely strong in training unstructured multimedia data. The network can be constructed comprising of one or more CNNs which are used for training samples. This can be further used for recommending images to the user.

- A hybrid recommendation system can be built using deep neural nets for music and video recommendations. The CNN-based ResNet model can be used to extract features from audio and video signals. It can also assist to alleviate the cold-start problem in audio and video recommendations.

- Graph-based convolutional neural networks can be applied for web-based recommender systems for recommendations on Pinterest and other social networks.

- RNNs can be used to predict what will a particular user purchase next, based on the click history profile. It helps to balance the trade-off between processing costs and prediction accuracy.

- Traditionally, most recommendation models are challenging in capturing the user's temporal intentions. They are also widely used in self-driving cars.

- For integrating deep learning models for an apparel recommendation system, a combination of deep learning models can be used to get some vital characteristics of the outfit used by the user. In this example, the recommendations will be based on the user and item attributes. The user attributes under consideration are: sex, age, and body mass index (BMI). The product features are the type of apparels the user is wearing. A photograph of the user will be required to generate the predictions. The garment attributes will be obtained from a full-body image of the user. A pose calculator can be used to find if the user is complete or not. The estimator detects 20–25 key points of a person. If it understands at least 15–17 points, we assume that the person is complete. The You Only Look Once (YOLO) classifier is used which is one of the most accurate image classifiers. The face detection model can be built that detects the different views of human faces. For age and sex detection, one can use a convolutional neural network. The outfit features are compared to the apparels in the records and the recommendations are made by an embedding. Further, it suggests similar apparels to the ones the user is currently wearing.

10.6 Tuning Hyperparameters in Deep Neural Networks

The success rate of a deep neural network model lies in setting the most optimum values of the hyperparameters under consideration. One may feel that the hyperparameters are set correctly, but often they might not work on certain part of your dataset or even outliers. Various hyperparameters while modeling a neural network are as follows:

- Learning rate
- Mini-batch size
- Number of hidden units
- Number of layers
- Learning rate decay
- Activation functions

It is difficult to decide which hyperparameter is most vital in a problem. One of the ways to tune is to sample a grid with n hyperparameter settings, and then try all settings combinations on the problem.

In general, the input data will be split into three parts:

- Training set
- Development set
- Testing set

A model is built using the training set, and then hyperparameters are optimized on development set as much as possible. Once the model is ready, the model is evaluated using the testing set. If the model is underfitting it is said to have a "high bias," whereas if the model is overfitting it is said to have a "high variance." The model being constructed must have minimum bias as well as variance.

- If the algorithm has a high bias:
  - o Try to increase the number of layers in your neural network.
  - o Try a different model that is suitable for your data.
  - o Try to run it for a longer duration.
- If the algorithm has a high variance:
  - o Pass more data.
  - o Try regularization.
  - o Try a different model that is more suitable for your data.

The various solutions available for regularization are as follows:

- L2 regularization: This is a hyperparameter setting that reduces the chances of model overfitting. It achieves this task by minimizing the values of the weights to as small as possible but not zero.
- Dropout: Dropout is a regularization technique applied during training. It is often applied during forward propagation and backpropagation.

- Data augmentation: Data augmentation is a method to increase the size of the training dataset by taking help from existing samples. The main advantage of data augmentation is the reduction of overfitting.
- Early stopping: In this technique the training set and the development set cost is plotted together for each iteration. At some iteration, the development set cost will stop decreasing and will start increasing. The point at which the training set error and development set error are best is picked, i.e., the cost should be the lowest.

10.7 Open Issues in Research

- Dynamically changing user preferences in retail market
- Lack of relevant data (domain specific, problem specific, outliers)
- Creating more robust neural networks
- Understanding and tuning the behaviour of the model under consideration
- Using generative adversarial networks (GANs) to build adaptive recommender engines
- One can inspect and evaluate a recommender engine based on customer satisfaction rate and usability aspects rather than only focussing on traditional evaluation metrics

10.8 Conclusion

Deep learning is becoming more and more useful as well as important for solving complicated research problems around us. At the same time, it provides many viable solutions for day-to-day life. This chapter covers the core applications of deep learning, which is recommendation systems. It highlights the need of recommendation systems and various systems that are under practice. It emphasizes on the deep learning architectures for building recommender systems. The chapter also provides many applications of recommender systems where deep learning is involved. Finally, the chapter covers hyperparameter tuning, which is one of the most vital stages during the training and testing process. At the end, the chapter delivers open issues in research in analytics and predictions.

References

1. Zhang, S., Yao, L., Sun, A. and Tay, Y., 2019. Deep Learning Based Recommender System. *ACM Computing Surveys*, 52(1), pp. 1–38.
2. Marr, B., 2020. *How Much Data Do We Create Every Day? The Mind-Blowing Stats Everyone Should Read*. [online] Forbes. Available at: https://www.forbes.com/sites/bernardmarr/2018/05/21/how-much-data-do-we-create-every-day-the-mind-blowing-stats-everyone-should-read/

3. Mackenzie, I., Meyer, C. and Noble, S., 2020. *How Retailers Can Keep Up With Consumers.* [online] https://www.mckinsey.com. Available at: https://www.mckinsey.com/industries/retail/our-insights/how-retailers-can-keep-up-with-consumers

4. Falk, K., 2019. *Practical Recommender Systems.* [ebook] Manning Publications. Available at: https://www.manning.com/books/practical-recommender-systems

5. Banda, T. and Avina, A., 2020. *Building A Recommendation System Using Deep Learning Models.* [online] dzone.com. Available at: https://dzone.com/articles/building-a-recommendation-system-using-deep-learni

6. Enríquez, J., Morales-Trujillo, L., Calle-Alonso, F., Domínguez-Mayo, F. and Lucas-Rodríguez, J., 2019. Recommendation and Classification Systems: A Systematic Mapping Study. *Scientific Programming*, 2019, pp. 1–18.

7. Drachsler, H., Hummel, H. and Koper, R., 2009. Identifying the Goal, User model and Conditions of Recommender Systems for Formal and Informal Learning. *Journal of Digital Information*, 10, pp. 4–24.

8. Bharadhwaj, Homanga, A Homin Park, and A Brian Y. Lim. 2020. "Recgan: Recurrent Generative Adversarial Networks For Recommendation Systems". In *12Th ACM Conference On Recommender Systems*, 372–376. Vancouver, British Columbia, Canada: Association for Computing Machinery. https://dl.acm.org/doi/10.1145/3240323.3240383.

9. Diaz-Aviles, Ernesto. 2020. "A Glimpse Into Deep Learning For Recommender Systems". *Medium.* https://medium.com/libreai/a-glimpse-into-deep-learning-for-recommender-systems-d66ae0681775.

10. Batmaz, Zeynep, Ali Yurekli, Alper Bilge, and Cihan Kaleli. 2018. "A Review On Deep Learning For Recommender Systems: Challenges And Remedies". *Artificial Intelligence Review* 52 (1): 1–37. doi:10.1007/s10462-018-9654-y.

11. Mu, Ruihui. 2018. "A Survey Of Recommender Systems Based On Deep Learning". *IEEE Access* 6: 69009-69022. doi:10.1109/access.2018.2880197.

12. Taheri, S. M., and I. Irajian. 2018. "*Deepmovrs: A Unified Framework For Deep Learning-Based Movie Recommender Systems*". In *2018 6Th Iranian Joint Congress On Fuzzy And Intelligent Systems (CFIS)*, 200–204. IEEE. https://ieeexplore.ieee.org/document/8336633.

13. Zhang, Jianyun, and Xianling Lu. 2020. "A Multi-Trans Matrix Factorization Model With Improved Time Weight In Temporal Recommender Systems". *IEEE Access* 8: 2408–2416. doi:10.1109/access.2019.2960540.

14. Venil, P., G. Vinodhini, and R. Suban. 2019. "*Performance Evaluation Of Ensemble Based Collaborative Filtering Recommender System*". In *2019 IEEE International Conference On System, Computation, Automation And Networking (ICSCAN)*, 1–5. IEEE. http://doi: 10.1109/ICSCAN.2019.8878777.

11

Application of Data Science in Supply Chain Management: Real-World Case Study in Logistics

Emir Žunić

University of Sarajevo, Bosnia and Herzegovina

Kerim Hodžić and Sead Delalić

University of Sarajevo and Info Studio d.o.o. Sarajevo, Bosnia and Herzegovina

Haris Hasić

Tokyo Institute of Technology, Japan and Info Studio d.o.o. Sarajevo, Bosnia and Herzegovina

Robert B. Handfield

North Carolina State University and Supply Chain Resource Cooperative, NC, United States

CONTENTS

11.1 Introduction

Supply chain management (SCM) represents a set of complex processes that need to be adapted to create a workable and cost-effective system. In practice, SCM consists of a complete set of steps from production to delivery to end users. Distribution companies are a significant part of the whole system. If only distribution companies are observed, then SCM involves the process of order planning, warehousing, and transportation to end customers.

Distribution companies' workflow consists of several steps that must be planned in detail to ensure the cost-effective operation of the company. In the first step, they have to plan and order goods from manufacturers. When the ordered items arrive, it is necessary to find an appropriate position in the warehouse for each item. During that process, each item is labeled. In the next step, customers make orders. When the ordering process is complete, it is necessary to collect orders from the warehouse and prepare them for transport. The final step in the system is the transport of goods to final customers. The complete process is shown in Figure 11.1.

In the process of order planning, it is necessary to make a prediction of sales and accordingly order enough goods to satisfy each customer, but at the same time not create excessive inventory that unnecessarily increases the cost of all warehouse processes. During the process of receiving goods in the warehouse, it is necessary to label and place the received goods in appropriate locations in the warehouse. When choosing a location, it is possible to achieve savings in further warehouse operations.

The warehouses consist of racks. Each rack contains a number of pallet locations arranged by floors. All products are stored in pallet places and usually each pallet place contains only one type of item. There are aisles between the racks, which are called parallel aisles. At certain positions in the racks, there are also aisles to improve the mobility through the warehouse. They are called cross aisles. Workers move on foot, with picking carts or forklifts through the aisles, and perform common tasks. After receiving customer orders, the process of collecting orders is initiated. The collection process depends largely on the type, size, and warehouse layout. During the order picking process, it is necessary to comply with multiple rules and restrictions, both when selecting locations and determining the order of visits. According to Bartholdi and Hackman (2014), the ordering process takes

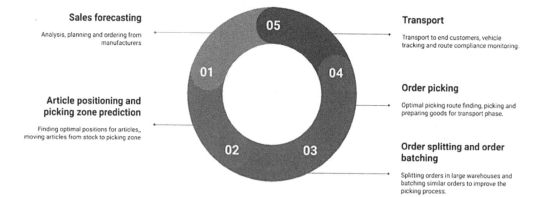

Sales forecasting

Analysis, planning and ordering from manufacturers

Article positioning and picking zone prediction

Finding optimal positions for articles,, moving articles from stock to picking zone

Transport

Transport to end customers, vehicle tracking and route compliance monitoring.

Order picking

Optimal picking route finding, picking and preparing goods for transport phase.

Order splitting and order batching

Splitting orders in large warehouses and batching similar orders to improve the picking process.

FIGURE 11.1
The Complete Categorization of SCM Processes

more than 50% of the total warehouse operation cost, and good organization of this process is of great importance.

Order picking is a process where a worker is walking and collecting ordered items. The worker is usually using a picking cart to collect and store items. Occasionally, items are located in higher pallet places and cannot be hand-picked. Pallet places where workers can collect items by hand are called the picking zone. Other pallet places are called the stock zone. When items are in the stock zone, the forklifts have to be used to move the items to the picking zone. The use of forklifts during the order picking is significantly slowing down the process. Therefore, the picking zone must be carefully planned to avoid the use of forklifts whenever possible. During the usual warehouse operations, certain locations are occasionally emptied, in which case the movement of goods within the warehouse takes place. More frequent items are being moved to better empty locations.

Large distribution companies own large-scale warehouses. In such warehouses, items from one order are often at different parts of the warehouse, and the process of order picking can be a tedious task for a single worker. In this case, the process of splitting orders into a series of smaller ones is initiated. In practice, the process usually consists of dividing the warehouse into sectors, with each of the smaller orders belonging to exactly one sector. In this case, the total distance traveled increases, but at the same time workers collect orders with a smaller mass and volume. The order batching process is used to optimize the order-picking process. Order batching is a process where one worker collects more than one order at a time. After all orders have been collected, they are prepared and sorted by vehicles for transport to final customers. Driving routes are created, where customers and the order of visits are determined for each vehicle. A number of realistic constraints have to be satisfied to make each route feasible.

By automating and improving each of these processes, it is possible to achieve significant financial savings and to facilitate and simplify the operation of the warehouse. Each of these processes should be monitored through the information systems that most often represent a combination of warehouse management systems (WMS) and transportation management systems (TMS). When all the data is properly collected in the information systems, it is possible to leverage the data and the optimization. The optimization of these processes is the subject of extensive scientific research. Although individual process optimization improves company performance, the greatest savings can be achieved through balanced optimization, planning, and coordination of all processes.

This chapter presents the concept of a supply chain management system improved by the artificial intelligence algorithms. Smart supply chain management includes inventory and procurement planning from manufacturers, acceptance of goods, activities of collecting and moving goods within the warehouse, as well as the process of optimizing deliveries to end customers. The delivery optimization process consists of planning the fleet of vehicles, scheduling customers by vehicle, and planning the optimal delivery route. In doing so, it is necessary to comply with many real constraints in order to obtain feasible and cost-effective routes. This chapter describes a number of improvements to the complete transportation system, including GPS vehicle tracking and route compliance, and the use of GPS data collected to improve future route proposals. The concept has been further improved by introducing a 3D-visualization warehouse and route optimization for traveling merchants. This concept has been implemented in a number of large distribution companies in Bosnia and Herzegovina.

By including all those improvements and optimizations in a smart SCM concept, it is estimated that the business in the real-world case study has improved by ~30% in organizational terms and in terms of human and other resources, while the financial side has improved by as much as approximately 30% to 40% of operational costs. The satisfaction of system users and workers, as well as customers and suppliers, has greatly increased, which is certainly one of the most important factors for the successful operation of the company

11.2 Related Work

As described in the introduction section, there are three main process categories in the SCM for distribution companies: order planning operations, warehousing-related operations, and transportation-related operations. All of these categories are further divided into subcategories that revolve around specific tasks that have been the subject of research in many different contexts. Therefore, a considerable amount of literature exists if all these tasks are included, but most of it is done within a specific environment or described through a specific case study. To fully encompass the gist of these researchers and place them into an SCM-related context, they will be described through individual research parts of the warehouse optimization project carried out in Bosnia and Herzegovina.

A successful order-planning approach in this context needs to start with the analysis of collected historical sales data as it is described in the work from Zunic and colleagues, [2] where the Prophet algorithm from Facebook is adapted for the sales forecasting task. Here, a pre-developed algorithm was successfully adapted to work in a retail sales analysis context, and it achieved reasonable results in terms of generating quarterly and monthly sales forecasts. A more detailed look at retail sales analysis approaches shows that three main approaches exist for this goal: time-series forecasting, ANN-based forecasting and hybrid approach forecasting. According to the analysis of multiple comparative studies like those from Aras et al.,[3] Alon et al.,[4] and Au et al.,[5] the best-performing models are the hybrid approaches, which indicates the complexity of the problem. Additional research on the topic of analysis of the warehouse sales data, which were implemented in this context, include the works from Golic et al. [6] and Zunic et al. [7] in which the outlier/anomaly detection task is tackled. These approaches were developed to help identify and exclude anomalous data during the main prediction of warehouse sales data. More insights on building efficient and sustainable supply chains are extensively described in the research by Handfield et al. [8–10]

After the retail sales data analysis, the strategic placement of the items in the warehouse racks is the next task. This is thoroughly analyzed in the related research from Zunic et al. [11] and Nogo et al., [12] where predictive analysis techniques and associative rules were applied for this task. In the former research, the historical sales data and the current status of the racks are analyzed to determine the best possible positioning of the items given the current context and existing constraints. In the latter research, the storage assignment is further improved by discovering association rules through the analysis of the same real-world data using various techniques like Apriori, FP-Growth, and ECLAT algorithms. Further research from Kofler et al. [13] and Fumi et al. [14] introduces different takes on this storage assignment problem. After the items are successfully stored, the order planning process, which covers the input of the wares in the warehouse, is finally completed. However, one more transitional step for planning the capacity and the strategic replenishment of the picking zone remains. This warehouse-specific task is covered in detail in the research from Zunic et al. [15] where the historical sales data is used to strategically place the most frequently sold items to more accessible locations and re-sort the cluttered warehouse storage racks over time. This leads to easier navigation of forklifts and more efficient order picking, which is a process covered by the warehousing-related operations category.

The two initial tasks during the handling of incoming orders are order splitting and order batching. To optimize the workflow in the warehouse, large orders are split into smaller parts through a process called order splitting. To minimize the traveled distance of the warehouse workers, some of these parts, which are not necessary from the same order, are batched and picked up together. The detailed approaches to handle these tasks are described in the research from Delalic et al. [16] and Zunic et al. [17] respectively. The former research approach utilizes the similarity of the process of order splitting with the vehicle routing problem and applies different approaches in solving it. Some notable approaches are described in the research from Kritikos and Ioannou [18] and Gendreau et al. [19]

The efficiency of the order-picking process is impacted by the warehouse layout. This is an important constraint that needs to be catered to while designing a warehouse, but in situations where the optimization needs to be performed on a fixed layout, different techniques need to be applied. This aspect of the optimization is described through the research from Zunic et al. [20] and Zunic et al. [21] where order-picking optimization is designed mainly to be robust against the constraints that come with different layout approaches. This is a very important aspect of the optimization processes inside a warehouse because of the effect that the layouts can have on the overall performance, as described in the research from Gu et al. [22] and Gue and Meller. [23] Furthermore, additional approaches for the navigation in various layouts are described in the research from Roodbergen and De Koster. [24–25] Finally, to increase the overview and navigation possibilities, a position-based visualization of the warehouse was developed through the research of Cogo et al. [26] This allowed the workers and the management of the warehouse to have a better overview of the situation in the warehouse and to plan the inventory process accordingly.

After the processes inside the warehouse have been optimized, the final task is the delivery of the items to the final customers. Given the specific context of delivery vehicle routing in Bosnia and Herzegovina, multiple research approaches have been covered and thoroughly described through the extensive research from Zunic et al. [27–35] on this topic. All described individual research projects include a systematic literature overview and most of them achieve satisfactory results given the environment in which they are applied. In the following sections of the chapter, all of these approaches will be summarized and the benefits of each part toward building a completely automated logistics warehouse will be illustrated and analyzed.

11.3 Smart Supply Chain Management Concept

The whole concept consists of nine segments: demand forecasting and stock optimization, including outlier (anomaly) detection, product positioning, picking zone prediction, order splitting, order batching, order picking, 3D visualization, vehicle routing during the delivery of goods, and traveling merchants cluster-based route improvements as an additional step in a whole concept. Each segment offers the possibility of optimizing and improving the company workflow. By optimizing individual processes, significant improvements are achieved. However, the greatest power of the concept is visible through the optimization and cooperation of all these segments.

Goods are ordered from the manufacturer based on sales history and previous experience. With the right quantity of ordered items, the cost of storage is reduced and the processes in the warehouse are simplified. When items arrive at the warehouse, it is necessary to place them in the best position. This will affect and improve the order-picking process. Also, at the beginning of each day, appropriate quantities of goods are prepared in the picking zone to speed up the order picking process. End customers send their orders online or orders are collected by travel merchants. By optimizing the routes of traveling merchants, significant savings are achieved, and the number of visited customers and picked orders is increased. Large orders are split into a series of smaller ones to reduce the workload of workers. As the transport of goods is the most expensive process, driving routes are created. Based on the routes, a picking plan is made and order batches are created. Orders are collected and prepared by vehicles and later transported to the end customers. Warehouse visualization and GPS vehicle tracking allow easy tracking of all processes, and the data collected is used for further performance improvements for segments. Therefore, proper linking of all steps, achieved a functioning system which significantly increases the performance of work. Each of these segments with the obtained results will be described in detail in the following subsections.

11.3.1 Demand Forecasting and Stock Optimization

For the successful delivery of goods to end customers, the number of items stored in warehouses is crucial. The number of items should be kept within the previously determined limit, because too many items can slow down the operation of the warehouse and increase costs, while even greater damage occurs if the warehouse does not have enough items to deliver to the end customer. In addition to the financial cost, there is a reduction in the company's reputation, which leaves long-term consequences. In the best case, the number of items in the warehouse matches the number of items ordered by end customers. That is, of course, an impossible task to reach in reality, but the main goal is to converge to that number. This problem is called *demand forecasting* in the literature. The problem is based on the analysis of historical data and their use for sales forecasting. It is very important to take into account the periods of the year and weeks like holidays and weekends, and also different planned or unplanned discounts. For the purpose of this project, a few different approaches were implemented in order to achieve better results. Their implementation and results comparison are given in the next paragraphs.

Some of the approaches described in the previous section explained picking-zone prediction modules. Those two modules have some similarities. The picking-zone predictions are predicting orders for a day, while te demand forecasting is usually trying to predict sales for the period between two weeks and three months. Adaptive shifted median approach is explained in detail in the paper by Zunic et al. [15] This approach showed better results for the picking zone prediction than demand forecasting, as it does not take into account holidays and discounts. The picking zone prediction is more fault tolerant, because in the case of wrong prediction, items can be transferred from the stock zone. Demand forecasting based on the prophet algorithm showed better results for product that have a long history of sales data. For the best results, minimum length of data history is 39 months. At least 24 months of sales data are observed, as well a a year of backtesting data and 3 months to find the accuracy of 3 months forecasts. Figure 11.2 shows one backtesting step for a chosen product.

An approach based on LSTMs produced better results for shorter predictions (daily instead of monthly). The probable reason is the existence of a larger number of data for

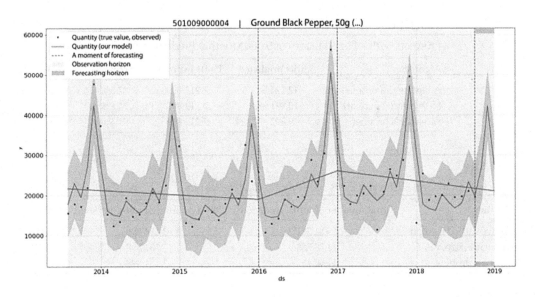

FIGURE 11.2
Illustrative Backtesting Experiment (Step 1 of 12) [2]

TABLE 11.1

All Product Daily Prediction Results

Algorithm	Units predicted	Units exported	Accuracy
Adaptive shifted median	502 137	314 120	92.9%
LSTM neural network	416 889	314 120	88.9%
Facebook's prophet	487 779	314 120	83.9%

TABLE 11.2

Products with a Long History of Sales Daily Prediction Results

Algorithm	Units predicted	Units exported	Accuracy
Adaptive shifted median	391 233	171 123	91.2%
LSTM neural network	280 234	171 123	91.3%
Facebook's prophet	251 031	171 123	94.1%

training phase. Table 11.1 shows summarized results for all approaches based on the total number of predicted product units and accuracy with different analysis for all products and daily predictions, and Table 11.2 shows results only for products that have a sales history of 24 months and longer. Table 11.3 and Table 11.4 show the same, but for monthly predictions.

The data that is gathered can always be susceptible to mistakes. This is also the case with historical sales data, which is used in forecasting. Those mistakes are called anomalies and can cause fake peaks in the data, which inherently leads to less accurate predictions. In order to avoid such situations, an important step is to identify and eliminate those

TABLE 11.3

Products with a Long History of Sales Monthly Prediction Results

Algorithm	Units predicted	Units exported	Accuracy
Adaptive shifted median	12 124 581	7 212 899	87.8%
LSTM neural network	10 391 938	7 212 899	74.6%
Facebook's prophet	9 892 871	7 212 899	91.4%

TABLE 11.4

Products with a Long History of Sales Monthly Prediction Results

Algorithm	Total number of units predicted	Total number of units exported	Accuracy
Adaptive shifted median	6 781 711	3 134 898	89.7%
LSTM neural network	4 678 788	3 134 898	77.5%
Facebook's prophet	4 800 481	3 134 898	97.8%

anomalies and use only accurate data as input to prediction algorithms. Such anomaly detection algorithms which are utilized in this project and are described in the research papers by Golic et al. [6] and Zunic et al. [36]

11.3.2 Product Positioning

One important step in supply chain management and important module in the smart WMS is to optimize product storing positions in the warehouse. The main goal is to gather the most frequently ordered products near the place where orders are stored and also to store products that are usually ordered together near each other. When products come to the warehouse, they enter the warehouse input location from where they are later transferred further into the warehouse. When orders are collected, they are usually stored near the warehouse exit location from where they are later transferred to the final customers. In order to make the order collecting process faster, it is important to have more frequently ordered products stored near the exit location which leads to a less traveling distance for workers collecting orders. Warehouses can be divided into sectors like food, cosmetics, low temperature room, and so on but can also be free for all products to be placed in every location. Algorithm implementation and results can differ in those cases as it is shown in next paragraphs. In a smart WMS there are two modules dealing with situations where products have to be placed in their racks. One is, as already mentioned, product positioning on arrival at the warehouse, and second is when the picking zone is being prepared and products are moved from stock zone to picking zone. Described methods can be used in those both cases. Another approach is to use this algorithm when moving products to the stock zone, and to move products to the nearest free location in the picking zone when it is preparing. The second approach benefits decrease the forklift traveling time and distance. The algorithm is such that it looks at best vacant warehouse locations and proposes them as a list of suggested locations. The most frequent items converge over time to the best locations. In completely empty warehouses, it can be used for the initial arrangement of products and in such cases this approach gives the best results. In addition to this approach, the association rules can be used to gather products frequently ordered together, as described in Nogo et al. [12]

The algorithm consists of four steps. The first step is to calculate grades for every warehouse location. Location grade is calculated as distance between that location and warehouse exit location. Locations that are nearer to the exit location get better grades. The algorithm for calculating distance between every warehouse location is described in Zunic et al. [11] The second step is to determine all the products that need to be placed in the warehouse, and calculate the rating (grade) for each product. The grade can be calculated based on the order frequency which product was part of. Frequency is calculated with different factors for periods of the last year, quarter, and month. Then both grading scales are scaled and products with better grades are paired with free locations. The algorithm is shown in 11.1 and elaborated in detail as a part of the author's previous work on this subject. [11]

ALGORITHM 11.1   CALCULATION OF POSITION/PRODUCT GRADE

```
function CalculateProductPositionGrades
        Require:
        aid - Identification number of the entering item.
        sec - Sector of the entering item.
        ig ← CalculateItemGrade(aid);
        positions ← GetListOfFreePositions(sec);
        cwgb ← CalculateCurrentWarehouseGradeBalance(sec);
        For p in positions do
                result.Add(p.id, ig/p.grade, cwgb - ig/p.grade);
        End
        //optional
        calculateAssociationRulesForWholeBatch();
        return result;
End
```

Chosen metrics for results comparison is average total length of the path needed to be taken by the worker to collect all daily orders. Tables show the average daily length difference in time from the time algorithm is implemented in the warehouse. Table 11.5 shows how number order size impacts the results. It is clear that for the biggest orders a worker has to walk almost full path in the warehouse, but for smaller orders results are much better. Results are also significantly dependent on the initial product positioning.

TABLE 11.5

Average Picking Route Length Reduction Compared in Order Size

Number of products on the order	1 month after	1 year after
20+	8.3%	9.3%
10–20	7.7%	8.9%
5–10	8.1%	13.7%
0–5	5.6%	19.4%

TABLE 11.6

Average Picking Route Length Reduction in
Different Layouts Compared

Number of sectors	1 month after	1 year after
0	7.8%	18.9%
2	11.3%	13.5%
3+	9.7%	11.2%

TABLE 11.7

Average Picking Route Length Reduction for
Empty and Full Warehouse

Warehouse state	1 month after	1 year after
Empty	18.5%	19.1%
Full	9.1%	16.6%

Table 11.6 shows how the number of warehouse sectors impact on the results where warehouses that are not organized in sectors shows best results. Reason for that is more space for an algorithm to take into account when calculating positions for every product. Table 11.7 shows results of the simulation where the whole warehouse is emptied and then the algorithm suggested a new position for every product.

Another measure that can be used to analyze the results is changes in the positioning of certain items in the warehouse. Figure 11.3 shows a comparison before and after the implementation of the proposed method.

The marked pallet places represent the ten most frequent products in the warehouse. The left image shows the position before using the algorithm, while the right image shows the positions one month after implementation. It is easy to notice that there has been a change in positioning, and that the homogeneity of positions has increased. The most frequent items were not scattered around the warehouse, and the positions were moved toward the central aisle. The central aisle is a frequent part of the warehouse, and the most prestigious locations are located near it.

11.3.3 Picking Zone Prediction

Warehouse racks are consisted of two main zones: picking (golden) and stock zone. Picking zone is part of the racks from which items can be picked by hand. Those are usually the first two or three rack floors. Stock zone is everything above. When there are not enough items to be picked, then the forklift has to be used to get the product from the stock zone. This consumes more time and energy. In order to further improve the order picking process, the picking zone has to be prepared and enough product units have to be transferred before the picking process begins. Picking zone preparation is usually done daily, early in the morning. It is necessary to predict how many items will be ordered tomorrow, which is not a simple problem to solve. The problem has some similarities with demand forecasting and stock planning in supply chain management. In some companies who had implemented a transport management

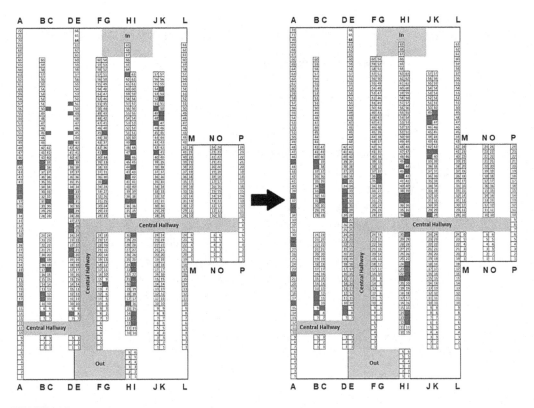

FIGURE 11.3
Most Frequently Ordered Products Location Change [11]

system, orders were gathered day before they were transported to the final customers, and they were transferred day after they were collected. In those cases, product and number of product units are known before as exact numbers which simplifies this process a lot.

During system development, different algorithms for picking zone preparation were implemented. The main idea is based on a shifted median where historical sales data is sorted and then value that is on 0.9 positions is taken into consideration; position 0 is lowest value, on position 1 is highest value, and on position separates all values in half. On this value different modifications based on different periods of time are made. The heuristics-based approach is implemented. The supervised learning is used as a part of the solution. The concept is shown in Figure 11.4.

Different implementations with comparisons are explained in detail in one of the author's previous papers. [15] The second approach is based on Prophet algorithm by Facebook and backtesting strategy, which is explained in this paper [2]. Third approach is based on LSTM neural networks and that approach is described in this paper [37]. When prediction is calculated for every product, workers get the list of the amount of every product that is missing in the picking zone. If there is little difference between predicted value and amount that is currently in the picking zone, then the picking zone refill can cause a lot of transfers. That is the reason why refillment filters are implemented as shown in Algorithm 11.2.

ALGORITHM 11.2   PREDICTION OF THE PICKING ZONE (WITH FILTER)

```
function PickingZonePredictionFilter
        Require:
        pza - Number of item units currently in the picking zone;
        sza - Number of item units currently in the stock zone;
        pv - Predicted number of item units;
        mv - Difference between pv and pza;
        sm - Shifted median;
        pv ← predictValue(item)
        If (sza > 0 and pv > pza) then
                If ((pv <= 100 and pza <= sm and mv/pv > 0.2) or
                        (pv > 100 and pv <= 500 and mv/pv > 0.15) or
                        (pv > 500 and pv <= 1000 and mv/pv > 0.1) or
                        (pv > 1000 and mv/pv > 0.05)) then
                                // Display the mv value on workers screen
                                SuggestMissingValue();
                End
        End
End
```

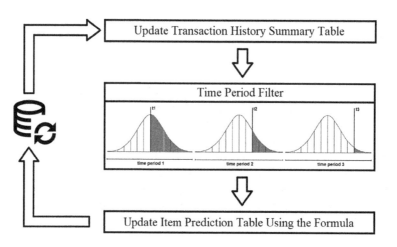

FIGURE 11.4
Flow Diagram of the Proposed Picking Zone Prediction Model [15]

For results analysis, different metrics were used. First is prediction accuracy, which is calculated as a percentage of ordered product units per order and per product that is completely gathered from the picking zone. Higher value is better. The number of product units suggested to be prepared in the picking zone is used as the second metric. The lower number is better. The reason is that the picking zone has limited space, and it must not become overcrowded with products. Table 11.8 shows comparison between different approaches.

TABLE 11.8

Different Algorithms Results—Comparison Analysis

Approach	Total number of units	Accuracy
Shifted median	536,225	91.2%
Adaptive shifted median	502,137	92.9%
LSTM neural networks	416,889	88.9%
Facebook's Prophet	487,799	83.9%

The third metric is the decrease in the total number of warehouse transfers per day, excluding picking zone preparation period which showed a decrease of between 30% and 50% depending on a day. In those transactions under 1% were from stock to pick zone.

11.3.4 Order Splitting

Distribution companies work with different items and usually distribute items in large geographic areas. Warehouses are used to store large quantities of goods. This means that large-scale warehouses are needed. When orders from customers are made, orders need to be collected from the warehouse. Workers need to walk through different parts of the warehouse to collect the order. For larger orders, total mass and volume can exceed the picking cart capacity, the total distance traveled may be significantly higher than in smaller warehouses, and the picker may spend a considerable amount of working time collecting a small number of orders. In addition, it is physically and psychologically easier to handle the collection of a larger number of smaller orders.

Therefore, the original orders are separated into a series of smaller orders. The original order is considered collected when all smaller orders have been collected and merged together. In practice, the most commonly encountered approach is to split orders based on previously defined sectors. Sectors are defined either as separate spaces in a warehouse (e.g., a chamber) or based on the type of goods stored in pallet locations.

The method of warehouse sectoring has several advantages. The main advantage is the division of the large warehouse into several smaller parts, where each picker is in charge of his own part of the warehouse. Based on this, each worker collects a smaller order and each worker is thoroughly familiar with his part of the warehouse. However, this approach does not represent an optimal division as the total distance traveled to collect the original order increases significantly. The reason for the increase is the fact that when order splitting is done, orders are created with a small number of items or certain items can be collected along the way (the picker already passes by the location with items, but that location does not belong to his sector, so the items are not picked). Small orders are not balanced. Occasionally, there is a low number of items in some sectors, which makes the order picking unprofitable and it is an additional disadvantage of this method of order splitting.

An innovative approach based on the VRP and a popular nature-inspired metaheuristic algorithm inspired by the ant colonies (ACO) is implemented and explained [17]. This approach consists of two main steps: calculating the number of smaller orders and the process of order splitting.

The total number of small orders is determined based on a few values: total mass (m_{tot}), total volume (V_{tot}), distances between each two pallet places in the order, maximal mass (m_{max}) and volume (V_{max}) one picker can take, the number of available pickers, and the maximal distance one picker can travel (d_{max}). A simple greedy algorithm is used to approximate the total route length (d_{tot}). The number of small orders is given by:

$$k = \left\lceil \max\left\{ c_d \cdot d_{tot} / d_{max}, c_m \cdot m_{tot} / m_{max}, c_V \cdot V_{tot} / V_{max} \right\} \right\rceil,$$

where parameters c_d, c_m and c_V are constant values.

Order splitting is the second step. In this process, each item should be placed in one of the k smaller orders. The problem is solved as the traveling salesman problem (TSP) using the ACO algorithm, where each pallet place is equivalent to a customer and each worker is added as a special customer to the TSP. The location of the special customers is the location of the starting pallet place, and the distance between each two special customers is set to a large value. This guarantees that two special customers will never be consecutive customers in the route. For each worker, the route is represented as the sequence of customers between two special customers in the final route. The objective function is calculated as:

$$D + \max_{i=1,k} \left(c_m \cdot m_i + c_V \cdot V_i + c_d \cdot d_i \right).$$

The length of all routes is marked by D, while m_i, V_i, d_i are total mass, volume, and length of the route i. Constants c_m, c_V and c_d depend on the warehouse settings and preferences.

The results of the implemented approach based on the ACO algorithm are compared with two standard approaches in warehouse operation. In the first approach, orders are not split, while in the second approach, orders are split into predefined sectors. The approach was tested on 1000 large orders. The order is considered to be large if it has twenty or more picking locations. The average mass is 236.51 kilogram. The average number of locations is 34.37. Predefined route length limit for workers is exceeded in more than 729 orders, and 545 orders exceed the mass and volume limit. When the algorithm is implemented, route length, mass, and volume limits are not exceeded. Compared to the predefined sector splitting, the algorithm gave significantly shorter routes (~40%).

11.3.5 Order Batching

Order batching is done to improve the picking process in the warehouse. The complete order batching concept consists of several steps. As the first step, customers make orders. Each order is divided in one of two different approaches. The simplest approach to divide orders is by splitting them to predefined sectors. If the orders are divided by the previously defined process, then the sector for each order is determined after the division. This way, the order batching process complexity is decreased. The sector for each of the final orders is determined by checking the dominant sector among locations in the order. The dominant sector is the sector to which most item locations belong.

Once all orders have been collected in the information system, the vehicle routing process is done. In this process, all orders are assigned to vehicles. The order picking process is done vehicle by vehicle. When orders for one vehicle are collected, orders for the next vehicle are collected. In case the routes have not been created before, orders are collected in a previously defined order (e.g., by creation time or by priorities).

Then the order batching process is done. In this process, order batches are created and pickers collect all orders from the batch at one time. When all parts of the original order are collected, everything is checked, and the process of order splitting and batching is done.

The order batching problem is a problem of creating optimal order batches. This process determines which orders should be collected together. The goal of the process is to optimize the distance traveled during the order picking for each vehicle and sector. This process is a hard optimization process, so it cannot be solved by checking all possible solutions. If route planning is not done earlier, then batches are created only by sectors or predefined groups.

In this approach, the Bat algorithm (BA) is implemented for order batching. The BA is a metaheuristic algorithm which is primarily created to solve continuous optimization problems. [38] In literature, many adaptations of the BA are created for problems of combinatorial optimization, where order batching also belongs. The complete pseudocode for the discrete BA is given in Algorithm 11.3.

ALGORITHM 11.3 THE MODIFIED BA FOR ORDER BATCHING OPTIMIZATION

```
Define the objective function f(x)
Initialize the bat population X = x_1, x_2, x_3 ... x_n
Find the best bat in population x_best
For each bat x_i in the population X do
        Initialize the pulse rate r_I
        Initialize the velocity vi
        Initialize the loudness A_I
End
Repeat
        For each bat x_I in the population X do
                Generate new solution
                Generate the random number rand
                If rand > r_I then
                        Generate solution around the best bat
                End
                If rand < A_I and f(x_I) < f(x_best) then
                        Accept the new solution
                        Increase r_I
                        Reduce A_I
                End
        End
End
```

The code in Algorithm 11.3 is the modified discrete bat algorithm used as the traveling salesman solver [39]. The goal is to minimize the traveled distance. Because for each order dozens of locations are visited, and the total number of smaller orders to be batched can be in the hundreds, it is not practical to calculate all distances between locations and to solve multiple TSP problems to find the total distance. In our approach, the objective is modified as follows.

All constraints have to be included. For a picker, a maximum number of orders to be picked at a time is determined. That number is usually determined by the number of compartments on the picking cart. At the same time, maximum volume and mass for each picker is determined and calculated in the objective function. When some of these constraints are violated, the returned value shows that the solution is not feasible. The goal is for the batch order to contain as few racks as possible, and to minimize the distance of the outermost pallet locations within each rack. One bat is created by shuffling all orders. Each subsequent order is added to the batch if possible, otherwise a new batch is created. All bats in the initial population are created as described. Pulse rate and loudness are defined and modified by the original formulas [38]. The velocity depends on the bat's distance. The distance is calculated as follows. For each order, corresponding batches are compared in both bats. For each order in the observed batches, the distance is increased if it is not contained in both batches.

A new solution from the existing one is created by choosing one of the three equally possible methods: two random orders swap batches, one random order creates a new batch, or one random order leaves the batch and joins existing one. The implemented concept was tested in the large real-world warehouse. For each vehicle, routes are created, and orders are divided by predefined sectors or by the previously defined algorithm. The algorithm was tested for 50 days of warehouse operation where more than 8200 orders were observed. The population of 50 bats is used. Initial loudness is set to be a real number between 0.7 and 1, and the initial pulse rate is set as a random number between 0 and 0.4. Parameter alpha is set to 0.98, as well as the gamma. The maximum number of iterations is set to 30,000, and the bat algorithm runs exactly 10 times for each instance. The algorithm assumes that maximum 4 orders and 100 kilograms can fit to a cart.

The approach was compared to two other approaches. In the first approach, orders were not batched. In the second approach, the greedy approach was used to batch order, where batches are created by batching orders by creation time. The bat algorithm outperforms both approaches. The first approach is improved by 61.2%, and the second approach is improved by 16%. The results confirmed that the concept of order batching can significantly improve warehouse operations, even by more than 50%. The only disadvantage of this process is the fact that the merging of collected orders must be further verified. In practice, this is not an additional effort, as the orders collected are already verified before loading to transport vehicles.

11.3.6 Order Picking

Order picking is the most expensive process in warehouse operation. It consists of several steps. A list of pallet places that picker need to visit to collect the order is created. Additional information about those locations is also collected. Pickers walk through the warehouse and pick items in the picking cart. The number of locations a worker should visit varies. It is often necessary to visit dozens of locations, and the best order of locations to be visited has to be determined. Seemingly, it is a classic traveling salesman problem (TSP).

In practice, there are many constraints and limitations. One of the constraints is the priority of the items. Priority is determined based on the weight, volume, or fragility of the item. Lighter or fragile items should not be placed at the bottom of the cart, so they have to be picked at the end. Perishable goods are collected at the end of orders (e.g., ice cream and similar goods). Defined differently, there are priority classes for items in the collection process. Orders with fewer locations were obtained, so that the optimal picking route problem can be solved with simpler approaches such as simpler approaches (2-opt, 3-opt).

As stated [20], 2-opt and 3-opt give routes with less than 5% and 3% error, respectively. The algorithm was tested on 5,000 orders in the real warehouse. The presented approach

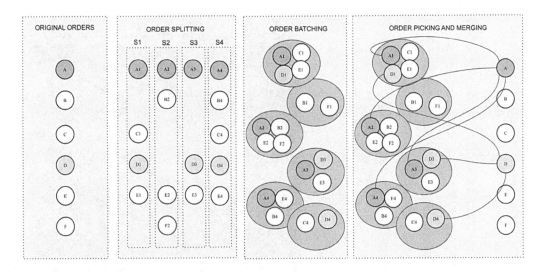

FIGURE 11.5
Complete Order Collecting Process Consisting of Order Splitting, Order Batching, Order Picking, and Merging

with priorities was compared to the previously used algorithm based on the item's brand and commodity group. The workers path shortens by 41.3% on average. The time savings is hard to calculate in real conditions, because the time the worker spends collecting items from the pallet place is the same in both approaches, and it depends on the item type and other factors. However, based on the estimations, the time savings is about 30%.

As it can be observed, one of the most important components for the algorithm is the process of calculating the distance between the locations used in the warehouse. It is necessary to create a simple and fast way to calculate the distance between warehouse locations. In this concept, the generic approach for distance calculation in the warehouse of general layout is implemented. The algorithm is based on dynamic programming.

As described in previous sections, the order collecting process in the smart SCM consists of several parts. Large orders or orders in large warehouses are divided into several smaller orders. Orders in the same sectors are batched when possible. Larger orders are created, but they are picked on a smaller warehouse area. When all parts of the original orders are collected, they are merged to the original order and the order is ready to be delivered to the end customer. This process is shown in Figure 11.5. Original orders *A* and *D* are marked. As can be seen, order *A* is divided into four smaller orders (*A1, A2, A3, A4*), and the order *D* is divided into three smaller orders (*D1, D3,* and *D4*). Then, batches are created and the order picking process for each batch can begin. When all parts of the original orders *A* and *D* are collected, they are merged together and the order picking process for the original orders is done.

11.3.7 33D Warehouse Visualization

The research done by Cogo et. al. [26] describes the development of a tool that is mainly aimed to facilitate the overview of the current situation in the warehouse racks and detect possible outliers and represent them through visual indications. A novel data visualization method in 3D space which includes all of the information about specific rack positions is developed which operates in real-time based on the information stored in the

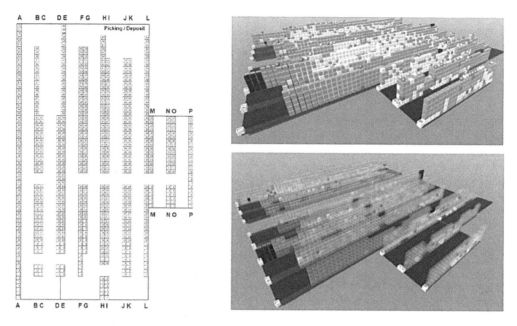

FIGURE 11.6
a) The general warehouse layout and examples of the developed b) marker-based and c) transparency-based 3D visualization approaches.

main database. Three different views are possible: qualitative view, quantitative view, and cumulative view. Given that all data is fetched, analyzed, and visualized in real-time, multiple different challenges in terms of precision and recall speed needed to be addressed.

In Figure 11.6, the actual translation of the 2D warehouse layout (a) to a position-based 3D visualization based on markers, and (b) object transparency is depicted. This way of representing available and unavailable warehouse racks offers a more comprehensive environment for humans to understand and react to cluttering problems that can arise in such dynamic environments. Furthermore, this representation can also assist with the navigation of workers through the warehouse, especially if the warehouse in question has big dimensions with a high amount of different products.

This position-based 3D visualization approach enabled quicker responses with additional information about object positioning or the spatial relation of different objects. Queries that seek information lower than the minimum hierarchy level can be shown without omitting data and queries that seek multiple types of data are limited by available pallet space. This approach also facilitated the general overview possibilities and added a more comprehensive and intuitive view of the storage racks status, which is especially useful for the higher levels of management.

11.3.8 Smart Data-Driven Transport Management System (TMS)

The next step after collecting the orders in the warehouse is the transport to the final customers. Throughout the approach, smart TMS optimization represents a very important component. Transport represents one third of the total cost of the logistics process. At the same time, the successful implementation of transport systems significantly reduces this cost. Transport is the last step in the complete process of production, storage, and delivery of goods to the end user. Manufacturers and distributors achieve maximum profit only in the case of optimal organization of the transport process. Logistic planning cannot obtain its total potential without a qualitative transportation system. Therefore, a successfully implemented transport system increases efficiency and reduces cost. By successfully solving the vehicle routing problem, the efficiency of the entire company is significantly increased.

The proposed approach of the optimal creation of transport routes is described in detail [27–28]. The approach consists of two main modules: (i) algorithm for solving the rich VRP, and (ii) parameter tuning process for the proposed algorithm. Realistic VRP problems are solved by a combination of several approaches, and the two major subcategories are: (i) a clustering solution based on the distribution of customers into the geographically remote regions (modeled on the experiential thinking of transport managers), and (ii) a multi–phase algorithm which creates the optimal routes for visiting remaining customers not belonging to any of the clusters, using the remaining available vehicle fleet. The proposed algorithm for solving rich VRP consists of several phases. Real-world constraints are included in the routing process through penalties. Therefore, the algorithm requires the initial setting of a large number of parameters and constant values that significantly affect the speed and quality of the solution. Due to the large amount of historical data, it is possible to do a dynamic parameter adjustment. The entire approach is described as adaptive and data-driven, as presented in Figure 11.7.

The results obtained by the described procedure are feasible in practice, which is one of the most important components for any company. In practice, the highest cost occurs in the case of non-delivery of orders to end customers, where in addition to the financial cost, the previously mentioned damage to reputation occurs.

The algorithm is adapted to solve the problem of multiple depots. GIS (geographic information system) and GPS (global positioning system) data are taken into consideration in the very approach, aside from the historical ones. This data is also used in an innovative way and to adjust some of the parameters of a VRP problem, which in practice is extremely difficult to define. All of the above is implemented as part of the web platform used for several large distribution companies in southeast Europe. The basic components shown in Figure 11.7 will be briefly presented hereafter.

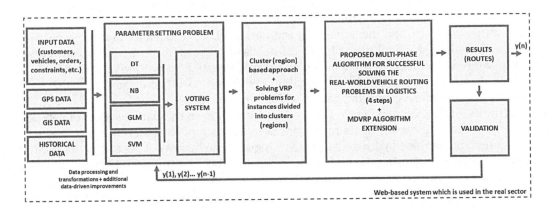

FIGURE 11.7
Proposed Smart TMS Approach

11.3.8.1 Solving VRP Problems for Instances Divided into Regions (Clusters)

The first phase of the approach is to create the clusters for all the customers to be served. Clusters are created depending on the distance of their center from the depot. Initial cluster creation is possible by using simple clustering algorithms such as k-medoids, hierarchical clustering, or K-means.

Aside from clustering methods, heuristic approaches also give good results. In this way a group of several hundred (or even several thousand) customers can be divided into several remote clusters, which significantly reduces the complexity of a problem in the next phases of the proposed approach. Also, if all customers ready to be served are concentrated around the depot, the number of clusters equals zero, so this step is ignored in the entire approach and we move to the next level.

As part of the SCM concept, several different approaches to creating clusters have been implemented and compared. A standard K-means algorithm has been implemented, as well as manual clustering based on the location of customers. In the manual approach, the corresponding region is defined in advance for each city and place, and customers are divided by the specified regions. The K-means algorithm shows a lack of ability to adapt to the routing problem, and ultimately leads to satisfactory solutions with tangible improvements. The latter approach has yielded satisfactory results in the case of less urban regions, as it is based on the many years of experience of transport managers. In the case of routing problems where a large number of customers are in cities or other urban regions, the algorithm encounters a problem of increased complexity.

Therefore, a metaheuristic approach was implemented using the Firefly algorithm (FA). The FA is inspired by the luminous behavior of fireflies, where fireflies with brighter light attract less bright fireflies. [40] The Firefly algorithm has been implemented to a number of hard optimization problems, [41] and has shown quality results in the field of clustering. [42] For SCM purposes, the basic FA is tailored to solve the clustering problem.

Therefore, the number of clusters has to be determined and the initial population has to be defined. It is necessary to define the objective function, the motion operator, and the distance of the agents. The number of clusters was determined by analyzing the number of customers and vehicles. The goal function is based on the analysis of the total distance of customers from the center of the corresponding cluster, as well as on the basis of the difference in the number of the most numerous and the cluster with the smallest number of customers. The initial population was selected based on the location of the customers, where a certain number of customers are selected for each individual. To calculate the distance and the movement of the fireflies, for each center of one individual, the nearest center of the other is chosen, and the movement is done based on the distance of those centers.

The algorithm gave quality results for the needs of routing problems, and solved previously observed problems in urban areas, but also automated the process of customer clustering. Based on the tested 30-day routing, compared to other approaches, the VRP algorithm based on FA clustering gave 10–15% better results.

In the example shown in Figure 11.8, special vehicles from the available fleet of vehicles during the creating the transport routes are used for each of the individual clusters, and they cannot be combined with each other. Customers who do not belong to any of the clusters are optimized by using the remaining vehicles in the next approach phase and can be inter-combined in one or more transport routes. Generally, customers are concentrated around the depot without the cluster, while remote customers belong to appropriate clusters, which is usually the approach unacceptable in practice. Also, if there are not enough customers to use the most cost-efficient vehicle, those who do not belong to any of the clusters and are on the route of the vehicle can be joined to the given cluster.

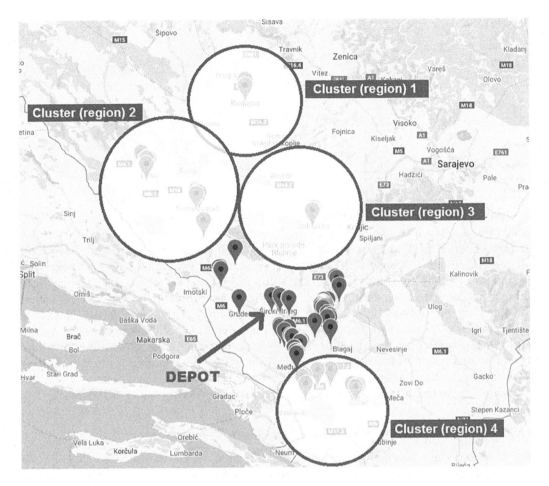

FIGURE 11.8
Customers Divided into Geographically Separated Regions (Clusters)

The number of clusters is determined in a way that within every cluster, there has to be:

$$\frac{\textit{The number of customers}}{\textit{The total number of customers}} \geq \frac{1}{\textit{The number of remaining vehicles in fleet}} \cdot 100 [\%].$$ The num-

ber of clusters described in this way should exceed the number of available vehicles from the fleet. If that happens, smaller neighboring clusters will be put together into the bigger ones (regions). If there is not any possibility of cluster unification because of the ordered capacity of the goods compared to the dimensions and constraints of the available vehicles, in this case additional (fictitious) vehicles with a significantly higher delivery cost are introduced. Any company can rent additional vehicles from the external companies delivering goods as their primary business.

11.3.8.2 Multiphase Adaptive Algorithm for Solving Complex VRP Problems

After the initial division into regions, a multiphase algorithm has been proposed for the remaining customers and the available fleet, which can optimally solve realistic VRP problems and meet a number of practical constraints. Algorithms consist of several phases, which are shown in Figure 11.9, and each of the phases is described in detail [27].

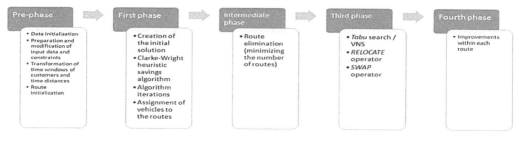

FIGURE 11.9
Phases of the Proposed Algorithm

The proposed algorithm that solves such a defined problem consists of four successively linked phases. The initial solution is created in the first phase, which improves in further phases. The modification Clark-Wright was implemented for these purposes. The second phase follows, which decreases the total number of routes. The solution obtained from the second phase of the algorithm is the initial solution for the local search. Tabu search algorithm is implemented as the third phase. Since this phase proved to be the most important for obtaining the optimal solution, the implementation and the variable neighborhood search (VNS) were made in this phase. After finalizing Tabu/VNS search, phase four is initiated (post-phase), which tries to find the optimal order of customers in each route. Then the attempt of additional vehicle redistribution is being made for already defined transport routes because vehicles from the fleet proved to be used in a better way, and at the same time to unload some vehicles, which makes the very routes more balanced.

11.3.8.3 Dynamic Adjustment of the Algorithm Control Parameters

The proposed algorithm contains a series of parameters and values whose values can be set after analysis of historical data. The entire approach consists of a segment that continuously and dynamically adjust parameters of the algorithm as show in Figure 11.10.

Four prediction models [27–28] have been implemented: generalized linear models (GLM), naïve Bayes algorithm (NB), support vector machines (SVM), and decision trees (DT). In the next step, a decision system was created that finds the result with the best predictive accuracy during every routing was implemented.

Each of the parameters of the proposed algorithm is determined independently. First step was data preprocessing, excluding only those from the history with all constraints being set. The next step is removing the redundant attributes and normalizing of the input values. Then we determine the significance of the input attributes for each of the target attributes. Minimum descriptor length (MDL) was used to determine the attribute significance, while one decimal rounded normalization process of the attributes was performed.

11.3.8.4 Improvements of the Proposed Routes Based on GPS Data

In order to analyze and validate the proposed routes in practice, it is necessary for the vehicles used in transport routes to have GPS coordinates of their movements collected. The accuracy of GPS data is extremely important to properly use for the purpose of analysis and the improvement of the very transport routes. Therefore, an algorithm for detecting anomalies in GPS records was implemented. The algorithm is described in more details [29]. The process consists of four steps: detection of the anomalies of the first type,

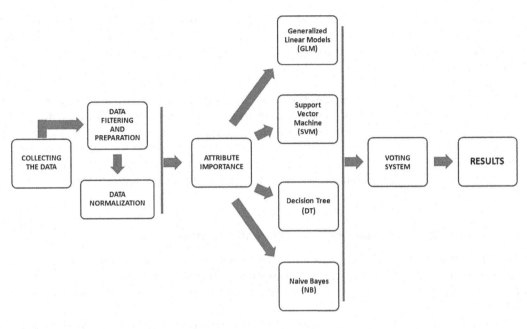

FIGURE 11.10
Dynamic Adjustment of Parameters and Constants

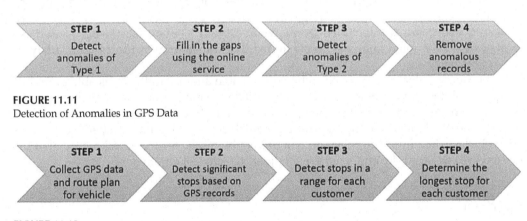

FIGURE 11.11
Detection of Anomalies in GPS Data

FIGURE 11.12
Route Analysis Based on GPS Data

completing of the routes, detection of the second type anomalies, and removing anomalous records. The complete process is shown in Figure 11.11.

Similarity was observed in the process of detection of anomalies of the second type in GPS coordinates with the process of detection of QRS complex of ECG signals. The AF1 algorithm was used for the detection of possible anomalies, although it is primarily used for the detection of the QRS complex. [29] Using such filtered and exact GPS data, the analysis of the transport route is performed at the end of each day, based on real GPS data.

The process of analyzing the proposed routes based on GPS data is presented in Figure 11.12.

In the first step presented in Figure 11.12, all GPS records for the observed vehicle are extracted and sorted by time of their occurrence. A driving plan has also been prepared and sorted out for the observed day and the vehicle. In the second step, it is necessary to deactivate every possible stop the customer makes. Of course, it is not necessary to deactivate every vehicle stopping, because it usually happens during the traffic jams or at the traffic lights.

The proposed algorithm detects stopping longer than 60 seconds. In the third step, all the stoppings are deactivated within the predefined range for each of the customers (usually of several hundred meters). The last step includes determining the longest stopping and service time for each of the customers. If more than one customer can be found in a single stop, the stopping time is proportionally divided concerning the predicted serving time of the algorithm for each of these customers. In addition, GPS data have been created in an innovative way to correct errors in customers' locations, [30] and to improve input parameters of the proposed algorithm.

11.3.8.5 Results: Smart Data-Driven Transport Management System

Detailed comparative analyses have been performed for each of the segments of smart TMS system [27–30]. The most significant results, performed on the benchmark data of a distribution company, also advertised to other researchers [31–33] are presented in this work.

Ten different days were used for testing the proposed multiphase algorithm. Real-world data was used to check the results. Analyzing the results, it is shown that the results in Tabu local search are better than using the VNS search in the same phase of the proposed algorithm.

Results with comments included are shown in Table 11.9 (when Tabu search is used as a local search). The main goal was to create feasible transportation routes that satisfy all constraints being set.

The proposed algorithm proved to be very reliable and accurate and is able to find an adequate solution for extremely complex input data. A small number of available vehicles and a heterogeneous fleet makes the optimal solution difficult to find. Optimality of the solution mostly depends on the algorithm parameters, as well as the number of customers and vehicles. Therefore, a comparison of a prediction model for the access component follows, which dynamically and adaptively adjusts the control parameters.

TABLE 11.9

Test Results (Real-World Dataset)

Instance	Num. of customers	ALGORITHM solution cost	Available vehicles in fleet	Number of used vehicles	Comment
19062018	107	124.848	8	5	All constraints met
14062018	119	174.167	8	6	All constraints met
13062018	78	166.557	8	4	All constraints met
12062018	110	136.453	8	5	All constraints met
07062018	129	176.774	8	7	All constraints met
05062018	124	150.113	8	6	All constraints met
30052018	94	225.582	6	6	All constraints met
29052018	115	154.490	7	6	All constraints met
28052018	101	254.256	7	7	1 Vehicle vol. exceeded by 0.13%
08052018	91	116.134	7	5	All constraints met

TABLE 11.10

Comparative Results of Used Regression Models

Parameter	DT	NB	GLM	SVM
ToleranceWeight	81.336	84.323	92.039	96.642
ToleranceVolume	79.928	80.905	82.193	90.450
PenaltyDelay	81.555	82.007	85.059	89.707
PenaltyCustomersVehicles	82.309	85.314	92.044	96.647
CostIncreasing	78.998	80.229	81.883	90.286
PenaltyVolumePercentage	83.892	84.934	89.673	92.003
PenaltyWeightPercentage	84.801	84.956	90.309	92.976

In order to make a knowledge base of the management parameters better, the algorithm has been initiated for 5,632 times with all the constraints satisfied. The algorithm was tested for different input parameters. [33] According to the results, each control parameter SVM is concluded to have given better prediction results compared to the GML algorithm, shown in Table 11.10, while the prediction models based on decision tree algorithms and naïve Bayes theorem always showed significantly worse results.

Comparison analysis of confidentiality/accuracy, marked as Predictive Confidence [%], was made for each of the control parameters. A detailed analysis of the influence of input attributes on the defined control parameters was performed, too. Available fleet of vehicles (number and type of vehicle) has the greatest influence on the results, as well as constraints such as time windows, SDVRP (Site-Dependent Vehicle Routing Problem), constraints, and so on. Practical application of algorithms for solving VRP problems has become popular for the last twenty years by rapid development of information technology. Increasing the processing power of the computers (servers), availability of vector maps for road navigation, and publicly available satellite systems for global positioning have created preconditions for successful application of knowledge concerning this problem in everyday planning of distribution in the economy.

During the testing period of three months, it is important to emphasize several results obtained. All the routes obtained were feasible and complied with all previous restrictions. Significant savings were observed in the complete transport process, and the importance of the described concept was confirmed in practice.

From the results shown in Table 11.11, it can be seen that the application of algorithms has significantly increased the application of the created routes in practical conditions. At the same time, 57 instead of 55 vehicles were used during the ten test days, and the total length of the obtained routes was increased. As previously emphasized, the feasibility of routes is the most important factor, and the optimality of the obtained routes often impairs

TABLE 11.11

Comparative Results Before and After the Proposed Approach

	Average number of used vehicles	Average vehicle distance [km]	Percentage of feasibility of routes in real environment
BEFORE using the proposed approach	55/10 = 5.5	129.761	79.65%
AFTER using the proposed approach	57/10 = 5.7	137.915	98.25%

the practical feasibility. Routes are created so that minor distortions (which occur in practice due to objective reasons) impair the feasibility of the complete route. Therefore, the total cost increases significantly because individual customers are not served.

11.3.9 Cluster-Based Improvements to Route-Related Tasks

To improve the quality of the generated routes, two additional pieces of research have been published by Zunic et al. [34–35] that focused on the utilization of clustering algorithms. More specifically, the utilization of the DBSCAN clustering algorithm for the pre-determination of routing regions based on the generated clusters and K-means clustering algorithm for the generation of specific routes. However, this research does not only highlight this clustering-based approach, but it rather underlines the importance of a strategic approach to the development process. Similar to the previous sections, this method has also been tested through two real-world case studies in warehouses located in Bosnia and Herzegovina. The main improvement was reflected through the fact that the routing efficiency is significantly improved, while critical constraints were respected.

The main process begins with the analysis of historical data, based on which the weekly frequencies of the visits are determined. This results in a set of geographical locations that need to be visited in the following work week. The goal of the first phase of the approach is to divide the fetched geographical locations into regions called macro-clusters, through the usage of DBSCAN clustering algorithm. This algorithm is chosen since it does not require a predetermined number of clusters, but rather naturally forms sensible location clusters. However, it produces outlier locations which need to be assigned to their nearest macro-clusters. In this way, an easier approach to the generation of balanced routes in the later stages of the approach is enabled. After the macro-clusters have been created, the individual routes are generated by the K-means algorithm. The satisfaction of the work hours constraint is checked for each individual macro-cluster. If this constraint is respected, the process terminates for this respective macro-cluster. If not, the K-means algorithm is applied to split the macro-cluster into multiple parts. The number of K-means clusters is gradually increased until all routes are manageable or the formation of empty clusters is detected. This implies that there are some regions that are densely populated and cannot be further split into clusters. These cases are handled by dividing the cluster into the smallest number of equal parts, which guarantee that all routes are manageable. After this iterative process has concluded, the final step is to check whether some of the routes can be aggregated.

The flow diagram and an appropriate visual representation of the whole process are depicted in Figure 11.13(a) and (b), respectively.

The two problems that are solved in the research are conceptually very similar. Because of that, the same metrics can be used to assess whether any improvement has been made. To highlight the achieved results the results from the first research will be analyzed in more detail. The comparison, in this case, was done between the previously used ad hoc approach to routing, the TSP solution applied on the collection of all locations, and finally the proposed approach based on clustering. The period of three weeks spanning from 2019/08/05 to 2019/08/26 was analyzed and the results in terms of the minimum number of representatives needed, an average number of generated routes and additional quality indicators are presented in Tables 11.12, 11.13, and 11.14, respectively.

The clustering-based approach significantly outperforms the previously utilized ad hoc approach by reducing the minimum amount of needed representatives almost in half.

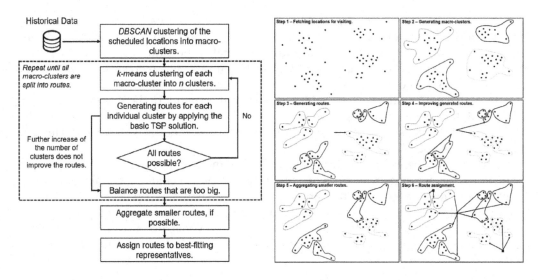

FIGURE 11.13
Clustering-Based Route Approach a) Flow Diagram and b) Visual Illustration

TABLE 11.12

The Minimum Number of Employed Representatives

Time Period	*ad hoc*	Basic TSP	Clustering TSP
Daily	66	35	**30**
Weekly	88	43	**37**
Total	92	44	**37**

TABLE 11.13

Average Number of Generated Routes

Time Period	*ad hoc*	Basic TSP	Clustering TSP
Daily	65.8	41.3	**34.7**
Weekly	236	121.1	**87**
Total	502	243	**174**

TABLE 11.14

Additional Quality Indicators of the Generated Routes

Time Period	*ad hoc*	Basic TSP	Clustering TSP
Most Frequent Route Length	6	18	19
Longest Route	48	38	20
Average Route Length	8.77	12.63	**14.93**
Average Time Duration (h)	4.13	6.04	**6.94**

Compared to the TSP-based approach, the improvement is smaller. As far the average number of generated routes is concerned, this number is also cut in half, which indicates the increase in overall route quality. The additional quality indicators confirm the superiority of the new approaches, which is highlighted the most in the average route length and duration. The average route length is 6.94 hours, which is very close to the set working time limit of 8 hours. From this point, it is clear that the quality of the routes is increasing while all of the constraints are still respected. This also showcases the advantage over the TSP-based approach because the average number of working hours is closer to the limit by almost a whole hour.

The case study described the technical as well as the social implications of the implementation of such a system. Besides just the technical improvement, the main goal was to highlight the importance of the human factor during system development. Overall, this is a sensitive subject, which can cause development projects to fail. If the developed approach is not properly utilized, the final goal is lost. Because of this, good communication and cooperation on all management levels is the key to a successful implementation and integration of any system.

11.4 Summary Results

The concept was created as one integrated unit through many years of research and practical work in the field of supply chain management. It was designed gradually, and the collected experiences were built into the complete operation of the system. Each part of the concept was carefully analyzed after implementation, and the results are described in earlier sections of the chapter. The complete concept was subsequently implemented under different conditions in many warehouses and organizations: gradual introduction of parts into existing organizations, parallel introduction of all parts into existing organizations, and parallel introduction of all parts into new organizations. In all cases where it was possible to do an analysis, the concept showed significant improvements over the approaches used previously. For results and comparison, the most significant case is certainly the introduction of the concept of smart SCM in existing organizations.

In earlier sections, the results of individual parts of the concept are listed. The overall effect of the concept implementation is difficult to calculate precisely, because the complete work of a company depends on a number of factors that change over time and are difficult to fully simulate. According to an exhaustive analysis conducted among management and workers in warehouses with implemented smart SCM, enviable results were obtained.

Improvements have been made to a number of frequently encountered problems. The level of unnecessary stock was reduced but the number of items was maintained, which allows uninterrupted operation of the warehouse and regular delivery to end customers. By reducing inventory, cash flow improved and warehousing costs were reduced. Expired items do not appear in warehouses, the return of goods is reduced, the workload of workers is reduced, and the use of forklifts is optimized. The process of collecting orders has been accelerated, and the workload of workers during the process itself has been reduced. Training time for new workers has been drastically reduced and kept to a minimum. Workers do not have to make independent decisions and assumptions in the processes, so it is enough to follow the recommendations of the system. The number of workers needed

TABLE 11.15

Experimental Results by Implementing Each Algorithm and the Summary Results

Implemented approach	Compared method	Results
Demand forecasting and sales prediction	Prediction based on personnel's experience	5–10% stock decrease
Product positioning	Predefined product places	~20% shorter routes
Picking zone prediction	Prediction based on personnel's experience	~35% more orders gathered from picking zone
Order splitting	Predefined sectors	~40% shorter routes
Order batching	No batching	61.3% shorter routes
	Greedy approach	16% shorter routes
Order picking	Algorithm based on item's brand and commodity groups	41.3% shorter routes
Transport management system	Predefined regions (clusters) based on Transport managers experiences	~20% routes are more feasible ~30% of cost savings
Route optimization for traveling merchants	Predefined routes defined by the geolocations of the cities	~40% more effective routes ~50% less workforce required
Complete concept	**Standard SCM**	**30–40% of cost savings**

for the warehousing has been reduced, and workers have been relocated to other positions, leading to increased productivity.

The system supports the growth of the company and the use of large warehouses by introducing the splitting and order batching, connecting to the transport system has significantly simplified and accelerated the loading and preparation process. Transport optimization has drastically reduced the number of unvisited customers and customers to whom goods have not been delivered, the number of used vehicles was reduced, the route planning process is automated, delivery monitoring is automated and simplified, and significant savings in transport have been achieved.

Table 11.15 shows the experimental results for each part of the smart SCM with appropriate comparisons to the previously used methods and approaches. Although all of these factors are difficult to combine into a single outcome, after exhaustive analysis it is estimated that the business has improved by ~30% in organizational terms and in terms of human and other resources, while the financial side has improved by as much as approximately 30% to 40% of operational costs. Based on all the above, the proposed concept significantly outperforms the results of earlier approaches.

The satisfaction of system users and workers, as well as customers and suppliers, has greatly increased, which is certainly one of the most important factors for the successful operation of the company.

11.5 Conclusion

This chapter describes the concept of a smart SCM system that connects the process of ordering goods from manufacturers, the process of receiving and moving goods in a warehouse, the process of collecting orders, splitting large orders and batching smaller ones in large warehouses, the process of optimizing and monitoring the transport of goods. The sales prediction is the first process to optimize for significant savings because increased number of articles in the warehouse directly increases costs of warehouse operation, and, at the same time, the lack of items in the warehouse prevents delivery to end users which damages the company's reputation. All warehouse operations need to be optimized to increase the warehouse efficiency and optimize the process of order picking. Once the orders have been collected, it is necessary to optimize the loading of goods into transport vehicles, which is achieved by timely route planning and the collection of orders along previously prepared transport routes whenever possible. The process of transportation is one of the most complex and expensive processes in the operation of a distribution company. The GPS vehicle tracking system monitors the compliance of the proposed routes, but at the same time gathers important data that is used to improve TMS. An additional component in the whole concept is the optimization of routes for commercial travelers, which ensures the optimal way of visiting customers.

Simultaneously using all the proposed algorithms, a system was created for efficient and synchronized operation of distribution companies. The complete concept was developed and tested over several years of warehouse operations and subsequently implemented in several new warehouses and companies. Using the system enables easy and quick training of new workers, and automation of a series of processes in warehouse operations. The system has shown excellent results compared to traditional SCM systems, where great savings have been achieved in each of these processes. The introduction of some of the described algorithms has achieved savings of more than 50% over the previous results and the complete concept can make a significant difference in the warehouse workflow and efficiency.

The problem of supply chain management contains a number of optimization problems, the solution of which can significantly reduce labor costs, which causes a number of positive effects. Therefore, in the future, it is planned to improve the described concept, as well as the analysis the possibilities of additional automation and optimization of processes. It is planned to gather additional data and experience in using the system from actual users, and to use the collected data for further improvements. The system will allow additional constraints within the algorithms.

Conflict of Interest

The authors declare that they have no conflicts of interest.

References

1. Bartholdi, J.J., and Hackman, S.T. (2014). *Warehouse and Distribution Science, Release 0.96. Supply Chain and Logistics Institute, School of Industrial and Systems Engineering, Georgia Institute of Technology, Atlanta, GA.* August, 2014.
2. Zunic, E., Korjenic, K., Hodzic, K., and Donko, D. (2020). Application of Facebook's Prophet Algorithm for Successful Sales Forecasting Based on Real-World Data. *International Journal of Computer Science & Information Technology (IJCSIT)*, 12(2), April 2020. DOI: 10.5121/ijcsit.2020.12203.

3. Aras, S., Deveci Kocakoc, I., and Polat, C. (2017). Comparative Study on Retail Sales Forecasting Between Single and Combination Methods. *Journal of Business Economics and Management*, 18(5), 803–832. DOI: 10.3846/16111699.2017.1367324.

4. Alon, I., Qi, M., and Sadowski, R.J. (2001). Forecasting Aggregate Retail Sales: A Comparison of Artificial Neural Networks and Traditional Methods. *Journal of Retailing and Consumer Services* 8(3), 147–156. DOI: 10.1016/S0969-6989(00)00011-4.

5. Au, K. F., Choi, T. M., and Yu, Y. (2008). Fashion Retail Forecasting by Evolutionary Neural Networks. *International Journal of Production Economics* 114(2), 615–630. DOI: 10.1016/j.ijpe. 2007.06.013.

6. Golic, M., Zunic, E., and Donko, D. (2019). *Outlier Detection in Distribution Companies Business using Real Data Set. IEEE EUROCON 2019 - 18th International Conference on Smart Technologies.* DOI: 10.1109/EUROCON.2019.8861526.

7. Zunic, E., Tucakovic, Z., Hodzic, K., and Delalic, S. (2019). *Multi-level Generalized Clustering Approach and Algorithm for Anomaly Detection in Internal Banking Payment Systems. IEEE EUROCON 2019 - 18th International Conference on Smart Technologies.* DOI: 10.1109/EUROCON.2019.8861903.

8. Handfield, R., Jeong, S., and Choi, T. (2018). Emerging Procurement Technology: Data Analytics and Cognitive Analytics. *International Journal of Physical Distribution & Logistics Management*, 0960–0035. DOI: 10.1108/IJPDLM-11-2017-0348.

9. Valadares de Oliveira, M.P., and Handfield, R. (2019). Analytical Foundations for Development of Real-time Supply Chain Capabilities. *International Journal of Production Research*, 57(5). DOI: 10.1080/00207543.2018.1493240.

10. Moheb-Alizadeh, H., and Handfield, R. (2019). Sustainable Supplier Selection and Order Allocation: A Novel Multi-objective Programming Model with a Hybrid Solution Approach. *Computers & Industrial Engineering*, 129, pp. 192–209. DOI: 10.1016/j.cie.2019.01.011.

11. Zunic, E., Hasic H., Hodzic, K., Delalic, S., and Besirevic, A. (2018). *Predictive Analysis based Approach for Optimal Warehouse Product Positioning. In proceedings of MIPRO 2018 - 41st International Convention on Information and Communication Technology, Electronics and Microelectronics.* DOI: 10.23919/MIPRO.2018.8400174.

12. Nogo, A., Zunic, E., and Donko, D. (2019). *Identification of Association Rules in Orders of Distribution Companies' Clients. IEEE EUROCON 2019 - 18th International Conference on Smart Technologies.* DOI: 10.1109/EUROCON.2019.8861951.

13. Kofler, M., Beham, A., Wagner, S., and Affenzeller M. (2014). Affinity Based Slotting in Warehouses with Dynamic Order Patterns. In: Klempous R., Nikodem J., Jacak W., Chaczko Z. (eds) *Advanced Methods and Applications in Computational Intelligence. Topics in Intelligent Engineering and Informatics*, vol. 6. Springer, Heidelberg. DOI: 10.1007/978-3-319-01436-47.

14. Fumi, A., Scarabotti, L., and Schiraldi, M. (2013). The Effect of Slot-Code Optimization in Warehouse Order Picking. *International Journal of Engineering Business Management* 5(1). DOI: 10.5772/56803.

15. Zunic, E., Hodzic, K., Hasic, H., Skrobo, R., Besirevic, A., and Donko, D. (2017). *Application of Advanced Analysis and Predictive Algorithm for Warehouse Picking Zone Capacity and Content Prediction. In Proceedings of ICAT 2017 - 26th International Conference on Information, Communication and Automation Technologies.* DOI: 10.1109/ICAT.2017.8171629.

16. Delalic, S., Zunic, E., Alihodzic, A., and Selmanovic, E. (2020). The *Order Batching Concept Implemented in Real Smart Warehouse. IEEE / 43rd International Convention on Information, Communication and Electronic Technology (Mipro 2020).* Paper Accepted.

17. Zunic, E., Delalic, S., Tucakovic, Z., Hodzic K., and Besirevic A. (2019). Innovative Modular Approach based on Vehicle Routing Problem and Ant Colony Optimization for Order Splitting in Real Warehouses. *Computer Science and Information Systems, ACSIS*, 20, 125–129. DOI: 10.15439/2019F196.

18. Kritikos, M.N., and Ioannou, G. (2010). The Balanced Cargo Vehicle Routing Problem with Time Windows. *International Journal of Production Economics*, 123(1), 42–51. DOI: 10.1016/j.ijpe.2009.07.006.

19. Gendreau, M., Hertz, A., and Laporte, G. (1994). A Tabu Search Heuristic for the Vehicle Routing Problem. *Management Science*, 40(10). DOI: 10.1287/mnsc.40.10.1276.

20. Zunic, E., Besirevic, A., Skrobo, R., Hasic, H., Hodzic, K., and Djedovic, A. (2017). *Design of Optimization System for Warehouse Order Picking in Real Environment. In Proceedings of ICAT 2017 - 26th International Conference on Information, Communication and Automation Technologies*. DOI: 10.1109/ICAT.2017.8171630.

21. Zunic, E., Besirevic, A., Delalic, S., Hodzic, K., and Hasic, H. (2018). *A Generic Approach for Order Picking Optimization Process in Different Warehouse Layouts. In Proceedings of MIPRO 2018 - 41st International Convention on Information and Communication Technology, Electronics and Microelectronics*. DOI: 10.23919/MIPRO.2018.8400183.

22. Gu, J., Goetschalckx, M., and McGinnis, L.F. (2010). Research on Warehouse Design and Performance Evaluation: A Comprehensive Review. *European Journal of Operational Research*, 203(3), 539–549. DOI: 10.1016/j.ejor.2009.07.031.

23. Gue, K.R., and Meller, R.D. (2009). Aisle Configurations for Unit-load Warehouses. *IIE Transactions*, 41(3), 171–182. DOI: 10.1080/07408170802112726.

24. Roodbergen, K.J., and De Koster, R. (2001). Routing Methods for Warehouses with Multiple Cross Aisles. *International Journal of Production Research*, 39(9), 1865–1883. DOI: 10.1080/00207540110028128.

25. ———— (2001). Routing Order Pickers in a Warehouse with a Middle Aisle. *European Journal of Operational Research*, 133(1), 32–43. DOI: 10.1016/S0377-2217(00)00177-6.

26. Cogo, E., Zunic, E., Besirevic, A., Delalic, S., and Hodzic, K. (2020). *Position based Visualization of Real World Warehouse Data in a Smart Warehouse Management System. In Proceedings of 19th International Symposium INFOTEH-JAHORINA (INFOTEH)*. DOI: 10.1109/INFOTEH48170.2020.9066323.

27. Zunic, E., Donko, D., and Buza, E. (2020). An Adaptive Data-Driven Approach to Solve Real-World Vehicle Routing Problems in Logistics. *Complexity*, 2020. DOI: 10.1155/2020/738670.

28. Zunic, E., and Donko, D. (2019). *Parameter Setting Problem in the Case of Practical Vehicle Routing Problems with Realistic Constraints. In Proceedings of the 2019 Federated Conference on Computer Science and Information Systems, FedCSIS 2019*. DOI: 10.15439/2019F194.

29. Zunic, E., Delalic, S., Hodzic, K., and Tucakovic, Z. (2019). *Innovative GPS Data Anomaly Detection Algorithm inspired by QRS Complex Detection Algorithms in ECG Signals. In Proceedings of EUROCON 2019 - 18th International Conference on Smart Technologies*. DOI: 10.1109/EUROCON.2019.8861619.

30. Zunic, E., Delalic, S., and Donko, D. (2020). Adaptive Multi-phase Approach for Solving the Realistic Vehicle Routing Problems in Logistics with Innovative Comparison Method for Evaluation based on Real GPS Data. *Transportation Letters*. DOI: 10.1080/19427867.2020.1824311

31. Zunic, E. (2018). Real-world VRP Benchmark Data with Realistic Non-standard Constraints - Input Data and Results. *4TU.Centre for Research Data*. DOI: 10.4121/uuid:598b19d1-df64-493e-991a-d8d655dac3ea

32. ———— (2019). Real-world MDVRP Data with Realistic Constraints. *4TU.Centre for Research Data*. Dataset DOI: 10.4121/uuid:b5013b9c-c462-479d-ad06-2ad15cc034e4.

33. ———— (2018). Real-world VRP Data with Realistic Non-standard Constraints - Parameter Setting Problem Regression Input Data. *4TU.Centre for Research Data*. Dataset. DOI: 10.4121/uuid:97006624-d6a3-4a29-bffa-e8daf60699d8.

34. Zunic, E., Hasic H., and Delalic, S. (2020) *Strategic Development, Improvement and Integration of Representative Routing in Warehouse Management Information Systems. In Proceedings of ICCMB 2020, January 31-February 2, 2020, Tokyo, Japan*. DOI: 10.1145/3383845.3383855.

35. ———— (2020) Strategic Approach to Implementation and Integration of Routing-based Tasks in Warehouse Management Information Systems. *International Journal of e-Education, e-Business, e-Management and e-Learning (IJEEEE)*. DOI: 10.17706/ijeeee.2020.10.4.294-311

36. Žunić, E., Tucaković, Z., Delalić, S., Hasić, H. and Hodžić, K. (2020). *Innovative Multi-Step Anomaly Detection Algorithm with Real-World Implementation: Case Study in Supply Chain Management. IEEE / ITU International Conference on Artificial Intelligence for Good (AI4G 2020)*. Paper Accepted.

37. Hodzic, K., Hasic, H., Cogo E., and Juric, Z. (2019). *Warehouse Demand Forecasting based on Long Short-Term Memory Neural Networks. In Proceedings of ICAT 2019 - XXVII International Conference on Information, Communication and Automation Technologies,* Sarajevo, Bosnia and Herzegovina. DOI: 10.1109/ICAT47117.2019.8939050.

38. Yang, X. S. (2011). Bat Algorithm for Multi-objective Optimisation. *International Journal of Bio-inspired Computation,* 3(5), 267–274. arXiv:1203.6571 [math.OC].

39. Osaba E. Yang X. S. Diaz F. Lopez-Garcia P. and Carballedo R. (2016). An Improved Discrete Bat Algorithm for Symmetric and Asymmetric Traveling Salesman Problems. *Engineering Applications of Artificial Intelligence,* 48 59–71. DOI: 10.1016/j.engappai.2015.10.006

40. Yang, X. (2010). Nature-Inspired Metaheuristic Algorithms. *Nature-Inspired Metaheuristic Algorithms Second Edition.* ISBN: 1905986289, 9781905986286

41. Yang, X. S., and He, X. (2013). Firefly Algorithm: Recent Advances and Applications. *International Journal of Swarm Intelligence.* DOI: 10.1504/ijsi.2013.055801

42. Senthilnath, J., Omkar, S. N., and Mani, V. (2011). Clustering Using Firefly Algorithm: Performance Study. *Swarm and Evolutionary Computation.* DOI: 10.1016/j.swevo.2011.06.003

12

A Case Study on Disease Diagnosis Using Gene Expression Data Classification with Feature Selection: Application of Data Science Techniques in Health Care

Abhilasha Chaudhuri and Tirath Prasad Sahu

NIT Raipur, India

CONTENTS

12.1 Introduction

We are living in a data-driven era that has influenced our lives in many ways, and the field of health care is not an exception. A huge amount of data is being generated in health care through clinical trials, electronic medical records, billing, genetic information, hospital management databases, medical imaging, scientific articles, pathology lab networks, and so on. This large amount of data is not useful until there is some way to discover knowledge and information out of it (Leskovec, Rajaraman, and Ullman, 2020). This is where the data science field blends with the health care field. The use of data science in the field of health care is featured in this chapter (Chaudhuri and Sahu, 2020a). Data science is the method by which data is organized, processed, and analyzed to extract information and insights from a vast and diverse collection of data. Techniques like mathematical and statistical modeling, machine learning, data mining, and deep learning are used by data scientists. Data science is used in many areas of health care, such as medical image analysis, drug discovery, genetics and genomics, predictive medicine, virtual assistance for patients, hospital operations, disease diagnosis, and disease prevention. These use cases of data science in health care are described in this chapter. Health care is a high-stakes field because apart from money, life is also at stake. Therefore, techniques and models that are being used need to be very accurate and efficient. The accuracy of a model depends upon the quality of data that is being fed to the model during the learning phase. In the healthcare industry, data inaccuracies like missing data and imbalanced data are very common issues and will be discussed in this chapter. Feature engineering is the solution to these kinds of problems. It is believed that genetics and genomics will have a major influence on the future of the healthcare industry, as it will unveil new dimensions like personalized medicine, disease prediction, and genetic engineering. This application area is presented as a case study in this chapter.

The chapter's main goals are as follows:

- To describe key application areas of data science in the health care field.
- To highlight issues and challenges faced by data scientists due to the specific nature of data in this field.
- To present feature engineering techniques as a solution to the above-mentioned problems.
- To demonstrate the benefits of feature selection before the classification of gene expression dataset in form of a case study.
- To demonstrate the use of the binary particle swarm optimization algorithm for the feature selection task.

For a better understanding of the concepts presented in the chapter, various open-source tools are also described.

12.2 Data Science in Health Care

"Hiding within those mounds of data is knowledge that could change the life of a patient or change the world." —Atul Butte, Stanford University

Healthcare is the most emerging and challenging application of data science techniques. Figure 12.1 illustrates some significant applications of data science techniques in the field of health care, and is discussed in Section 12.2.1 to Section 12.2.8.

12.2.1 Drug Discovery

One of the most substantial applications of data science is drug discovery (Vamathevan et al., 2019). Drug discovery is a complex and time-consuming task that involves multiple disciplinary approaches. Pharmaceutical companies have a large amount of data about previous drugs' clinical trials, experiments, simulations, finances, and other important aspects. This is where data science can be helpful; data science can give useful insights into the drug discovery process by predicting the success rate of certain types of experiments. Data science can forecast how a particular chemical compound would react with a particular biological entity. This technology is also helpful in simulating the lab experiments; data science–aided lab simulations make the process fast, easy, and more accurate. Moreover, with the help of machine learning (which is the inseparable part of data science), it is possible to test the effect of chemical compounds on all possible combinations of cell types and different genetic mutations. This would not be possible without the help of machine learning. Data science makes the process of drug discovery more fast, easy, economic, and safe.

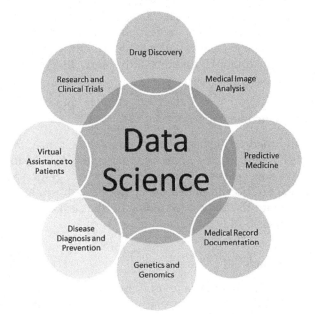

FIGURE 12.1
Applications of Data Science in Health Care

12.2.2 Medical Image Analysis

Medical image analysis is a prominent field of research for data scientists (Carneiro et al., 2017). Various types of medical imaging methods are used to treat various disorders, such as X-ray, mammography, magnetic resonance imaging (MRI), sonography, computed tomography, and so on (Komura and Ishikawa, 2018). Medical professionals understand these images and treat the patients accordingly, but due to the lack of the experts and large number of patients, hospitals have long queues of the patients waiting for doctors and medical experts. Data science is a helpful tool to solve this problem. The expert systems that analyze these medical images can detect tumors and anomalies with good accuracy. These expert systems cannot replace the expertise of doctors, but they can help in making a fast decision. These automated tools help medical experts screen the images, generate reports, and support the decision-making process.

There are many algorithms available that can detect cancerous tumors from mammographic images (Shen et al., 2019) with great accuracy. Automated systems are available to detect various skin diseases. The stones and other anomalies can be detected by different machine learning systems trained on ultrasound images (Giger, 2018). Hence, we can say that the field of medical image analysis is the hot spot for data scientists since long, and it will continue to be the major area of research in the future also.

12.2.3 Predictive Medicine

With the recent advancements in the predictive capabilities of data science, medical professionals have started to work toward the improvement in quality of life of individuals and better working environments for doctors and medical professionals. Patients' data related to their clinical notes, previous medications, lifestyle, eating habits, genetic structures, and so on are recorded. These datasets are processed through data science techniques to find the correlations and associations between entities and make predictions. The effects of lifestyle and genetic structures on the particular drug and the treatment given to patients are analyzed. The individuals can receive suggestions about their diet and lifestyle habits based on their previous medical records and genetic structures. Therefore the data science is used for predictive medication (Hernandez and Zhang, 2017) by many cancer research institutes and other healthcare providers.

12.2.4 Medical Record Documentation

All the paperwork and medical history of the patients is digitized and available in soft copy. In this way, when a person goes to the hospital his medical history will be available at the hospital with just some clicks; this eases the process of getting admitted, treatment, referring to another expert/doctor, and transfer from one hospital to another. All these things will be possible with the help of technologies like support vector machine, optical character reader, and other tools.

12.2.5 Genetics and Genomics

A lot of information is encoded in the genes of living organisms, including human beings. How the information is transferred from one generation to another, how the creatures adapt to their environments, how a drug will affect in the body of an individual are some of the questions whose answers are hidden in the genome of the organisms. Ever since the success of the whole genome project (Reuter et al., 2018), researchers are working on these types of problems. There is a large volume of data available that needs to be studied (Gibbs, 2020). Data science technologies are being applied to these datasets. Personalized drugs, genetic risk prediction, and personalized medical treatment are some of the most inspiring applications in the field of genetics and genomics.

12.2.6 Disease Diagnosis and Prevention

Data scientists have made expert systems that can detect irregular heartbeats from ECG signal more quickly than a cardiologist, can differentiate between benign and malignant skin lesions from skin images, and can interpret MRI, X-Rays, and mammograph with the same accuracy as radiologists. With the help of genetic study, we can also get advanced intimation of the chances of getting certain types of diseases and thus implement measures to prevent that. In this way, data science is a great tool for disease diagnosis and prevention.

12.2.7 Virtual Assistance to Patients

This is the latest application of data science technology to the health care sector. In many cases like common cold, fever, headache, or a routine visit during/after treatment, it is not necessary to visit the doctor. Patients can tell the symptoms online or through some applications, and receive medication and advice. For this purpose, natural language processing (NLP) tools are very beneficial. This saves the patients' time, and also helps doctors to focus on more critical cases. A mobile application is also helpful to make healthy choices, healthy routine, and track one's health. These types of virtual tools are also helpful for elderly persons for their routine checkups, for the patients that are recently discharged from hospitals to connect with their doctors for follow-ups, for pregnant women to continuously monitor their baby's movement, for individuals with diabetes and hypertension, and many other situations. In the pandemic or other situations like COVID-19, these types of virtual assistance to patients have emerged as an essential tool.

12.2.8 Research and Clinical Trials

Data science has an obvious application in the field of research in the health care sector. Different types of data are being collected and generated with the help of various tools like microarray technology, medical imaging devices, ECG, EEG, psychological treatment related questionnaire, and so on. These data are being analyzed using the data science techniques to have deeper insights, validate a hypothesis, make informed decisions, and draw conclusions.

Clinical trials are a long process in which large volumes of data are generated. It is essential to organize the data in order to preserve the information contained in it so that it can be analyzed in later stages. Data science techniques are very helpful in managing and analyzing the clinical trial data in an efficient and fast manner.

12.3 Issues and Challenges in the Field of Data Science

The expert systems trained using machine learning algorithms undoubtedly have the capacity to help the health care industry in many aspects as discussed in Section 12.2.

FIGURE 12.2
Issues and Challenges in the Field of Data Science

However, there are a lot of challenges and issues with the data that need to be addressed. Data, being the backbone of data science technology, has to be accurate, consistent, balanced, and it should be available in sufficient volume that is suitable to train machine learning algorithms. After all, an algorithm's performance is only as good as the quality of data it is being trained upon. In this section, the issues and challenges about the data in the health care sector will be discussed. Figure 12.2 shows the existing issues and challenges that are faced by the data scientists when they design some expert systems.

12.3.1 Inconsistent, Missing, and Inaccurate Data

It is true that there are volumes of electronics health records present. However, they are not in a suitable format for machine learning algorithms. There is a lot of work to be done before the available data will be usable for data science technologies. Different institutes, or even in the same institute, the data have been stored in different formats over time because they have software systems to record these data and those softwares were designed with some other purpose in mind. This means the existing data is not consistent. Moreover, the data has lots of missing values due to various reasons like privacy issues, non-availability of information, merging of inconsistent formats, and so on. The data is also inaccurate due to errors introduced by the data entry operators, lack of sufficient expertise in the particular field (of the person who is recording the data in the system), and so on.

12.3.2 Imbalanced Data

A dataset consists of two things: the number of features that describe various characteristics and the number of samples or instances. The dataset is said to be imbalanced when the ratio between the number of features and number of instances is very big. One of the highly imbalanced datasets is the gene expression dataset obtained by microarray experiment that consists of tens of thousands of features and only tens/hundreds of instances. For example, consider the gene expression dataset of lung cancer; it has 12533 features and only 181 instances. It is very difficult to train a machine learning model on these types of datasets. These types of imbalanced datasets are not limited to gene expression data, some of the image classification, face recognition, and text classification datasets are also highly imbalanced. This is a challenge for data scientists to devise some mechanisms to train the mathematical model on the imbalanced datasets.

12.3.3 Cost of Data Collection

In the field of health care, the data is collected by conducting some pathological or medical imaging tests. Some of these tests (like whole genome sequencing or gene expression profiling) are very costly, therefore it is difficult to collect the large volumes of data in such fields to train the machine learning models. Also, the cost involved with creating and maintaining the database in the proper format (as per the requirement of data scientists) is also very costly. These issues pose the challenges for the data scientists to get the appropriate datasets as per their needs.

12.3.4 Huge Volume of Data

On one hand, where it is very difficult to collect large volumes of data due to high cost; on the other hand, there is a huge amount of data available in the health care sector (Mehta and Pandit, 2018), and it is very difficult to process and handle this big data. A lot of research is ongoing to address the issue of big data in the field of health care. These high volumes of data are related to the medical insurance industry, pharmaceutical companies, medical equipment design and manufacturing, and so on.

12.3.5 Ethical and Privacy Issues

Apart from the technical issues discussed above, the health care field also needs to deal with ethical and privacy issues. It is not ethical to use or share patients' data without their consent. Also, the privacy of the patients should be maintained all the time. Whenever a new drug is introduced, its ethical implications are also considered. Ethical and privacy issues are also have an important role in medical insurance agencies. The genetic databases of individuals are also a very sensitive database that should be handled with privacy issues in mind.

12.4 Feature Engineering

This section discusses the solution to the issues discussed in Section 12.3. Feature engineering is the technique of extracting/finding such features from raw data that improves the performance of machine learning algorithms. Feature engineering includes feature extraction, feature selection, and feature weighting. These techniques are discussed in detail in this section.

12.4.1 Feature Extractions

Feature extraction techniques extract new features from the dataset by some linear or non-linear combinations of the original features. New features are less in numbers than the original number of features, in this sense feature extraction is a dimensionality reduction technique that reduces the dimension, computational time, and effort, and improves the accuracy and performance of the machine learning algorithms. Principal component analysis (PCA) and linear discriminant analysis (LDA) are two main feature extraction techniques.

12.4.2 Feature Selection

Feature selection is a technique for reducing dimensionality that selects the subset of features from the original feature set in such a way that the output of the machine learning model improves. Feature selection technique falls under three categories: filter, wrapper, and embedded techniques (Ang et al., 2016; Abhilasha, Chaudhuri, and Sahu, 2020b). Each of these techniques is discussed here.

12.4.2.1 Filter Method

Filter methods select the feature subset on the basis of the characteristics of the dataset. They study and recognize the hidden pattern in the dataset on the basis of some statistical and information-theoretic measures. The classifier is not involved during the feature selection process. Therefore, these are considered more generalized, fast, and cost-effective feature selection methods. The process of feature selection through the filter method is shown in Figure 12.3. The best feature subset is first found and then applied to the classifier to evaluate the performance of the feature selection method.

12.4.2.2 Wrapper Method

Wrapper methods for feature selection involve the classifier in each step for selecting features as it is depicted in Figure 12.4. They employ some search techniques like forward

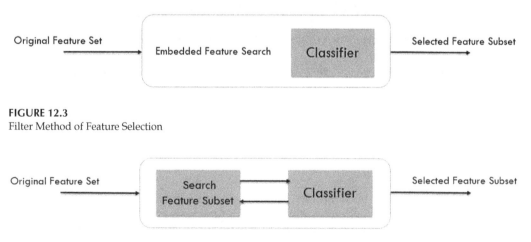

FIGURE 12.3
Filter Method of Feature Selection

FIGURE 12.4
Wrapper Method of Feature Selection

FIGURE 12.5
Embedded Method of Feature Selection

selection and backward elimination to select a feature subset, then the selected feature subset is evaluated by the classifier to get some accuracy. Next, some other feature subset will be tried until the feature subset with maximum accuracy is discovered. Then this feature subset will be designated as finally selected feature subset. Wrapper-based feature selection is more time consuming than filter methods because they involve the classifier in each step.

12.4.2.3 Embedded Method

Embedded methods have the qualities of both filter and wrapper methods. The process of feature selection through the filter method is shown in Figure 12.5.

It is implemented by algorithms that have their own built-in feature selection methods (Han, Kamber, and Pei, 2012).

12.4.3 Feature Weighting

Feature weighting techniques reduce data dimensionality by assigning weights to features according to their importance. More important features are assigned greater weight values. A threshold is set to remove the less important features. Feature weighting technique is considered more flexible than feature selection techniques (Han, Kamber, and Pei, 2012) because here feature weights can be any real number between 0 and 1. However, in feature selection it can take only two values either 0 or 1, where 0 means feature is not selected and 1 means feature is selected. In this way, we can say that feature selection is a special case of feature weighting where feature weights are restricted to binary values.

12.4.4 Model Evaluation Metrics

Many algorithms and techniques are available for feature selection and classification. Now the question is how we can compare those models in order to choose the best suitable model. For a model generated using imbalanced data, the implementation of incorrect evaluation metrics may be risky. Different model evaluation metrics are available in the literature. For instance, consider an imbalanced data related to a rare disease; the data contains the details of 100 individuals out of which 97 are healthy and 3 have the disease. If the model classifies all the samples as healthy, the model will have 97% accuracy. However, such a model will be of no use. Therefore we need other metrics apart from accuracy. These metrics are discussed here.

i.   *Recall/Sensitivity:* Sensitivity tests the proportion of positives correctly identified (for example, the percentage of sick people correctly identified as having any disease).

ii. *Precision/Specificity:* Specificity tests the proportion of negatives correctly identified (e.g., the number of healthy persons correctly identified as not having a certain disease).

iii. *AUC:* AUC-ROC curve is an output calculation at different threshold settings for classification problems. ROC is a probability curve, and AUC is a degree or separability metric. It tells how much model one can differentiate between groups. The higher the AUC, the better the model is to differentiate between patients with illness and no illnesses.

12.5 Case Study of Disease Diagnosis Using Gene Expression Data Classification

Gene expression profiling has become possible through microarray technology, which generates high throughput data. This high throughput data is about the expression level of genes. The aim of this gene expression profiling is to study different diseases at genetic level. It is important to understand the practical implications of the study related to classification of gene expression datasets. Classification of the gene expression dataset is important in disease diagnosis and prognosis. It is also helpful in making personalized drugs that are targeted for specific genes that are responsible for any particular diseases. When the genetic traits of an individual are known, doctors can suggest taking preventive actions in order to avoid some genetic diseases. Diseases can be treated at genetic (root) level instead of symptomatic level. Different datasets are available related to diseases like colon cancer, lung cancer, ovarian cancer, leukemia, and so on.

In this case study, we will see what is a gene expression dataset, how data science technology is helpful in extracting knowledge out of it, and what are the challenges in doing so.

12.5.1 Introduction to Gene Expression Dataset

In this section, we will discuss what exactly a gene expression dataset is and how it is created. The gene expression dataset is created through microarray technology, which is a major breakthrough in the field of molecular biology because it has the capability to reveal valuable information about the organism's functionality. DNA (Deoxyribonucleic acid) microarrays are created by robots that place thousands of gene sequences on a microscopic slide. At first, the complementary cDNA of a healthy sample and cancerous samples are taken. Then they are labeled with fluorescent dyes of different colors; after this the dyed cDNAs of both normal and cancerous samples are mixed in equal amounts. And then these probes are hybridized to microarray slide. For each spot on the microarray slide, the microarray slide is now scanned using a special scanner which measures the fluorescent intensity. The scanner returns an image which is then processed with image processing softwares that convert it into the form of a matrix (i.e., tabular format) in which each row represents a particular gene and each column denotes a sample or appoint of time when the gene expressions are monitored. This process is shown in Figure 12.6. A more detailed explanation of this process is beyond the scope of this book, the readers interested in more details can refer to Brazma and Vilo (2001).

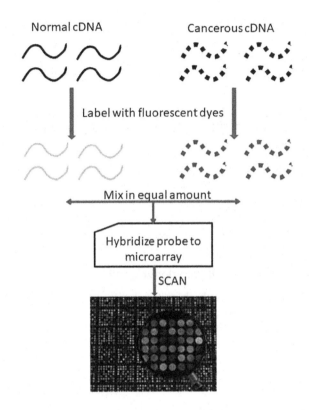

FIGURE 12.6
Microarray Technology

12.5.2 Challenges in Gene Expression Data

The gene expression data obtained from the microarray experiment as mentioned in Section 12.5.1 is very high dimensional. It has thousands of genes and only tens or hundreds of samples. This makes the gene expression dataset very imbalanced and poses many difficulties in training of machine learning model (Bolón-Canedo, Sánchez-Maroño, and Alonso-Betanzos, 2016; Pes, 2019). In order to overcome these difficulties, the dataset needs to be balanced, i.e., the feature to sample ratio need to be made small. This can be achieved by either reducing the number of features or increasing the sample size. It is not possible to increase the sample size due to the high price associated with gene profiling and other practical problems. However, we can reduce the number of features because all the genes of the dataset are not equally important, therefore we can select only the important genes and discard the noisy/irrelevant genes (Ghosh et al., 2019). This process is called feature selection.

A large number of feature selection methods are available in the literature (Ang et al., 2016). Now, we need to decide which feature selection technique is suitable for our application. Let us say we have a dataset with N features, therefore there will be 2^N possible combinations of feature subsets that can be selected by the feature selection problem. That means we can consider the feature selection problem a combinatorial optimization problem that has a very large search space. Meta-heuristic optimization algorithm has been proven very good in searching the large search space in a reasonable amount of time (Talbi, 2009). Many metaheuristic based wrapper feature selection approaches are available in the literature. Metaheuristic algorithms like genetic algorithm (GA) (Kabir, Shahjahan, and Murase, 2011), ant colony optimization (ACO) (Kashef and Nezamabadi-pour, 2015), particle swarm optimization (PSO) (Mirjalili and Lewis, 2013), and artificial bee colony (ABC) (Zorarpac and Özel, 2016) algorithms are popular wrapper-based feature selection methods available in the literature.

12.5.3 Feature Selection and Classification of Gene Expression Data Using Binary Particle Swarm Optimization

Feature selection and classification of gene expression data is done using the binary particle swarm optimization algorithm (Mirjalili and Lewis, 2013; Xia et al., 2020). Consider a gene expression dataset related to central nervous system (CNS); it has 7129 genes and 60 samples. It is a binary classification dataset, i.e., it has two classes. This dataset can be downloaded from http://csse.szu.edu.cn/sta/zhuzx/Datasets.html.

12.5.3.1 Binary Particle Swarm Optimization Algorithm

The working of PSO is inspired by the bird flocks. Suppose it has P birds in the flock, i.e., population size is P. The solution space is N dimensional. Here N is 7129 because the number for features are 7129. The position of a bird i is denoted by X_i, and its value is updated per Equation 12.1.

$$X_i^{t+1} = X_i^t + V_i^{t+1} \tag{12.1}$$

Where X_i^t is the value of ith position vector at iteration t and V_i^{t+1} is the velocity of the ith particle in iteration $t+1$, which is given by Equation (12.2):

$$v_i^{t+1} = wv_t^i + c_1 \times rand \times \left(pbest_i - X_i^t \right) + c_2 \times rand \times \left(gbest_i - X_i^t \right) \tag{12.2}$$

Where *rand* is the uniformly generated random number, *c1* and *c2* are called acceleration constants, w is called inertia weight, $pbest_i$ is the personal best position of the particle I until now, and $gbest_i$ is the global best position of all the particles obtained so far. The term wv_t^i denotes the exploration capability of the algorithm, term $c_1 \times rand \times \left(pbest_i - X_i^t \right)$ represents the importance given to self-learning by an individual particle, and the term $c_2 \times rand \times \left(gbest_i - X_i^t \right)$ represents the weight given to social interaction-based learning.

PSO is originally designed to work in continuous search space but feature selection is a binary problem, therefore the conversion of continuous search space is done with the help of transfer function as mentioned in Equations (12.3) and (12.4).

$$x_i^k (t+1) = \begin{cases} 0 \, if \, rand < T\left(v_i^k (t+1) \right) \\ 1 \, if \, rand \geq T\left(v_i^k (t+1) \right) \end{cases} \tag{12.3}$$

$$T\left(v_i^k (t+1) \right) = \frac{1}{1 + e^{-v_i^k (t+1)}} \tag{12.4}$$

The overall working of the PSO algorithm is given in Figure 12.7. To understand how feature selection is done using the algorithm mentioned here, let us take a detailed view.

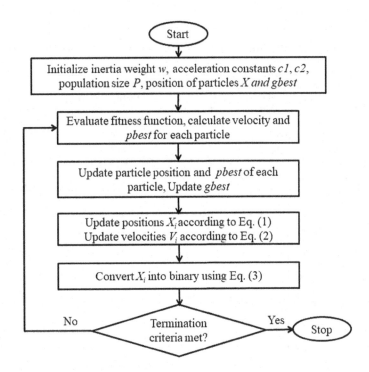

FIGURE 12.7
Flowchart of Binary Particle Swarm Optimization Algorithm

12.5.3.2 Working of Feature Selection Using BPSO

First of all, the number of features in the dataset need to be determined; here the dataset has 7129 features. Then population size will be decided, let us say population size is 30. A two-dimensional 30×7129 matrix will be created. Each row of the matrix represents a particle or candidate solution vector, and each column represents one feature of the dataset. The solution vector can contain only two values, either 0 or 1 where 0 represents that corresponding feature is not selected and 1 indicates that corresponding feature is selected. The population is initialized randomly and values of parameters c1, c2, and w are set.

In the second step (step 2), the fitness of each solution is determined. Here classification accuracy is selected as a fitness function (also called the objective function) of the BPSO algorithm to maximize the classification accuracy with a particular set of features. After calculating the fitness of each solution, *pbest* of each particle and *gbest* are decided.

Now, the position of each particle is updated as per Equations (12.1) and (12.2). At this point of time, the position values of particles have again became continuous; therefore it is again converted into binary using the transfer function as mentioned in Equations (12.3) and (12.4). The termination criterion is checked now. If the termination criterion is met, the process is stopped here. Otherwise it is repeated, and the process from step 2 is performed again and again until the stopping criterion is met.

12.5.3.3 Result and Discussion

Feature selection on gene expression dataset improves the accuracy of the classification task. In order to establish this fact we evaluate the fitness of each solution by considering

TABLE 12.1

Comparative Analysis of Classification Accuracies of Different Classifiers with and without Feature Selection

Classifier	Accuracy without feature selection	Accuracy with BPSO-based feature selection	Improvement
KNN	63.3	90.26	26.96
Decision Tree	68.3	91.67	23.37
Naïve Bayes	62.6	89.72	27.12
Logistic Regression	60.0	74.26	14.26

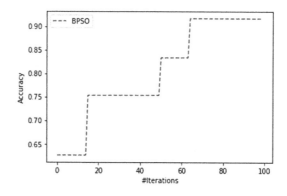

FIGURE 12.8
Convergence Curve of BPSO-Based Classification

four classifiers: KNN, decision tree, naïve Bayes, and logistic regression. The results of feature selection using BPSO with each algorithm. It is evident from the careful observation of Table 12.1 thatclassifier on CNS gene expression dataset are shown in Table 12.1. The accuracies mentioned in Table 12.1 are the average of 10 independent runs of each accuracy is improved significantly when the feature selection is done irrespective of the classifier. The reason behind this is that when irrelevant, redundant, and noisy features are removed each classifier performs better. Therefore, it is recommended to apply feature selection technique before classification task. Naïve Bayes classifier has achieved highest improvement of 27.12 percent, but decision tree classifier has the highest accuracy. The convergence curve of the decision tree classifier with BPSO-based feature selection technique is shown in Figure 12.8 because it has given the maximum accuracy. Other classifiers also have a similar convergence curve; they converged between 55–70 iterations.

12.6 Public Dataset and Codes in the Field of Data Science for Health Care

Many datasets related to various diseases are publicaly available at the repositories like (i) the machine learning repository of University of California Irvine (UCI) (https://archive. ics.uci.edu/ml/datasets.php); (ii) Kaggle is a great platform to find publicly available datasets (https://www.kaggle.com/datasets); and (iii) health care datasets are made available at https://data.gov.in/ by the Indian government.

Apart from the data, some codes of the commonly used data science techniques are also freely available at some of the platforms. These are very useful to begin learning data science techniques. Some of the well-known resources are https://www.kaggle.com/notebooks and https://github.com/donnemartin/data-science-ipython-notebooks. Readers are encouraged to explore these public repositories of data and code related to data science techniques to get some hands-on experience on the topics discussed in this chapter.

12.7 Conclusion

The techniques and tools of data science are very important in the field of health care and medicine because of the high volume and dimensionality of the data. Feature engineering techniques are an essential data preprocessing step that improves the performance of the machine learning models. It can be concluded that the use of data science and machine learning in the field of healthcare will result in a better medical facility by shortening the waiting time for treatment, efficient diagnosis of the disease through medical imaging, and personalized medicine through genetic and genomics.

The future of the health care sector lies in the considerate and strategic application of data science technologies. Well-planned application of advanced data science technologies will lead to better and personalized care for patients, as well as a better working atmosphere for health care facilitators.

References

Ang, Jun Chin, Andri Mirzal, Habibollah Haron, and Haza Nuzly Abdull Hamed. 2016. "Supervised, Unsupervised, and Semi-Supervised Feature Selection: A Review on Gene Selection." *IEEE/ACM Transactions on Computational Biology and Bioinformatics* 13 (5). IEEE: 971–989. doi:10.1109/TCBB.2015.2478454.

Bolón-Canedo, Verónica, Noelia Sánchez-Maroño, and Amparo Alonso-Betanzos. 2016. "Feature Selection for High-Dimensional Data." *Progress in Artificial Intelligence* 5 (2). Springer Berlin Heidelberg: 65–75. doi:10.1007/s13748-015-0080-y.

Brazma, A., and J Vilo. 2001. "Gene Expression Data Analysis." *Microbes and Infection / Institut Pasteur* 3 (10): 823–829. doi:10.1016/S0014-5793(00)01772-5.

Carneiro, Gustavo, Yefeng Zheng, Fuyong Xing, and Lin Yang. 2017. *Deep Learning and Convolutional Neural Networks for Medical Image Computing. Advances in Computer Vision and Pattern Recognition*. doi:10.1007/978-3-319-42999-1_2.

Chaudhuri, A, and T P Sahu. 2020a. "PROMETHEE-Based Hybrid Feature Selection Technique for High-Dimensional Biomedical Data: Application to Parkinson's Disease Classification." *Electronics Letters*. IET.

Chaudhuri, Abhilasha, and Tirath Prasad Sahu. 2020b. "Feature Selection Using Binary Crow Search Algorithm with Time Varying Flight Length." *Expert Systems with Applications*, 168: 114288.

Ghosh, Manosij, Shemim Begum, Ram Sarkar, Debasis Chakraborty, and Ujjwal Maulik. 2019. "Recursive Memetic Algorithm for Gene Selection in Microarray Data." *Expert Systems with Applications* 116. Elsevier Ltd: 172–185. doi:10.1016/j.eswa.2018.06.057.

Gibbs, Richard A. 2020. "The Human Genome Project Changed Everything." *Nature Reviews Genetics*. doi:10.1038/s41576-020-0275-3.

Giger, Maryellen L. 2018. "Machine Learning in Medical Imaging." *Journal of the American College of Radiology*. doi:10.1016/j.jacr.2017.12.028.

Han, Jiawei, Micheline Kamber, and Jian Pei. 2012. *Data Mining: Concepts and Techniques. Data Mining: Concepts and Techniques*. doi:10.1016/C2009-0-61819-5.

Hernandez, Inmaculada, and Yuting Zhang. 2017. "Using Predictive Analytics and Big Data to Optimize Pharmaceutical Outcomes." *American Journal of Health-System Pharmacy*. doi:10.2146/ajhp161011.

Kabir, Md Monirul, Md Shahjahan, and Kazuyuki Murase. 2011. "A New Local Search Based Hybrid Genetic Algorithm for Feature Selection." *Neurocomputing*. doi:10.1016/j.neucom.2011.03.034.

Kashef, Shima, and Hossein Nezamabadi-pour. 2015. "An Advanced ACO Algorithm for Feature Subset Selection." *Neurocomputing*. doi:10.1016/j.neucom.2014.06.067.

Komura, Daisuke, and Shumpei Ishikawa. 2018. "Machine Learning Methods for Histopathological Image Analysis." *Computational and Structural Biotechnology Journal*. doi:10.1016/j.csbj.2018.01.001.

Leskovec, Jure, Anand Rajaraman, and Jeffrey David Ullman. 2020. *Mining of Massive Datasets. Mining of Massive Datasets*. doi:10.1017/9781108684163.

Mehta, Nishita, and Anil Pandit. 2018. "Concurrence of Big Data Analytics and Healthcare: A Systematic Review." *International Journal of Medical Informatics*. doi:10.1016/j.ijmedinf.2018.03.013.

Mirjalili, Seyedali, and Andrew Lewis. 2013. "S-Shaped versus V-Shaped Transfer Functions for Binary Particle Swarm Optimization." *Swarm and Evolutionary Computation* 9. Elsevier: 1–14. doi:10.1016/j.swevo.2012.09.002.

Pes, Barbara. 2019. "Ensemble Feature Selection for High-Dimensional Data: A Stability Analysis across Multiple Domains." *Neural Computing and Applications*. 32, 5951–5973. doi:10.1007/s00521-019-04082-3.

Reuter, Miriam S., Susan Walker, Bhooma Thiruvahindrapuram, Joe Whitney, Iris Cohn, Neal Sondheimer, Ryan K.C. Yuen, et al. 2018. "The Personal Genome Project Canada: Findings from Whole Genome Sequences of the Inaugural 56 Participants." *CMAJ*. doi:10.1503/cmaj.171151.

Shen, Li, Laurie R. Margolies, Joseph H. Rothstein, Eugene Fluder, Russell McBride, and Weiva Sieh. 2019. "Deep Learning to Improve Breast Cancer Detection on Screening Mammography." *Scientific Reports*. doi:10.1038/s41598-019-48995-4.

Talbi, El Ghazali. 2009. *Metaheuristics: From Design to Implementation. Metaheuristics: From Design to Implementation*. doi:10.1002/9780470496916.

Vamathevan, Jessica, Dominic Clark, Paul Czodrowski, Ian Dunham, Edgardo Ferran, George Lee, Bin Li, et al. 2019. "Applications of Machine Learning in Drug Discovery and Development." *Nature Reviews Drug Discovery*. doi:10.1038/s41573-019-0024-5.

Xia, Xuewen, Ling Gui, Guoliang He, Bo Wei, Yinglong Zhang, Fei Yu, Hongrun Wu, and Zhi Hui Zhan. 2020. "An Expanded Particle Swarm Optimization Based on Multi-Exemplar and Forgetting Ability." *Information Sciences*. doi:10.1016/j.ins.2019.08.065.

ZorarpacI, Ezgi, and Selma Ayşe Özel. 2016. "A Hybrid Approach of Differential Evolution and Artificial Bee Colony for Feature Selection." *Expert Systems with Applications*. doi:10.1016/j.eswa.2016.06.004.

13

Case Studies in Data Optimization Using Python

Jahangir Alam

AMU, India

CONTENTS

13.1 Introduction

Statistics, probability, and linear algebra topics that are recommended to any newcomer to learn in the field of data science and machine learning (ML). High-performance computing (HPC), machine learning, data science, and big data are buzz words these days. In order to provide companies with a competitive advantage in the modern virtual world, data scientists are discovering new ways to exploit leverage of the big data available to them. These scientists are generally equipped with combination of skills, which include programming, soft skills, and analytics (optimization, machine learning, and statistical techniques). It would not be out of context to mention here that in the present digital world companies regard data scientists as their wildcards or maybe gold miners who dig for chunks of gold underground.

For a successful career in these fields, the value of strong basis in these topics is beyond argument. However, the topic of data optimization, while undermined, is also equally important to everyone willing to pursue a successful career in these fields. The importance of optimization as an essential step in every major social, economic, business, and personal decision that is taken by a group of individuals, an individual, software personal decision agents, and intelligent machines, can't be underestimated.

The ingredients of AI, big data, and machine learning algorithms are incomplete without optimization. The optimization process starts with formulating a cost function and finishes with maximizing or minimizing the formulated function using one or another optimization procedure under given constraints. What affects the accuracy of the results is the selection of appropriate optimization procedure. The application area of optimization is too wide, and it is always difficult to find a real-life situation where it can't be applied. Due to such a broad application area, optimization has been widely researched in academia as well as industry.

An optimization problem is defined as a problem where we maximize or minimize a real valued function by carefully choosing input values from an allowed set of values and compute the values of the real valued function. It means that when we consider optimization, we always strive to find the best solution. Optimization is an essential step in modeling and problem solving related to AI and allied fields like machine learning and data science. A large number of data science and machine learning problems ultimately converge to optimization problems. As an example, consider the approach of a data analyst who solves a machine learning problem for a large dataset. First of all, the analyst expresses the problem using a suitable group of prototypes (called models) and transforms the information into a format acceptable by the chosen group. The next step is to train the model. This is done by optimizing the variables of the prototype with regard to the selected regularization function or loss function using a core optimization problem. The process of selecting and validating the model requires the core optimization problem to be solved several times. Through these core optimization problems, the research related to the field of machine learning, data science, and mathematical programming is related to each other. At one end, mathematical programming provides the definition of optimality conditions, which guide the analyst to decide what constitutes an optimal solution, and at the other end, algorithms of mathematical programming enable data analysts with procedures required to train large groups of models.

The general form an optimization problem is:

$$\min_{z} f(z)$$

$$\textit{Subject to}: g_i(z) \le 0 \quad i = 1, 2, 3 \ldots, n$$

$$h_j = 0 \quad j = 1, 2, 3 \ldots, p$$

$$z \in \Delta$$

Where:

- Δ, is an m-dimensional set of real numbers or integers or positive semi-definite matrices.
- $f : \Delta^m \rightarrow \Delta$, is referred to as an objective function to be minimized over the m-variable vector space z.
- $g_i(z) \le 0$, are called inequality constraints and $h_j = 0$ are called equality constraints, and

- $n \geq 0, p \geq 0$.
- The problem is referred to as unconditional optimization problem if $n = p = 0$.
- The above general form defines what is known as a minimization optimization problem. There also exists a maximization optimization problem, which could be understood by negation of the objective function. Solution of an optimization problem refers to determine $z \in \Delta$, to minimize/maximize the objective function f subject to inequality constraints $g_i(z) \leq 0$ and equality constraints $h_j = 0$.

Any problem that starts with the question "What is best?" can almost always be formulated as an optimization problem (Boyd and Vandenberghe, 2004). For example:

- Which is the best route from Aligarh to Prayagraj?
- Which method should be adopted to produce shoes to maximize the profit?
- What is finest college for my son?
- What is the best fuel for my car?
- How to allocate oil fields to bidding companies to maximize the profit?

To help formulate the solutions to such problems, researchers have defined a framework into which the solvers fit the questions. This framework is referred to as a model. The ultimate feature of a model is that it has constraints and a function referred to as objective, which must be achieved under the given constraints. In other words, the constraints are obstacles in the way of achieving the objective. If a solver is capable to clearly state the constraints and the objective function, he is nearer to a model. Figure 13.1 illustrates the solution procedure for an optimization problem.

There are different classes of optimization problems. For a particular class of optimization problem, the solution procedure refers to an algorithm that leads to a solution (up to some desired accuracy) for a given problem (an instance of the class) of that class. Efforts on developing viable algorithms for various classes of optimization problems, developing S/W packages to solve them, and analyzing their properties are being put since late 1940s. The viability of various algorithms significantly depends on factors like the particular form of constraints and objective functions, number of constraints and variables, and special features such as sparsity. If each constraint function of the problem depends on only a small portion of the variables, the problem is referred to as sparse. This is unexpectedly hard to solve the generalized optimization problem when constraint and objective functions are smooth (e.g., polynomials) (Boyd and Vandenberghe, 2004). So it is imperative that attempts to solve the general optimization problem include certain kinds of compromise, such as not finding the exact solution, long execution time, and so on. There are, however, few exceptions to this general rule. Efficient algorithms do exist for a particular class of problems that can solve sufficiently large problems with thousands of constraints and variables reliably. Linear programming and least squares problem belong to those classes of optimization problems. Convex optimization is also an exception to the general

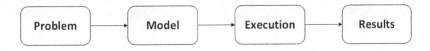

FIGURE 13.1
Steps to Solve an Optimization Problem

rule of solving optimization problems (Agrawal et al., 2018). Efficient algorithms do exist for convex optimization problems that can reliably solve the large optimization problems efficiently. General non-convex optimization problems are proved to be *NP*-hard (Boyd and Vandenberghe, 2004).

In the optimization field, the emphasis is switching to data driven optimization from model based optimization. In this approach data is the main source around which the optimization problem is formulated. The size of the optimization problem is becoming large as the size of data to be processed through the problem is also large. This leads to significant increase in solution time and complexity of the problem. In other words, we can say that large optimization problems, including big datasets, require large interaction with a human solver to find a feasible solution and require a longer solution time.

The rest of the chapter is organized as follows. Section 13.2 discusses optimization in the context of data science and machine learning. Section 13.3 presents a review on related research. Section 13.4 presents various tools that are used to solve the optimization problems and justifies author's choice for a specific tools (Google OR-Tool). Section 13.5 presents Python's prerequisites for running the models formulated in this chapter. Section 13.6 presents detailed case studies along with modeling process, code, and results. Section 13.7 concludes the chapter.

13.2 Optimization and Data Science

The present era is being driven by social media, big data, data analytics, AI, machine learning, deep learning, and IoT (Internet of things), along with high-performance computing. This is the reason that almost every industry is on big data adoption curve. The most valuable asset for most of businesses today is the data captured and reserved by them. In this highly professional environment, the effective use of data can lead to better decision-making in business and other fields. Another aspect of this scenario is that if the businesses fail to optimize their data, instead of gaining anything significant from their large data they are only going spend their precious resources and time digging through the data.

Day by day, organizations are becoming data dependent, a state that is rapidly increasing. The data may come from various sources and may be in different formats or may be unstructured at all. However, in most of the cases, it is inaccurate, inconsistent, and redundant. These variances make it difficult to handle the data for organizations which then struggle to get the relevant information in a suitable manner. This indicates that there is a need to optimize the data. Data optimization means collecting all the data at your disposal and managing it in a way that maximizes the speed and comprehensiveness with which critical information can be pull out, analyzed, and utilized.

As far as machine (and deep learning) is concerned, all machine learning algorithms can be viewed as solutions to optimization problems and it is interesting that even in cases, where the original machine learning technique has a basis derived from other fields for example, chemistry, physics, biology, and so on one could still interpret all of these machine learning algorithms as some solution to an optimization problem. A basic understanding of optimization helps in:

- Deeply understand the working of machine learning algorithms.

- Rationalize the working of the algorithm. That means if we get a result that we want to interpret and we had a deep understanding of optimization, we will be able to realize why we got the result.

- And at an even higher level of understanding, we might be able to develop new algorithms ourselves.

13.3 Literature Review

Based on the objective and constraint functions, a taxonomy of optimization problems exists. There are many classes of mathematical optimizations: linear, semi definite, quadratic, integer, nonlinear, semi-infinite, geometric, fractional, goal, and so on. As an example, a linear mathematical optimization has a linear constraint and objective functions. The NEOS optimization guide (The NEOS, 2020) and the glossary of mathematical optimization (MPG, 2020) provide complete descriptions of these problems. Each class of optimization problems is a diverse research field with wide-ranging mathematical background and procedures.

Surrogate assisted optimization techniques are employed to provide solutions to single or multi-objective computationally expensive optimization problems (Chugh et al., 2017; Jin, 2011). Computationally expensive problems are those problems for which evaluating constrained and/or objective functions take longer than the reasonable time during simulated experiments. In optimization problems involving large data, the timing complexity is not high due to the evaluation of the objective and/or constraint functions, but is because of the large size of data. In surrogate-driven optimization, surrogate functions are trained using a small model of expensive function evaluations. These surrogate functions produce approximate solutions but are computationally inexpensive (Chugh et al., 2017; Jin, 2011).

For mathematical background and algorithms related to nonlinear optimization, several good resources are available (Nocedal and Wright, 1999; Bertsekas, 2004; Bazaraa, Sherali, and Shetty, 2006). Convex optimization including semi-definite optimization is covered in (Boyd and Vandenberghe, 2004); Diamond and Boyd, 2016). Goberna and Lopez (1998) provide semi-infinite algorithms and mathematical background. Nemhauser and Wolsey (1999) provide information about integer and combinatorial optimization.

Researchers have noticed that the connection between machine learning models and optimization models, and this field is constantly advancing. Use of mathematical optimization in the field of machine learning has led to advanced research in this area. In the area of neural networks researchers have gone from backpropagation (Hinton and Williams, 1986) to exploit the use of unconstrained nonlinear optimization (Bishop, 1996). The backpropagation worked fine, so programmers simulated gradient descent to have a deep insight into its properties (Mangasarian and Solodov, 1994). Advances in kernel methods (Cortes and Vapnik, 1995) have made mathematical optimization terms like duality and language multipliers, quadratic program, and so on more realistic for machine learning students. To exploit the mathematical optimization tree more into depth with special focus on convex optimization, machine learning, and data science, researchers are working on novel methods and models. As a result of the advances in mathematical optimization, a rich set of ML models are being explored without much worries about the algorithms (Bergstra et al., 2015). Conversely machine learning and data science have inspired advances in mathematical optimization. The optimization problems emerging from AI, data mining, data science, machine learning, and deep learning are way ahead in size of the problems which have been reported in literature.

The relationship between data science, machine learning, and optimization becomes complicated when machine learning mixes two things, i.e., methods and modeling. In such cases, machine learning is more like operation research (OR). Historically, mathematical optimization is a branch of OR. OR is related to system modeling while optimization analyzes and solves that model. Both the analysts (i.e., OR or ML) formulate problems in real world using a model, derive the main problem and solve it using an optimization model. So, the OR and machine learning analysts face the same kind of issues, and it is not a matter of surprise that both can explore the same set of tools (Radin, 1998).

As in machine learning, mathematical optimization also has large number of problems for benchmarking. A benchmark performance evaluator measures speed of algorithms referred to as performance of algorithm (Dolan and More, 2002). Karush-Kuhn-Tucker optimality conditions (KKT, 2020) are applied to measure the quality of the solution. Quality of solution is a function of the amount of the deviation from the constraints and objective value. All these metrics related to solution quality are generally not reported in machine learning literature. It has been observed that small adjustment or tuning in the model can lead to much better solutions (Sonnenburg, Schafer, and Scholkopf, 2006; Shalev-Shwartz and Singer, 2006). In Sonnenburg, Schafer, and Scholkopf (2006 and Shalev-Shwartz and Singer (2006), the authors have reformulated the models and the new procedures reproduce the problem into a collection of simpler familiar problems, which could be solved easily.

In some cases, machine learning models are made convex. This is done by defining an appropriate definition for system boundaries wherein parameters are treated as fixed. For a fixed-ridge parameter, ridge regression is a convex unconstrained quadratic problem. The cross-validation procedure (Golub and Mattvon, 1997) defines the ridge parameter within boundary and the problem is converted into nonconvex.

Artificial intelligence and data science are comprehensive fields that encompass miscellaneous techniques, measures of success, and objectives. One branch of these fields is related to find the viable solutions to some well-known problems in the field of optimization (Blank and Deb, 2020). This chapter introduces the reader to the art of developing models for some well-known optimization problems and the science behind of implementing these models in Python. As pointed out earlier, the intention of the author is not to help the user become a skillful theoretician but a skillful modeler. Therefore, little of mathematical principles related to the subject of optimization is discussed. This has been done by undertaking some case studies in the related field.

13.4 Taxonomy of Tools Available for Optimization

Over the years, a sizeable number of specialized languages have been designed by the researchers in the field of mathematical optimization. Figure 13.2 proposes a taxonomy of these languages and lists various languages or software tools available in each category of the taxonomy. As shown in Figure 13.2, optimization tools can be classified into two categories: modeling tools and solving tools. Whereas modeling languages provide specific

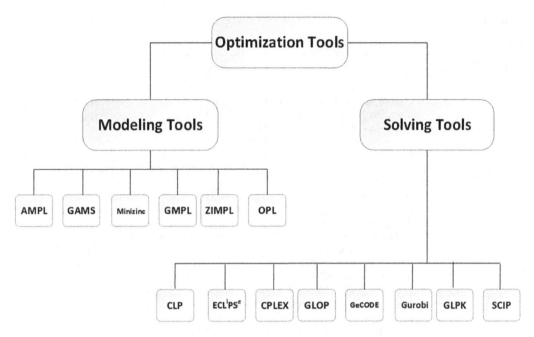

FIGURE 13.2
Taxonomy of Optimization Tools

vocabulary, formal constructions, and grammar for specifying the models, the solving languages can take as input the models programmed in certain modeling languages and provide the solution.

This section briefly introduces some prominent tools under each category and justifies why we have chosen Python-based approach over the other approaches available for modeling and solving the optimization problems.

13.4.1 Modeling Tools

Table 13.1 summarizes various modeling tools available for optimization problems.

13.4.2 Solving Tools

Table 13.2 summarizes various solving tools available for optimization problems.

13.4.3 Justification for Selecting OR-Tools

From subsection 13.4.2, it is clear that a model is formulated in a modeling language and then the model is fed to solver (a different language) to get the results. This happens because there exists a parser between the modeler and solver languages, which translates the modeler language code into a format known to the solver. Figure 13.3 shows a parser between a modeler and a solver. If the parser doesn't translate into the format known to a specific solver, that solver can't be used with the modeling language. This is a major drawback of modeler and solver model. In addition to the above, there are very limited modelers and solvers that integrate with high-level languages like Python or R. If one of these is

TABLE 13.1

Summary of Various Modeling Tools

S.No.	Tool	Description
1.	AMPL	To promote rapid development and reliable results, the AMPL supports the entire life cycle of optimization modeling (AMPL, 2020). It supports a high-level algebraic representation of optimization models, which is close to the ways people think about the models. It provides special tools for modeling large scale optimization problems. A command line language for analyzing and debugging of models and a debugging tool for manipulation optimization strategies and data are also provided with the system. AMPL's APIs for C, C++, MATLAB, JAVA, R, Python, and so on to ensure easy integration.
2.	GAMS	GAMS is a high-level language that supports both optimization and mathematical programming (GASM, 2020). It provides a language compiler for analyzing and debugging the models and several associated solvers. Real-world optimization problems can quickly be transformed into computer code using GAMS modeling language. Its compiler puts the model in a format that can easily be understood by associated solvers. As many solvers are supported by GAMS format, it provides users the flexibility of testing his model on various solvers.
3.	Minzinc	Minzinc is an open-source and free framework for modeling of the constraint optimization problems (The MiniZinc, 2020). It could be used on model constraint optimization problems in a solver independent high-level language. This is done by taking benefit of a large library of predefined constraints. Models formulated with Minzinc are compiled into another high-level language referred to as FlatZinc. FlatZinc is a solver input language and is understood by a large number of solvers.
4.	GMPL	It stands for GNU mathematical programming language. GMPL is a modeling language intended for describing mathematical programming models (GLPK, 2020). To develop a model in GMPL, a high-level language is provided to the user. The model consists of data blocks and a set of statements defined by the user. A program referred to as model translator analyzes the user-defined model and translates it into internal data structures. This process is referred to as translation. The translated model is submitted to the appropriate solver for getting the solution of the problem.
5.	ZIMPL	ZIMPL is a relatively small language (ZIMPL, 2020). ZIMPLS facilitates to formulate the mathematical model of a problem into a (mixed-)integer mathematical or linear program. The output is generated in .mps or .ls file format that can be understood and answered by a MIP or LP solver.
6.	OPL	Optimization Programming Language (OPL) is an algebraic modeling language. It facilitates an easier and shorter coding mechanism compared to a general-purpose programming language (The IBM ILOG, 2020). A part of the CPLEX (IBM, 2020) software package, it is well supported by IBM through its ILOG CPLEX and ILOG CPLEX-CP optimizers. OPL supports integer/(mixed)-integer, constraint and liner programming.

compatible the other doesn't have support. These constraints make the use of modeler and solver limited. Another aspect of this incompatibility is that a large number of modelers have support for some mathematical optimization problems. From his past experience, the author has learnt that use of specialized modeler and solver languages should be avoided and one must use a high-level language, e.g., C, C++, Python, R, interfaced with a library that supports multiple solvers. Google's Operation Research Tools (OR-Tools) come into picture to support this idea. It is a well-structured, comprehensive library that offers a user-friendly interface. It effectively supports constraint programming and has special routines for network flow problems. In this chapter the author will demonstrate only a very small portion of this encyclopedia of optimization.

TABLE 13.2

Summary of Solving Tools

S.No.	Tool	Description
1.	CLP	CLP (COIN-OR): CLP also referred to as COIN-OR (Computational Infrastructure for Operations Research). It is written in C++ and is an open-source mathematical programming solver. COIN-OR is run by the educational, non-profit COIN-OR Foundation (COIN-OR, 2020). It is accommodated by the Institute for Operations Research and the Management Sciences (INFORMS). Many peer-reviewed journals in the field of optimization use this tool to cross-check the results claimed by researchers.
2.	ECL^{i}PS^e	It is an open-source software. This tool is especially used for cost-effective deployment and development of applications related to scheduling, planning, resource allocation, transportation, timetabling, and so on (constraints programming) (ECLiPSe, 2020). For teaching combinatorial problem solving, e.g., constraint programming, modeling, and mathematical programming, it is an ideal tool. It supports several constraint solvers, a control and high-level modeling language and libraries. It easily interfaces with third-party software.
3.	CPLEX	Informally referred to as CPLEX, it stands for IBM ILOG CPLEX. Optimization Studio is an award-winning optimization studio. In 2004 work on CPLEX was awarded an impact prize by Institute for Operations Research and the Management Sciences (INFORMS). The name CPLEX is given to the software because of the fact that it implements well-known simplex method in C programming language. As of now it has support for other types of mathematical optimization and interfaces with other languages including C. CPLEX has the power to solve very large linear programming problems using either dual or primal variants of the well-known simplex method or the barrier interior point method.
4.	GLPO	This refers to Google's linear programming system. The primary linear optimization solver for well-known OR-Tools is GLOP (OR-Tools. 2020). According to Google, its memory is efficient, fast, and numerically stable. The author has exploited OR-Tools using Python while solving the case studies scenarios present in this chapter.
5.	GeCode	It is free and open-source toolkit (C++) for solving constraints satisfaction problems. It stands for Generic Constraint Development Environment (GECODE, 2020). It is in fact a library that is extensible and modular. It provides a state-of-the art performance constraint solver. According to the developer, GeCode is open, comprehensive, well-documented, parallel, efficient, portable, and tested.
6.	GurOBI	It is a commercial solver and developers claim that it is the fastest solver on Earth (GUROBI, 2020). It has support for various optimization problems such as quadratically constrained programming, linear programming, mixed integer linear programming, and so on.
7.	GLPK	It stands for GNU Linear Programming Kit (GLPK, 2020). It is a set of procedures written in ANSI C and is used to solve large-scale linear programming, mixed-integer programming, and other related problems. It is supported in the form of a callable library.
8.	SCIP	It stands for Solving Constraint Integer Programs (SCIP, 2020). Developed at Zeus Institute at Berlin, Germany, it is currently one of the fastest free solvers for mixed integer nonlinear programming (MINLP) and mixed integer programming (MIP). It is supported as a C callable library.

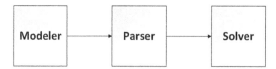

FIGURE 13.3
Parser Between Modeler and Solver

OR-Tools have been awarded four gold medals in the 2019 MiniZinc Challenge, the international constraint programming competition (OR-Tools, 2020). Some other important features of OR-Tools are listed below (Bodnia, 2020):

- **Stability and Continuous Development:** OR-Tools are continuously updated, bugs are fixed, and new features are added by a dedicated team of programmers.
- **High Performance:** Complex calculations are performed using multithreaded algorithms optimized for the purpose. This leads to get the results at a faster pace without acquiring sophisticated hardware.
- **Flexibility:** It implies that best results could be obtained with minimal expenses on infrastructure.
- **Resource Utilization:** Guarantees the best use of available resources by exploiting vacant space or idle time.

Looking at the above properties of Google's OR-Tools the author has selected them for the proposed case studies.

13.5 Case Studies Python Prerequisites

Python has become a popular choice of programmers for both optimization and data analytics (Zegard and Paulino, 2015). This section briefly guides the reader to download and install the Python packages required to perform the case studies presented in this chapter. The author assumes that Python is installed on your system. For the consideration that the required libraries are better supported by Python 2, the author has used Python 2.7.x, where x stands for any version released later than Python 2.7.10. Table 13.3 shows step-by-step process to install required Python packages or libraries.

13.6 Case Studies: Solving Optimization Problems Through Python

As stated earlier, the main goal of this chapter is to demonstrate the reader how to solve real-life optimization problems through Python and Google's OR-Tools. In this section the author has selected certain optimization problems and demonstrated how they could be solved using OR-Tools and Python. The simplest problems are like those encountered in a first course on optimization. The nature of these problems is algebraic, which means they

TABLE 13.3

Python Commands to Install Required Packages

Step 1:	**Upgrade pip** **Launch the Window's command prompt as an administrator and to upgrade pip type in the following:**

```
python -m pip install - -upgrade pip
```

Step 2:	**Install Packages** To install any package using pip, launch the Window's command prompt as an administrator and use the following command (general form):

```
python -m pip install package_name
```

Step 3:	<div align="center">**OR-Tools Installation**</div>

The command to install OR-Tools is as follows:

```
python -m pip install ortools
```

OR

```
!pip install ortools
```

(For users working with Jupyter Notebook or Google Colab platform)

Note: For the purpose of installing packages two options, namely **conda** and **pip,** are there. These case studies use Python Packaging Authority's (PPA) recommended tool pip for installing packages from the Python Package Index (PyPI). With pip, Python software package are installed as wheels or source distributions. pip is already installed with all versions of Python after 2.7.9.

can be formulated and solved (not always) by applying simple liner algebraic techniques. In Case Study 1, the author considers one such problem and shows how to model and solve the problem.

13.6.1 Case Study 1: Product Allocation Problem (Swarup, Gupta, and Mohan, 2009)

An electronics company has three operational subdivisions—Fabrication, Testing, and Packing, with a capacity to produce three different types of components, namely E_1, E_2, and E_3, yielding a profit of Rs. 4, Rs. 3 and Rs. 5 per component. Component E_1 require 4 minutes in fabrication, 4 minutes in teasing, and 12 minutes in packing. Similarly, component E_2 requires 12 minutes in fabrication, 4 minutes in testing, and 4 minutes in packing. Product E_3 requires 8 minutes in each subdivision. In a week, total run time of each subdivision is 90, 60, and 100 hours for fabrication, testing, and packing respectively. The goal is to model the problem and find the product mix to maximize the profit.

- **Modeling the Problem**

Table 13.4 summarizes the data of the problem:
   The general steps to model a problem are as follows:

   i. Read the problem carefully and precisely.

   ii. Identify what is required to solve the problem, and based on that identify the decision variables.

   iii. To streamline the constraints or of the objective function, define auxiliary variables. They may also help in the presentation of the solution and analysis.

   iv. Derive algebraic equalities or inequalities directly involving the decision variables or indirectly the supplementary (auxiliary) variables. This is done by transforming each constraint into an algebraic inequality or equality.

TABLE 13.4

Product Allocation Problem Data

	Subdivisions			
	Fabrication (in minutes)	Testing (in minutes)	Packing (in minutes)	Profit/ Component (In. INR)
E_1	4	4	12	4
E_2	12	4	4	3
E_3	8	8	8	5
Availability (minutes)	90×60	60×60	100×60	

v. Formulate the objective function for the quantity to be maximized or minimized.

vi. Choose an appropriate solver and run the model.

vii. Solution should be displayed in proper manner.

viii. Validate the model and the results. Identify whether the solution appropriately satisfy the constraints. Is the solution implementable and leads to proper solution? If not, consider finetuning the model.

Figure 13.4 pictorially represents the complete process.

The above steps implemented for Case Study 1 problem are as follows:

Step 1: Let a, b, and c denote the weekly production units of components E_1, E_2, and E_3 respectively. The key decision that is to be made is to determine the weekly rate of production of these components so that the profit could be maximized.

Step 2: Since negative production of any component makes no sense, we have values of a, b, and c bounded by inequalities shown in Equation 13.1:

$$a \geq 0, b \geq 0, \text{and} c \geq 0 \qquad (13.1)$$

Step 3: The constraints are the limiting weekly working hour of each subdivision. Production of one unit of component E_1 requires 4 minutes in fabrication. The quantity being a units, the requirement for fabrication for component E_1 alone will be $4a$ fabrication minutes. Similarly, b units of product E_2 and c units of product E_3 will require $12b$ and $8c$ fabrication minutes respectively. Thus the total weekly requirement of fabrication minutes will be $4a + 12b + 8c$, which should not exceed the available 5,400 minutes. So, the first constraints can be formulated as shown in Equation 13.2:

$$4a + 12b + 8c \leq 5400 \qquad (13.2)$$

Step 4: Similarly, the constraints for testing and packing subdivisions can be formulated as shown in Equations 13.3 and 13.4:

$$4a + 4b + 8c \leq 3600 \qquad (13.3)$$

$$12a + 4b + 8c \leq 6000 \qquad (13.4)$$

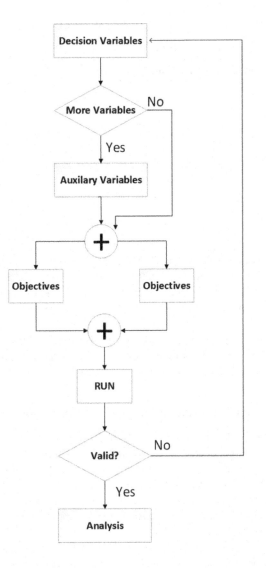

FIGURE 13.4
Flowchart for Modeling and Solving an Optimization Problem

Step 5: The objective is to maximize the weekly total profit. Assuming that all components produced are immediately sold in the market, the total profit is given by Equation 13.5:

$$z = 4a + 3b + 5c \qquad (13.5)$$

Clearly, the mathematical model for the problem under consideration can be summarized as shown in Table 13.5.

Step 6: The author selects Google's OR-Tool GLOP solver and Python language to run the above model. The Python code used to solve the model are listed Table 13.6:

A model is coded in Python in the same way as shown in above solution code. The line sol = pywraplp.Solver.CreateSolver('Product Allocation Problem', 'GLOP') invokes

TABLE 13.5

Summarized Mathematical Model for Product Allocation Problem

Mathematical Model for Product Allocation Problem
Find a, b, and c so as to maximize:
$$z = 4a + 3b + 5c$$
Subject to the constraints:
$$4a + 12b + 8c \leq 5400$$ $$4a + 4b + 8c \leq 3600$$ $$12a + 4b + 8c \leq 6000$$ $$a \geq 0, b \geq 0, \text{ and } c \geq 0$$

Google's own GLOP solver (OR-Tools 2020) and names it as sol. The OR-Tools could be interfaced with a variety of solvers. Altering a solver, say CLP (COIN-OR) (COIN-OR, 2020) or GLPK from GNU (GLPK, 2020) is just a matter of altering this line.

Step 7: The optimal solution to the product allocation problem, therefore, is shown in Table 13.7:

Hence maximum profit that could be earned is: 4(300) + 3(225) + 5 (187) = **Rs. 2810**.

Step 8: Model validation: If the solution obtained is correct, then it should satisfy every constraint. Table 13.8 validates the model:

13.6.2 Case Study 2: The Transportation Problem (Swarup, Gupta, and Mohan, 2009)

XYZ makes trailers at plants in Frankfurt, Copenhagen, and Seoul, and ships these units to distribution centers in London, Paris, New York, and Tokyo. In planning production for the next year, XYZ estimates unit shipping cost (in US dollars) between any plant and distribution center, plant capacities, and distribution center demands. These numbers are given in the Table 13.9.

XYZ faces the problem of determining how much to ship between each plant and distribution center to minimize the total transportation cost, while not exceeding capacity and while meeting demand.

(a) Formulate a mathematical model to minimize the total shipping cost.

(b) Set up and solve the problem on a spreadsheet. What is the optimal solution?

Steps 1 and 2: From the statement of the problem, it is clear that twelve decision variables are required to make the decision stated in the problem. The decision variables could be expressed $x_{11}, x_{12}, x_{13}, x_{14}, \ldots, x_{32}, x_{33}, x_{34}$.

Step 3: Let c_i be the cost of shipping one unit of trailer from plant i to distribution center j. Therefore the cost of shipping units x could be expressed as $c_{ij}x_{ij}$.

Steps 4 and 5: The objective function to be minimized and the applicable constraints therefore could be formulated as shown in Table 13.10. Equation 13.6 expresses the objective function while Equations 13.7 to 13.11 express the constraints.

Steps 6 and 7: As is obvious from the mathematical model of the problem, the solution to the model requires the use of two-dimensional subscripted variables and Python dictionaries to be utilized. The author selects Google's OR-Tool GLOP solver and Python language to run the above model. Python code to solve the model and output obtained are shown in Table 13.11:

TABLE 13.6

Python Code to Solve Product Allocation Problem

Python Code for Product Allocation Problem

```python
#Install Required Package
!pip install ortools #Execute only once
#Import required functions
from __future__ import print_function
from ortools.linear_solver import pywraplp
# Invoke the solver with GLOP.
sol = pywraplp.Solver.CreateSolver('Product Allocation Problem', 'GLOP')
# Populate variables a,b,c
a = sol.NumVar(0, sol.infinity(), 'a') #Enables the constraint a>=0
b = sol.NumVar(0, sol.infinity(), 'b') #Enables the constraint b>=0
c = sol.NumVar(0, sol.infinity(), 'c') #Enables the constraint c>=0
print('Decision variables =', sol.NumVariables())
#Formulate First Constraint 4a + 12b + 8c <= 5400
cst1 = sol.Constraint(0, 5400, 'cst1')
cst1.SetCoefficient(a, 4)
cst1.SetCoefficient(b, 12)
cst1.SetCoefficient(c, 8)
#Formulate Second Constraint 4a + 4b + 8c <= 3600
cst2 = sol.Constraint(0, 3600, 'cst2')
cst2.SetCoefficient(a, 4)
cst2.SetCoefficient(b, 4)
cst2.SetCoefficient(c, 8)
#Formulate Third Constraint 12a + 4b + 8c <= 6000
cst3 = sol.Constraint(0, 6000, 'cst3')
cst3.SetCoefficient(a, 12)
cst3.SetCoefficient(b, 4)
cst3.SetCoefficient(c, 8)
print('Total constraints =', sol.NumConstraints())
# Formulate the objective function z = 4a + 3b + 5c
objf = sol.Objective()
objf.SetCoefficient(a, 4)
objf.SetCoefficient(b, 3)
objf.SetCoefficient(c, 5)
objf.SetMaximization()
sol.Solve()
print('Product Allocation Problem Solution:')
print('Objective value =', objf.Value())
print('a =', a.solution_value())
print('b =', b.solution_value())
print('c =', c.solution_value())
```

Output

```
Decision variables = 3
Total constraints = 3
Product Allocation Problem Solution:
Objective value = 2812.5
a = 300.00000000000006
b = 225.0
c = 187.49999999999997
```

Note: All Python code used in this chapter has been run using Jupyter Notebook and Google Colab web applications. These applications allow users to share and create documents that contain equations, live code, narrative text, and visualizations (Jupyter, 2020). Code is available on author's repository at Github. URL to access the code is: https://github.com/jahangir-amu2020/ORCS.

TABLE 13.7

Optimal Production per Week

Product	Units to be produced per week
E_1	300
E_2	225
E_3	187

TABLE 13.8

Model Validation

Constraint Calculated Value	Equality/Inequality	Satisfied/Unsatisfied
4(300) + 12(225) + 8(187) = 5396	<= 5400	Satisfied
4(300) + 4(225) + 8(187) = 3596	<= 3600	Satisfied
12(300) + 4(225) + 8(187) = 5996	<= 6000	Satisfied

TABLE 13.9

Unit Shipping Cost (in US Dollars) Between Plants and Distribution Center, Plant Capacities, and Distribution Center Demands

Plant	Distribution Center				Capacity
	London	Paris	New York	Tokyo	Capacity
Frankfurt	35	40	60	120	12000
Copenhagen	30	30	45	130	8000
Seoul	60	65	50	100	5000
Demand	9000	3000	9500	1500	

Step 8: Model Verification: This could be done in the same way as we did in the last step of Case Study 1. We notice that all constraint are satisfied, so the model is valid.

13.6.3 Case Study 3: The Assignment Problem (Swarup, Gupta, and Mohan 2009)

As the last case study of this introductory chapter, the author presents a solution for another important optimization problem referred to as the assignment problem. After carefully examining the assignment problem, it is easy to conclude that the transportation problem is a special case when the objective is to assign a certain number of resources to the equal number of activities at a maximum profit (or minimum cost) is actually named as an assignment problem. Another form of assignment problem is referred to as an unbalanced assignment problem in which number of resources are greater than the number of activities to be performed.

Following is an example of an assignment problem:

A department head has four subordinates and four tasks to be performed. The subordinates differ in efficiency, and the tasks differ in their intrinsic difficulty. His estimate of the time each subordinate would take to perform each task is given in Table 13.12:

How should the head allocate the task to subordinates (one task to each) so as to minimize the total time to complete the tasks?

TABLE 13.10

Mathematical Model for Transportation Problem

Mathematical Model for the Transportation Problem

Find $x_{11}, x_{12}, x_{13}, x_{14}, \ldots, x_{32}, x_{33}, x_{34}$ so as to minimize:

$$z = \sum_{i=1}^{3} \sum_{j}^{4} c_{ij} \cdot x_{ij} \tag{13.6}$$

or

$$z = 35x_{11} + 40x_{12} + 65x_{13} + 120x_{15} + \ldots + 100x_{34}$$

Subject to the following capacity and demand constraints:

$$\sum_{i=1}^{3} x_{i1} \geq 9000, \sum_{j=1}^{4} x_{1j} \leq 12000 \tag{13.7}$$

$$\sum_{i=1}^{3} x_{i2} \geq 3000, \sum_{j=1}^{4} x_{2j} \leq 8000 \tag{13.8}$$

$$\sum_{i=1}^{3} x_{i3} \geq 9500, \sum_{j=1}^{4} x_{3j} \leq 5000 \tag{13.9}$$

$$\sum_{i=1}^{3} x_{i4} \geq 1500 \tag{13.10}$$

$$x_{ij} \geq 0 \text{ for all } i, j \tag{13.11}$$

Step 1: To mathematically express the above assignment problem we consider the generalized form of an assignment problem in which n resources are to be assigned to n activities. The cost of assigning resource i to activity j is known as c_{ij}. Table 13.13 describes the cost matrix for the problem.

The cost matrix is same as it is with the transportation problem. However, this time the requirement at each of the destinations and the availability at each of the resources is unity (1). This is because of the fact that assignments are to be made on one-to-one basis.

Step 2: Let x_{ij} denotes the assignment of the ith resource to j^{th} activity, such that:

$$x_{ij} = \begin{cases} 1, \text{if resource i is assigned to activity j} \\ 0, \text{Otherwise} \end{cases} \tag{13.12}$$

Step 2: Following above notions, the generalized assignment problem can be mathematically formulated as shown in Table 13.14:

Steps 3, 4, and 5: Based on above general mathematical formulation, the problem considered in the present case study could be formulated as shown in Table 13.15:

Steps 6 and 7: As obvious from the mathematical model of the problem, solution to the model requires the use of two dimensional subscripted variables and Python dictionaries to be utilized. The author selects Google's OR-Tool CBC solver (a MIP solver) and Python language to run the above model.

TABLE 13.11

Python Code to Solve Transportation Problem

Python Code for Transportation Problem

```
#Install Required Package
!pip install ortools #Execute only once
#Import required functions
from __future__ import print_function
from ortools.linear_solver import pywraplp
def transmodel():
  "Initialize Problem Data"
  pd = {}
  pd['cbound'] = [12000,8000,5000]
  pd['dbound'] = [9000,3000,9500,1500]
  pd['obcoeff'] = [
                  [35,40,60,120],
                  [30,30,45,130],
                  [60,65,50,100],
                  ]
  pd['ncc'] = 3
  pd['ndc'] = 4
return pd
pd = transmodel()
solver = pywraplp.Solver.CreateSolver('simple_mip_program', 'GLOP')
inf = solver.infinity()
x={}
#Create Variables and enforce greater than zero constraints
for i in range(pd['ncc']):
  for j in range(pd['ndc']):
    x[i, j] = solver.NumVar(0, inf, ")
print('Number of variables =', solver.NumVariables())
#Enforce Capacity Constraints
for i in range(pd['ncc']):
  constraint = solver.RowConstraint(0, pd['cbound'][i], ")
  for j in range(pd['ndc']):
    constraint.SetCoefficient(x[i,j], 1)
#Enforce Capacity Constraints
for i in range(pd['ndc']):
  constraint = solver.RowConstraint(pd['dbound'][i],inf, ")
  for j in range(pd['ncc']):
    constraint.SetCoefficient(x[j,i], 1)
print('Number of constraints =', solver.NumConstraints())
# Formulate the objective function
objf = solver.Objective()
for i in range(pd['ncc']):
  for j in range(pd['ndc']):
    objf.SetCoefficient(x[i,j], pd['obcoeff'][i][j])
objf.SetMinimization()
solver.Solve()
print('Transportation Problem Solution:')
print('Objective value =', objf.Value())
for i in range(pd['ncc']):
  for j in range(pd['ndc']):
    print('x[', i, j,']', ' = ', x[i,j].solution_value())
```

Python Code for Transportation Problem

Output

```
Decision variables = 12
Total constraints = 7
Transportation Problem Solution:
Objective value = 1010000.0
x[ 0 0 ] = 9000.0
x[ 0 1 ] = 999.9999999999998
x[ 0 2 ] = 0.0
x[ 0 3 ] = 0.0
x[ 1 0 ] = 0.0
x[ 1 1 ] = 2000.0000000000002
x[ 1 2 ] = 5999.999999999999
x[ 1 3 ] = 0.0
x[ 2 0 ] = 0.0
x[ 2 1 ] = 0.0
x[ 2 2 ] = 3500.0
x[ 2 3 ] = 1500.0
```

TABLE 13.12

Time Required by Each Subordinate to Perform Each Task

Tasks	Subordinate			
	A	B	C	D
T_1	18	26	17	11
T_2	13	28	14	26
T_3	38	19	18	15
T_4	19	26	24	10

TABLE 13.13

Cost Matrix for Assignment Problem

Resources	Activities				Available
	A_1	A_2	...	A_n	
R_1	c_{11}	c_{12}	...	c_{1n}	1
R_2	c_{21}	c_{22}	...	c_{2n}	1
R3	c_{31}	c_{32}	...	c_{3n}	1
...	...	...	...	...	...
R_n	c_{n1}	c_{n2}	...	c_{nn}	
Required	1	1	1	1	1

Python code to solve the model is available at author's repository and can be accessed using the URL: https://github.com/jahangir-amu2020/ORCS/blob/master/Case-Study-3.pdf.

The code also illustrates how to solve the assignment problem using a mixed-integer programming (MIP) solver.

TABLE 13.14

Mathematical Model for Generalized Assignment Problem

Mathematical Model for the Generalized Assignment Problem

Minimize:

$$z = \sum_{i=1}^{n}\sum_{j=1}^{n} c_{ij}.x_{ij} \qquad (13.13)$$

Subject to the constraints:

$$\sum_{i=1}^{n} x_{ij} = 1 \text{ and } \sum_{j=1}^{n} x_{ij} = 1; \text{ where } x_{ij} = 0 \text{ or } 1 \qquad (13.14)$$

$$Subject\ to: g_i(z) \le 0 \quad i = 1,2,3\ldots$$

TABLE 13.15

Mathematical model for case study assignment problem

Mathematical Model for the Case Study Assignment Problem

Minimize:

$$z = \sum_{i=1}^{4}\sum_{j=1}^{4} c_{ij}.x_{ij} \qquad (13.15)$$

Subject to the constraints:

$$\sum_{i=1}^{4} x_{ij} = 1 \text{ and } \sum_{j=1}^{4} x_{ij} = 1; \text{ where } x_{ij} = 0 \text{ or } 1 \qquad (13.16)$$

$$h_j = 0 \quad j = 1,2,3\ldots$$

13.7 Conclusions

In the past few years, research in mathematical optimization, machine learning, and data science have become highly interrelated. Branches of mathematical optimization are being fully exploited by machine learning researchers. With the help of available mathematical optimization modelers, algorithms, and robust solvers, data scientists have an ideal toolkit for exploring new machine learning problems. Machine learning models so obtained require highly efficient and accurate modelers and solvers. As pointed out earlier, not all models support all solvers, so we must use the modeler and solver in combination with some high-level language like C/ C++/ Java or Python.

In this chapter the author has focused on Google's Operation Research Tools (OR-Tools) and has shown that how some well-known optimization problems can be solved using OR-Tools in combination of Python language. In each case, first a mathematical model has been developed, which is the primary aim of the author. The model has then been coded and solved using OR-Tools and Python. To keep the subject matter simple and easy for all those who are entering in the field of data science and optimization, the author has only focused on simple optimization problems like transportation problem, assignment problem, and so on. The author has focused on the general steps of developing, solving, and validating the mathematical model of an optimization problem and has demonstrated these steps by developing, solving, and validating three important classes of optimization problem using Python and OR-Tools. Other optimization problems can also be modeled and solved using the concepts presented in this chapter and the author intends to take this assignment in future. The chapter can be effectively used to create easy yet powerful and efficient models for optimization problems.

References

Agrawal, A., Verschueren, R., Diamond, S., and S. Boyd. 2018. A rewriting system for convex optimization problems. *Journal of Control Decision* 5(1):42–60

AMPL. 2020. "AMPL streamedlined modeling for real optimization." (accessed October 17, 2020) https://ampl.com/

Bazaraa, M., Sherali, H., and C. Shetty. 2006. *Nonlinear Programming Theory and Algorithms.* Wiley

Bergstra J., Komer B., Eliasmith C., Yamins D., and D.D. Cox. 2015. Hyperopt: a Python library for model selection and hyperparameter optimization. *Computational Science & Discovery.* 8(1)

Bertsekas, D.P. 2004. *Nonlinear Programming.* Athena Scientific, Cambridge

Bishop, C. 1996. *Neural Networks for Pattern Recognition.* Oxford University Press, Oxford.

Blank J., and K. Deb. 2020. pymoo: multi-objective optimization in python. *IEEE Access* 8: 89497–89509

Bodnia V. 2020. Google OR-Tools business value and potential. (accessed October, 2020) https://freshcodeit.com/google-or   tools#:~:text=The%20primary%20purpose%20of%20using,%2C%20graph%20algorithms%2C%20and%20more.

Boyd S., and L. Vandenberghe. 2004. *Convex Optimization,* Cambridge University Press, The Edinburgh Building, Cambridge

Chugh, T., Sindhya, K., Hakanen, J., and K. Miettinen. 2017. Handling computationally expensive multiobjective optimization problems with evolutionary algorithms: a survey. *Soft Computing* 23: 3137–3166

COIN-OR. 2020. "Computational Infrastructure for Operations Research" (accessed October, 2020) https://en.wikipedia.org/wiki/COIN-OR

Cortes, C., and V. Vapnik. 1995. Support-vector networks. *Machine Learning* 20(3): 273–297

Diamond, S., and S. Boyd. 2016. CVXPY: A Python-Embedded Modeling Language for Convex Optimization. *Journal of Machine Learning Research.* 17(83): 1-5

Dolan, D. and J. More. 2002. Benchmarking optimization software with performance profiles. *Mathematical Programming* 91(2):201–213.

ECLiPSe. 2020. "The ECLiPSe Constraint Programming System." (accessed September, 2020) http://eclipseclp.org/

GASM. 2020. "GAMS System Overview" (accessed August, 2020). https://www.gams.com/products/gams/gams-language/

GECODE. 2020. "Generic constraint development environment." (accessed August, 2020) https://www.gecode.org/

GLPK. 2020. "GNU Linear Programming Kit." (accessed August, 2020) https://www.gnu.org/software/glpk/

Goberna, M.A., and M.A. Lopez. 1998. *Linear Semi-Infinite Optimization.* John Wiley, New York.

Golub, G.H., and U. Mattvon. 1997. Generalized cross-validation for large scale problems. *Journal of Computational and Graphical Statistics* 6(1):1–34.

GUROBI. 2020. "GUROBI Optimization." (accessed August, 2020) https://www.gurobi.com/

Hinton, G.R., and R. Williams. 1986. Learning internal representations by error propagation. *Parallel Distributed Processing*. 1: 318–362 Cambridge, MIT Press

IBM. 2020. "IBM ILOG CPLEX Optimization Studio." (accessed August, 2020) https://en.wikipedia.org/wiki/CPLEX

Jin, Y. 2011. Surrogate-assisted evolutionary computation: recent advances and future challenges. *Swarm Evol. Comput.* 1(2): 61–70

Jupyter. 2020. "The Jupyter Notebook Site." (accessed August, 2020) https://jupyter.org/

KKT. 2020. "Karush–Kuhn–Tucker conditions" (accessed August 2020) https://en.wikipedia.org/wiki/Karush%E2%80%93Kuhn%E2%80%93Tucker_conditions

Mangasarian, O.L., and M.V. Solodov. 1994. Serial and parallel backpropagation convergence via nonmonotone perturbed minimization. *Optimization Methods and Software* 4(2):103–116.

MPG. 2020. "Mathematical programming glossary" (accessed August, 2020). https://glossary.informs.org/ver2/mpgwiki/index.php?title=Main_Page).

Nemhauser, G., and L. Wolsey. 1999. *Integer and Combinatorial Optimization*. Wiley.

Nocedal, J., and S.J. Wright. 1999. *Numerical Optimization*. Springer, New York.

OR-Tools. 2020. "Google OR-Tools." (accessed August, 2020) https://developers.google.com/optimization

Radin, R.L. 1998. *Optimization in Operations Research*. Prentice-Hall, New Jersey

Shalev-Shwartz, S., and Y. Singer. 2006. Efficient learning of label ranking by soft projections onto polyhedral. *Journal of Machine Learning Research* 7:1567–1599

SCIP. 2020. "Solving Constraint Integer Programs" (accessed September, 2020) https://www.scipopt.org/

Sonnenburg, G. R., Schafer, C., and B. Scholkopf. 2006. Large scale multiple kernel learning. *Journal of Machine Learning Research.* 7:1531–1565.

Swarup, K., Gupta P.K., M. Mohan. 2009. *Operation Research*. Sultan Chand & Sons, New Delhi (35)

The IBM ILOG. 2020. "The IBM ILOG Optimization Programming Language" (accessed August 2020) https://www.ibm.com/support/knowledgecenter/SSSA5P_12.8.0/ilog.odms.studio.help/pdf/opl_languser.pdf

The MiniZinc. 2020. "The MiniZinc Website." (accessed August, 2020) https://www.minizinc.org/

The NEOS. 2020. "The NEOS optimization guide" (accessed August, 2020) https://neos-guide.org/content/optimization-introduction

Zegard, T., and G.H. Paulino. 2015. GRAND3 - ground structure based topology optimization for arbitrary 3D domains using MATLAB. *Struct Multidisc Optim* 52(6):1161–1184

ZIMPL. 2020. "Zuse Institute Mathematical Programming Language." (accessed September, 2020) https://zimpl.zib.de/

14

Deep Parallel-Embedded BioNER Model for Biomedical Entity Extraction

Ashutosh Kumar and Aakanksha Sharaff

National Institute of Technology, Raipur, India

CONTENTS

14.1 Introduction

Biomedical text data gradually increases day by day, and a strong methodology is needed in order to obtain meaningful and essential data from different biomedical text data. This chapter utilizes text mining component of the information extraction (IE) of a sub-domain called named entity recognition (NER). The biomedical text dataset can be labeled through named entity recognition (NER). NER immediately identifies the entity's name from the particularly interesting domain. Most of the entities, such as protein name, disease, gene name, chemical, and medicine are needed to mark in the biomedical text-domain. Most of the researchers have concentrated on the extraction of protein and gene entities in the modern past, while some study is on the extraction of disease entities. Biomedical named entity recognition (BioNER) is a little bit hard as compared to the general NER because biomedical named entity recognition has verity in naming convention, alias entities, organism, and abbreviation that can share common name genes or protein that refer different context to different biological entities. For example, a biomedical entity called p53 refers to the name of the protein entity in one context. Similarly, p53 corresponds to a molecular protein weight of 53 KD. Different NER approaches have been expanded to include biomedical text names as a machine-based learning, a rule-based approach, and a dictionary-based approach to solving this kind of problem. Thousands of biomedical literatures are published every day in thousands of journals, resulting in new terms and spelling variations are generated in biomedical word. Due to less prediction ability, the dictionaries and rules-based methods of NER are not sufficient. Then, the ML-based solution joins the picture here. For biomedical named entity recognition, the ML-based way is more accurate and stable since it has the potential to manage extensive dimensional vector feature data for text analysis and can anticipate new words or variants depending on learning trends. A robust and high-performance entity recognition model is required for testing, capable of fully capturing context words. The usage of different word characteristics, such as stemming and lemmatization, morphological attributes, suffixes and prefixes, word type, weight of character, orthographic characteristics such as word formation, marks, digits, and so on have been created to construct biomedical NER semantic characteristics such as word windows and conjunctions. Binarian encoding function sets would be used for ML input to train the structure decision of the named entity recognition via an annotation in the testing dataset defined.

Most studies operate on the single domain only in the last few years, for example, a gene or a chemical or a disorder or protein terms only. But no analysis has been performed together on the three datasets, as mentioned in the literature. In order to automatically identify and mark the correct entity in a given document, this chapter explored numerous fields together (disease, gene, protein, and chemical name). The primary purpose of this analysis is to deal with polysemic terms, which are the primary cause of lower recall. The combined architecture referred to in this chapter deals with a single model of all three styles of fields.

Discuss the model of multitasking instruction, which is used at the same time to prepare a specific model for different activities [1]. Other datasets obtained for different yet similar activities will influence MTL [2]. However, gene extraction is entirely distinct from the chemical entity extraction. Both activities include studying specific common characteristics that can help access the biomedical text's linguistic expression. Crichton et al. (2017) built a multitasking model that involves annotations of multiple individuals trained by various datasets. The multitask-learning model was suggested by Wang et al. [4]. The single task NER model performs well compared to other states-of-the-art approaches. For the proposed model, this literature review stimulates us; the model proposed is a summary of various versions. As before, the traditional multitask learning approach uses just a single-task paradigm [5]. Different datasets were prepared for a particular type of task by the proposed technique. For a specific class of entity, the model proposed is used to create an annotated data collection, tailored for its own entity type. The key benefits of multitasking learning methods are that they contribute to high recall and low precision. Models targeted at several tasks of learning also train various kinds of entities to have a more comprehensive training dataset. There is more coverage with various medical entities, which contributes to a higher recall. On the other side, MTL models teach a combination of various types of entities, generating differences between different types of entities, resulting in lower precision. Another explanation why the named entity recognition in the biomedical domain is said to be problematic is that NER labeled as a separate form of an entity depending on the textual sense [6]. Several false prediction tents on polysemic have been listed in this chapter. A term, for example, may be used as a name for a disease and a name for a gene. This mystified entity dilemma tends toward the false-positive incidence in a model allocated for the named disease entity wrongly named gene as a disease. For example, deep learning combined with CRF, i.e., BI-LSTM-CRF models, wrongly labeled disease entity as a gene called "BRCA1," an entity type of disease since the name of the disease appears in the training dataset as "BRCA1 anomalies" or "brca1 deficient." Furthermore, in the training data collection, "VHL" is annotated as a "disorder that confuses the model since" VHL "is often used to label the gene, which turns the gene into a disease after mutation." This is the product of this mutation. A suggested model is added to address the false positive that occurs because of the polysemous terms, in which the outputs of the chemical and gene model are used for the "BRCA1." As forecast as a virus, it advises the disease model to recognize "BRCA1" as a virus, so that predicting the disease model as a disease is not suitable. Each model is taught independently to the entity type and taught again, utilizing the results of another model to teach the other entity type.

14.1.1 Rule-Based NER Approach

Rule-based NER systems are dependent on hand-made rules. On the basis of syntactic-lexical patterns and domain-specific gazetteers, [7] rules can be formulated. Many applications take this approach. Typical rule-based structures use internal and external proof, and word-trigger dictionaries to find support. A professional linguist manually constructs the rules. The benefits of such methodology are the precision, robustness, and coverage of the data collected. Briefly, this method has been well appreciated in literature so far. Experimental results suggest that the approach improves reminder while it has marginal effects on precision.

14.1.2 Directory-Based NER Approach

In this method, the directory is located to a full name entity from a certain dictionary document, and different terms have been implemented in biomedical text mining [8]. The "HUGO" instance is a language that supplies 21,000 humans. UniProt gene [9] entities are commonly used in the Swiss-Prot [10] archive, which includes 180,000 protein documents. BioThesaurus involves the collection of several million genes and proteins depicted in the UniProt entries included in the process database via a cross-reference. In comparison to a machine-based learning method, the major benefit of the dictionary-based framework over the machine-based learning framework is that each case has an external identifier that provides metadata to the names obtained from the annotation. However, owing to the cause of the uncertainty of the term, this method has many problems, including false positives. The false negative covers spelling variants and synonyms. This method relies on the curation and development of a specific domain lexicon, which involves millions of entities. Campagna et al. [11] utilized the variant generator and string control methodology to fix string control approaches, heterogeneity spelling problems, and a higher GENIA corporate F-score than the precise algorithm.

14.1.3 Machine Learning–Based NER Approach

ML-based is the strongest and commonly utilized in text mining. The highest result obtained with a machine-based learning method is the BioCreative II gene or protein tasks. In consideration of named entities recognition, a variety of supervised learning approaches were used, such as CRF [12], Hidden Markov Model (HMM) [13], and Hidden Markov Model (SVM) [14]. Methods for guided learning use annotated document corpus only. They are resolving the sparse data challenge that has surfaced on a small dataset by utilizing a wide variety of functionality. Few semi-monitored learning approaches have been utilized recently by broad unnoted text firms. A sufficient set of functions, represented by the named entity, is an integral part of the ML strategy [15]. Morphological trends, POS marking, spelling term creation, lemmatization, tokenization, and contextual function conjunction are primarily used [16].

14.1.4 Deep Learning–Based NER Approach

DL-based NER models have dominated in recent years and have obtained state-of-the-art results. Deep learning helps to find hidden features automatically compared to feature-based approaches. We shall then quickly clarify what profound learning is and why profound NER learning is. We discuss NER methods dependent on DL. Deep learning is a machine learning field consisting of several computing layers that have many levels of data [17]. Artificial neural networks include forward and backward passes as standard layers. Effects can be calculated and distributed in the future using a nonlinear function, weighted as a whole in the previous layer. In reverse, the gradient of an objective function is determined in the derivatives chain rule for the weight of a module stack. The greatest benefit of deep learning is the ability of both vector and neural processing to acquire representation and semanticist composition. This lets a machine provide raw data such that latent representations and care are automatically discovered to be identified or located. Three main benefits lie in the usage of deep learning techniques in NER. First, a non-linear transition produces non-linear input-to-output mappings. DL models are able to acquire complex data attributes by utilizing nonlinear active functions (e.g., HMM log-linear and linear CRF) compared to linear functions. Secondly, the creation of NER is an immense amount of work to understand deep learning. The standard approaches to characteristics involve comprehensive technical knowledge and experience. On the other side, DL models are powerful to automatically learn valuable representations and raw data variables. Third, the deep neural NER models can be influenced by a gradient descent into a final frame. This allows us to build dynamic NER systems.

The remaining structure of the chapter is described as follows: Section 14.2 describes the related work-related in the area of BioNER. In Section 14.3, we describe the proposed methodology using biomedical datasets. In Section 14.4, varied evaluation parameters, including the dataset description, have been shown. Section 14.5 discusses the results and compares them with its competitor system. Section 14.6 is the last section of this chapter, which tells about the overall gist of this chapter in its future direction.

14.2 Related Work

The volume of biomedical text is growing rapidly. PubMed Central has accessibility of 6 million full-text biomedical publications in 2020 [18]. One obstacle to the usage of biomedical text data is that reading or even locating the knowledge is too large for an individual. This has escalated to a requirement that useful knowledge is collected automatically. Biomedical text mining will convert the lengthy method into fully automated operation [19]. NER is the automated system of identifying and labeling persons in certain texts. Typical entities cover gene, chemical, disease, and protein in the biomedical domain. BioNER is an important source for many downstream text mining technologies, including medication extraction [20] and disease management [21]. BioNER is also used to develop a ground-breaking biomedical entity discovery method that enables users to search bio-entities in challenging issues. NER is primarily based on a dictionary, laws, and artificial learning methods in biomedical text mining [22]. Dictionary frameworks provide a basic and intuitive structure but cannot include unknown entities or polysemic words that render a bad recall [23]. Moreover, it takes substantial manual labor to create and preserve a robust and up-to-date dictionary. The rule-based methodology is more flexible, but manual feature sets are required to adopt a model to a dataset [24]. The rules will reach a high degree of accuracy, but will make false predictions if a new term is unavailable in a sentence in the training data. Usually, this out-of-vocabulary phenomenon also arises in the biomedical context, when a new biomedical word, such as a new drug name, is popular in this area. Recent studies revealed the efficacy of the techniques focused on deep learning. NER performance was demonstrated in the biomedical text by Sahu and Anand's [25] Recurrent Neural Network (RNN). Sahu and Anand's model includes a short-term bidirectional memory network (BiLSTM) and CRF. The importance of deep learning techniques was shown in recent studies. Sahu and Anand show how the Recurrent Neural Network (RNN) identifies a biological entity. The suggested Sahu and Anand models are the combination of conditional random field (CRF) with word level (WL) and character level (Cl) embedding, bidirectional long short-term memory (Bi-LSTM), but the benefits of CL and WL embedding have not been identified by the Bi-LSTM-CRF model [26]. Habib and colleagues [27] paired the Lample and colleagues [28] Bi-LSTM-CRF model with the word embedding of Pyysalo and colleagues [3]. Habibi used CL-based term incorporation to gather characteristics such as spelling in bio-medical institutions. Habibi and colleagues [27] in BioNER highlight the ability of character-level word embedding. While the simulations demonstrated the influential outcome, there remains a very difficult challenge in the field of identification of biomedical named entities. First, to handle the limited volume for training data requirements for the assignment of BioNER. A gold standard dataset is composed of one or two annotation types. NCBI corpora mainly includes annotation of diseases, and this corpus does not include all other agent forms such as genes and proteins. Whereas in JNLPBA corpora, there are only gene and protein annotations. Therefore, for any entity, a limited sum of overall annotated data is damaged.

14.3 Methodology

The baseline is based on the state-of-the-art OntoNotes 5.0 and CoNLL-2003 text data NER architecture. The proposed methodology contains three types of inputs: a word, character, and case input level, each of which is encoded in Figure 14.1 for a particular element of the document. The design begins the separate processing of the three inputs, but fuses them into a further phase. This architecture is based on several atomic activities or layers, which we explain as follows: Mapping of character into a 97-character vocabulary to 30-dimensional integration, arbitrarily initialized U from (−0.5, 0.5). The number and words of sample inputs per batch ("w") differ from batch to batch. There were 52 maximum characters per term ("c"). The character level feedback is used to minimize the possibility of overfitting through dropout layers with a drop rate of 0.5. Figure 14.1 show the model architecture, and rectangles with operating name in bold black letters represent the operations.

14.3.1 Character Embedding

Char_input maps an arbitrarily initialized U (−0.5, 0.5) vocabulary of 97 potential characters in 30-dimensional embedding. The amount of input samples ("b") and the word count ("w") per sample varies from batch to batch. There were 52 maximum characters per word ("c").

14.3.2 Dropout Layer

Character-level feedback is used to minimize the possibility of char dropout1 and char dropout two over fitting at drop rate 0.5 in Figure 14.1. Rectangles with operational names in bold black letters are represented.

14.3.3 1D Convolutional Layer

The single dimension input with three widths of 30 kernels is handled by char convolution. This layer is then followed by a 1-d max pool (char max pool) procedure of 52, which essentially compiles character measurements to size 1. Drafting from a uniform Glorot distribution initializes the kernel. Conditions of bias are initialized to zero.

14.3.4 Word Embedding Layer

We use the Wikipedia 5 Giga embeddings and Glove Wikipedia 2014 with 6B.

14.3.5 Casing Embedding Layer

Casing input maps into Vca-dimensional embeddings a vocabulary of "Vca" casing forms. Eight casing is considered by default as numeric, all-out, all-low, mainly numerical, initial upper, contain a digit, padding, and others (if no one of those cases is applicable and more than 50% of the word is numerical).

14.3.6 Concatenation Layer

Merge-concatenate blend computed character-level (30-dimensional vector per sample input), casing (Vca-dimensional) and word-level (50-dimensional) and data into 80 + Vca-dimensional vectors.

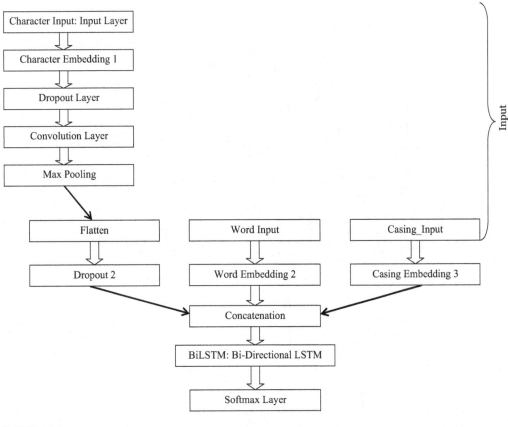

FIGURE 14.1
Flow of the Proposed Work

14.3.7 Bidirectional LSTM (BLSTM)

A BiLSTM measures the series of inputs from the opposite direction to a hidden sequence forward and a hidden sequence backward. The encoded vector consists of the concatenation of the final outputs forward and backward, where the output sequence of the first hidden layer is located.

14.3.8 Mathematical Definition

The detailed architecture of the proposed work shown in Figure 14.2 and Table 14.1, Table 14.2, and Table 14.3 shows hyperparameters with its description values.

14.3.8.1 Input/Output Layer

The formal definition of the proposed model is start with the input sequence X. Let assume the input sequence $x = x_1, x_2, x_3, \ldots x_T$, where T denotes sequence length and the RNN memory at step t is denoted by Y_t.

$$Y_t = \left(\sigma \left(W_x x_t + W_y Y_{t-1} + b_t \right) \right) \tag{14.1}$$

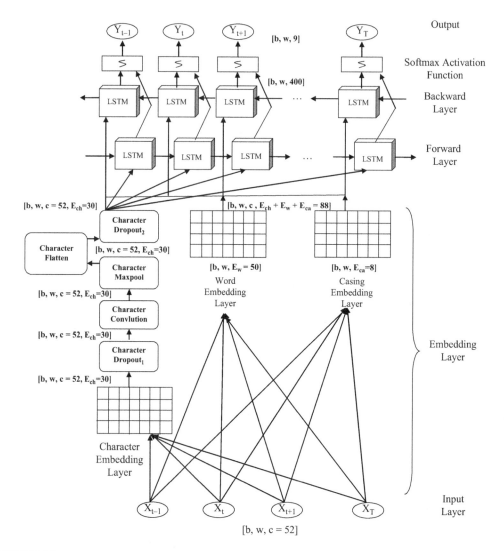

FIGURE 14.2
Architecture of the Proposed Work

TABLE 14.1

Embedding Layer Description

S.No.	Hyperparameters	Description
1.	Character Embedding Layer	Time_Distribution (Embedding (input_dim = 97, output_dim = 30, initialize = Random_Uniform (−0.5. +0.5)))
2.	Word Embedding Layer	Embedding (input_dim = V_w, output_dim = 50, initialize = Random_Uniform (−0.5, +0.5))
3.	Cassing Embedding Layer	Embedding (input_dim = V_{ca}, output_dim = 8, initialize= Random_Uniform (−0.5, +0.5))

TABLE 14.2

Tensor Legend Size Description

S.No.	Legand Tensor Size
1.	Number of batch size = "64"
2.	Number of sample in batch = "b"
3.	Maximum number of words in batch = "w"
4.	Chapter vocablary size = "97"
5.	Words vocabulary size = "V_w"
6.	Casing vocabulary size = "V_{ca}"
7.	Characters embedding dimension = "E_{ch}"
8.	Words embedding dimension = "E_w"
9.	Casing embedding dimension = "E_{ca}"

TABLE 14.3

Another Remaining Hyperparameter Value

S.No.	Hyperparameters	Description
1.	Character Dropout$_1$	Dropout Rate (0.5)
2.	Character Convolution	Time Distribution (Convolution One-Dimension (Kernal_Size = 3, filters = 30, strides =1, padding = "Same", activation "tanh"))
3.	Character Maxpool	Time Distribution (MaxPooling One-Dimension (Pool_Size = 52))
4.	Character Flatten	Time Distribution (flatten)
5.	Character Dropout$_2$	Dropout Rate (0.5)
6.	Bi-LSTM Merging	Bidirectional (LSTM (units = 200, dropout = .5, return_sequence = 1, recurrent _dropout = 0.25))
7.	Activation Function Merging	Time Distribution (Dense (Unit=9, activation = "Softmax"))

Where σ is used to non linear function or sigmoid function (in our case we uses Softmax activation function), W_h *and* W_x is used for weight matrices, and b_t is a constant bias. The output of the RNN is denoted by Y and the sequence of the output is $Y = y_1, y_2, y_3, \ldots y_T$. The corresponding probability can be calculated by Equation 14.2 and the condition probability can be calculated by Equation 14.3.

$$P(x_1, x_2, x_3, \ldots x_T) = p(x_1)p(x_2 | x_1)p(x_3 | x_1, x_2) \ldots p(x_T | x_1, \ldots x_T)) \tag{14.2}$$

$$p(x_t |, x_1 |, \ldots |, x_{t-1}) = \sigma(h_t) \tag{14.3}$$

14.3.8.2 LSTM

Forget Gate: Forget gate is denoted by f_t and the value of the f_t lay between 0 and 1. The f_t can be calculated by the Equation 14.4.

$$f_t = \sigma\left(W_{fh}[h_{t-1}], W_{fx}[x_t], b_f\right) \tag{14.4}$$

Bias value is denoted by $\mathbf{b}_f$.

Input Gate: This gate has two layers: 1) the sigmoid layer, and 2) the tanh stratum. The sigmoid layer specifies which values to be upgraded, and the tanh layer generates a vector of new nominee values that will be applied to the LSTM memory. The outputs of these two layers are computed through Equations 14.5, 14.6, and 14.7.

$$t = \sigma\left(\mathbf{W}_{i_h}\left[\mathbf{h}_{t-1}\right],\mathbf{W}_{i_x}\left[\mathbf{x}_t\right],\mathbf{b}_i\right) \tag{14.5}$$

$$c_t = \tanh\left(\mathbf{W}_{c_h}\left[\mathbf{h}_{t-1}\right],\mathbf{W}_{c_x}\left[\mathbf{x}_t\right],\mathbf{b}_c\right) \tag{14.6}$$

$$c_t = \mathbf{f}_t * \mathbf{c}_{t-1} + \mathbf{i}_t * \mathbf{c}^{\sim}{}_t \tag{14.7}$$

Output Gate: The output of the LSTM gate can be calculated by Equations 14.8 and 14.9.

$$\mathbf{o}_t = \sigma\left(\mathbf{W}_{o_h}\left[\mathbf{h}_{t-1}\right],\mathbf{W}_{o_x}\left[\mathbf{x}_t\right],\mathbf{b}_o\right) \tag{14.8}$$

$$h_t = \mathbf{o}_t * \tanh\left(\mathbf{c}_t\right) \tag{14.9}$$

Sigmoid and Softmax Layer

The sigmoid-level takes in input x and uses the sigmoid-function for output y for any value in x. There are no parameters w for the sigmoid function, too. It only applies for each input value a fixed transformation shown below. Figure 14.3 show the activation function flow.

$$y_i = \frac{1}{1+e^{-xi}} \tag{14.10}$$

$$\frac{\partial E}{\partial x_i} = \frac{\partial E}{\partial y_i} \cdot \frac{\partial y_i}{\partial x_i} = \partial yi.\frac{\partial y_i}{\partial x_i} \tag{14.11}$$

$$\frac{\partial y_i}{\partial x_i} = \frac{e^{-xi}}{\left(1+e^{-xi}\right)^2} = y_i.\left(1-y_i\right) \tag{14.12}$$

$$\therefore \frac{\partial E}{\partial x_i} = \delta\, yi \cdot yi \cdot \left(1-yi\right) \tag{14.13}$$

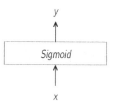

FIGURE 14.3
Activation Function

$$\partial x = [c] = \delta y \odot y \odot (1-y) \tag{14.14}$$

Note that in this layer, $m = n$.

δx is of size $m \times 1$, δy is of size $n \times 1$, y and $(1-y)$ are of size $n \times 1$

$$\delta x = \delta y \odot y \odot (1-y) \tag{14.15}$$

$$\delta w = \text{N.A.} \tag{14.16}$$

Softmax Layer

The Softmax layer normalizes its inputs x for outputs y, using the equation below, to generate the output sum of values 1. This layer generates outputs that can be represented as distributions of probabilities. It is also used very much in networks that forecast class input probabilities. Notice that yj output is a function of all xi inputs.

$$y_i = \frac{e^{x_i}}{\sum_{k=1}^{m} e^{x_k}} \tag{14.17}$$

$$\frac{\partial E}{\partial x_i} = \sum_{j=1}^{n} \left(\frac{\partial E}{\partial y_j} \cdot \frac{\partial y_j}{\partial x_i} \right) \tag{14.18}$$

$$\text{If } i = j, \frac{\partial y_i}{\partial x_i} = \frac{\partial}{\partial x_i} \left\{ \frac{e^{x_i}}{\sum_{k=1}^{m} e^{x_k}} \right\}$$

$$= \frac{e^{x_i} \left(\sum_{k=1}^{m} e^{x_k} \right) - \left(e^{x_i} \right)^2}{\left(\sum_{k=1}^{m} e^{x_k} \right)^2}$$

$$= \frac{e^{x_i}}{\sum_{k=1}^{m} e^{x_k}} - \frac{\left(e^{x_i} \right)^2}{\left(\sum_{k=1}^{m} e^{x_k} \right)^2} \tag{14.19}$$

$$= \frac{e^{x_i}}{\sum_{k=1}^{m} e^{x_k}} \left(1 - \frac{e^{x_i}}{\sum_{k=1}^{m} e^{x_k}} \right)$$

$$= y_i \cdot (1 - y_i)$$

$$= y_i \cdot (1\{i = j\} - y_j)$$

$$\text{If } i \neq j, \frac{\partial y_i}{\partial x_i} = \frac{\partial}{\partial x_i}\left\{\frac{e^{x_j}}{\sum_{k=1}^{m} e^{x_k}}\right\}$$

$$= \frac{-e^{x_i} \cdot e^{x_j}}{\left(\sum_{k=1}^{m} e^{x_k}\right)^2} \tag{14.20}$$

$$= \frac{-e^{x_i}}{\sum_{k=1}^{m} e^{x_k}} \cdot \frac{e^{x_j}}{\sum_{k=1}^{m} e^{x_k}}$$

$$= -y_i \cdot y_j$$

$$= y_i \cdot \left(\mathbf{1}\{i = j\} - y_j\right)$$

$$\therefore \frac{\partial E}{\partial x_i} = \sum_{j=1}^{n} \delta y_j \cdot y_i \cdot \left(\mathbf{1}\{i = j\} - y_j\right)$$

$$= \sum_{j=1}^{n} J_{ij} \times \delta y_j \tag{14.21}$$

$$\text{where } J_{ij} = y_i \cdot \left(\mathbf{1}\{i = j\} - y_j\right)$$

$$\delta x = \left[\frac{\partial E}{\partial x_i}\right]_i = J \times \delta y$$

$$\tag{14.22}$$

Note that in this layer, $m = n$

δx is of size $m \times 1$, J is of size $m \times n$, δy is of size $n \times 1$

$$\boxed{\begin{aligned} \delta x &= J \times \delta y \\ \delta w &= \text{N.A.} \end{aligned}} \tag{14.23}$$

14.4 Evaluation

All the experimental requirements for the evaluation of the proposed model are described in this section, including corpora description, competitor system, dataset generation, evaluation matrices, hyperparameter setting, training procedure, and hardware and software requirements, which are described as follows.

14.4.1 Corpora Description

The same biomedical datasets are considered for comparison of the proposed model in previous biomedical NER studies. The three datasets, namely NCBI, [29] JLNPBA, [30] BC4CHEMD, [31] are used for evaluation of the proposed model. The statistics of the dataset are described in Table 14.4.

TABLE 14.4

Biomedical Dataset Description

S.NO.	Corpus	Entity Type	#annotation	#Sentences	Data Size
1.	NCBI-Disease	Disease	6,881	7,639	793 abstract
2.	JNLPBA	Protein/Gene	35,336	22,562	2,404 abstract
3.	BC4CHEMD	Chemical	84,310	86,679	10,000 abstract

\# Total no. of.

14.4.1.1 NCBI

The NCBI corpus is a series of 793 abstracts thoroughly noted as guides to and conceptualizations that serve as a platform for the bio-healthy culture that processes natural languages. Two annotators with illness references and their related definitions in Medical Topic Headings (MeSH) [32] or Online Mendelian Inheritance in Man (OMIM) [33] have been manually annotated per the PubMed abstract. The manual curation was performed during PubTator, involving pre-annotations as a pre-step for manual annotation. NCBI for identification and normalization of disease names was introduced and was carried out in several trials of this role.

14.4.1.2 JLNPBA

In 2004, the JNLPBA shared the highest result in acknowledgment among bio-medical entities and achived 72.55% of the F-score for the reliable emulate [34] achieved by Zhou and Su. While this discovery is far older than many other metrics, the success of the recently proposed methods is still competitive.

14.4.1.3 BC₄CHEMD

The BioCreative IV Chemical and Drug named entity recognition corpus (BC4CHEMD) consists of 10,000 abstracts annotated for chemical and drug names in a common class, chemical [3]. BC4CHEMD corpus data is accessible in the TAB-separated standoff format from http://www.biocreative.org/and and describes typical preparation, creation, and test subsets [35].

14.4.2 Competitor System

The performance of the proposed methodology is compared with **Wang and colleagues** [4] multitask model. Similar corpora as baseline used to perform the experiment to evaluate the result. Even though a direct comparison is not required, the proposed methodology achieves an average of **+1.32** % more F-score as compare to Wang et al.'s multitask model, which shows a promising result.

14.4.3 Evaluation Measure

This section analyses the model's efficiency in terms of precision (P), recall (R), and F-score (F). The mathematical formula to calculate F-score, recall, and precision are described in Equations (14.24), (14.25), and (14.26) [36].

$$Precision(P) = \frac{Z}{X} \tag{14.24}$$

$$Recall(R) = \frac{Z}{Y} \tag{14.25}$$

$$F - Score(F) = 2 * \frac{(P.R)}{(P+R)} \tag{14.26}$$

Where

X is used for an entire predicted entity present in the biomedical text document sentence.

Y is used for the entire actual entity present in the biomedical text document sentence.

Z is used for the correct overall biomedical entity.

14.4.4 Hyper-Parameter Setting

The proposed methodology used the same setup for proposed model experiments over datasets in order to make a fair comparison. Table 14.5 shows the values of the hyperparameters used in the experiment.

14.4.5 Hardware/Software Requirement

8 GB of RAM with Intel I-7 processor is used to perform this experiment. 1050 TI with Cuda-enabled nvidia graphics processor GPU is used to support the proposed deep learning-based model, and the module is designed over Python language.

14.5 Result and Discussion

In this section, the combined impact of word embedding, character embedding, and casing embedding is clearly noticed in Table 14.6, which is performed over three biomedical datasets, namely NCBI, JLNPBA, and BC_4CHEMD. The proposed model marked +1.32 % more average F-score than its competitor models. JLNPBA achieved +9.68 % as compared to the Wang MTM model. Also the result obtained by JLNPBA is much higher as compared to the

TABLE 14.5

Hyperparameter Values

S.No.	Parameters	Values
1.	Epoch	100
2.	Dropout Rate	0.50
3.	Batch Size	32
4.	Learning Rate	0.02
5.	Sequence Length	100
6.	Embedding	Glove

TABLE 14.6

Performance comparison

S.No.	Datasets	Proposed model			Wang MTM et al. [4]		
		Precision	Recall	F1 Score	Precision	Recall	F1 Score
1.	NCBI-disease	79.90	82.50	81.20	85.86	86.42	86.14
2.	JNLPBA	80.40	86.20	**83.20**	70.91	76.34	73.52
3.	BC4CHEMD	90.78	87.01	88.85	91.30	87.53	**89.37**
	Average	**83.69**	**85.24**	**84.41**	82.95	83.30	83.09

other deep learning models. The comparison of the proposed MTM model with the Wang MTM model is shown in Table 14.6. The problem of supplying limited annotated samples was discussed with the proposed model in several domains. However, this challenge was not presented to our understanding of medical texts that are highly troublesome. Medical text in the EHRs is mainly distinct from other firms so that unclinically educated readers can barely comprehend the EHR text because of the common usage of technical words, the unofficial acronyms, and shorthand. The traditional transfer learning methods from other annotated non-medical corpus (e.g., using standard Wikipedia vocabulary or Glove embedding models) are not that successful. Therefore, we conclude that contributions like this paper are incredibly significant. In addition to the final model, our analyses are also crucial to this task with many observations. Our experiment findings over the baseline model suggest that pre-trained text-based weights near the target domain significantly improve efficiency. The change we find particularly dramatic for the first stages of learning appears to fade after extended knowledge toward an asymptotic positive constant. Our proposed model improvement reveals that the optimizer option has a more significant impact on the F1 score than using train word embedding (TE) and batch normalization (BN). This is in accordance with a recent analysis examining the effect of different hyper-parameters on NER activities. Combine our third improvement with pre-training data, and the result is decreased performance. This can be clarified in two possible forms. First of all, on different datasets, we have optimized hyperparameters. Second, when the model is trained in the first dataset and then refines the weights in the next dataset, the initial values may be considered incorrect and have to be adjusted even further than when weights are randomly initialized, which means that different pre-trained weights have to be produced. Finally, the fourth development revealed that custom word embedding learned from the same area as the goal challenge in text enhances efficiency in specific tasks. Yet, we have some gaps in our analysis, and these can be discussed in the future. Firstly, the changes were sequentially implemented to further enhance the efficiency of the objective assignment through separate arrangements. Given this constraint in the search room, the findings of this analysis can be called conservative. Finally, an F1 score of 84.41% is still quite disappointing in comparison to the performance big annotations produce.

14.6 Conclusions and Future Work

Finally, we refer to a variety of potential avenues of changes to the BioNER multitask model. First, it could be an excellent way to merge the single task and multitask models.

Secondly, we will create a coherent framework to identify various forms of biomedical entities with high accuracy and productivity if we further address the issue of boundaries and conceptual model conflicts. We suggested a multitask computational method for the identification of biomedical entities. The proposed methodology is straightforward and does not involve manual feature engineering, but is superior to advanced systems and many efficient BioNER dataset neural network models. Detailed analysis showed us that high performance is achieved with a marginal additional training time of the multitask model and confirmed that the significant advantages are mainly the extent to which information is shared between the types of biomedical entities on a character and word level. Finally, we illustrate some more ways of improving the BioNER model with multiple functions. Next, it may be fruitful to merge one-task and multitask models.

Conflict of Interest statement

The authors declare that they have no conflict of interest.

Abbreviations

NER   Named entity recognition
BioNER   Biomedical named-entity recognition
BILSTM   Bidirectional long short term memory
CE   Character embedding
WE   Word embedding
MTM   Multitask model
Casing embedding

Acknowledgment

Both the authors of this chapter are always thankful to the National Institute of Technology Raipur and Department of Computer Science and Engineering to provide the necessary infrastructure and facilities for the support of this research.

References

1. Dewangan, J.K., Sharaff, A., and Pandey, S. 2020. Improving topic coherence using parsimonious language model and latent semantic indexing. *ICDSMLA* 2019. 823–830.
2. Smith, V., Chiang, C.K., Sanjabi, M. and Talwalkar, A.S. 2017. Federated multi-task learning. *Advances in Neural Information Processing Systems* 30: 4424–4434.

3. Crichton, G., Pyysalo, S., Chiu, B. and Korhonen, A. 2017. A neural network multi-task learning approach to biomedical named entity recognition. *BMC bioinformatics*. 18(1), 368.

4. Wang, X., Zhang, Y., Ren, X., Zhang, Y., Zitnik, M., Shang, J., Langlotz, C. and Han, J. 2019. Cross-type biomedical named entity recognition with deep multi-task learning. *Bioinformatics*. 35(10), 1745–1752.

5. Sharaff, A. and Nagwani, N.K. 2017. Effect of N-Grams Technique in Preprocessing of Email Spam Filtering. *International Journal of Applied Evolutionary Computation (IJAEC)*. 8(1), 26–37.

6. Kumar, A. 2020. Disambiguation Model for Bio-Medical Named Entity Recognition. In: Dash S., Acharya B., Mittal M., Abraham A., Kelemen A. (eds) *Deep Learning Techniques for Biomedical and Health Informatics. Studies in Big Data*, vol 68. Springer, Cham. https://doi.org/10.1007/978-3-030-33966-1_3.

7. Gorinski, P.J., Wu, H., Grover, C., Tobin, R., Talbot, C., Whalley, H., Sudlow, C., Whiteley, W. and Alex, B. 2019. Named entity recognition for electronic health records: A comparison of rule-based and machine learning approaches. *arXiv preprint arXiv:1903.03985*.

8. Lowe, D.M. and Sayle, R.A. 2015. LeadMine: a grammar and dictionary driven approach to entity recognition. *Journal of cheminformatics*. 7(1), 1–9.

9. Dimmer, E.C., Huntley, R.P., Alam-Faruque, Y., Sawford, T., O'Donovan, C., Martin, M.J., Bely, B., Browne, P., Mun Chan, W., Eberhardt, R. and Gardner, M. 2012. The UniProt-GO annotation database in 2011. *Nucleic Acids Research*. 40(D1), D565–D570.

10. Boutet, E., Lieberherr, D., Tognolli, M., Schneider, M. and Bairoch, A. 2007. Uniprotkb/swiss-prot. *Plant Bioinformatics*. 89–112.

11. Campagna, G., Xu, S., Moradshahi, M., Socher, R. and Lam, M.S. 2019, June. Genie: A generator of natural language semantic parsers for virtual assistant commands. In *Proceedings of the 40th ACM SIGPLAN Conference on Programming Language Design and Implementation*. 394–410.

12. Liu, Z., Tang, B., Wang, X. and Chen, Q. 2017. De-identification of clinical notes via recurrent neural network and conditional random field. *Journal of Biomedical Informatics*. 75, S34–S42.

13. Cheng, J., Park, J.H., Cao, J. and Qi, W. 2019. Hidden Markov model-based nonfragile state estimation of switched neural network with probabilistic quantized outputs. *IEEE Transactions on Cybernetics*. 50(5), 1900–1909.

14. Huang, S., Cai, N., Pacheco, P.P., Narrandes, S., Wang, Y. and Xu, W. 2018. Applications of support vector machine (SVM) learning in cancer genomics. *Cancer Genomics-Proteomics*. 15(1), 41–51.

15. Sharaff, A. and Soni, A. 2020. Time and feature specific sentiment analysis of product reviews. In *Cognitive Informatics, Computer Modelling, and Cognitive Science*. 255–272.

16. Sharaff, A., Khaire, A.S. and Sharma, D. 2019, May. Analysing Fuzzy Based Approach for Extractive Text Summarization. *2019 International Conference on Intelligent Computing and Control Systems (ICCS)*. 906–910.

17. Shen, Y., Yun, H., Lipton, Z.C., Kronrod, Y. and Anandkumar, A. 2017. Deep active learning for named entity recognition. *arXiv preprint arXiv:1707.05928*.

18. Topper, L. and Boehr, D. 2018. Publishing trends of journals with manuscripts in PubMed Central: changes from 2008–2009 to 2015–2016. *Journal of the Medical Library Association: JMLA*. 106(4), 445.

19. Kilicoglu, H. 2018. Biomedical text mining for research rigor and integrity: tasks, challenges, directions. *Briefings in Bioinformatics*. 19(6), 1400–1414.

20. Christopoulou, F., Tran, T.T., Sahu, S.K., Miwa, M. and Ananiadou, S. 2020. Adverse drug events and medication relation extraction in electronic health records with ensemble deep learning methods. *Journal of the American Medical Informatics Association*. 27(1), 39–46.

21. Zayed, H.S., Medhat, B.M. and Seif, E.M. 2019. Evaluation of treatment adherence in patients with Behçet's disease: its relation to disease manifestations, patients' beliefs about medications, and quality of life. *Clinical Rheumatology*. 38(3),761–768.

22. Elkin, P.L., Schlegel, D.R., Anderson, M., Komm, J., Ficheur, G. and Bisson, L. 2018. Artificial intelligence: bayesian versus heuristic method for diagnostic decision support. *Applied Clinical Informatics*. 9(2), 432.

23. Xiaofeng, M., Wei, W. and Aiping, X. 2020. Incorporating token-level dictionary feature into neural model for named entity recognition. *Neurocomputing*. 375, 43–50.

24. Salah, R.E. 2017. Arabic rule-based named entity recognition systems progress and challenges. *International Journal on Advanced Science, Engineering and Information Technology*. 7(3), 815–821.

25. Sahu, S.K. and Anand, A. 2016. Recurrent neural network models for disease name recognition using domain invariant features. *arXiv preprint arXiv:1606.09371*.

26. Kumar, A. and Sharaff, A. 2020 Performance enhancement of gene mention tagging by using deep learning and biomedical named entity recognition. *Intelligent Data Engineering and Analytics*. 637–645.

27. Habibi, M., Weber, L., Neves, M., Wiegandt, D.L. and Leser, U. 2017. Deep learning with word embeddings improves biomedical named entity recognition. *Bioinformatics*. 33(14), i37–i48.

28. Lample, G., Ballesteros, M., Subramanian, S., Kawakami, K. and Dyer, C. 2016. Neural architectures for named entity recognition. *arXiv preprint arXiv:1603.01360*.

29. Doğan, R.I., Leaman, R. and Lu, Z. 2014. NCBI disease corpus: a resource for disease name recognition and concept normalization. *Journal of Biomedical Informatics*, 47, 1–10.

30. Huang, M.S., Lai, P.T., Tsai, R.T.H. and Hsu, W.L. 2019. Revised JNLPBA corpus: A revised version of biomedical NER corpus for relation extraction task. *arXiv preprint arXiv:1901.10219*.

31. Akhtyamova, L. and Cardiff, J. 2020, May. LM-based Word Embeddings Improve Biomedical Named Entity Recognition: a Detailed Analysis. *International Work-Conference on Bioinformatics and Biomedical Engineering*. 624–635.

32. Shu, F., Qiu, J. and Larivière, V. 2019. Mapping the Life Science using Medical Subject Headings (MeSH). *ISSI* 1927–1932.

33. Amberger, J.S. and Hamosh, A. 2017. Searching online mendelian inheritance in man (OMIM): a knowledgebase of human genes and genetic phenotypes. *Current Protocols in Bioinformatics*. 58(1), 1–2.

34. Wang, X., Yang, C. and Guan, R. 2018. A comparative study for biomedical named entity recognition. *International Journal of Machine Learning and Cybernetic*. 9(3), 373–382.

35. Zhou, J. and Fu, B.Q. 2018. The research on gene-disease association based on text-mining of PubMed. *BMC Bioinformatics* 19(1), 37.

36. Sharaff, A., Nagwani, N.K. and Dhadse, A. 2016. Comparative study of classification algorithms for spam email detection. *Emerging Research in Computing, Information, Communication and Applications*. 237–244.

15

Predict the Crime Rate Against Women Using Machine Learning Classification Techniques

P. Tamilarasi and R. Uma Rani

Sri Sarada College for Women (Autonomous), Salem, Tamil Nadu, India

CONTENTS

15.1 Introduction

In India, women's security has become a very big challenge. In our nation, people treated Durga and Lakshmi as goddesses, whereas crime rates are continuously increasing against

TABLE 15.1

Statewise Crimes Recorded against Women in India

States	Crimes Types
Meghalaya ,Arunachala Pradesh	1000
Jammu and Kashmir, Himachal Pradesh	5000
TN, Gujarat, Punchab, haryana	10,000
Rajasthan Madyapradesh	30,000
Maharastra, Delhi, UP	30,000

women. Domestic aggression, rape, kidnapping, and sexual harassment are some important crime types against women. These are missiles handled by a male to express male power. The Indian government formed so many acts to try to control this type of violence. The Dowery Prohibition Act 1961, the Protection of Women from Domestic Violence Act 2005, and the Immoral Traffic Act 1956 are some examples of offense underneath the special and local laws. Table 15.1 shows the statewise crimes recorded against women in India.

15.1.1 Data Analytics

Today data is one of the most essential resources in industry apart from volume. Data is priceless when it comes to making decisions. In this world, big data is several-million-dollar businesses, and price for data are rising very quickly in the market. Data usage is not new, since industry began using it long years ago. Data analytics is a mixture of some procedures and skills such as data management, data mining, and predictive analytics. Both Excel and Tableau are important tools for data analytics. Some other tools are also available for complex data, tools mainly used in programming languages like Python, R programming, Java, Microsoft SQL, Scala, and other very familiar data analytics tools. Data analytics has three types: structured, unstructured, and semistructured. These are based on huge volume, huge velocity, and different kinds of data. Today data analytics, along with machine learning techniques, are widely used for prediction. In this chapter we work to predict the crime rate against women using various types of classification techniques. This technique has performed better than other machine learning algorithms. The following Figure 15.1 shows the data types of analytics.

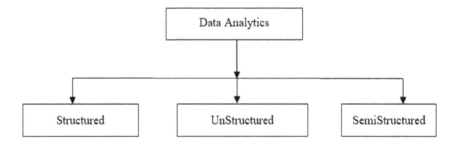

FIGURE 15.1
Types of Data Analytics

15.1.1.1 Structured Data

This type of dataset is used to analyze the data effectively. It is stored in the table form of an SQL database along with rows and columns, which are managed by a formatted repository of databases. Structured data has a relational key so it is used to map the predesigned attribute easily. These types of data are usually used for development and to manage information without difficulties. Relational data are an example of structured data.

15.1.1.2 Unstructured Data

Unstructured data doesn't have a predefined format, so it is very difficult to handle and understand. That's why these types of data are not a high-quality fit for SQL databases. IT industries offer many platforms for managing and organizing unstructured data. Word is the best example of an unstructured data platform. These types of data are using different kinds of business and analytics.

15.1.1.3 Semi-Structured Data

Semi-structured data data are the parts of structured and unstructured data that cannot be stored in a relational database because these types of data have no format—so they don't have any tabular form. The data are extracted from semi-structured format using different kinds of tools, like graphs and objects. XML is the best example of semi-structured data. This type of data analysis is very easy to compare to unstructured data.

15.2 Machine Learning

Machine learning is a division of artificial intelligence, and the main objective is to make the computer process through training data. Machine learning algorithms prediction is based on past or historical data and identifies patterns from collected data. Machine learning uses different areas, such as image processing to predict feature values, speech recognition, and recommended systems. It is classified into three categories: supervised, unsupervised, and reinforcement. Figure 15.2 describes the types of ML and its algorithms.

15.2.1 Supervised Machine Learning

These types of algorithms are the main part of machine learning, and they are designed to gain knowledge by exemplar. In these algorithms, the input data pairs with exact output. These algorithms predict the output based on training data, which are associated with the correct output. After the training process, these algorithms get new input and decide which label classified the recent input variable based on prior training data. The main aim of this algorithm is to predict the label for the new input variable. Supervised m achine learning is classified into two types: classification and regression.

$$\mathbf{y} = \mathbf{f}(\mathbf{x}) \qquad (15.1)$$

In the above equation, x is the new input variable and y is the predicted output variable.

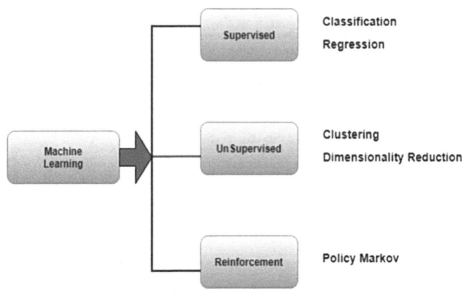

FIGURE 15.2
Types of Machine Learning Algorithms

15.2.2 Unsupervised Machine Learning

Unsupervised machine learning has only input variable x, which does not have a parallel output variable y. The main aim of these types of algorithms is to form the subajacent structure or delivery so the information can gain knowledge regarding the data. This type of algorithm is not like supervised because this algorithm does not predict the correct output. Both the clustering and apriori algorithms are examples of unsupervised machine learning.

15.2.3 Reinforcement Machine Learning

These types of algorithms are essential for evolving the independent system which are based on the arrangement of labeled data and communicate with the received data. The reinforcement method is called exploration. This technique is easy and very simple. The conclusion is observed, and the second action is considered the result as the first action. Q-learning, temporal differences, and Monte Carlo tree search are some examples of reinforcement machine learning algorithms.

15.3 Data Analytics and Its Classification

Analytics is the discovery of meaningful patterns in the data. Both statistics and programming are simultaneously executing analytics, and operation research is also used to qualify the implementation. Analytics usually support data visualization to promulgate insight. Data analytics is mainly used in business to express, predict, and develop business. Data

FIGURE 15.3
Classifcation of Data Analytics

analytics is divided into four categories: predictive, descriptive, prescriptive, and diagnostic analytics. Figure 15.3 shows the classification of analytics.

15.3.1 Predictive Analytics

Predictive analytics predict future data values using historical and present data. Predictive analytics development is based on six steps:

1. Project describtion
2. Data gathering
3. Processing the analysis
4. Model
5. Deployment
6. Monitoring

15.3.2 Descriptive Analytics

Descriptive Analytics is a traditional type of business intelligence and data analysis that attempts to give an illustration or abstract of truth. It describes the incomprehensible structure to either tell or set up data for additional analysis. It utilizes two main systems, which are data aggregation and mining. These are used to account for precedent dealings. It provides historical data in a simple understandable format for the gain of large business spectators. Statistical methods are generally used in this analytical type.

15.3.3 Prescriptive Analytics

This is a statistically based model that is used to make recommendations that depends upon the results of algorithms. This type of analytics is not commonly used in machine learning, due to multifarious prerequisites needed in the area of machine learning; however, it can be used in an adaptive and learning experience area.

15.3.4 Diagnostic Analytics

Diagnostic analytics get data from descriptive analytics for further analysis and inform the response for the query. This type of analysis is mostly used in root cause analysis. The process for executing diagnostic analysis includes skills such as data invention, drill-through data mining, and drill down.

15.4 Literature Survey

So many researchers use machine learning classification techniques in various places and areas. This chapter discusses such types of predictions and works based on the classification techniques. The authors use different types of classification algorithms, such as support vector machines (SVM), decision trees (DTs), random forests, and boosted decision trees in remote sensing, and also implement nonparametrically and optimization techniques in machine learning. Finally, these authors conclude the result based on accuracy. Here the decision tree algorithm is very slow and gives less accuracy if the data size is high. The researcher implemented several types of data mining techniques along with some theories like choice, conflict, sociological, and psychological theories to predict the crime rates (Sreedevi, 2018). The researcher proposed various types of supervised machine learning algorithms and classified diabetes datasets along with 786 attributes, and also implemented many algorithms. Finally, the SVM gave better accuracy compared to other classification algorithms (Osisanwo, 2017). The writer implemented many classification techniques to predict the categorical class labels and classified new data into class labels, which are based on the training data set (Gorade, 2017). Different kinds of classification methods are used in robotics and describe well-suited classification methods for Robo (Hormozi et al., 2012). The author concluded the result of SVM and neural networks (NN) performed better than other classifier procedures based on mail messages that distinguished the message as spam and nonspam. Finally, the author conveys the result, which is based on the dataset. If the dataset range is high, the SVM and NN will give better accuracy (Muhammad, 2015). Crimes are happening regularly which is a big headache for crime departments. Specifically, a crime against women is the most important focused area for the police department. The author used different types of methods like simple, weighted moving average and wilder smoothing along with time-series analysis techniques for predicting crime rates for future (Motwani, 2018). The biographer compared four different types of classification models along with SVM in linear and nonlinear separable methods and also implemented a kernel trick for nonlinear mapping. At last, the author concluded the result based on accuracy, which is calculated by the confusion matrix. The SVM brings better accuracy than the other three algorithms (Mohamed, 2017). Machine learning is a very important technique in today's world for prediction. Student dropouts from school are government-focused areas in developing countries. The main reason for imbalanced learning is classified using machine learning to find the reasons and conclude the results based on the classification. It is useful to control such types of problems in the future (Mduma, 2019). The novelist proposed two classification procedures, SVM and random forest) to predict the crime categories based on existing prediction used clustering techniques. In this work he concluded the results from random forest had given the highest accuracy, even higher than SVM (Zaidi et al., 2019). Classification is used in many areas like image processing, predicting, and datamining. The main purpose of classification is to develop an uncomplicated and unambiguous function for a class tag in provisions of predictor attributes to the rate of the class tag, which is unidentified (Reddy, 2018). The researcher proposed a new journal performance factor to identify the best journal and also focused to discover the missing parameters, which are not in earlier papers. Bayesian classification is used to classify the developed method and compare the outcome with prior results (Saeed Iqbal, 2013). The developer proposed a context-aware system for predicting smartphone data usage for each person through ten classification procedures (Sarker, 2019). Crime forecasting is an efficient approach for recognizing and analyzing style in the offense. Using different data ming techniques to predict the crime region for avoiding crime incidents and taking the action to control the crime (Shiju Sathyadevan, 2014). The creator proposed three classification methods for classifying the diabetes dataset and evaluating these algorithms using recall, e-measures, precision, and accuracy. Finally, the naïve Bayes has given better outcomes than the other two of decision and SVM (Sisodiaa, 2018). Crimes are the most important social crisis that affects lifestyle or quality of life. This is believed to be the main issue for whether or not the persons settle or travel to a safe place. The author executed naïve Bayes and decision tree techniques for finding a crime place. The decision tree has given better accuracy compared with Naive Bayes (Tahani Almanie, 2015). The instigator used clustering with classification for predicting the crime against women. K-means clustering is used to find similar types of crimes, and classification is used to classify the clustered data that has brought the better result to find out the crime patterns (Yadav, 2017).

Table 15.2 shows the past work in crimes against women data using machine learning algorithms.

15.5 Methodologies

The following figure illustrates the workflow of this paper. There are six methods used to predict the crime rate. Figure 15.4 describes the workflow of crime prediction using machine learning algorithms.

15.5.1 Data Preprocessing

Data preprocessing is a fundamental step in machine learning that helps to boost the data to high quality and promote the data with meaningful insight. Data preprocessing is a data mining model that is mainly used to change the data from unrefined to clear form. There are seven basic steps in data preprocessing:

TABLE 15.2

Past Work in Crime against Women Data

S.No	Writer	Title	Applications	Existing	Proposed	Measurement
1	Lavanyaa And Akila	Crime against Women Analysis and Prediction in Tamilnadu Police Using Data Mining Techniques	Weka Tool	Rule induction, Decision Tree and Euclidian distance	Classification and Prediction	Use a decision tree to classify a crime data against women and predict the better crime rate by calculating the Euclidian distance
2	Rishabh Singh and Rishabh Reddy	K-means Clustering Analysis of Crimes on Indian Women	Rapid miner Tool	K-means Cluster	Analysis and Prediction	Use a K-means clustering model to find a crime rate against women in India.
3	Bhajneet Kaur, Laxmi Ahuja	Crime against Women: Analysis and Prediction Using Data Mining Techniques	Python	Different Machine Learning Techniques	Analysis and Prediction	The author used different ML algorithms to predict the crime rate against women
4	G.Vicente, T.Goicoa and P.Fernanddez	Crime against women in India: unveiling spatial patterns and temporal trends of dowry deaths in the districts of Uttar Pradesh	-	Spatio Temporal Model	Spatio pattern Analysis	Spatio Temporal model analysis to expose a whole image of the geological and temporal patterns of crimes against women in UP.

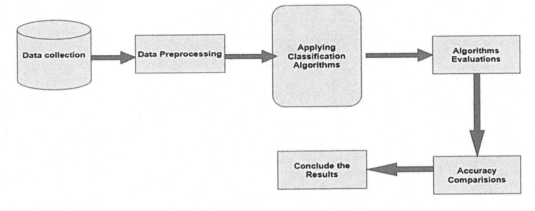

FIGURE 15.4
Work Flow of Crime Prediction

1. Collecting data
2. Import all needed libraries
3. Import the file
4. Finding the lost values
5. Training the definite data
6. Dividing the dataset
7. Attribute scaling

The crime against women dataset collected from data.gov.in has several features. All attributes are based on crime types. In this dataset, crimes are recorded statewide in India from 2001 to 2014. Python has the most extensively used preprocessing libraries. Python built-in libraries make specific data preprocessing work in machine learning; there are Numpy, Pandas, and Matplotlib. Numpy is a primary systematic computation in Python that is used to include the mathematical functions in the code. Numpy is also used for adding matrices and multidimensional array in the program. Pandas is used for data management and analysis. These libraries are mainly used for importing and manipulating the dataset. Based on the libraries, data structures, and several analytical tools these can be easily used in Python. Matplot is mainly used for graphical representation of the dataset. It has 2D plotting libraries. It also provides high-quality figures.

The third step is importing the libraries from the current directory to the working directory using spider IDE. The fourth step is handling missing values in the dataset. This is important because based on this step only can we conclude the results accurately, otherwise the result will be faulty or nonaccurate. Typically, missing data is handled in two ways. We can remove specific rows and evaluate the mean values. When the rows have more than 75% null values, that row is removed from the dataset. This method is recommended when the dataset has sufficient samples. After removing the row, ensure there is no residue or no extras of preconception. The calculating mean method is helpful for a numerical field like age, year, or salary. Fill the mean, median, and mode values to a specific missing place in a row or column. This method will give better results compared to deleting row methods. This method is also efficient in machine learning. This type of missing value handling is mostly used in linear regression. The definite attributes have two different types: nominal and ordinal. These types of elements contain two or more than

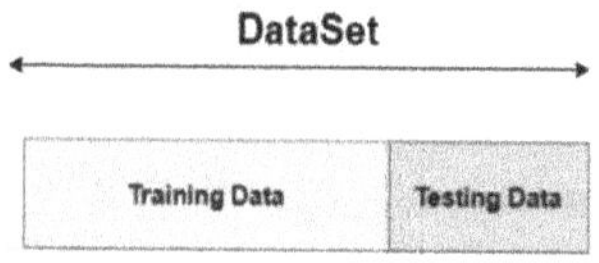

FIGURE 15.5
Training and Testing Data

STATE/UT CRIME HE/		2001	2002	2003	2004	2005	2006	2007	2008	2009	2010	2011	2012
ANDHRA P	RAPE	1150	1340	1237	1443	1415	1360	1436	1531	1487	1761	1758	1664
ARUNACH	RAPE	51	61	35	56	38	40	57	37	60	49	47	47
ASSAM	RAPE	928	1019	1188	1233	1406	1290	1477	1445	1644	1629	1470	1626
BIHAR	RAPE	1400	1304	1120	1157	1455	1451	1816	1464	1086	892	1185	1327
CHHATTIS	RAPE	1134	1214	1020	1144	1107	1211	1146	1108	1128	1198	1257	1214
GOA	RAPE	14	12	36	48	34	20	25	41	56	50	34	61
GUJARAT	RAPE	401	378	356	481	501	539	503	529	610	617	621	647
HARYANA	RAPE	539	511	523	573	627	772	607	849	848	866	801	940
HIMACHAI	RAPE	152	204	146	187	176	131	197	182	250	197	187	259
JAMMU &	RAPE	222	203	266	271	248	301	331	234	303	266	349	388
JHARKHAN	RAPE	637	873	759	759	732	943	886	802	765	836	758	780
KARNATAK	RAPE	361	357	410	397	381	475	518	642	595	771	837	842
KERALA	RAPE	712	600	517	562	506	666	555	623	694	659	1226	1259
MADHYA F	RAPE	3212	3926	3694	4181	3900	3878	4131	3875	4243	4387	4593	4822

FIGURE 15.6
Standardizing the Different Range of Features

two categorical values. The nominal variable has no fundamental ordering. For example, gender is a definite attribute because it has two principles, which are male and female. An ordinal type element is placed in a clear order. For example, temperature has three categories, which are low, medium, and high. The dataset is further divided into two parts as training and testing, which is useful for training the machine learning model, and testing is used to test the model. The training data's are divided as 70%, 30% and 80%, and 20%. Here 70%, 80% for training data size, and 30%, and 20% for testing the data. Figure 15.5 shows the data division of train and test.

Feature Scaling is the last step in data preprocessing. This is mainly used for standardizing the autonomous attribute to a definite range. In other words, it is used to limit the element ranges. Figure 15.6 shows the different ranges of features in the crime dataset. In this dataset, state-wise total crimes are recorded against women in India from 2001 to 2012.

In Figure 15.6 the year fields are different in range. If we compute any two values from 2001 to 2012, it will give the wrong result. To eliminate this problem, feature scaling method is necessary. Mostly the ML algorithms are performed by Euclidian distance. Equation 15.2 is used to calculate the Euclidian distance.

$$d(A,B) = \sqrt{(x_1 - x_2)^2 + (y_1 - y_2)^2} \tag{15.2}$$

A few ML algorithms are used for feature scaling. K-nearest neighbor as well as Euclidian distance calculate in perspective to size and thus all features should be scaled equally. K-means utilizes Euclidian distance calculation. Here, feature scaling is substance. Scaling is difficult while executing principal component analysis (PCA). PCA aims to get the attributes in high variance. The variance value is high while the skew value is high. Gradient descent also used for feature scaling when the variable is uneven. Some options for feature scaling include:

1. MinMax scaler
2. Robust Scaler
3. Unit Vector
4. Standard Scaler
5. Power Transform
6. Max's abs
7. Quantile Transform

MinMax Scaler: This type of scaler is used when the standard deviation is small and the goal is to transform the feature to a given range. If the training data value is between 0 and 1, the data minimize the range to –1 to 1. Equation 15.3 shows the MinMax scaler formula.

$$x_{new} = \frac{x - x_{min}}{x_{max} - x_{min}} \tag{15.3}$$

Standard Scalar: Standard scalar treats all features normally. It set the range of the values between 0 to 1. Here 0 is a center value, and 1 is a standard deviation. Equation 15.4 is used to calculate the Standard Scaler.

$$x_{new} = \frac{x - \mu}{\sigma} \tag{15.4}$$

Max abs Scaler: It is similar to the Maxmin scaler, and scales all features in maximum absolute value. The maximum absolute value of each feature is 1.0.

Robust Scaler: This is robust for outliers. If the dataset contains more outliers, then the standard deviation is not functioning well.

Quantile transformer scaler: It is applied for quantile information. It changes the features to normal or even distribution. It is also used to reduce the outliers, so it is called a robust preprocessing scheme. Rank scaler is another name for quantile transformer.

Power Rransformer Scaler: The power scaler discover the optimal factor to alleviate conflict and minimize skewness during maximum probability evaluation.

Unit Vector Scaler: This is like max-min scaler. It will be useful when the feature is in inflexible boundaries. This is also provides the range of the features in 0, 1. Equation 15.5 is used to calculate the Unit Vector Scaler.

$$x' = \frac{x}{\|x\|} \tag{15.5}$$

15.6 Machine Learning Classification Models

Machine learning classification is divided into two parts. There are linear models and non-linear models.

Linear model classification: Linear model classification is divided into two parts. There are support vector machines and logistic regression.

Nonlinear Model Classification: Nonlinear models are also further divided into five parts, which are K-nearest neighbors, naïve Bayes, decision tree classification, random forest, and kernel SVM.

15.6.1 Naïve Bayes

Naïve Bayes is a great machine learning procedure that is applied to classification. This is a conservatory of the Bayes in which every feature presumes sovereignty. It employs different tasks, like spam filtering and text classification. It helps to predict the dataset category; with this it can achieve a multiple set prophecy. When the postulation of liberty is true, naïve Bayes is greatly more accomplished than the other procedures, such as logistic regression. Moreover, it needs fewer data for training.

15.6.1.1 Drawbacks of Naïve Bayes

If the unqualified element belongs to a kind that does not pursue the training data, after that the algorithm will provide it a likelihood of 0 and it will reduce it from making every prediction. Naïve Bayes assigns sovereignty between its attributes. In real-time, it is hard to collect data that grip overall autonomous elements.

15.6.2 Decision Tree Algorithms

Decision tree algorithms are a supervised learning system that can be helpful for each classification and regression harms, but it is chosen to resolve the classification issue. This is a tree format classifier; wherever internal nodes signify the elements of a dataset, twigs signify the resulting policy and every leaf node denotes the result. The decision tree has two nodes; there are the decision nodes and the leaf nodes. The decision node helps to create any conclusion and it contains several branches; here the leaf node is the result of an individual's decisions and does not hold any additional branches. The choice or the analysis performs on the origin of attributes of the assigned dataset. It is used for graphical representation to obtain all the likely solutions to a dilemma based on specified rules. This is called a decision tree because it is in a tree structure. It begins with the root node and enlarges on more branches. Cart algorithm is used to create a tree; it means classification and regression tree. The decision tree split the subtree based on the yes or no questions. Figure 15.7 describes the common configuration of decision trees. The following are the terms of decision trees.

RootNode: It is the origin of decision trees that denotes the entire dataset. Further, it is divided into two or more sets.

Leaf Node: Finishing output nodes are called leaf nodes and cannot be divided further.

Splitting: This process is used for dividing the decision or root node as subnodes based on the condition.

Pruning: Pruning is an important method in a decision tree; it is used to eliminate the unnecessary branches from the tree.

Parent and Child Node: The origin or starting nodes are called parent nodes and all other nodes are called child nodes.

15.6.3 K-Nearest Neighbors Model

This is the simplest model to compare to all other supervised techniques. K-nearest neighbor is one of the simplest machine learning algorithms based on the supervised learning

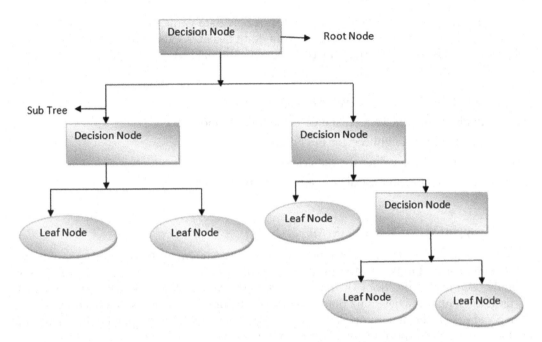

FIGURE 15.7
Configuration of Decision Tree

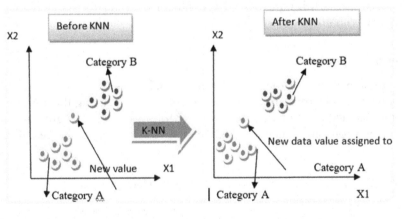

FIGURE 15.8
Before and After Categorization of K-NN

technique. K-NN model considers the comparison among the new arrival data and obtainable data, and places the new data into the class that is mainly like to the obtainable type. A K-NN algorithm registers all the offered data and categorizes the latest data based on the resemblance. It means these algorithms are well suited for regression, and it can be easily classified also, so it is usually used in classification techniques. The nonparametric type algorithm is K-NN, which means it does not create any consideration on original data. This algorithm has another name called *lazy learner algorithms* because it does not train from the training data, instead it learns from stored data at the time of classification. Figure 15.8 is an example of K-NN.

Consider A and B is a two category and x1 is new data value that has arrived. We want to understand which categories the new data point lies in. K-NN used to solve these types of problems. It is used to identify the type in particular data record. The following steps are basic for K-NN execution.

Step 1: Select the K value. This is for K neighbors

Step 2: Evaluate the Euclidian distance value for neighbor

Step 3: Consider the neighbour for Euclidian

Step 4: Count the data values for each class

Step 5: Place the new data value to the maximum number of neighbor

15.6.4 Support Vector Machine (SVM)

This is one of the most popular methods of supervised learning. It has two types of linear and nonlinear methods. SVM is used for classification as well as regression, but this is mainly used in classification. The main aim of the SVM is to place the decision line, which is used to identify the new data point in correct categories. This line is called a hyperplane. The SVM selects the maximum data, which helps to create the hyperplane. The maximum values are called support vectors. Figure 15.9 shows the SVM functions.

SVM are classified into two types:

Linear SVM: This type of SVM us categorized the data values by using a straight line. That line is called linear. These data are called linearly separable data.

Non-Linear SVM: In this type of SVM, the categorized data does not base on the straight line. This type of classification is called nonlinear types of classification.

15.6.5 Logistic Regression

Logistic regression is one of the most familiar machine learning techniques; it appears below the supervised learning models. It is utilized for forecasting the definite dependent variable by a specified position of independent attributes. Logistic regression forecasts the result of uncompromising dependent elements. Consequently, the result must be an

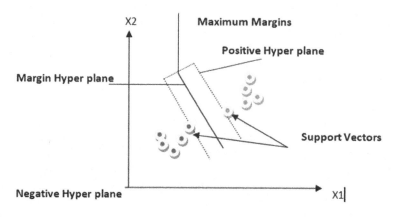

FIGURE 15.9
SVM Function

unqualified or discrete value. This can be both Yes or No, 0 and 1, or true or false (although as a substitute of the correct value as 0 and 1, it produces the probabilistic results which recline between 0 and 1). Logistic regression is greatly related to the algorithms of linear regression, excluding how they are used. Linear regression helps unravel regression troubles, while logistic regression deciphers classification troubles. Instead of placing the regression line in logistic algorithms, we can fit the S-shaped function of logistics. It predicts two types of values 0 and 1. The curve following the logistics procedure specifies the likelihood of incredible, such as whether the units are damaged or not, a mouse is heavy or not based on its weight, and so on. Logistic regression is an imperative machine learning procedure since it has the capability to supply possibilities and categorize new data using assiduous and detach datasets. Logistic regression can be helpful to organize the annotations using the dissimilar categories of data and can effortlessly establish the most successful elements used for the categorization. Figure 15.10 describes the logistic regression function.

Sigmoid model of logistic: This model is a mathematical model used to plot the forecasted results to likelihood. It delineates any genuine significance into one more value inside a limit of 0 and 1. The significance of the logistic regression has to be placed between 0 and 1, it cannot leave outside the limit, so its shape is a curve similar to the S shape. The S-form camber is called the sigmoid procedure or the logistic function. In logistic regression, we employ the idea of the threshold significance, and it describes the likelihood of both 0 and 1. The ideal is higher than the threshold value to be liable to 1, and an assessment under the threshold values be liable to 0. Logistic is divided into three categories: binomial, multinomial, and ordinal.

Binomial: Here can be just two probable kinds of the dependent variables, like 0 or 1, true or false, pass or fail, and so on.

Multinomial: There can be three or more feasible disordered categories of the dependent attributes in multinomial logistic regression, such as "cow," "cat," or "goat."

Ordinal: There can be three or further probable prearranged kind of reliant attributes available in ordinal logistic regression, such as "low temperature," "medium temperature," or "high temperature." The dependent element must be categorized in the environment and the independent elements should not be different collinearity. These are hypotheses for logistic regression.

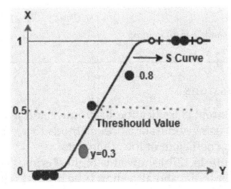

FIGURE 15.10
Logistic Regression Function

```
In [3]: crimecorr=crimerate.corr(method='pearson' )
   ...: crimecorr
Out[3]:
          2001      2002      2003    ...      2010      2011      2012
2001  1.000000  0.980241  0.916131   ...  0.819025  0.795074  0.792900
2002  0.980241  1.000000  0.955917   ...  0.860366  0.839692  0.836142
2003  0.916131  0.955917  1.000000   ...  0.849112  0.834932  0.830904
2004  0.948498  0.979695  0.975789   ...  0.914238  0.899889  0.897842
2005  0.936671  0.967900  0.975356   ...  0.925052  0.910845  0.907268
2006  0.923227  0.957574  0.961209   ...  0.938137  0.924406  0.922354
2007  0.907861  0.940223  0.936107   ...  0.958365  0.944619  0.941447
2008  0.879770  0.907190  0.903864   ...  0.979099  0.968738  0.965096
2009  0.850861  0.884045  0.879631   ...  0.992522  0.985457  0.982618
2010  0.819025  0.860366  0.849112   ...  1.000000  0.994942  0.992666
2011  0.795074  0.839692  0.834932   ...  0.994942  1.000000  0.996485
2012  0.792900  0.836142  0.830904   ...  0.992666  0.996485  1.000000
```

FIGURE 15.11
Correlation Coefficient for Crime Dataset

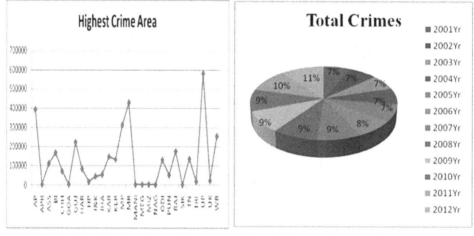

(a): Highest Crime Registered Area   (b): Highest Crime Registered Year

FIGURE 15.12
Highest Crime Recorded Area (a) and Year (b) in India

15.7 Result and Discussions

This chapter proposed different classification techniques and evaluated the results based on the accuracy while also using some statistical methods to predict the crime rate. Figure 15.11 shows the correlation coefficient of the crime data.

Figure 15.12 (a) and Figure 15.12(b) shows the highest crimes against women in a registered area (UtterPradesh) in India, and also shows the highest crime recorded year (2011). The below Figure 15.13 confirms maximum level of crimes registered against women 18–30

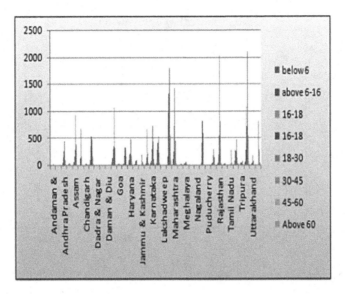

FIGURE 15.13
Agewise Crimes Recorded Against Women in India

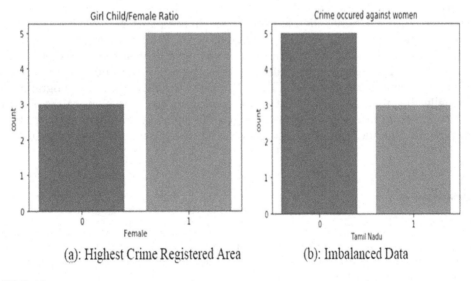

(a): Highest Crime Registered Area   (b): Imbalanced Data

FIGURE 15.14
Comparision of Crime Ratio (a) and Imbalanced Data (b)

years old. Figure 15.14 (a) shows that more crimes are recorded against women than girl children, and Figure 15.14 (b) shows the unbalanced dataset. The maximum data point has negative class. To avoid such types of issues, we need to balance the data. Finally estimate the machine learning algorithms performance based on the banced data. Here K-NN has given better accuracy compared to other models. Figure 15.15 shows the different ML models performance outcomes.

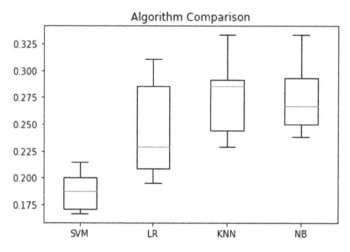

FIGURE 15.15
Machine Learning Algorithms Accuracy Comparisons

15.8 Conclusion

To determine the crime rate against women is essential for our nation, as it helps the crime department to take the right action to avoid crime. In this panicked time, it is very difficult to control crime against women. Using different types of machine learning classification techniques, we can find out the regular crime region and agewise crime prediction against women easily. This chapter implemented various types of classification techniques on balanced data to identify the crime rate. This algorithm classified crimes by geographic location. Finally, the algorithm performance evaluated using the confusion matrix. The K-NN supervised machine learning algorithms has given better accuracy when compared to other algorithms. To continue to improve accuracy, we can use different statistical methods.

References

Tahani Almanie, Rsha Mirza and Elizabeth Lor. "Crime Prediction based on Crime types and using spatial and Temporal Criminal Hotspots." *International Journal of Data Mining & Knowledge Management Process*, 2015.

G. Goicoa, T. Vicente. "Crime against women in India: unveiling spatial patterns and temporal trends of dowry deaths in the districts of Uttar Pradesh." *Journal of the Royal Statistical Society: Series A (Statistics in Society)* , 2019.

M. Sudhir Gorade. "A Study of Some Data Mining Classification Techniques." *International Research Journal of Engineering and Technology*, 2017.

Hadi Hormozi, Elham Hormozi, and Hamed Rahimi Nohooji. "The Classification of the Applicable Machine Learning methods in Robot Manipulators." *International Journal of Machine Learning and Computing*, 2012.

Saeed Iqbal, Muhammad Shaheen, Fazl-e-basit. "A Machine Learning Based Method for Optimal journal Classification." *The 8th International Conference for Internet Technology and Secured Transactions*, IEEE, 2013.

Bhajneet Kaur. *"Crime against Women: Analysis and Prediction using Data Mining Techniques." ComitCon-2019: International Conference on Machine Learning, Big Data, Cloud and Parallel Computing*, 2019.

S. Lavanyaa, D. Akila. "Crime against Women Analysis and Prediction in Tamilnadu Police Using Data Mining Techniques." *International Journal of Recent Technology and Engineering (IJRTE)*, 2019.

Neema Mduma, Khamisi Kalegele, Dina Machuve. "A Survey of Machine Learning Approaches and Techniques for Student Dropout Prediction." *Data Science Journal*, 2019.

Amr E. Mohamed, "Comparative Study of Four Supervised Machine Learning Techniques for Classification." *International Journal of Applied Science and Technology*, 2017.

Mayank Motwani, Pratha Purwar. "An Efficient Approach towards Crimes against Women using TimeSeries algorithm." *International Journal of Computer Applications*, 2018.

Iqbal Muhammad, Zhu Yan. "Supervised Machine Learning Approach: A Survey." *ICTACT Journal of Soft Computing*, 2015.

F.Y. Osisanwo. "Supervised Machine Learning Algorithms: Classification and Comparision." *International Journal of Computer Trends and Technology (IJCTT)* , 2017.

Iqbal H. Sarker "Efectiveness analysis of machine learning classifcation models for predicting personalized context-aware smartphone usage." *Journal of Big Data*, 2019.

Devan M. S Shiju Sathyadevan, S. Surya Gangadharan. "Crime Analysis and Prediction Using Data Mining." *First International Conference on Networks & Soft Computing, IEEE*, 2014.

Ishabh Singh, Rishabh Reddy. "K-means Clustering Analysis of Crimes on Indian Women." *Journal of Cybersecurity and Information Management (JCIM)*, 2020.

Deepti Sisodiaa. "Prediction of Diabetes using Classification Algorithms." *International Conference on Computational Intelligence and Data Science*, Elsevier, 2018.

M. Sreedevi, A. Harsha Vardhan Reddy, CH. Venkata Sai Krishna Reddy. "Review on Crime Analysis and Prediction using Data Mining Techniques." *International Journal of Innovative Research in Science, Engineering and Technology*, 2018.

Reddy R. Vijaya Kumar, D. U. R. Babu. "A Review on Classification Techniques in Machine Learning." *International Journal of Advance Research in Science and Engineering*, 2018.

Chhaya Yadav. "Improving the Performance for Crime Pattern Analysis Using." *International Journal of Advance Research Ideas and Innovations in Technology*, 2017.

Nur Ain Syahira Zaidi, Aida Mustapha, Salama A. Mostafa, Muhammad Nazim Razali. "A Classification Approach for Crime Prediction." *International Conference on Applied Computing to Support Industry: Innovation and Technology*, Springer, 2019.

16

PageRank–Based Extractive Text Summarization

Supriya Gupta, Aakanksha Sharaff and Naresh Kumar Nagwani

National Institute of Technology, Raipur, India

CONTENTS

16.1 Introduction

In natural language processing applications, text summarization is the most important application. It helps reduce the amount of original text and extracts only the significant information from it. Text summarization is also referred to as data reduction process. It comprises creating an outline of the original text that permits the user to acquire primary snippets of data accessible from that text, however with a lot shorter understanding time. This chapter provides a brief overview of different types of text summarization techniques and explains about an inventive unsupervised methodology to construct text summaries through hassle-free sentence extraction and sorting them byranks obtained from a graph-based ranking algorithm. The above automatic summary generation method is further evaluated and compared with the benchmark results.

This chapter involves various sections that focus on topics related to the proposed project. Section 16.2 explains the research work on text summarization. Further Section 16.3 gives the brief application of text summarization. Section 16.4 explains the proposed work and PageRank algorithm. Section 16.5 shows the result and analysis part obtained from the successful execution. Section 16.6 depicts the conclusion of the complete project and summarizes the whole chapter.

16.1.1 Types of Text Summarization Process

The text summarization process can be classified upon different basis like:

Figure 16.1 describes the categorization of the text summarization process. As shown, text summarization can be divided into different types on the basis of what can again be further sub-classified.

Based on Number of Document

Text summarization can be further sub-categorized based on the number of a document:

- **Single:** As the outline is brief, precise, and express, it turns out to be increasingly significant. One document can be made out of some subdocuments. They can be made out of some subdocument's document's laid uncommon accentuation on various perspectives although these reports were all encompassed a similar subject [1].

- **Multiple:** Multi-document summary is the method that manages heaps of information in multiple related supply documents that comprises simply the essential material or primary ideas in less area [2]. Currently, a multi-document report has become a big subject in automatic summarization.

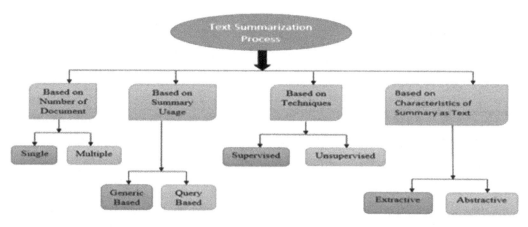

FIGURE 16.1
Types of Text Summarization Process

A. **Based on Summary Usage**

Text summarization can be further sub-categorized based on summary usage listed as:

- **Generic Based:** Generic summaries don't target any explicit cluster, as it addresses a broad community of readers [3].

- **Query Based:** Query or topic-focused queries are customized to the particular needs of an individual or a specific group, and speak to a specific topic. Query-based text summarization is planned for extracting basic information that answers the query from the original text [4]. The appropriate answer is introduced in a negligible, regularly predefined, number of words.

B. **Based on Techniques**

Text summarization can be further sub-categorized based on techniques listed as:

- **Supervised:** Supervised text summarization is a lot of like supervised keyphrase extraction. Essentially, on the off chance that you have an assortment of documents and human-generated summaries for them, you can learn highlights of sentences that make them a great possibility for incorporation in the summary [5].

- **Unsupervised:** Unsupervised keyphrase extraction evacuates the requirement for training data. It moves toward the issue from an alternate angle [6]. Rather than attempting to learn explicit features that describe key phrases, the TextRank algorithm misuses the structure of the content itself to decide key phrases that seem "central" to the text similarly that PageRank chooses significant webpages.

C. **Based on Characteristics of Summary as Text**

Text summarization can be categorized into numerous categories based on characteristics of summary as text given as:

- **Abstractive Summarization:** Abstractive summarization systems modify the document by using new phrases, rephrasing, or using such words that are not present in the original text. The model has to initially comprehend the document and then express that with new words and phrases for a perfect abstractive summary. It comprises of complex features like a generalization, paraphrasing, and incorporating real-world knowledge.

- **Extractive Summarization:** Extractive text summarization generates summaries by combing different parts of sentences copied from the original source text. In such cases, a significant advance is regularly that of scoring the significance of various sentences [7]. In this, a subset of critical data is pulled and afterward joined again to frame a summary.

16.1.2 PageRank Algorithm

The PageRank set of rules were designed and advanced with the aid of Page and Brin around 1998. It became essentially applied within the prototype of Google's seek engine. The cause in the back of this set of rules is to calculate the popularity, or the significance, of a webpage, on the idea of the interconnection of the web. The ideas are that a web page that includes a greater incoming hyperlinks performs a biger function than a web page that includes much less incoming hyperlinks. Moreover, a web page with a hyperlink from a web page that is thought to be of excessive significance is likewise huge. PageRank belongs to the most mainstream ranking algorithms and was structured as a technique for Weblink analysis. The PageRank algorithm is used in calculating the weight for web pages, the same principle used in the Google search engine to assign a rank to a web page as per search result. [1,8–10]

16.2 Related Work

Complicated morphological structure present within the Arabic language causes difficulty in extracting nouns that are to be utilized as an attribute for the summarization process. Al Khalil morphological analyzer is employed to require care of the matter of noun extraction. The projected technique is based at the graph-primarily based totally system, throughout which the record resembles the graph while the vertices of the graph suit sentences. A changed PageRank algorithmic rule is implemented with associate preliminary score for every node this is the range of nouns at some stage in this sentence [11].

The category of extractive document summarization contains a fuzzy rule-based system that describes the fuzzy rule that helps in recognizing and choosing the most relevant sentences and concepts in every text document in the research paper [12]. The category of summarization using FRQ-CL depicts the novel medicine summarization system addicted to a mixture of clustering and frequent itemsets mining with an abstract illustration of biomedical text to boost the standard of generated summaries [13].

Query-based text summarization helps to extract sentences by finding the linguistics connection score between the query and input text document [8]. RNN depicts extracts salient sentences from the supply document then more cluster them to get a summary, while not ever-changing the source text [9]. Yang has worked on the category of single document extractive summarization, which depicts neural network–based encoder to make representations for sentences and apply a binary classifier [10]. He has also worked on the category of keyword extraction, AKE automatic keyword/keyphrase extraction, and TS textual summarization is focused on presenting key-information [1].

These ranks are assigned to sentences and therefore the sentence is taken out of the summary per scoring, while abstractive summarization delivers an abstract summary that comes with words and phrases distinctive to those appearing source documents. Subsequently, abstract could be a summary that comprises ideas or concepts taken from the initial document but are re-interpreted and presented in an alternate type. It wants extensive natural language processing [2]. Consequently, it's considerably perplexing to extract summarization. Summarization tasks will be categorized into supervised and unsupervised. A large amount of data is required with a label or annotation of learning ways. These systems confer with two classes wherever abbreviated sentences are known as good samples, and sentences that don't seem to be during this summary are known as negative samples. To create sentence classification, some common reduction methods are utilized. Support vector machine (SVM) and artificial neural networks are good examples. They manufacture a summary by accessing solely the target documents. Such programs use heuristic levels to remove the foremost vital sentences and to create a summary. The strategy employed in the unsupervised system is consolidated [14].

Another common type is that the web-based summarization. Users get ample knowledge over the web nowadays. Online material doubles per annum. As a result, users have to undergo several links to grasp which document is very important and which isn't, and within the first attempt most users abandon their searches. Radev proposed an efficient programme capable of summarizing clusters of related documents that may help users discover the outcomes of the recovery [4].

In email based, more often than not, summarization is an additional range of summarization inside e-mail conversations are summarized. Emails, nevertheless, appear inside mailboxes due to the fact of that email overloading troubles exist and a superb deal of time is spent reading, arranging, and archiving incoming mails. There are different ways to make use of of email summaries. Within the commercial enterprise world, email summarization should be used as organizational reminiscence inside of summaries whose messages precede commercial enterprise decisions. Personalized summaries include the exclusive information the patron dreams. In updating the summary, customers are give the idea to own primary facts on the topic and totally want the latest updates of the article [3].

Web 2.0 has created the construction of Internet sites corresponding to social networking sites, social media, blogs, and so on. When people express their feelings or give updates on a product, organization, service, or topic, text summarization (TS) and sentiment analysis (SA) formulate concepts and work along to form those summaries. Such abbreviations establish and explain concepts initially based on behavior rather than based on polarity (good, bad, or neutral). A summary of the analysis, a summary of human history, and Wikipedia articles, all comprise this class [15].

Research Gap

During research, it is found that the previous models are not able to create optimal summaries as an output due to various flaws in the process. It has been observed that the cosine similarity is evaluated alongwith PageRank algorithm with a lower number of nodes. The PageRank algorithm is used as a base and this can be further enhanced for improving the quality and accuracy of the generated summaries.

16.3 Proposed Work

To style a new learning rule which will extract the optimum coefficients but not user interaction, and will thus offer the user a summary close to a semi-synthetic summary. To identify and compare various algorithms, output parameters can be used to tune parameters and improve the accuracy of the new text summarization algorithm.

Figure 16.2 describes the methodology of the research as it is a stepwise procedure. Initially the articles are combined together to form a text, then the text is split into sentences. Further vectors are applied and then the similarity index is calculated. Moreover, it is described in the graph; after calculating sentence ranking, the summary is generated.

16.3.1 Text Summarization Approach

- Data preparation for effective summarization
- Text pre-processing
- Text processing
    - ✓ Feature extraction from documents using NLP techniques
    - ✓ Feature comparison for effective summary generation

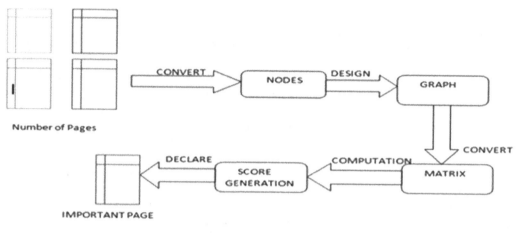

FIGURE 16.2
Methodology

- Text summarization engine model
  - ✓ Selection of text summarization algorithm
  - ✓ Comparison of generated summary with a gold-standard summary document

16.3.2 Text Pre-Processing Techniques

A. **Tokenization:** Tokenization is additionally called feature extraction in text mining. The extraction of features from an email into a vector space is called feature extraction.

B. **Stopping:** In this period of pre-processing, non-informative words like "the," "is," "was," and "were" are eliminated. The noninformative words are those words in the text collection that do not have any huge importance [16]. For the maximum part, the stopping is actualized with the assistance of preserving up a stop list, which contains of all stop phrases required to be removed from the textual content series to install the textual content series organized for analysis.

C. **Stemming:** Stemming may be a procedure of emission for the standard person morphological and inflexional endings from words in English. The motivation at the back of stemming is to differ over the phrases to their root bureaucracy for that reason that each one the occurrences of the phrases are given constantly in the textual content collection for superb analysis [17].

D. **Noise removal:** Eliminating obscure text or symbols or word from features, e.g., symbols like, and so on.

16.4 PageRank Methodology

PageRank is an algorithm utilized in the natural language process to get a summary of the documents. The algorithmic rule is used to calculate the rank of web content. TextRank algorithmic rule supported PageRank algorithmic rule. PageRank works on the likelihood distribution; it represents the likelihood that someone indiscriminately clicking on links can reach any particular page.

In contrast to other ranking algorithms, PageRank incorporates the effect of both approaching and outgoing links into one single model, and along these lines, it creates just one lot of scores:

$$PR(Vi) = (1-d) + d * \sum_{Vj \in \ln(Vi)} \frac{PR(Vj)}{|Out(Vj)|} \tag{16.1}$$

In the above expression, d is a damping factor whose probability is set somewhere in the range of 0 and 1 (say damping factor). Where pr(vi) is the cutting-edge rank of the sentence (vi). The probability of surfer now no longer preventing to click on at the hyperlink is given via way of means of damping problem d. Higher the value of d masses of apparently the surfer clicking at the hyperlink. For every one all told those algorithms, ranging from randomized values appointed to every node inside the graph, the computation emphasizes until convergence under a given threshold is accomplished. Within the wake of going for walks the algorithm, a score is expounded to every vertex that speaks the "importance" or "power" of that vertex within the graph. Notice that the ultimate word values do not appear to be motivated via way of means of the selection of the preliminary price; simply the quantity of iterations to convergence can also additionally properly be unique (Figure 16.3).

Let N be the full number of pages. A matrix N×N is defined by defining the (i, j) entry as:

$$A_{ij} = \begin{cases} \dfrac{1}{L(j)} & \text{transition from j to i} \\ 0 & \text{otherwise} \end{cases} \tag{16.2}$$

The graph is used to symbolize connections amongst pages. A website is implied via way of means of a node and an arrow from web page A to web page B implies that there's a hyperlink from web page A to web page B. The quantity of outgoing hyperlinks is a crucial parameter. We use the notation "out-diploma of a node to square for the amount of out-going hyperlinks contained in a very web page. This graph is typically said due to the fact the net graph. Each node inside the graph is recognized with a web page. We we're going to use the term "node" and "web page" interchangeably.

In our example, we considered the matrix having order 5 × 5. As such, we consider 5 nodes in our example. The Matrix A can be given as follows:

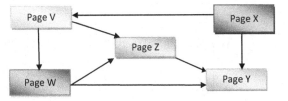

FIGURE 16.3
Page Node Links

$$
A = \begin{array}{c} \\ V \\ W \\ X \\ Y \\ Z \end{array}
\begin{array}{ccccc}
V & W & X & Y & Z \\
\end{array}
\left(\begin{array}{ccccc}
0 & 0 & \frac{1}{2} & 0 & 0 \\
\frac{1}{2} & 0 & 0 & 0 & 0 \\
0 & 0 & 0 & 0 & 0 \\
0 & \frac{1}{2} & \frac{1}{2} & 0 & 1 \\
\frac{1}{2} & \frac{1}{2} & 0 & 0 & 0
\end{array}\right)
$$

Let L(p) be the amount of out-going links in page P. There are five pages. Page V consists of a link to page W, a link to page X, a link to page Y, and a link to page Z. Page V consists of two single links to page W and Z. Page W points to pages Y and Z, page X points to pages V and Y, and page Z points to page Y. They're depicted by the subsequent graph. We've $L(V) = 2, L(W) = 2, L(X) = 2, L(Y) = 0, L(Z) = 1$

In the above example, the sum of the entries in each column is equal to 1, except Y since there is no outward transition from node Y, hence it is a dead node. mMatrix is alleged to be column-stochastic if the entries are non-negative and therefore the sum of the entries in each column is capable 1. The matrix A isn't column-stochastic as there's no outgoing link from node Y.

To find the score of each page we performed the following iteration.

Iteration 1:

$$
A = \begin{array}{c} \\ V \\ W \\ X \\ Y \\ Z \end{array}
\begin{array}{ccccc}
V & W & X & Y & Z \\
\end{array}
\left(\begin{array}{ccccc}
0 & 0 & \frac{1}{2} & 0 & 0 \\
\frac{1}{2} & 0 & 0 & 0 & 0 \\
0 & 0 & 0 & 0 & 0 \\
0 & \frac{1}{2} & \frac{1}{2} & 0 & 1 \\
\frac{1}{2} & \frac{1}{2} & 0 & 0 & 0
\end{array}\right)
\times
\left(\begin{array}{c}
1 \\ 1 \\ 1 \\ 1 \\ 1
\end{array}\right)
$$

$$
R[\text{Iteration } 1] = \left(\begin{array}{ccccc} \frac{1}{2} & \frac{1}{2} & 0 & 2 & 1 \end{array}\right)
$$

Iteration 2:

$$
A = \begin{array}{c} \\ V \\ W \\ X \\ Y \\ Z \end{array}
\begin{array}{ccccc}
V & W & X & Y & Z \\
\end{array}
\left(\begin{array}{ccccc}
0 & 0 & \frac{1}{2} & 0 & 0 \\
\frac{1}{2} & 0 & 0 & 0 & 0 \\
0 & 0 & 0 & 0 & 0 \\
0 & \frac{1}{2} & \frac{1}{2} & 0 & 1 \\
\frac{1}{2} & \frac{1}{2} & 0 & 0 & 0
\end{array}\right)
\times
\left(\begin{array}{c}
1/2 \\ 1/2 \\ 0 \\ 2 \\ 1
\end{array}\right)
$$

$$R[\text{Iteration 2}] = \begin{pmatrix} 0 & 1/4 & 0 & 5/4 & 1 \end{pmatrix}$$

Iteration 3:

$$A = \begin{matrix} & \begin{matrix} V & W & X & Y & Z \end{matrix} \\ \begin{matrix} V \\ W \\ X \\ Y \\ Z \end{matrix} & \begin{pmatrix} 0 & 0 & \frac{1}{2} & 0 & 0 \\ \frac{1}{2} & 0 & 0 & 0 & 0 \\ 0 & 0 & 0 & 0 & 0 \\ 0 & \frac{1}{2} & \frac{1}{2} & 0 & 1 \\ \frac{1}{2} & \frac{1}{2} & 0 & 0 & 0 \end{pmatrix} \end{matrix} \times \begin{pmatrix} 0 \\ 1/4 \\ 0 \\ 5/4 \\ 1 \end{pmatrix}$$

$$R[\text{Iteration 3}] = \begin{pmatrix} 0 & 0 & 0 & 9/8 & 1/8 \end{pmatrix}$$

Iteration 4:

$$A = \begin{matrix} & \begin{matrix} V & W & X & Y & Z \end{matrix} \\ \begin{matrix} V \\ W \\ X \\ Y \\ Z \end{matrix} & \begin{pmatrix} 0 & 0 & \frac{1}{2} & 0 & 0 \\ \frac{1}{2} & 0 & 0 & 0 & 0 \\ 0 & 0 & 0 & 0 & 0 \\ 0 & \frac{1}{2} & \frac{1}{2} & 0 & 1 \\ \frac{1}{2} & \frac{1}{2} & 0 & 0 & 0 \end{pmatrix} \end{matrix} \times \begin{pmatrix} 0 \\ 0 \\ 0 \\ 9/8 \\ 1/8 \end{pmatrix}$$

$$R[\text{Iteration 4}] = \begin{pmatrix} 0 & 0 & 0 & 1/8 \end{pmatrix}$$

Iteration 5:

$$A = \begin{matrix} & \begin{matrix} V & W & X & Y & Z \end{matrix} \\ \begin{matrix} V \\ W \\ X \\ Y \\ Z \end{matrix} & \begin{pmatrix} 0 & 0 & \frac{1}{2} & 0 & 0 \\ \frac{1}{2} & 0 & 0 & 0 & 0 \\ 0 & 0 & 0 & 0 & 0 \\ 0 & \frac{1}{2} & \frac{1}{2} & 0 & 1 \\ \frac{1}{2} & \frac{1}{2} & 0 & 0 & 0 \end{pmatrix} \end{matrix} \times \begin{pmatrix} 0 \\ 0 \\ 0 \\ 1/8 \\ 0 \end{pmatrix}$$

$$R[\text{Iteration 5}] = \begin{pmatrix} 0 & 0 & 0 & 0 & 0 \end{pmatrix}$$

Its proved by the above example that if one of the nodes will be a dead node (as page *Y* is a dead node) since there is no outward transition from Page *Y*, then iteration must be end to zero matrix.

From R [Iteration 3] and R [Iteration 4], it shows that Page Y has approximately the same value as compared to other page nodes. So Page Y has the highest score. Also, Page Y has 3 incoming links, another page has one or two incoming links. It shows that Page Y is more important than any other pages or nodes that are present in graph.

From the above example, it can be concluded that the page or node with the highest score has more important than any other nodes.

16.4.1 PageRank Algorithm:

Step 1: Initialize x to an N × 1 column vector with non-negative components.

Step 2: x by the product A × x until it converges.

Step 3: Update the respective row by multiplying updated (Most recent) vector with Matrix A.

Step 4: Continue Step 2 and Step 3 until we do not find appropriate value at any node between adjacent iteration.

Step 5: Find out such node per Step 4, and declare that node with high score.

Step 6: The node declare per Step 5 is important node than other nodes as it has maximum inward link.

16.4.2 TextRank Algorithm

The TextRank algorithm is based on the PageRank algorithm. Keyword extraction and text summarization basically use the TextRank Algorithm. The Sentence Extraction implemented in Python uses Text Summarization. The most significant task and the core of this algorithm are to get the most pertinent Sentences to form the bit of the content from the huge number of text. The top sentences from the original sauce text are extracted using the TextRank Algorithm.

Cosine Similarity - As per the vector representation given below, the similarity between two sentences Si and Sj is determined as the cosine similarity, which is identified to the angle of the vectors Si and Sj and is determined according to Eq.

$$sim_{cos}\left(Si,Sj\right) = \frac{\sum_{k=1}^{m} W_{ik}W_{jk}}{\sqrt{\sum_{k=1}^{m} W_{ik}^2 * \sum_{k=1}^{m} W_{jk}^2}} \tag{16.3}$$

where m represents the total number of terms in the document, W_{ik} represents the weight of the term k in the sentence Si and W_{jk} represents the weight of the term k in the sentence Sj.

16.5 Experimental Setup and Methodology

To measure the result of the PageRank algorithm hardware and software are a must.

Hardware Used:- Laptop or Computer with minimum requirements like 4GB RAM, 64 bit- OS, Processor- Intel i3@2.00 GHz.

Software Used:- Google Colab Cloud-based Platform for Python.

Google Colab is also known as Collaboratory. It is a Jupiter environment provided and supported by Google with the option to work with CPUs, GPUs, and even TPUs. It's like any other Jupyter notebook where we can code in Python and write descriptions as markdown along with all the other Jupyter features and a lot more.

The algorithm involved to perform for the successful execution of this process is as follows.

Step-1: Tokenize words in each sentence
A list of tokenized sentences will be generated in this step.

Step-2: Build a Similarity matrix
The similarity between two sentences will be found by Cosine similarity which will be used to measure the distance between two sentences.

Step-3: Run PageRank Algorithm
The PageRank algorithm can be run on it as now we do have the similarity matrix. On the off chance that followed the PageRank Article, the accompanying code is comparative and straightforward. The PageRank matrix will be created which will have the score of all sentences with the most significant sentence containing the highest score.

Step-4: Extract top sentences
Finally, the top sentences will be extracted from the PageRank matrix.

16.6 Result and Analysis

The two fundamental parameters are the Compression ratio and Retention ratio helps in evaluating the summary generated by Summarization Process. Compression Ratio, i.e. generated summary length in respect of golden summary, and the Retention Ratio i.e. the proportion of central information is retained.

$$\text{Compression Ratio} : CR = (\text{length S}) / (\text{length T}) \tag{16.4}$$

$$\text{Retention Ratio} : RR = (\text{info S}) / (\text{info T}) \tag{16.5}$$

Length S defines the number of the sentence in the text
Length T defines the number of the sentence in the Summarized text
Info S defines the number of words in Text
Info T define the number of words in the summarized text

In our example for TextRank algorithm length S=36 and length T=19.So, according to Equation (16.4), the Compression Ratio is 19/36=0.5277. And info in T=295 info in S=126. So. According to Equation (16.5), the Retention Ratio is 126/295=0.42711. The experiment is performed on two types of datasets to compare the output parameters using four different types of ROUGE values. Inputs fed to our text summarization model are documents from BBC News Summary and DUC2001 datasets. The top-scoring sentences are extracted to obtain the summaries as a result. This system generated summary is then compared with the reference summaries and ROGUE-1, ROUGE-2, ROUGE-L, and ROUGE-4 techniques are used to compare average Recall, Precision, and F-Score values.

The TextRank algorithm, which internally utilizes the PageRank technique, is combined with cosine distance to evaluate dissimilarity from a graph-based structure of sentences. The algorithm performance is directly proportional to the similarity measure. This model is unsupervised, hence does not require training and is language independent apart from the cosine distance evaluation. It has been observed that this approach improves the relevance of evaluated summaries.

Average Recall

Average recall, as mentioned in Table 16.1 and Figure 16.4, lists the ROUGE scores calculated using our model on DUC-2001 and BBC News Summary datsets. It is observed that the different set of documents produce different kind of summaries. The ROUGE score values for recall states the relevant content from the retrieved document.

TABLE 16.1

Analysis of Average Recall

Task-Name	ROUGE 1	ROUGE 2	ROUGE L	ROUGE SU4
Business-1	0.40588	0.22222	0.38889	0.26234
Political-1	0.36585	0.20812	0.36697	0.24974
Technology-1	0.46488	0.43056	0.50327	0.4426
Technology-2	0.43226	0.15646	0.32222	0.22158
DUC-2001-5089	0.5	0.13402	0.26027	0.23913
DUC-2001-5267	0.40187	0.12745	0.25581	0.17938
DUC-2001-6110	0.51429	0.22772	0.40506	0.26804
DUC-2001-6455	0.32353	0.10309	0.23171	0.13913

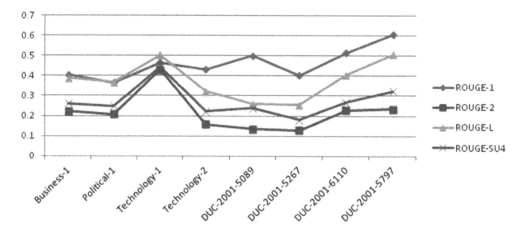

FIGURE 16.4
Average Recall Graph

Average Precision

Table 16.2 and Figure 16.5 list the ROUGE scores calculated for average precision using our model on DUC-2001 and BBC News Summary datsets. The ROUGE score values for precision depicts the relevant content from the full text document.

Average F-Score

Table 16.3 and Figure 16.5 list the ROUGE scores calculated for Average F-Score using our model on DUC-2001 and BBC News Summary datsets. The ROUGE score values for F-Score states the relevant content from the retrieved document.

Algorithms and model comparison over DUC2001 dataset is presented in Table 16.4.

Table 16.4 and Figure 16.6 depict the comparative analysis of ROUGE 1 & ROUGE 2 scores over a number of state-of-art algorithms. Our proposed model is found to be superior than the other models which are compared empirically.

TABLE 16.2

Analysis of Average Precision

Task-Name	ROUGE 1	ROUGE 2	ROUGE L	ROUGE SU4
Business-1	0.4726	0.25532	0.38043	0.29706
Political-1	0.57692	0.328	0.51282	0.39333
Technology-1	0.91447	0.84354	0.85556	0.86338
Technology-2	0.54472	0.19492	0.37662	0.27257
DUC-2001-5089	0.31098	0.08176	0.18095	0.14286
DUC-2001-5267	0.36752	0.11607	0.31429	0.16262
DUC-2001-6110	0.35762	0.15753	0.3299	0.1844
DUC-2001-6455	0.32353	0.10309	0.29231	0.13913

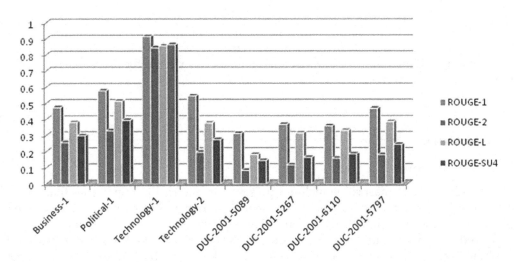

FIGURE 16.5
Average Precision Graph

TABLE 16.3

Analysis of Average F-Score

Task-Name	ROUGE 1	ROUGE 2	ROUGE L	ROUGE SU4
Business-1	0.43671	0.23762	0.38462	0.27862
Political-1	0.44776	0.25466	0.42781	0.3055
Technology-1	0.61641	0.57011	0.63374	0.5852
Technology-2	0.48201	0.17358	0.34731	0.24444
DUC-2001-5089	0.38346	0.10156	0.21348	0.17886
DUC-2001-5267	0.38393	0.1215	0.28205	0.17059
DUC-2001-6110	0.42187	0.18623	0.36364	0.21849
DUC-2001-6455	0.32353	0.10309	0.2585	0.13913

TABLE 16.4

Comparative Analysis of ROUGE Scores

S. No.	Algorithm/Model	ROUGE 1	ROUGE 2
1	Proposed Model	**0.5284**	**0.2033**
2	LexRank	0.4468	0.1989
3	UnifiedRank	0.4538	0.1765
4	FEOM	0.4773	0.1855
5	DE	0.4786	0.1853
6	NetSum	0.4643	0.177
7	CRF	0.4551	0.1733
8	SVM	0.4463	0.1702
9	Manifold ranking	0.4336	0.1664
10	QCS	0.4485	0.1852

Figures 16.4, 16.5, and 16.6 shows the different types of datasets (DUC Document Understanding Conference and BBC News Dataset) in X axis and the precision, recall, and F-score values in Y axis accordingly.

16.7 Conclusion

The efficient text summarization includes present advantages like summaries that reduce the reading time required for large documents. It makes the selection process more convenient while researching documents. The effectiveness of indexing can be hugely improved via ranking and scoring sentence graphs through automatic text summarization. The human summarizers are more biased than the rank-based extractive text summarization algorithms. We have compared various algorithms' performance with the proposed method and observed decent improvisation over the state of art techniques. Methods like

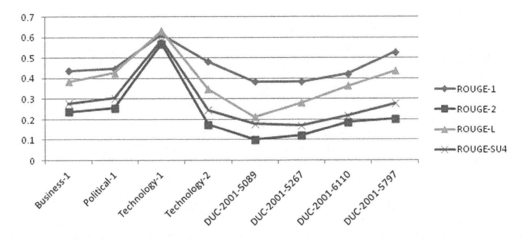

FIGURE 16.6
Average F-Score Graph

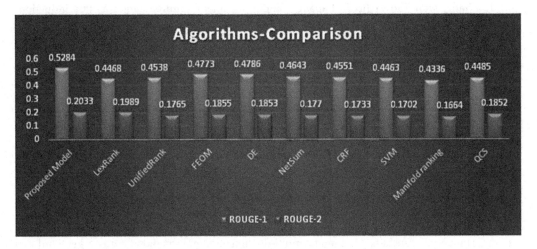

FIGURE 16.7
Algorithm Comparison Graph

unified rank and lex rank in which graphs are generated display better results when compared with supervised techniques (SVM, NetSum, and CRF). We have found cosine similarity works efficiently with the PageRank algorithm. After comparing different algorithms, it is clearly indicated that the metaheuristic approach combined with different sentence similarity methods can be further explored.

References

1. Zara Nasar, Syed Waqar Jaffry, Muhammad Kamran Malik, "Textual keyword extraction and summarization: State-of-the-art" *Information Processing and Management* 56 (2019).

2. Nabil Alami, Mohammed Meknassi, Noureddine En-nahnahi, "Enhancing unsupervised neural networks based text summarization with word embedding and ensemble learning", *Expert Systems With Applications* (2019).
3. K. Srinivasa Rao, D.S. R. Murthy, Gangadhara Rao Kancherla, "Semantic similarity based automatic document summarization method", *International Journal of Engineering and Advanced Technology (IJEAT)* 8 ISSN: 2249 – 8958, (2019).
4. Yangbin Chen, Yun Ma, Xudong Mao, Qing Li, "Multi-task learning for abstractive and extractive summarization" *Science and Engineering* (2019).
5. H. Xu, Z. Wang, X. Weng, "Scientific literature summarization using document structure and hierarchical attention model", *IEEE Access*, vol. 7, pp. 185290–185300 (2019).
6. Fábio Bif Goularte, Silvia Modesto Nassar, Renato Fileto, Horacio Saggion, "A expert systems with applications" 115, 264–275 (2019).
7. Krishnan Ramanathan, Yogesh Sankarasubramaniam, Nidhi Mathur, "An evolutionary framework for multi-document summarization using Cuckoo search approach", *MDSCSA Applied Computing, and Informatics* (2017).
8. Nazreena Rahman, Bhogeswar Borah, "Improvement of query-based text summarization using word sense", *Complex & Intelligent Systems*, 6, 75–85 (2020).
9. Yangbin Chent, "Multi task learning for abstractive and extractive summarization" *Science and Engineering* (2019).
10. Liu Yang, Ivan Titov, Mirella Lapata, "Single document summarization as tree induction", *Human Language Technologies* vol 1 (2019).
11. Reda Elbarougy, Gamal Behery, Akram El-Khatib, "Extractive arabic text summarization using modified PageRank algorithm" *Egyptian Informatics Journal* 21 (2020).
12. A.D. Dhawale, S.B. Kulkarni, V. Kumbhakarna, "Survey of progressive era of text summarization for indian and foreign languages using natural language processing", *Innovative Data Communication Technologies and Application* (2020).
13. Oussama Rouane, Hacene Belhadef, Mustapha Bouakkaz, "Combine clustering and frequent itemsets mining to enhance biomedical text summarization", *Expert Systems With Applications* 135 (2019).
14. Deepa Anand, Rupali Wagh, "Effective deep learning approaches for summarization of legal texts", *Journal of King Saud University - Computer and Information Sciences* (2019).
15. Marzieh Oghbaie, Morteza Mohammadi Zanjireh, "Pairwise document similarity measure based on present term", *Journal of Big Data* (2018).
16. Nabil Alami, "Using unsupervised deep learning for automatic summarization of arabic documents", *Arabian Journal for Science and Engineering* (2016).
17. YE Feiyue, XU Xinchen, "Automatic multi-document summarization based on keyword density and sentence", *Word Graphs Journal of Shanghai Jiaotong University (Science)* (2018).

17

Scene-Text Analysis

Tanima Dutta, Randheer Bagi and Hari Prabhat Gupta

IIT (BHU), Varanasi, India

CONTENTS

17.1 Introduction

Due to rapid development in the technology, resource-constrained devices are increasing, leading to a volcanic generation of multimedia content over the Internet and broadcast. Therefore, a huge unstructured dataset has been created for data scientists to analyze. The presence of text in these datasets is crucial, and it is essential to investigate to find out some meaningful information. The text that appears in the scene images is called scene text. Scene text contains a lot of valuable information that helps in analyzing and understanding the scenes. Texts in billboards, guideposts, notices, doorplates, and traffic signs have salient semantic clues that help in scene understanding. Therefore, the texts play an eminent role in the analysis of the scene images. It is rather easy to detect the text instances from the printed document than the scene images because of the underlying complex backgrounds have a broad range in terms of orientation, shape, color, textures, lighting/illumination conditions, and font. Scene images have found great attention because of their broad range of day-to-day applications, like the driver assistance system, text preserving animations, human-computer interaction, and robotics navigation. Thus, scene-text analysis can help in real-time applications. Scene-text analysis is broadly categorized in three ways: scene-text detection task, scene-text recognition method, and scene-text spotting system.

- **Scene-Text Detection:** This is the task that determines the presence of text instances in a scene image and localizes that text instance using bounding boxes or polygons. A general architecture of scene-text detection using deep convolutional networks is depicted in Figure 17.1.

- **Scene-Text Recognition:** This is defined as assigning the label to the detected text instances using prior knowledge. A general architecture for recognizing scene-text instances via deep sequential networks is shown in Figure 17.2.

- **Scene-Text Spotting:** The task of localizing and classifying text instances in a scene image in a unified manner is known scene-text spotting. A general architecture of scene-text spotting via deep neural networks is shown in Figure 17.3.

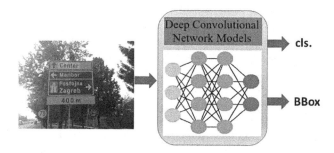

FIGURE 17.1
Overall Architecture of Text Detection Using Deep Networks in Scene Images

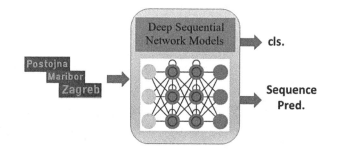

FIGURE 17.2
Overall Architecture of Scene-Text Recognition Using Sequential Deep Networks

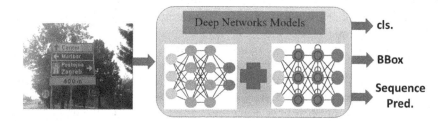

FIGURE 17.3
Overall Architecture of Scene-Text Spotting Using Deep Networks

Text plays an eminent role in analyzing and understanding scenes since text highlights important information relevant to the content of the scene. Moreover, some studies have validated that the intention of the person is mostly to focus more on text regions than any other objects present in a natural image because text helps portray the semantics associated with the context of the scene. Scene-text detection methods mostly include either direct regression, anchor-based, or segmentation-based approach. The direct regression for a positive sample regresses the bounding box directly, whereas anchor-based method uses anchors as a reference to regress. The first one predicts the bounding boxes for a group classification and regress them. In later ones, scene text is predicted with various shapes of anchors for different set of classifications followed by regressing them. In the segmentation-based approaches, pixel-level classification is performed to locate the text instances. However, these methods fail when the scene-text regions are near to each other.

Text recognition is also an essential part in the process of text analysis in scene images. Several recognition approaches based on sequence-to-sequence modeling are proposed in the literature that has made remarkable findings for text recognition. The recognition of scene text in the wild is complicated. There are variations in appearance, font type, visual layout, and underlying complex background. Various attention mechanisms, such as gated attention, spatial attention, and channel-wise attention are used to minimize false text recognition. The use of transformation techniques to transform arbitrary text instances into regular text instances is also popular. Text spotting is classified into two branches: text detection process and text recognition model. An independent analysis of detection with subsequent text recognition in scene images does not give complete information about the text present in natural images and their relationship. The text detection task is complementary to the text recognition job. Therefore, a combined approach of both of them attracts computer vision researchers. This combined approach is known as text spotting. In traditional approaches, both of these two branches are trained separately. Recently, end-to-end trainable deep neural networks with minimum overhead are proposed.

17.2 Literature Survey

We have discussed the popular scene-text spotting methodologies, along with scene-text detection models and scene-text recognition approaches for analyzing text instances using deep neural networks (in short deep networks).

17.2.1 Scene-Text Detection

The two important models that are effectively used in scene text detection are direct regression and anchor-based mechanism. EAST (Zhou et al., 2017) has designed a simple but powerful architecture using a deep learning model to achieve a fast text detector that produces detection results with high accuracy in natural scene images. The architecture is straightforward and estimates a quadrilateral shape to anticipate word-level and/or text-line-level text instances that have multiple orientations. The authors also elaborate the design of loss functions and neural network pipeline. Although these mechanisms are very effective, they suffer from some limitations like how the optimization of direct regression-based methods are challenging without anchor references. Therefore, the generation of appropriate anchors is also essential. Inappropriate anchors may degrade the robustness of a scene-text detector for complex scenes. To handle these problems, the authors introduce a hidden anchor mechanism (HAM) (Hou et al., 2020), where the anchors are predicted based on the hidden layer and the predicted weighted sum is directly integrated into the network for regression. HAM framework is a simple and easy way to support and optimize anchors using direct regression mechanisms. Besides, the authors handle long text detection using a post-processing technique, which is named as an iterative regression box. It added the additional cost of computation and generalized the HAM framework in detecting long texts.

The authors in (Raghunandan et al., 2019) have performed the task of text detection in scene video and images, as well as born-digital images. The evaluation of experimental results for localizing and recognizing multi-script text is challenging. Also, the texts have multiple orientation. First, the most significant bit is utilized to explore the bit plane. Furthermore, based on the structure of convex deficiency and concave deficiency of different parts of a text instance in bit planes, the authors choose the most suitable bit planes and named them candidate ones. In a candidate plane, the authors introduce pair components using mutual nearest neighbor to select text in distinguished pairs, which utilizes the gradient direction. These distinguished pairs of text, known as representative pairs, are responsible for text detection at the word level. They use sub-bands and the angular relationship between them. A fusion of bands is performed by fixing the window of each character to handle the arbitrary orientation of words in scene images. The features are extracted in the contourlet wavelet domain. The authors include support vector machine as a classifier for detecting characters. In the case of the recognition, the hidden Markov model is used.

The authors addressed the shortcomings of regression and segmentation-based approaches in scene-text detection in progressive scale expansion network (PSENet) by developing a kernel-based framework (Wang et al., 2019a). Most of the traditional techniques claim a quadrangle bounding box, which poorly localizes the arbitrary shape texts in the detection process. Also, when the two texts are in a close neighborhood, they mislead the detection process by generating false detection. In this case, the segmentation-based approach also fails to detect accurate text. Therefore, PSENet different scales of kernels are generated gradually to fit the text instances. The generated minimal scale kernels have large geometrical margins among them. Hence, it is a robust text detector that addresses the problem of partially intersected text instances and detects arbitrary-shaped text instances.

Scene-text detection using deep networks gained remarkable outcomes over a few years. However, due to the large variation in scene text in natural images, text detection methods suffer from false detection. To mitigate this issue, the authors in SPCNET (Xie et al., 2019) proposed a text detector using a deep network that utilizes the feature pyramid network (FPN) along with the an instance segmentation technique, and named the framework as supervised pyramid context network (Dollár et al., 2014). SCPNET takes advantage of both instance segmentation for semantic information and FPN for sharing information to accurately locate the text regions in scene images with minimum false detection. It also added marginal computational cost in the network. Dealing with the arbitrary-oriented text in scene-test detection is another major challenge. In the literature (Ma et al., 2018), the authors introduce a rotation-based framework using a deep network to detect text instances with arbitrary-orientations. They design rotation region proposal networks (RRPNs) to graft oriented text proposals that have angular information. Using the angular information of the grafted-oriented text proposals, the authors adapt bounding box regression to enhance the accuracy of fitting the proposals into the text regions for oriented text. Arbitrary-oriented proposals are used for classification of the text region by projecting to a feature map. It is a computationally efficient detector that localizes text proposals with multi-orientation.

The scene-text detection methods perform training to detect bounding boxes with word-level annotations and display the shortcomings in the case of an arbitrary shaped text representation. In CRAFT (Baek et al., 2019), the authors proposed a technique that measures each character and the affinity between each character for arbitrary shape text detection. They utilize character-level annotations of synthetic images to determine the ground-truths of natural images (real) to overcome the deficit of individual annotations at character-level. The training of the network is performed by using the affinity score of the characters. Also, it can detect arbitrarily oriented text, curved text, and deformed texts in a bottom-up manner. The use of a rectangular bounding box or quadrangle for text detection in traditional models may feel restrained in detecting long and arbitrarily text instances. Therefore, the authors in LOMO (Zhang et al., 2019) proposed a detection method that progressively localizes the long text instances multiple times. LOMO is the combination of three sub-branches: (I) direct-regressor that initially generates the text proposals in the form of a quadrangle; (ii) iterative refinement module then progressively refines the text proposals grafted previously; and (iii) shape expression module finally utilizes the geometric properties, such as text region representation, centerline of text instances, and border offsets of texts for reconstructing the more precise and accurate representation of text instances.

17.2.2 Scene-Text Recognition

The process of assigning the label to the text-detected text instances based on priory knowledge is known as scene-text recognition. The recognition task will become more challenging when the detected text has a complex background, and the text instances are in an arbitrary shape. In SCATTER (Litman et al., 2020), the authors introduced a scene-text recognition deep network architecture, which is named as a selective context attentional text recognizer. It is based on the BiLSTM (Graves and Schmidhuber, 2005) framework and utilizes the intermediate supervision in the training of a BiLSTM encoder with stacked block architecture. This improves the contextual information in the encoded feature map. In the decoding part, it uses the attention mechanism in a two-step process. In the first process, it re-weights the visual feature obtained from the convolutional neural network with contextual features grafted from the BiLSTM. In the second process, it considers feature as a sequence and accomplishes an intra-sequence relationship among them.

The recurrent neural network with attention mechanism was exploited recently to achieve a considerable gain in the text recognition process. It is found that the recurrent neural network with attention mechanisms in the deep network may suffer from attention drift in certain conditions. The semantic segmentation-based methods also face the problem of setting the threshold for text recognition over the segmented feature map. In Wan and colleagues (2020), the authors address the aforesaid problems by introducing an alternative approach in the form of TextScanner. It exhibits three main characteristics in the process of scene-text recognition. First, it produces a pixel-wise, multi-channel segmentation map for each character class, position, and sequence order. Second, it utilizes a recurrent neural network for context encoding modeling. Last, it predicts the character position and its class in parallel to make sure that the transcribed characters are in the correct order sequence. The recurrent neural network–based scene text recognition model limits computational efficiency due to time-dependent decoding manner. Also, the intrinsic property corresponding to semantic context help to capture the semantic information using one-way serial transmission. Therefore, the authors (Yu et al., 2020) have proposed a recognition framework of scene texts, which is an end-to-end trainable. The authors named the framework as a semantic reasoning network that couples the visual context information and semantic context information effectively for text recognition in scene images. They also introduce a global module for semantic reasoning that seizes the global semantic context during the multi-path concurrent transmission. The issue of perspective distortion and curve shape text is covered in the encoder-decoder framework. However, it still fails in text recognition when the scene text comes from the blurred image or uneven lighting/illumination condition. In Qiao et al. (2020b), the authors have proposed an encoder-decoder framework that incorporates local visual features in the absence of specific global semantic information. It is robust in nature and can recognize the low-quality scene texts. The problem of complex background, cluttered environment, uneven lighting condition, low resolution, perspective distortion, and arbitrary shape text in scene-text recognition is handled in several suboptimal deep network models proposed in the literature. In Wang and colleagues (2019a, b), the author addresses the problem of misalignment that occurs in the attention-based text recognition model between the intended character region and the selected attention region. They introduce a gated cascade attention module that increases the precision of alignment of attention region in an aggregated manner. They extracted more discriminative features from the feature maps using the channel attention and spatial attention modules in the text recognition network.

17.2.3 Scene-Text Spotting

The text detection process and the text recognition module work together in a unified network to perform scene-text spotting. It is the current trend in the field of multimedia for scene text analysis. Mask TextSpotter (Liao et al., 2019) has proposed an end-to-end trainable network that utilizes semantic segmentation in two-dimensional space to directly perform detection and recognition. It can handle the curve, arbitrary, and irregular text instances for scene text spotting. Mask TextSpotter incorporated a spatial attention mechanism that enhances the overall performance of the proposed network. In scene text spotting, most of the recent advances use a two-stage framework that uses a region-of-interest pooling, which degrades the spotting performance. The authors of CharNet (Xing et al., 2019) proposed a one-stage model for test spotting, which is named as convolutional character networks. It executes two tasks simultaneously in a single pass, i.e., it directly produces the output as a bounding box with word or character-level annotations. The detection branch uses the character as a basic element in the detection branch. The recognition branch is based on the recurrent neural network. It also designs a text detection model, which is iterative in nature and transforms the learning ability of characters from synthetic data for detection in real-world images. It can handle both multi-orientation texts as well as curved texts in the spotting process.

TextDragon (Feng et al., 2019) has proposed a text spotter that is trained in an end-to-end way for arbitrary shape texts. During the training, it uses only word or line-level annotations of the text instances. It handles the arbitrary scene text by generating a series of local quadrangles. Furthermore, it introduces the differentiable operator RoISlide. Using RoISlide, the rectified text regions are extracted from the features map in the detection branch. RoISlide helps in connecting the detection and recognition branch for arbitrary shape text spotting. To satisfy the accurate text recognition of arbitrary shape text and apply an optimal training strategy of scene text spotting, the authors of Text Perceptron

(Qiao et al., 2020a, b) developed a text spotting network, which is end-to-end trainable in nature. It is based on the segmentation and transforms the selected text regions into the regular structure without adding any additional parameters by designing a shape transform module. It combines detection and recognition as a single unit system for text spotting and optimizes it globally to enhance the spotting performance.

Different from the traditional approaches, the authors in Wang and colleagues (2020) use a set of points on the boundary of a text instance to localize in an end-to-end style. It spots the arbitrary scene text instances without annotating at the character level. In the case of the direct boundary point prediction, the authors adopt a two-step process. First, with the help of a two-stage convolutional neural network, the minimally oriented rectangular text box is detected. Second, on the detected oriented rectangular text box, the boundary point prediction is performed. The predicted boundary points provide a flexible way to spot the various shapes of text instances. It suppresses the background noise and precisely acquires the boundary points even for the arbitrary shape scene text. With the help of boundary points, the arbitrary or irregular shape scene text can be easily transformed into the horizontal text. This transformed text acts as an input to the recognition module. The boundary point can be easily rectified by optimizing the whole network as a single unit during back-propagation.

17.3 Experimental Results

The comparison of the performance of the existing state-of-the-art models in terms of text detection, text recognition, and text spotting on publicly available benchmark datasets.

17.3.1 Benchmark Datasets

ICDAR 2011: This is an English dataset that has 484 images. 229 images are used in the training process, and the remaining 255 are utilized for testing purposes. This dataset has a 1564 text instance. It provides character-level annotation as well as a word-level annotation.

ICDAR 2013: This dataset is released in Robust Reading Competition 2013 for focused classification, which is approximately the same as ICDAR 2011. It contains 462 images in total, where 229 images are taken in the training set, and the 233 images are considered in the test set. It includes 849 and 1095 instances in the in the training and testing sets, respectively. The words containing non-alphanumeric characters are removed. The dataset therefore carries 1015 cropped text instances, and there is no lexicon affiliated with ICDAR 2013. It has 215 duplicate texts that are included both in the training and testing datasets.

ICDAR 2015: This is introduced as incidental scene text detection, as well as recognition at Robust Reading Competition in 2015. The dataset includes 1000 and 500 images for training and test sets. All texts are in English. Quadrilateral boxes are used for annotations at the word level. The recognition task contains 2077 cropped text samples with about 200 irregular text instances. Google glasses are used to capture the text images. Therefore, the text may be blurred, small, and multi-oriented. There is no lexicon provided for the task of recognition.

ICDAR 2015 Video: For the reading text in the videos, the ICDAR 2015 dataset is extensively redesigned with new video sequences having scene text instances. In training, it has a set of 25 videos with 13450 frames, and in the testing, it has a set of 24 videos having 14374 frames. The ground truth data are updated at the frame and sequence level. It also supports recognition in an end-to-end way.

YVT Video: The YouTube Video Text3 (YVT) dataset is collected from YouTube. Scene text in the YVT dataset contains scene images like street signs, business signs, or words on a shirt. It includes 30 videos in total, in which 50% of videos is used in the training set and the rest as the test set. Every video has a quality of HD 720p. Each video is split into 15-second segments that have 30 frames per second.

ICDAR 2017 MLT: It comprises 10,000 natural images in total for a multi-lingual text dataset. It includes 7200 images in the training set, 1800 images in the validation set, and 9000 images in the test set. In this dataset, the images are collected from 9 languages that the text may be oriented in nature. It does not include text-spotting task.

MSRA-TD500: It is dedicated to detecting English and Chinese text instance of long and arbitrary orientation text. For the training, it has 300 images, and for testing, it has 200 images. The annotations are provided at the text-lines level instead of word and polygon box level. The images are gathered together from indoor spaces, like signs, caution plates, or doorplates of office or malls and outdoor streets using the help of a pocket camera.

SVT: It comprises 350 images and has 725 English text instances in total, where 100 images are considered in the training set and the other 250 are included in the test set. SVT has both character-level and word-level annotations. The dataset collected images mostly using Google Street View. The images have poor resolution. Some images have blurs or get damaged by noise. For recognition, it has an average of 50-word lexicon per image.

ICDAR 2017 RCTW: This is a large dataset containing Chinese or English scene text instances. It has 12,514 images in which 11,514 are used in the training set and 1000 are used for the test set. The dataset has collected images from street views, posters, and screenshot with the help of a camera, smart-phone, and other image capturing devices. Quadrangles are used to annotate words and text lines with multiple orientation in the scene images of the ICDAR 2017 RCTW dataset.

SCUT CTW 1500: The dataset contains long curve-text images. For training purposes, it has 1000 and 500 images in training and test sets. It has 10,751 bounding boxes, where 3530 are curve bounding boxes and have minimum one curve text per image. Text instances in CTW 1500 are labeled by 14-point polygons. The use of 14 points covers the scene text of arbitrary shape in the CTW 1500 dataset. The dataset is composed of images that are collected from different sources, such as websites and Google open-image library.

Total Text: This is also a curve-text dataset. The dataset is composed of 1555 images in total, where the training set has 1255 images and the test set has 300 images. It includes 11,459 cropped word images, and these images have text orientations like horizontal, vertical, multi-oriented, and curved shapes. For each text instance, the annotations are provided at word level.

IIT5K: It contains 5000 cropped images, which are collected from Google image search. In IIT5K, most of the text instances are regular samples for scene text recognition. It has 2000 images in the training set, and 3000 for the test set. Each test image is linked with a lexicon of 50 words and 1000 words. Also, a ground-truth word and few arbitrary selected words are present in the lexicon.

SVTP: It comprises 238 images in total, with 639-word patches. The images are collected from Google Street View with different angles. The non-frontal view angle snapshots increase the perspective distortions in the collected images. More specifically, it is created for the evaluation of perspective distorted scene images for text recognition. Each image in SVTP is linked with a lexicon of 50 words and full-word.

CUTE80: This dataset composed of 288 cropped texts corresponding to 80 high-resolution images. The text instances are mostly curved in nature. It is a lexicon-free dataset, which is designed for scene images with curved text recognition. It is a complex dataset because many images have perspective distortion, low resolution, and challenging backgrounds. The images are of indoor and outdoor scenes that are clicked using digital cameras and accumulated from the Internet.

17.3.2 Performance Metrics

There are many evaluation frameworks proposed for scene-text analysis in the literature. Most of the performance measures are computed using the confusion matrix. However, the confusion matrix is never considered as a performance measure. The performance metrics are mostly depending on the number associated with the confusion matrix. It has conclusions, like true positives, false positives, true negatives, and false negatives. 1 represents *yes* and 0 denotes *no*.

- **True Positives (TP):** This is the condition where the predicted output and the actual output are both 1.
- **True Negatives (TN):** This is the condition where the predicted output and the actual output are both 0.
- **False Positives (FP):** This is the condition where the predicted output is 1, but the actual output is 0.
- **False Negatives (FN):** This is the condition where the predicted output is 0, but the actual output is 1.

Therefore, in this chapter, based on the confusion matrix, we compare the results by calculating precision, recall, and f-score for the scene-text detection. We also compute the accuracy without different lexicons in the case of scene-text recognition. For scene-text spotting, the performance is evaluated by using a strong, weak, and generic approach, which is based on the lexicon provided in the datasets.

- **Precision:** The ratio between the number of true positives and the number of true positives plus the number of false positives is termed as precision. It is a measure of states that tell how many are actually positive among all the predicted positive classes. It helps to understand whether our model is performing well in an imbalanced dataset for the minority class. It is calculated by:

$$Precision = \frac{TP}{TP + FP} \qquad (17.1)$$

- **Recall:** The correlation between the number of true positives and the number of true positives plus the number of false negatives is denoted as recall. It only focuses on positive classes. Therefore, it is useful where the correct identification of negative classes does not play any role. Hence, a model that predicts more false negatives has a lower recall. It is best suited for binary classification. A recall is defined as:

$$Recall = \frac{TP}{TP + FN} \qquad (17.2)$$

- **F-score:** It is also known as the harmonic mean of precision and recall having a range from 1 to 0, where the maximum value is 1 in the best case and 0 in the worst scenario. It is computed by:

$$F-score = \frac{2 \times Precision \times Recall}{Precision + Reacll} \tag{17.3}$$

- **Accuracy:** It is defined as the fraction obtained by dividing the number of correct predictions by the total number of predictions. The accuracy, in the case of binary classification, is formulated by:

$$Accuracy = \frac{TP + TN}{TP + TN + FP + FN} \tag{17.4}$$

- **Strong (S):** A vocabulary of 100 words per image is provided for all words that appear in training and testing set of scene images.
- **Weak (W):** The lexicon covers all words that are present in the whole test set of scene images.
- **Generic (G):** The lexicon comprises approximately 90,000 words of vocabulary per scene image for the task of end-to-end recognition.

17.3.3 Evaluation for Scene-Text Detection Methods on Benchmark Datasets

In this section, we have compared seven recent scene text detection methods on various benchmark scene text datasets. Tables 17.1–17.7 show the results of detection methods with respect to precision, recall, and f-score. Precision has the highest value over the ICDAR 2015 dataset for the method HAM (Hou et al., 2020). Table 17.7 shows that recall is better than precision for the method shown in Raghunandan and colleagues (2019). Curve scene texts are compared in Table 17.2, Table 17.4, and Table 17.5 for the total text and CTW 1500 dataset. F-score in CRAFT for curve text dataset has the highest value.

Tables 17.1–17.5 have a comparison of methods for the multi-lingual dataset. Table 17.4 has the highest recall rate over ICDAR 2017 MLT dataset.

17.3.4 Evaluation for Scene-Text Recognition Methods on Benchmark Datasets

In this section, we analyze extensive experiments of different recognition methods to verify their effectiveness in Table 17.8. We compare five recognition methods for regular

TABLE 17.1

Scene-Text Detection on Various Datasets in HAM (Hou et al., 2020)

Datasets	Precision	Recall	F-score
ICDAR 2015	90.6	87.7	89.2
ICDAR 2017 MLT	82.5	62.3	71
MSRA-TD500	89.3	83.3	86.2
ICDAR 2013	94.5	83.5	88.7

TABLE 17.2

Scene-Text Detection on Various Datasets (Wang et al., 2019a, b)

Datasets	Wang et al. (Wang et al., 2019a, b)		
	Precision	Recall	F-score
ICDAR 2015	86.1	83.8	84.9
ICDAR 2017 MLT	73.7	68.2	70.8
CTW 1500	82.1	77.8	79.9
Total Text	84.5	75.2	79.6

TABLE 17.3

Scene-Text Detection on Various Datasets in SPCNET (Xie et al., 2019)

Datasets	Precision	Recall	F-score
ICDAR 2015	88.7	85.8	87.2
ICDAR 2017 MLT	73.4	66.9	70
ICDAR 2013	93.8	90.5	92.1
Total Text	83	82.8	82.9

TABLE 17.4

Scene-Text Detection on Various Datasets in CRAFT (Baek et al., 2019)

Datasets	Precision	Recall	F-score
ICDAR 2015	89.8	84.3	86.9
MSRA-TD500	88.2	78.2	82.9
ICDAR 2017 MLT	80.6	68.2	73.9
ICDAR 2013	97.4	93.1	95.2
Total Text	87.6	79.9	83.6
CTW 1500	86	81.1	83.5

TABLE 17.5

Scene-Text Detection on Various Datasets in LOMO (Zhang et al., 2019)

Datasets	Precision	Recall	F-score
ICDAR 2015	87.8	87.6	87.7
ICDAR 2017 MLT	80.2	67.2	73.1
Total Text	87.6	79.3	83.3
CTW 1500	85.7	76.5	80.8
ICDAR 2017 RCTW	79.1	60.2	68.4

TABLE 17.6

Scene-Text Detection on Various Datasets in RRPN
(Ma et al., 2018)

Datasets	Precision	Recall	F-score
ICDAR 2015	84	77	80
MSRA-TD500	82	69	75
ICDAR 2013	95	88	91

TABLE 17.7

Scene-Text Detection on Various Datasets (Raghunandan
et al., 2019)

Datasets	Precision	Recall	F-score
ICDAR 2011	76.3	81.1	78.6
ICDAR 2013	84.5	87.7	86
ICDAR 2015 Video	62.8	67.6	66.1
YVT Video	78.8	81.6	80.1
SVT	60.4	68.7	64.2

TABLE 17.8

Recognition Accuracy Results on Benchmark Datasets in Lexicon-Free Mode

Methods	IIIT5K	SVT	ICDAR 13	ICDAR 15	SVTP	CUTE 80
SCATTER (Litman et al., 2020)	93.7	92.7	93.9	82.2	86.9	87.5
TextScanner (Wan et al., 2020)	95.7	92.7	94.9	83.5	84.8	91.6
(Yu et al., 2020)	92.3	88.1	93.2	77.5	79.4	84.7
SEED (Qiao et al., 2020a, b)	93.8	89.6	92.8	80	81.4	83.6
(Wang et al., 2019a, b)	93.9	91.3	95.7	83.9	85.7	83.3

TABLE 17.9

Results on ICDAR2015

Methods	Word Spotting			End-to-End		
	S	W	G	S	W	G
Mask TextSpotter (Liao et al., 2019)	82.4	78.1	73.6	83	77.7	73.5
CharNet (Xing et al., 2019)	–	–	–	85	81.2	71
TextDragon (Feng et al., 2019)	86.2	81.6	68	82.5	78.3	65.1
Text Perceptron (Qiao et al., 2020a, b)	84.1	79.4	67.9	80.5	76.6	65.1
(Wang et al., 2020)	–	–	–	79.7	75.2	64.1

TABLE 17.10

Results on ICDAR2013

Methods	Word Spotting			End-to-End		
	S	W	G	S	W	G
Mask TextSpotter (Liao et al., 2019)	92.7	91.7	87.7	93.3	91.3	88.2
Text Perceptron (Qiao et al., 2020a, b)	94.9	94	88.5	91.4	90.7	85.8
(Wang et al., 2020)	–	–	–	88.2	87.7	84.1

(IIT5K, SVT, and ICDAR 2013) and irregular (ICADR 2015, SVTP, and CUTE 80) datasets. Regular datasets have horizontal text orientation, whereas the irregular datasets are more challenging, having arbitrary orientation and curve-text instances. The results in Table 17.8 demonstrate that TextScanner shows the highest accuracy over the IIIT5K, SVT, and CUTE 80 datasets. Literature (Wang et al., 2019a, b) represents a better result in accuracy for ICDAR 2013 and ICDAR 2015 datasets. SCATTER (Litman et al., 2020) method shows higher recognition accuracy for SVT and SVTP datasets.

17.3.5 Evaluation for Scene-Text Spotting Methods on Benchmark Datasets

In this section, we study the supremacy of scene-text spotting over ICDAR 2013 and ICDAR 2015 dataset. Table 17.9 and Table 17.10 show the results for word spotting and end-to-end recognition. The performance is computed for strong, weak, and generic lexicon.

In the case of word spotting in Table 17.9, TextDragon (Feng et al., 2019) exhibits higher performance in comparison to other methods with the strong and weak lexicon, whereas in generic lexicons Mask TextSpotter (Liao et al., 2019) have better results. When the methods are compared for end-to-end recognition, CharNet (Xing et al., 2019) shows better results for strong and weak lexicon, and Mask TextSpotter reflects better results for generic lexicon. Results in Table 17.10 are computed for various methods over ICDAR 2013 dataset. In the word spotting, Text Perceptron (Qiao et al., 2020a, b) shows effective results for strong, weak, and generic lexicons. In the case of end-to-end recognition, Mask TextSpotter executed better results with strong, weak, and generic lexicons.

17.4 Summary

In this chapter, we have discussed the recent advancements in the field of scene-text analysis. We have analyzed the limitations of traditional methods in the field of scene text detection, recognition, and spotting. In scene-text detection, we have seen how we are handling curve and arbitrary scene text in the detection process and illustrated the architectural difference between different models. In the scene-text recognition, we have seen various methods and attention mechanisms that are used in accurate text recognition. In the scene-text spotting, we discuss the different methods that are used in an end-to-end trainable style for network training without adding any additional computational overhead.

References

Baek Y., Lee B., Han D., Yun S., and Lee H. 2019. Character Region Awareness for Text Detection. *IEEE Conference on Computer Vision and Pattern Recognition*. 9365–9374.

Dollár P., Appel R., Belongie S., and Perona P. 2014. Fast feature pyramids for object detection. IEEE Transactions Pattern Analysis and Machine *Intelligence*, 36(8):1532–1545.

Feng W., He W., Yin F., Zhang X., and Liu C. 2019. TextDragon: An End-to-End Framework for Arbitrary Shaped Text Spotting. *IEEE International Conference on Computer Vision*. 9075–9084.

Graves A. and Schmidhuber J. 2005. Framewise Phoneme Classification with Bidirectional LSTM Networks. *International Joint Conference on Neural Networks*, 4:2047–2052.

Hou J., Zhu X., Liu C., Sheng K., Wu L., Wang H., and Yin X. 2020. HAM: Hidden Anchor Mechanism for Scene Text Detection. *IEEE Transactions on Image Processing*, 29:7904–7916.

Liao M., Lyu P., He M., Yao C., Wu W., and Bai X. 2019. Mask TextSpotter: An End-to-End Trainable Neural Network for Spotting Text with Arbitrary Shapes. IEEE Transactions on Pattern Analysis and Machine Intelligence. 1–17.

Litman R., Anschel O., Tsiper S., Litman R., Mazor S. and Manmatha R. 2020. SCATTER: Selective Context Attentional Scene Text Recognizer. *IEEE Conference on Computer Vision and Pattern Recognition*, 11:959–969.

Ma J., Shao W., Ye H., Wang L., Wang H., Zheng Y., and Xue X. 2018. Arbitrary-Oriented Scene Text Detection via Rotation Proposals. *IEEE Transactions on Multimedia*, 20(11):3111–3122.

Qiao L., Tang S., Cheng Z., Xu Y., Niu Y., Pu S., and Wu F. 2020a. Text Perceptron: Towards End-to-End Arbitrary-Shaped Text Spotting. *AAAI Conference on Artificial Intelligence*. 11: 899–907.

Qiao Z., Zhou Y., Yang D., Zhou Y., and Wang W. 2020b. SEED: Semantics Enhanced Encoder-Decoder Framework for Scene Text Recognition . *IEEE Conference on Computer Vision and Pattern Recognition*. 13:528–537.

Raghunandan K. S., Shivakumara P., Roy S., Kumar G. H., Pal U., and Lu T. 2019. Multi-Script-Oriented Text Detection and Recognition in Video/Scene/Born Digital Images. IEEE Trans. on Circuits and Systems for Video *Technology*, 29(4):1145–1162.

Wan Z., He M., Chen H., Bai X., and Yao C. 2020. TextScanner: Reading Characters in Order for Robust Scene Text Recognition. *AAAI Conference on Artificial Intelligence*, 12:120–127.

Wang H., Lu P., Zhang H., Yang M., Bai X., Xu Y., He M., Wang Y., and Liu W. 2020. All You Need Is Boundary: Toward Arbitrary-Shaped Text Spotting. *AAAI Conference on Artificial Intelligence*. 12:160–167.

Wang S., Wang Y., Qin X., Zhao Q., and Tang Z. 2019a. Scene Text Recognition via Gated Cascade Attention. *IEEE International Conference on Multimedia and Expo*. 1018–1023.

Wang W., Xie E., Li X., Hou W., Lu T., Yu G., and Shao S. 2019b. Shape Robust Text Detection With Progressive Scale Expansion Network. *IEEE Conference on Computer Vision and Pattern Recognition*, 9336–9345.

Xie E., Zang Y., Shao S., Yu G., Yao C., and Li G. 2019. Scene Text Detection with Supervised Pyramid Context Network. *AAAI Conference on Artificial Intelligence*. 9038–9045.

Xing L., Tian Z., Huang W., and Scott M. R. 2019. Convolutional Character Networks. *IEEE International Conference on Computer Vision*. 9126–9136.

Yu D., Li X., Zhang C., Liu T., Han J., Liu J., and Ding E. 2020. Towards Accurate Scene Text Recognition with Semantic Reasoning Networks. *IEEE Conference on Computer Vision and Pattern Recognition*. 12:113–122.

Zhang C., Liang B., Huang Z., En M., Han J., Ding E., and Ding X. 2019. Look More Than Once: An Accurate Detector for Text of Arbitrary Shapes. *IEEE Conference on Computer Vision and Pattern Recognition*, 10:552–561.

Zhou X., Yao C., Wen H., Wang Y., Zhou S., He W., and Liang J. 2017. EAST: An Efficient and Accurate Scene Text Detector. *IEEE Conference on Computer Vision and Pattern Recognition*, 2642–2651.

Index

Page numbers in *italic* indicate figures. Page numbers in **bold** indicate tables.

A

Abdi, S., *et al.*, 134
ACF, *see* auto-correlation (ACF)
ACO, *see* ant colonies algorithm (ACO)
AdaBoost, 58
Adam algorithm, 70, 72
ADAS-Cog, *see* Alzheimer's Disease Evaluation
  Scale (ADAS-Cog)
Aggarwal, C. C., 7
agriculture, 63
  plant disease, 68
  smart farming, 84; *see also* citrus diseases
    detection (deep learning)
Akaike information criterion (AIC), 117
Al Khalil morphological analyzer, 318
algorithm evaluation, 52–56
  absolute error (AE), 53
  binary classification, 55–56
  binary particle swarm optimization
    algorithm, 250–251, *251*, 252
  classification, 54–56
  clustering, 56
  confusion matrix, 55, *55*
  correlation terms, 54
  false negative, 55
  false positive, 55
  lazy learner algorithms, 307
  linear regression models, 53–54
  mean absolute error (MAE), 53
  mean squared error (MSE), 53
  multiclass classification, 56
  nature-inspired metaheuristic, 217, 219,
    224, 250
  recall, 55
  relative absolute error (RAE), 53
  relative squared error (RSE), 54
  root mean squared error (RMSE), 53
  sum of squared error (SSE), 53–54
  supply chain management case study, 213,
    213, 215, *216*, 217, **217**, 225–226, 233
  true negative, 55
  true positive, 55
Alon, I., *et al.*, 208
Alzheimer's disease

brain images, *163*
cognitive abilities, 155–156
dataset training loss values, *160*
deep brain stimulation (DBS), 152–153,
  155–163
feature evaluation, **159**
implementation results (DBS), 158–163
intelligence measurements, 156
methodology of DBS study, 157–158
mini-mental state test (MMSE), 155
neuropsychiatric symptoms (NPS), 155, *156*
perceptual variations, 155
risk assessment, 165, **165**
swarm Intelligence (SI) algorithms, 158, 162
symptoms, 156–157, *157*
validation accuracy, *160*
Alzheimer's Disease Evaluation Scale
  (ADAS-Cog), 155
Amazon
  recommender systems, 192
  user data mining, 26
Ambroise, C., *et al.*, 6
AMPL, **262**
Anand, A., and Sahu, S. K., 281
Anderson, T., 128
ANNs, *see* artificial neural networks (ANNs)
ant colonies (ACO) algorithm, 217–218
Apriori algorithm, 4–5
Aras, S., *et al.*, 208
ARIMA, *see* auto-regressive integration moving
  average model
artificial intelligence (AI), business leverage, 28
artificial neural networks (ANNs), 42, 46, 196
assignment problem case study, 270–274
  CBC solver, 271
  cost matrix, **273**
  mathematical model, **274**
  time required, **273**
association rules, 4–5
Au, K. F., *et al.*, 208
Aurobindo, S., 128
auto-correlation (ACF), 104, 120–121, 123–124
auto-regressive integration moving average
  (ARIMA) model, 117